THE
LANGUAGE ARTS
HANDBOOK

IRIS M. TIEDT

Director, South Bay Writing Project
San Jose State University

Prentice-Hall, Inc., Englewood Cliffs, New Jersey 07632

Library of Congress Cataloging in Publication Data

TIEDT, IRIS M.
  The language arts handbook.

  Includes index.
  1. Language arts (Elementary)   I. Title.
LB1576.T554   1983   372.6'044   82-16562
ISBN 0-13-522615-5

Editorial/production supervision and interior design by Kate Kelly
Manufacturing buyer: Ron Chapman
Cover design: Judy Winthrop

Printed in the United States of America

10   9   8   7   6   5   4   3   2   1

ISBN 0-13-522615-5

Prentice-Hall International, Inc., *London*
Prentice-Hall of Australia Pty. Limited, *Sydney*
Editora Prentice-Hall do Brasil, Ltda., *Rio de Janeiro*
Prentice-Hall Canada Ltd., *Toronto*
Prentice-Hall of India Private Limited, *New Delhi*
Prentice-Hall of Japan, Inc., *Tokyo*
Prentice-Hall of Southeast Asia Pte. Ltd., *Singapore*
Whitehall Books Limited, *Wellington, New Zealand*

CONTENTS

AN INVITATION . . .

Teaching the English language arts can be the most enjoyable and exciting experience you have ever had. I invite you now to venture forth on a lifetime voyage that will never end. We will not sail uncharted seas, for many have travelled this route before us. We will, however, explore territory that you have never seen before, and we will savor delights that you can scarcely imagine. Does that intrigue you? I hope so.

The Language Arts Handbook is designed to provide an overview of a field that is rich and extensive. I will introduce you to the varied topics of language, literature, and the language arts. I will suggest content and strategies of instruction and guide you toward further exploration. The rest, however, is up to you. You have the opportunity of touching the lives of children with magic.

I need you to carry out the stimulating, integrated language arts program that is outlined in the first chapter, for as the classroom teacher, you hold the key to what will happen in the lives of the students in your classroom. In Chapter 1, I share my ideas for teaching the language arts holistically with a strong focus on composition, and I try to guide you toward creating your own philosophy of instruction that will determine how and what you teach as you work with children.

Throughout this book, you will hear a strong emphasis on language, for language is both content and process. Language—thinking, listening, and speaking—provides the foundation from which we will build with children. It is an integral part of reading and writing programs at every level of instruction. Although I have focused separately on the language skills for purposes of discussion, chapter by chapter, in actuality language cannot be segmented in this way. As we talk about listening, therefore, we are also discussing speaking, and we are beginning to move toward writing and reading. Later, as we focus on composition, we include thinking, listening, and speaking as important ways of preparing to write.

Because language and the processes of using language underlie all of learning, special emphasis is given to language activities in other subject areas in the elementary school curriculum. In addition to suggestions given as we focus on each language skill, I have included a chapter that deals with language arts instruction across the curriculum. The "I-Search Paper," for example, engages the student in such oral language processes as interviewing and the production of a formal composition that is shared through reading. Literature is also suggested as a means of enriching learning in social studies, science, and even mathematics.

I have tried, furthermore, to present a happy combination of theory and practice. We need to be aware of theoretical backgrounds and research findings as we make curriculum decisions, for we base our choices of methods and materials on the knowledge that we have internalized whether it is explicit or not. A wealth of instructional strategies are described in each chapter to enable you to choose those that fit your immediate needs. I trust that you will feel free to adapt these ideas as you make them your own.

Special topics of concern to all teachers are included in this handbook to facilitate your meeting the needs of students in your classroom. Sections of chapters deal, for instance, with problems faced by handicapped students and those who do not yet speak English fluently. Multicultural teaching ideas are presented that will aid you in recognizing the diversity of our population. Many suggestions are made, too, for adapting methods to adjust your teaching to the ages and abilities of your students. I believe that a student-centered approach to teaching is vital if you want to teach effectively.

The Language Arts Handbook is unique in its efforts to provide a focus for language instruction that enables teachers to integrate learning activities efficiently for maximum effect. It also stresses the enjoyment of exploring language and literature with children which stimulates creativity and generates self-motivated learning. We will embark on this adventure now with the understanding that our trip will be educational but that it will also be exciting.

Bon Voyage!

Dr. Iris M. Tiedt

New Perspectives
for the Language Arts

1

Tell me, I forget. Show me, I remember. Involve me, I understand.

Ancient Chinese Proverb

INTEGRATING LANGUAGE ARTS INSTRUCTION
A Focus and Sequence for Teaching

Language arts instruction permeates the whole elementary school curriculum. We sing language; we use language to discuss issues in the social sciences; we explain mathematical processes verbally. Thinking itself necessitates a rich, precise, yet flexible language that facilitates analytical processes and also enables us to make the creative "leap." As we begin our investigation of the language arts and ways to improve instruction, therefore, we are undertaking a formidable task. On the other hand, this investigation will be a very exciting experience for you, as you discover the amazing qualities of our English language. Through you it will have a powerful impact on the lives of thousands of students.

This, then, is the intent of *The Language Arts Handbook*. In this first chapter we will examine the content comprised in the broad study of the language arts, and we will talk about teaching the language arts holistically so that students see the interrelationships among listening, speaking, reading, and writing and how these skills relate to the thinking process. We will emphasize involving students in a study of language as it functions in their daily lives, introducing them to the technical information about how our language system works as well as the lore and recreational aspects of linguistics that will generate a love of language that will last a lifetime.

As we introduce each chapter, you will find a benchmark exercise designed to help you begin thinking about the topics we will discuss. This activity will assist you in assessing where you are in relationship to this part of our study and to determine the need for more concentrated investigation. In the following benchmark we stress the teacher's role, the student as learner, and the language arts curriculum.

BENCHMARK

Discuss each of the following questions in a small group. Have someone record the main points made by members of your group. Share the ideas presented in the large group.

1. How would you describe the role of a teacher? List responsibilities that you see as appropriate to this role.

2. How might you, as a teacher, provide for the needs of individual children? Consider, for example, a handicapped child in a wheelchair, a very slow learner, and a highly gifted, creative student.

3. What would you want children to learn in your classroom related to language arts? State five objectives in terms of what students will be able to do at the end of the year.

In this introductory chapter you will explore the extent of the language arts and the many areas of study encompassed by this term. After reading the chapter and thinking about the ideas presented, you should be able to:

- discuss the interrelationships among the language skills
- analyze how thinking works in conjunction with the language skills
- define some of the needs of students in a classroom
- express your personal views of the teaching–learning process
- enumerate some of the goals for language arts instruction

CENTERING ON THE LEARNER

In 1979, the Year of the Child, many of us reviewed the statement adopted by the United Nations twenty years earlier making explicit the rights of the children of the world.

The Right to affection, love, and
     understanding.
The Right to free education.
The Right to full opportunity for
     play and recreation.
The Right to a name and nationality.

The Right to special care, if
handicapped.
The Right to be among the first to
receive relief in times
of disaster.
The Right to learn to be a useful
member of society and
to develop individual
abilities.
The Right to be brought up in a spirit
of peace and universal
brotherhood.
The Right to enjoy these rights,
regardless of race,
color, sex, religion,
national, or social
origin.

As we begin this study of language arts instruction in the elementary school, it is appropriate that we reaffirm our responsibility to children. We need to remind ourselves that classrooms exist for the good of children, not for providing the jobs of teachers and administrators or a marketplace for published materials. We need to think about the needs of children as students, as learners.

The Basic Needs of the Learner

As we prepare to work with students in the classroom, it is essential to identify the basic needs of children as they engage in the learning process. As we enumerate these basic considerations, we will develop a statement of the Rights of the Child as a Learner, which incorporates many of the components of the statement that you just read (see page 4).

As we think about the needs of children, and the rights we have listed, we may need to rethink practices that deny some of these rights. Evaluation techniques, for example, must reflect our recognition of the child's need for self-esteem. The handicapped child must feel accepted on entering the classroom with children who do not have the same handicap. We must call on all of our knowledge and resources to provide for the basic needs of children as learners.

Special Needs

In any classroom there are children who have special needs. As we move toward mainstreaming children with more pronounced handicaps, the number of children with special needs will increase. Special education has been developed as a field to meet these needs, but all teachers need to consider how to plan language arts instruction in classrooms that include the exceptional child. The needs of special children cover a wide range that demands a great deal from the classroom teacher, as demonstrated in this summary:

Rights of Children as Learners

Children have basic needs that affect their development.
Each child has a right to have these needs met
as part of the learning process.

The Right to Acceptance
Children have the right to know that their total being
is acceptable — language, skin color, mental abilities, handicaps.

The Right to Self-Esteem
Children have the right to know that they are
worthy beings. They have the right to value themselves
for whatever they are and whatever they do.

The Right to Growth
Children have the right to grow to the fullest of
their individual potentials.

The Right to Guidance
Children have the right to expect help from more
mature persons as they engage in living.

The Right to Schooling
Children have the right to free schooling, formal or
informal, with the best instruction and resources available
as they learn.

RETARDED LEARNING

Although teachers have been accustomed to providing for slower students by using
"remedial" techniques, the retarded learner is operating on a much lower level on
the scale of mental ability.

GIFTEDNESS

At the opposite end of the scale is the highly gifted child who has often been
ignored in planning instruction. We have a responsibility to provide for the growth
of these able learners.

VISUAL HANDICAPS

Children who are partially and/or totally blind can participate in such activities as listening to "lectures" or stories, but they require input through methods other than the visual, on which we depend heavily.

HEARING DEFICIENCIES

Children who have hearing losses depend on the visual methods of learning including sign and lip reading. They require special consideration when methods are largely oral.

EMOTIONAL DISTURBANCE

Perhaps the most difficult need to meet is the understanding and support required by the child who is emotionally upset. You will usually receive assistance from a counselor. The most severe cases are not, of course, mainstreamed into the regular classroom.

At all times our concern is for helping students grow to their fullest potential. Our expectations for the students and ourselves must, however, remain realistic. It should be remembered that most students do not fall into any of these special categories. These "nondistinguished" students should not be ignored as we strive to meet the more visible, demanding requirements of special children.

Meeting the needs of students and planning a curriculum that is student-centered is the focus of the next chapter. There we discuss the needs of children at different stages of development and such problems as providing a supportive climate for children in crisis.

The entire organization of this textbook has the student at the center, as shown in the diagram on page 6. The learner exists in a world of language as the brain begins to function. Gradually, the young learner develops thinking, listening, and speaking skills that are closely related to the later development of reading and writing. The sequence of the chapters reflects this perception of the child's growth.

Throughout the book I have tried to emphasize the interactive nature of these elements, which are singled out chapter by chapter for purposes of discussion. Although content about language, language skills, and literature is presented in each chapter, I have focused more heavily on the learning process, for it is my feeling that we have spent too much time talking about languaging. Now is the time for doing!

DEFINING THE LANGUAGE ARTS

The language arts comprise a large body of knowledge as well as all of the basic skills of language processing and communication. It is no simple task, therefore, to describe a curriculum that encompasses both content and process and also meets the needs of individual students. It is exciting to conceive of an elementary language arts curriculum such as Courtney Cazden envisions:

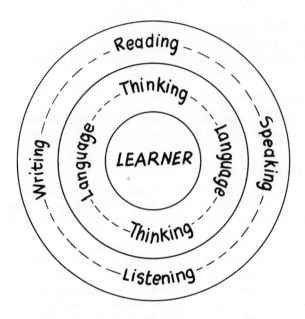

The Learner and the Language Arts

The elementary school must retain its concept of the whole, unfragmented learner; it must keep intentional activity at the core of the process of education; and it must always remember that the language arts are the curriculum area that cannot stand alone. Only linguists have language as their subject matter. For the rest of us—especially children—language is learned not because we want to talk about language, but because we want to talk and read about the world.[1]

The curriculum we develop must be student-centered. It must reflect the overriding goal of preparing children to live in an unpredictable future. The language arts curriculum should be sufficiently general to enable us to respond to a changing society, yet specific enough to be implemented in the classroom. Let us first delineate goals and objectives and then consider the content and processes that children need.

Establishing Goals

In expressing the goals for the curriculum we are designing, we are faced with a paradox that Margaret Mead recognized:

We are at the point where we must educate people in what nobody knew yesterday and prepare in our schools for what no one knows yet, but what some people must know tomorrow.[2]

[1]Courtney Cazden, "Commentary: Environments for Language Learning." *Language Arts.* 55, 6:682, September 1978.

[2]Margaret Mead, "That Each Child May Learn What It Is To Be Completely Human." (Address at 62nd Annual Convention of National Council of Teachers of English, Minneapolis, Minnesota, November 23, 1972.)

Clearly, we must focus on broad, flexible goals that will prepare today's children to deal with tomorrow's landscape. What knowledge will be of most worth? Two basic language processes stand out as vital to human existence: thinking and communicating. These processes are interactive and overlapping, as you will see in the delineation that follows.[3]

Thinking process The language arts program of the future must focus directly on thinking. Like listening, thinking occurs without visible behavior; there is no instruction designed to develop the efficiency and effectiveness of this process. Recently, however, there is renewed interest in the teaching of thinking as more has been learned about the interaction of the right and left hemispheres of the brain.

Focusing on thinking as a major goal for the language arts curriculum assumes that methodology will emphasize *inquiry* as children experiment and observe, as they collect raw data, and then make inferences, draw conclusions, and test their hypotheses. Direct instruction should develop such skills as comparing, evaluating, and decision making and encourage the use of divergent and convergent thinking.

Teachers have not, in general, been trained to teach the many thinking skills of a taxonomy that includes numerous specific competencies. The chapter on thinking will guide you through the components that make up the thinking process. We will also present strategies that involve students in problem solving as they move from relatively simple, concrete operations to increasingly complex and more abstract processes. Thinking will also be discussed as it relates to the focus of each of the succeeding chapters in the book.

In specifying objectives and planning instructions, it is important to recognize affective and cognitive elements of learning. We will aim at utilizing both hemispheres of the brain to reinforce learning as we strive to maximize what children can achieve. As Piaget noted, the affective and the intellectual cannot be isolated in life or in instruction:

> Affective life, like intellectual life, is a continuous adaptation, and the two are not only parallel but interdependent, since feelings express the interest and values given to actions of which intelligence provides the structure.[4]

Communication process The communication model for language arts includes the interactive processes of listening and speaking, reading and writing, as shown on the following chart.

Listening and speaking are related through their use of the oral language. The aural-oral language skills, listening and speaking, are the primary means of language learning; they continue, furthermore, to provide an essential foundation for all of learning. Through listening, the learner

---

[3]Iris M. Tiedt, "English in the Elementary School: What, How, and Why We Teach," in *Education in the 80s: English,* ed. R. Baird Shuman (Washington, D.C.: National Education Association, 1981).

[4]John H. Flavell, *The Developmental Psychology of Jean Piaget.* (New York: Van Nostrand, Reinhold Co., n.d.), p. 80.

Interrelationships of the Language Skills

SPOKEN LANGUAGE		WRITTEN LANGUAGE	
LISTENING (RECEIVED)	SPEAKING (PRODUCED)	READING (RECEIVED)	WRITING (PRODUCED)
Hearing phonemes (language sounds)	Producing sounds		
Understanding intonation meaning	Using intonation effectively		
Discriminating among sounds	Producing meaningful words		
Associating adult utterances with meaning	Speaking 2-word sentences grammatically		
Understanding words	Speaking longer, more complex utterances	Seeing adults read	
Understanding more complex structures	Learning to modify speech to fit listener, context	Hearing stories read from books	Observing adults writing
Listening to stories	Learning appropriate registers	"Pretend reading" from books	"Scribble" writing
FORMAL SCHOOLING			
Advanced listening skills	Learning to speak formally to group	Associating sounds with symbols	Learning to write symbols
Continued development of knowledge of language	Polishing speaking abilities	Associating symbols with meaning (words)	Writing words
		Learning meaning of punctuation	Writing sentences
			Using punctuation
		Reading fluently	Learning different forms of writing
		Using advanced reading skills	Polishing writing skills
		Reading for pleasure and information independently	Writing with style

receives input which is processed through the brain (thinking). The listener has a choice of (1) not responding at all or (2) responding through body movements or through speaking or writing. Speaking is a productive skill that requires knowledge and effort; it may or may not be addressed to a listener. In order for the message to be comprehended the listener is very much dependent on the ability of the speaker. Listening and speaking are discussed in Chapters 5 and 6.

The more sophisticated skills of reading and writing work with symbolic or written language. As children read, they should be made aware that someone wrote what they are reading. As they write, they should think about the person who will read what they have written. Ability to read and write are very much dependent on the child's oral language development. In order to comprehend, the learner will make inferences, attribute meaning to words, interpret metaphor—basic thinking processes that are essential to understanding. When producing written communication, on the other hand, the student must control the meanings of words, command concepts to be presented, and handle the intricacies of putting writing on paper. Clearly, the productive skill of writing is the most difficult of the language arts.

Thinking is inextricably tied to any linguistic function. Production of language depends on what each learner has stored in his or her brain. For this reason, we need to be concerned about providing input as we literally "feed the brain" of each child in the classroom. Thinking processes are limited by the learner's language abilities. Children need to be actively engaged in a rich environment that includes varied experiences and language. Our aim is to help children communicate, to bridge the transition from oral language to working with written language, always mediated by the thinking processes as shown in the following diagram.

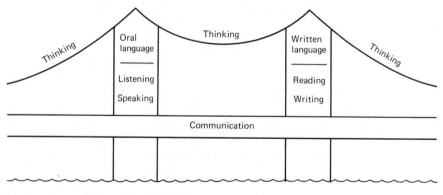

A Model for Bridging Language Development

DEVELOPING A LANGUAGE ARTS CURRICULUM

We need to design a developmental scope and sequence, and to consider the goals and objectives that we hope to achieve through language arts instruction. Only then will we be able to plan specific lessons to use with students in the classroom. In this section we will first look at a model that spells out the full range of the language arts program. We will examine the goals and objectives we will work toward as we help students develop language and thinking abilities.

An Integrated Model for the Language Arts

In order to conceptualize the structure of an integrated language arts program we need to examine the full extent of this complex process that brings thinking, listening, speaking, writing, and reading together and teaches concepts about both language and literature. The model below should enable you to visualize the total language arts program. This holistic approach to language arts is based on a strong experiential and oral language foundation. Without this foundation children are not ready to move to the more abstract use of language required as they work with letter symbols and express their original thoughts in writing.

It is usually assumed that the first stages of thinking and language develop in the home before the child enters school. Realistically, however, we often begin at this level with children from varied cultural backgrounds,

An Integrated Model for the Language Arts Thinking and Communication Skills

those with a limited knowledge of English, and those whose working parents may not have the time or energy to help them develop language. Introducing new processes is most effective when supported by the presentation of concepts, thinking processes, and vocabulary through listening and speaking activities. Oral language is essential for pre- and postreading and writing activities that guarantee the student's success; therefore, oral language will continue to be an integral part of the language arts program as children learn to read and to write.

The eight stages of development in the model are not totally discrete; they overlap as does any integrated approach to learning. Children may learn to analyze a process orally as they create a mural about the adventures of Curious George. The language–experience approach to reading will have them writing stories with the help of the teacher or an aide. Language skills cannot be developed in isolation; they support the total learning process as children discuss ideas and engage in projects that involve them in solving problems that require reading and writing for specific purposes.

The model indicates the range of instructional strategies that are possible within an integrated language arts program. Considering that students use language arts as they study all other subject areas, it can truly be said that language arts are taught throughout the total elementary school curriculum.

Goals for Thinking and Communicating

The goals stated for any language arts program must be comprehensive, broad, and flexible. They should encompass the interrelated skills of thinking, listening, speaking, reading, and writing, and they must be process-oriented. Such goals can be grouped under the following important thinking skills: (1) describing, (2) discriminating, (3) relating, (4) generalizing, (5) judging or evaluating, and (6) valuing. These goals can be applied to any aspects of the language arts program. Responses to literature in a reading program might be expected to fall under these goals as delineated here:

DESCRIBING

Students identify and describe such elements of literature as character, setting, plot, point of view, and dialogue in a narrative and use these models for their original narratives.

DISCRIMINATING

Students identify and discuss differences in the behavior of two characters or the handling of a topic by several authors.

RELATING

Students make connections, see similarities, and relate a tale they read to their world as they share the emotions expressed by a character or observe a different family's way of living.

GENERALIZING

Students state concepts abstracted from literature such as the universal need for love or the perception of death as part of life.

JUDGING OR EVALUATING

Students evaluate the content or style in writing by different authors.

VALUING

Students state what they like or admire and what they reject in the story they have read.[5]

Students who deal with such broad goals will be able to transfer their understanding to learning in any subject area. They will be able to describe objects, situations, and processes as they work in science. They will learn to compare and contrast as they discriminate between fact and opinion in history or two methods of solving a mathematical problem. Students will learn a variety of relationships such as cause and effect, as well as the language appropriate to expressing such relationships. They will also discover the skills and hazards of generalizing. As students advance in their language abilities, they will make judgments based on observation and discrimination, and they will begin developing their own set of values.

Students will use these levels of thinking as they work with new concepts and express their ideas. These skills will be part of the listening, speaking, reading, and writing processes because thinking is an integral part of each process. We need to make a point, however, of increasing student awareness of the kind of thinking they are using as they engage in classroom learning activities.

Content for the Curriculum

Selecting content to be taught is almost as important as establishing goals for instruction. As we examine the study of the English language, the whole field of children's literature, and the languaging skills that children need, it is clear that determining a scope and sequence of instruction is not a simple task. Under each of these aspects of the language arts we find substantial content to be shared with children. How we share this content, and methods of instruction, will be discussed in detail in Chapter 3, but teaching strategies will be found in every chapter as content is presented.

The English language   A study of the English language offers a wide variety of concepts. This study will offer many opportunities for speaking and writing about language as well as listening to language and reading the many books about language that have been written for young children. Students may not need the technical terms for the fundamental elements of a language, but they will certainly be dealing with all of them:

---

[5]Tiedt, "English in the Elementary School", p. 73.

PHONOLOGY (the study of the sounds used to produce a language)

Young children must be aware of the sounds they make as they learn to relate these sounds to the various spellings we use to represent the sounds. Phonology is the root of phonics in teaching reading.

MORPHOLOGY (the study of meaningful elements of a language)

As children learn to read and write, they learn the meaning of such morphemes as the *'s*, signalling possession, or the prefix *sub-*, which always means *under*.

GRAMMAR (the system of structuring sentences to convey meaning)

Students will become aware of how they use word order to give meaning to words or how the meaning of a word can change when it is placed in a different grammatical structure.

SEMANTICS (the study of meaning in language, both surface and deep-structured)

Expressing and gaining meaning is the ultimate reason for language.

The study of our rich English language deals with psychological and sociological issues as well. Fascinating information can be shared from the following areas of linguistic study:

Body language
    Example: How the body conveys meaning without words
Dialectology
    Example: Comparing British and American English
History of English
    Example: How spelling has changed over the years
Semantics
    Example: How the context of a sentence affects meaning
Usage
    Example: The levels of appropriateness of language
Wordplay
    Example: The euphemisms we invent for taboo subjects

Literature concepts   Literature written for children today is a never-ending source of amazement and delight. Books and materials suitable for stimulating children's thinking and language development range from the ABC and counting books to mature fantasies. We can enumerate many literary concepts that children begin assimilating as soon as they listen to stories. They will find the same concepts applicable to the composition process as they write original literature, for example:

Characterization
Plot development
Setting
Theme
Mood
Style

Children can experience all of the literary genres as they learn to read. They are establishing models for the composition of poetry, fiction, nonfiction, drama, biography, and films.

Perhaps one of the most important attributes of good literature, however, is what it says directly to the reader. The child laughs at the many problems Alexander lists (*Alexander's Terrible, Horrible, No-Good Very Bad Day* by Judith Viorst) but at the same time any boy or girl can empathize with his complaints, too. The book that tells of the death of a grandmother or the pain of adjusting to a divorce will touch the hearts of children who have had a similar experience. Children will shiver delightedly at the monsters in *Where the Wild Things Are* and share the terrors of their peers in *The Lion, The Witch, and The Wardrobe* as they follow a talented author into a fantasy world. A good book is a friend as we cope with what comes our way.

The languaging skills　In addition to the language and literature that they encounter, children also need to learn about the processes of using language. They need to talk about how to listen more effectively or how to revise their own writing, and they will learn the vocabulary associated with each process.

Students should also be shown the ways that the language arts are related. We can talk with them about the interdependence, for example, of the speaker and the listener, for neither can succeed without the cooperation of the other. They need to become aware of the way reading and spelling can support each other. Such information will increase student understanding and help students make generalizations about how language works.

Students should recognize, furthermore, that we learn how to use language effectively through using it. We can talk with them about the importance of reading frequently if they want to become good readers. The same is true for writing, speaking, and listening. At the same time, of course, we can let students know how they can operate more effectively, and we can design instruction to help them do so.

While we recognize the fact that no language skill can be developed in isolation and that the effective teacher will deliberately integrate instruction in order to maximize learning, there is a need to study each of the languaging processes as one component of the total language arts program. We need to look at listening as a separate process in order to help students become more aware of the problems of listening and how they can improve this essential skill. At the same time we will point out the interrelationships of listening and the other languaging skills. As we plan instruction designed to improve listening ability, we will use content from the fields of language and literature or one of the many other subjects taught in the elementary school. Ways of planning integrated units of study are illustrated in Chapter 3. Examples are also included in Chapter 14: Language Arts Across the Curriculum.

SUMMARY

Teaching the language arts presents a number of difficulties that are not typical of other subjects taught in the elementary school. Language arts encompass the study of language and literature, but includes teaching students how to use thinking, listening, speaking, reading, and writing more effectively. The latter skills comprise both content and method, and they are used to further learning in all other areas of the school curriculum. Writing is the most complex of the skills to learn because success in composition is based on success in the oral language skills as well as reading. It is further complicated by the physical act of handwriting and the necessity to spell words correctly.

At this stage we might observe:

1. Learning to use language successfully is closely integrated with a child's self-esteem. This concept will be developed in more detail in the next chapter.
2. To be most effective, instruction should be centered on the learner. Meeting children's needs is our top priority in planning instruction. Our aim is to help each child develop to his or her fullest potential.
3. Language arts instruction comprises thinking and communication processes. It includes the study of language, literature, and the development of languaging skills.
4. Goals for the language arts program comprise the thinking skills: description, discrimination, relating, generalization, evaluation, and valuing. These goals are applicable in any area of study and can be expressed both orally and in writing.

CHALLENGE

The Challenge section in each chapter gives you a chance to try out ideas that have been presented. It will encourage you to organize your thinking and the ideas you collect.

1. Organize a large ringed notebook to help you sort ideas for teaching the language arts. Label a divider for each of the chapter titles in this book. In each section insert lined paper for notes and writing assignments. Also insert a large manila envelope (punch holes along one side) to hold clippings you collect related to the topic of each section—word games, information about authors, useful addresses.

2. In the first section of your notebook begin a process journal. Here you will write comments and observations about the learning process you are experiencing as you explore language arts instruction. Make your first entry now, beginning with today's date. Write whatever you are feeling or thinking about what you have read, the classroom and being in this class, your expectations, and so on. This is a private journal to be shared only on a voluntary basis. Continue to make entries at least twice a week as you record your impressions of the process you are experiencing. (The process journal is an excellent device that you may use in your classroom with elementary school students.)

EXPLORING FURTHER

Blake, Howard E., *Creating a Learning-Centered Classroom; A Practical Guide for Teachers*. New York: Hart Publishing Co., 1977.

English Language Framework Writing Committee, California State Department of Education, *English Language Framework for California Public Schools*. The Department, 1976.

Froese, Victor and Stanley B. Straw, *Research in the Language Arts*. Baltimore, Md.: University Park Press, 1980.

Glatthorn, Allan A., *A Guide for Developing an English Curriculum for the Eighties*. Urbana, Ill.: National Council of Teachers of English, 1980.

Judy, Stephen N., *The ABCs of Literacy: A Guide for Parents and Educators*. New York: Oxford Univ. Press, Inc., 1980.

——— *Explorations in the Teaching of English* (2nd ed.). New York: Harper & Row, 1981.

Mandel, Barrett, ed., *Three Language-Arts Curriculum Models*. Urbana, Ill.: National Council of Teachers of English, 1980.

Moffett, James and Betty Wagner, *Student-centered Language Arts and Reading, K-13* (2nd ed.). Boston: Houghton Mifflin Co., 1976.

Shane, Harold G. and James Walden, Coordinators, *Classroom-Relevant Research in the Language Arts*. Washington, D.C.: Assoc. for Supervision and Curriculum Development, 1978.

Shuman, R. Baird, ed., *Education in the 80s: English*. Washington, D.C.: National Education Association, 1981.

Smith, Frank, *Comprehension and Learning; A Conceptual Framework for Teachers*. New York: Holt, Rinehart and Winston, 1975.

Stanford, Gene, *Developing Effective Classroom Groups; A Practical Guide for Teachers*. New York: A & W Visual Library, 1980.

Tiedt, Iris M., *Exploring Books with Children*. Boston: Houghton Mifflin, 1979.

Tiedt, Sidney and Iris M. Tiedt, *Language Arts Activities for the Classroom*. Boston: Allyn & Bacon, 1978.

Wolf, Maryanne et al., eds., *Thought & Language/Language & Reading*. Harvard Educational Review Reprint Series No. 14, 1980.

2

Children are the world's most valuable resource and its best hope for the future.

John F. Kennedy

CENTERING
ON THE STUDENT
Language and Learning Needs

"I holded the puppy," said Joey.
"Did you say you held the puppy?" asked his mother.
"No," he replied firmly, "I holded the puppy."

Joey is learning to speak English. He has listened to the language around him, and he has learned how to express action in the past tense. As he hears more language, his language ability will continue to grow.

In this chapter we will examine how children learn language, beginning in the home and continuing in the classroom. We will consider, in the light of what we know about language learning, how we can best assist language development. We will also explore the special language needs of children who are learning English for the first time.

In addition to a focus on language development, we will study the other needs of our students. The growth of self-esteem, for example, is of such primary concern that we will devote a number of pages to instruction designed to promote a positive self-image for each child.

Special attention must also be directed toward the needs of handicapped students who are being mainstreamed in the regular classroom. Individualization of instruction is clearly necessary to meet these students' needs as learners. Experiences designed to develop self-esteem will also be especially helpful for the handicapped student as well as for the student who is not proficient in using English.

BENCHMARK

Imagine a third-grade classroom. Think about the students in this room as you answer these questions.

1. What do you know about children at this age level? What might you expect them to be able to do? If you were to choose a book to read to this group, what kind of book would you choose?

2. What is the cultural and ethnic make-up of the community in which you live? Name the languages that are spoken in homes. List some of the religions that are represented. How will this cultural and ethnic background affect what goes on in the classroom?

3. How can a teacher accommodate the varied needs of students? Suggest a number of ways to individualize instruction to meet specific needs. How might a teacher help, for example, a deaf child, a child who just came from Vietnam, a child whose mother died?

After reading this chapter and trying the suggested activities, you will be able to:

• identify variations in children's mental and physical abilities
• discuss children's needs in terms of self-esteem and the understanding of others
• describe learning activities that develop self-esteem and the understanding of others
• discuss the importance of individualizing the language arts program
• suggest specific methods of meeting individual needs in the classroom

UNDERSTANDING STUDENT NEEDS

The children who come to us are not equal. They have varied abilities, distinctive personalities, well-established attitudes and values, and other characteristics that make them the individuals that they are.

The students who enter our classrooms, however, do have similar needs and the right to expect that their needs will be met. As pointed out in the first chapter, children have the following rights as learners:

1. Acceptance
2. Self-esteem
3. Growth
4. Guidance
5. Schooling

In this section we will first look at the characteristics of the students we teach that will influence language arts instruction. Because it is so important in developing curriculum and instruction, we will then examine language development in more detail.

The Characteristics of Students

Children have been living and learning for five years or more before they enter a classroom. Many factors influence their growth during this period of time—the home attitudes, inherited mental abilities, physical development, and native language. The thirty individuals in one classroom have experienced life differently and been shaped accordingly. We begin by getting acquainted with these students as individuals.

As Moffett and Wagner point out:

> Different individuals have dominances toward the physical, the emotional, the intellectual, or the intuitive. Some gravitate toward visual media, some toward auditory, some toward manipulatory, and some toward the kinesthetic (the body itself as medium). Some learn better from peers, some from elders, some from the same sex, some from the other sex, some from certain personality types, and so on. Each has learned the same words in different connections and has a different notion about what language, especially written language, is worth and what it can do for him. Youngsters the same age want to read very different things, and any one class may have a spread of reading maturity ranging over six to ten grades as measured by standardized reading tests.[1]

In this part of the chapter we will look at the variations we can expect to find in any classroom. We will summarize mental and physical variations first and then examine variations in cultural and ethnic backgrounds. We will also consider the needs of economically and sociologically deprived students.

Varying mental and physical abilities   Students in any single classroom show great diversity in physical and intellectual ability. Even the novice teacher soon learns that instruction must be adjusted to meet individual abilities. This adjustment must be made in terms of how information is presented as well as in terms of teacher expectations of what students can accomplish.

Slower learners may be able to learn the same concept that is presented to gifted students, but the learning process will take longer. Instruction should, therefore, include more repetition and be presented in smaller increments. The teacher will use more oral language to support reading and writing activities and will evaluate student progress based on individual growth. Instructional priorities must be established based on the student's most immediate need and the effort required for learning.

At the other end of the continuum is the creative, mentally gifted student. Sometimes, the gifted child is ignored or expected to work completely

---

[1]James Moffett and Betty Jane Wagner, *Student-centered Language Arts and Reading, K-13,* 2nd ed. (Boston: Houghton Mifflin Co., 1976), p. 26.

independently just because he or she can read well. The gifted student may be bored by school activities that provide no stimulus or opportunity to interact with other students. Bright students can be challenged to investigate topics of their own choice, to plan instructional presentations for other students, and to engage in classroom activities at a more sophisticated level. Again, evaluation is based on their achievement, their individual growth.

Physical abilities or handicaps must also be considered. The handicapped child may fit at any point on the intellectual continuum, for the deaf child or the paraplegic may have a brilliant mind. It is essential not to make assumptions about any child as we take special care to discover individual characteristics and needs. An important aspect of education for the handicapped student is access to "normal" persons, interaction with other children. The learning that occurs through mainstreaming programs is beneficial to all of the students involved.

As we consider the mental and physical variations among children, it should be noted that children are more alike than they are different. All children have the needs pointed out at the beginning of this section. Individual variation that makes teaching more complex may occur in the following areas:

MATURATION

Children are most frequently grouped according to chronological age. Children of the same age have not matured mentally or physically at the same rate, however, which requires adjustment in pacing of learning activities as well as the timing of the presentation of concepts.

LANGUAGE VARIATION

Children who learn English as a first language may speak widely different dialects. Other children have learned different languages as their native speech. For them English becomes a second language, and they may become fully bilingual. Teachers who recognize the language variations as normal aspects of language development in the classroom will provide support for each child's language growth.

SPEECH IMPAIRMENT

Most children with a speech impairment can function within the classroom with teacher and student support. Problems in articulating specific sounds such as /r/ or /l/ become evident as children enter kindergarten or first grade. Stuttering is a not uncommon disorder. Children who have such impairments should usually have special assistance, but they need to feel accepted in the normal classroom as they build self-confidence and learn with other students of similar age and ability.

MENTAL GIFTEDNESS

The gifted child often reads early and displays thinking abilities that stand out in that age group. Gifted or creative students may themselves need help in understanding their abilities and in learning how to get along with persons who are less advanced.

SENSORY HANDICAPS

Varying degrees of deafness or blindness may occur in students who are main-streamed in regular classrooms. Both teacher and students can learn to assist the sensory-handicapped student by substituting different modes of learning. The positive support and caring attitude demonstrated in the classroom benefits the entire group of students.

LEARNING HANDICAPS

Students may exhibit some degree of retardation or perceptual problems. A specialist should test these students, and recommend and assist with instruction designed to aid the specific handicap. Parental involvement will also be invaluable.

A number of generalizations will help classroom teachers deal effectively with exceptional children who are in their classrooms, for example:

1. As much as possible, treat the exceptional child as you would any other child in the room. Avoid oversolicitous behavior.
2. Individualize instruction so that the child can achieve at an appropriate level. Have realistic expectations.
3. Generate a classroom climate that engenders caring and supportive behavior for all children. Discuss diversity and the needs of everyone in the classroom.
4. Listen to children. Open channels of communication with the exceptional child so that he or she can ask for help as needed.
5. Establish clear priorities for the handicapped child's learning. Stress that which is most important, for example, oral language development.
6. Work closely with specialists who are assisting the child's learning. Communicate frequently with parents, and encourage them to play an active role in their child's growth.

Notice that the recommendations listed above are characteristic of good teaching that is helpful for *all* students. In the next chapter we will examine teaching practices in more detail.

Cultural and ethnic groups   Students come from varied cultural and ethnic backgrounds. Prior to the 1960s, the schools reflected the "melting pot" theory, the idea that all persons living in the United States should be as much alike as possible. Immigrants were pressured to learn English immediately, and there was often expressed hostility toward groups that resisted assimilation. Following World War I, for example, there was much antagonism toward German–Americans.

Today, however, in general, we respect the cultural diversity that exists in the United States. In 1968, Title VII of the Elementary and Secondary Education Act, mandated bilingual programs in schools throughout the country. Although there is controversy about the way to implement bilingual education, all schools are involved in working with students who first learned a language other than English. In 1976, the Office of Education funded bilingual programs across the country in forty-six languages, as listed here:

Bilingual Programs Sponsored by HEW
Forty-six Languages Represented

NATIVE AMERICAN LANGUAGES	EUROPEAN LANGUAGES	OTHER LANGUAGES
Indian	French	Arabic
Apache	Canadian French	Hebrew
Cherokee	Haitian Creole	Punjabi (India)
Choctaw	Greek	Samoan
Cree	Italian	Cambodian
Crow	Pennsylvania Dutch (Germanic)	Chinese
Eelaponke	Polish	Ilocano (Philippines)
Havasupai	Portuguese	Japanese
Keresan	Spanish	Korean
Lakota	Russian	Tagalog (Philippines)
Miccosukee-Seminole	Yiddish	Vietnamese
Mohawk		
Navajo		
Northern Cheyenne		
Paiute		
Papago		
Passamaquoddy		
Seminole-Creek		
Tewa		
Ute		
Walapai		
Eskimo		
Aleut		
Central Yupik		
Gwichin		
Inupik		

SOURCE: Department of Health, Education and Welfare.

Following the establishment of bilingual programs came an effort to teach broad multicultural concepts. Multicultural education is not a subject to be taught in isolation. It is more effectively taught as the subject matter for such basic instruction as reading or composition and is clearly related to social studies instruction. The teacher can work actively to dispel stereotyped perceptions of members of groups in the United States by showing students how to:

1. Use language that is free of racist and sexist terms or labels
2. Recognize that careless use of language and stereotyped perceptions can hurt human beings and limit their potential
3. Talk about people as individual human beings who have varied characteristics not limited by sex, race, class, or ethnic background.[2]

As teachers, we need to be aware of acceptable terminology as we talk about ethnic groups in the United States. The following group names are accepted:

[2]Pamela Tiedt and Iris M. Tiedt. *Multicultural Teaching: A Handbook of Activities, Information, and Resources* (Boston: Allyn & Bacon, Inc., 1979), p. 12.

22

Asian–Americans, Chinese–Americans, Japanese–Americans
Black Americans, Negro, Afro-American
Chicano, Mexican-American
Native Americans or specific Latino tribal names, as: Hopi, Aleut[3]

The term *race* is often used incorrectly and, therefore, should be discussed with children. Race is not synonymous with nationality, language spoken, culture, or color. A more scientific approach is recommended based on blood type or geography.

Multicultural education should be a serious concern as we plan language arts instruction. The selection of literature should include excellent books about children of varied cultures, ones that present accurate historical information. *Dragonwings* by Laurence Yep is about Chinese–Americans; it could be read aloud to upper elementary and junior high school students to provide insight into American history and a model for good writing. Language arts instruction should also be planned to promote self-esteem through oral and written activities. Students can learn to critique literature in terms of stereotyping and accuracy of information. The nature of our cultural heritage is a concern to all students at every age level. Multicultural education will be discussed in more detail in Chapter 14: Language Arts Across the Curriculum, for multicultural education should also "cross the elementary school curriculum."

Economically and socially deprived children   Many English-speaking children have special needs because they have not had an enriched childhood that supported language development. Economic, psychological, and sociological factors (for example, working parents, the high divorce rate, and single–parent homes) may deprive the child of experiences and linguistic input that would prepare him or her to enter kindergarten at an expected level of competency. These students need psychological support as well as assistance with language learning.

The disadvantaged child may be a Mexican-American boy living in California, an American Indian on a Utah reservation, a poor white from Appalachia, a Puerto Rican girl living in New York City or a black living along South State Street in Chicago. The point is that economic disadvantage is limited to no particular racial or ethnic group nor to any special locality; it is spread literally across our nation, for it is present in every city, in most small towns, and in many rural areas.

As Richard Corbin states in the excellent report published by the National Council of Teachers of English:

> Whatever the racial or ethnic background of these disadvantaged, their circumstances are much the same. They come from families that exist on annual incomes which fall below the established national minimum subsistence level, that have known little or no schooling, that have no job security. More than half have only one parent (generally the mother), and many have never known either parent. They come from families who seldom aspire, or when they do, aspire

[3]Ibid., p. 11.

unrealistically, who are often idle because few jobs are open to them. They are the people who exist—one can hardly say "live"—on the wretched rim of an otherwise affluent world. And they number not fewer than one quarter of our total national population.[4]

Studies have identified certain characteristics which are typical of children of all ages who are classified as deprived or disadvantaged. The typical economically disadvantaged child can be described thus:

1. Lacks self-confidence. Insecurity may cause unruly behavior in the classroom or juvenile delinquency. Attitude toward self and possibilities for success in life is negative. Feels that others view him as "a worthless individual." Racial discrimination has accentuated the poor self-image for the black child. The disadvantaged child is afraid, ill at ease in the school situation, lacks the security of a stable home, frequently moves and has little opportunity to develop friendships.
2. The home does not provide educational stimulus. The family is economically poor as well as educationally impoverished. Money is not available for books, magazines, or the daily newspaper; and even were money available, there is little desire for spending it in this way. More likely, money would be used to buy entertainment, food, or clothing. Paper, pencils, and crayons are not available in the home, nor are varied toys to stimulate play. There is no precedent for obtaining an education, as parents and grandparents have had little formal schooling. A college degree or even a high school diploma is beyond the aspirations of this child. There may be hostility toward teachers and the school, with the latter viewed as a jail and the teacher as jailer. The child may enter school already looking forward to dropping out. The experiential background of this child is limited with little opportunity to travel, to be read to, to visit museums, or to explore the world in general.
3. Not physically well cared for, and in many cases undernourished. The child shows evidence of neglected illness and may have physical handicaps that need attention. Regular visits to the dentist have not been made, and the child's eyes have not been checked. Lack of parental supervision and adequate sleeping facilities may mean this child will come to school tired and may arrive hungry, having had no breakfast.
4. Language skills are impoverished. The speech heard at home is meager with little elaboration. Mother directs the child's activities by single-word commands, saying "Here," to the young girl to whom she hands the baby. She does not elaborate as a more educated person tends to, "Here; hold Manny while I start peeling the potatoes for dinner. He keeps crawling under my feet, and I'm afraid I'll step on him." The working mother, who herself may not be physically well, is tired and is preoccupied by providing the essentials—food, beds, clothes, a roof overhead. Although there may be many people living in the same apartment, the extent of the vocabulary to which the child is exposed is actually small, and no one has time to sit talking to a child about games or to tell stories nor is the child particularly encouraged to talk. The child is left largely alone, often having little contact with the English language, especially in its standard dialects. Mexican-Americans or Puerto Rican children may have the further disadvantage of not speaking English at all or of living in a home where English

[4]Richard Corbin, "Literacy, Literature, and the Disadvantaged," in *Language Programs for the Disadvantaged* (Urbana, Ill.: National Council of Teachers of English, 1965), p. 6.

is not usually spoken. The English that this child learns is only that heard on the street. Proficient in neither language, entrance in elementary school requires the learning of English, therefore, as a foreign language for these children, who must become bilingual.

Our focus as teachers is not on the broad social problem of deprivation, however, but on helping the child who is the victim of deprivation; even more specifically, our concern in this book is for instruction in English as one part of the elementary school curriculum. In order to plan a program designed to aid the child in developing language skills, it is first necessary to determine the needs.

The needs of the deprived child are varied, and they include more than academic knowledge, for this child comes to school psychologically handicapped, a factor which impedes learning. The objectives of any program for compensatory education must be cognizant of the child's need to develop:

1. Language skills: thinking, listening, speaking, writing, reading (in the order named)
2. Feeling of personal worth; confidence in ability to succeed
3. Recognition of school as pleasant and learning as pleasurable
4. Enthusiasm and interest in environment; wide experimental background
5. Interest in others and respect for them; ability to work and play with others

LANGUAGE LEARNING

As we consider the needs of students, language development is a primary concern. The language arts teacher can plan more effectively if she or he knows how children acquire the ability to speak a language and the implications of this information for language instruction. As more and more students are learning English as a second language, we also must plan for students who have limited proficiency in using English.

In this section we will discuss the acquisition of a first language. Then we will look at the language environment to see how that affects language development. Third, we will discuss the needs of students who have limited or no proficiency with English.

Acquiring a First Language

How does a young child learn language? Who teaches children to talk? Language is a human development, and normally all human babies learn to speak a language, the language they hear around them. Lying in their cribs, infants experiment with the physical movements of their bodies; they move their tongues and babble noises. At this stage children make many strange sounds, some that are not used in the language of their families; potentially, they could learn any language equally well. Gradually, however, they learn to focus on the sounds around them and to speak the language that they hear daily. They are highly motivated to learn so they keep practicing with no formal instruction and no one to evaluate their success.

We can assume that all children have linguistic competence, the ability to learn language. Noam Chomsky argues that children must have an innate ability to grasp language, which is the only explanation of how they can learn the complex grammar system of a language at such an immature stage. They begin learning this system before the age of one when they are scarcely intellectually developed, and they learn without formal instruction. Children abstract syntactic generalizations, moreover, from a fragmentary, incidental presentation of language. Even dull children learn language, and they learn from children around them, rather than adults.[5]

Children have learned most of the syntax of their native language before entering school, and they have developed a large speaking and listening vocabulary. We can observe their knowledge of grammar through their linguistic performance, and many students of child language have now written grammars of specific young children to demonstrate this cognitive development. What is particularly fascinating about children's acquisition of language, however, is that they develop an approach to learning that is individualized in the truest sense. It is self-motivated and self-designed. Children select what they need from their language environment. They learn through:

Real discovery techniques from the language environment
Making and correcting their own "errors" or miscues
Self-initiated and self-motivated learning
Positive reinforcement and encouragement
Feedback and expansion by children and adults around them

Notice, particularly, that there is no negative aspect to this early learning program. The child initiates it joyfully, feels successful and secure in learning, and would probably continue to approach learning positively if there were no interference. What happens to this enthusiasm when we adults design the program, select the input, and evaluate progress?

Many students of child language have analyzed the speech of young children to demonstrate the development of linguistic knowledge. Researchers note that dull children tend to lag behind brighter children at various stages—that is, a dull five-year-old may speak much like a bright four-year-old. Children of upper socioeconomic groups tend to develop at faster rates. Boys lag behind girls in development of speech, and children who are multiple births (twins, triplets, the famous quintuplets) tend to be retarded in linguistic development.[6] Excellent summaries of research in the field of child language can be read in the *Encyclopedia of Educational Research,* written by Dorothea McCarthy (1950), John Carroll (1960), and Robert L. Ebel (1969). A one-volume summary of developments in this field is *Child Language: A Book of Readings,* edited by Aaron Bar-Adon and Werner F. Leopold (Prentice-Hall, Inc., 1971).

[5]Noam Chomsky, "Language and the Mind," *Psychology Today,* February 1969.

[6]Dorothea McCarthy, "Language Development," *Encyclopedia of Educational Research,* ed. W.S. Monroe (New York: Macmillan Publishing Co., Inc., 1950), pp. 165–72.

Brown and Bellugi studied the development of syntax in two young children, Adam and Eve. They identified three processes in the children's acquisition of syntax:

Imitation and reduction (repeating one or two words)
Imitation with expansion (repeating a word or two plus additional idea)
Induction of latent structure (demonstrating generalization about grammar)

Adam and Eve began with single word sentences—for example, "Bad." From these holophrases their speech progressed to two-word sentences, such as "See truck." Gradually additional words were added to the child's speech, and more complex syntactic structures appeared.[7] By the age of four, therefore, the child has acquired the basic syntactic structures of English. McNeill notes that: "On the basis of a fundamental capacity for language, each generation creates language anew, and does so with astonishing speed."[8]

As Chukovsky listened to children's speech, he realized that it was not only fascinating "but also had an intrinsically high instructive value." He observed children's language "to discover the whimsical and elusive laws of childhood thinking."[9] He noted the child's creative use of language and invention of words and concluded that: "If his former talent for word invention and construction had not abandoned him, he would, even by the age of ten, eclipse any of us with his suppleness and brilliance of speech."[10]

Children learn language through hearing the speech of those around them; however, the process used is not imitation per se. The role of imitation in learning language needs clarification because children are not just repeating sentences they hear. Children actually construct a grammar based on the language they hear. They constantly test it by using it, polishing it over a period of years, until it closely approximates adult knowledge of the full syntax of English. What is amazing, furthermore, is that children all around the world learn their native language in much the same way. This fact supports the existence of linguistic universals, characteristics common to all language.[11]

The Language Environment

The language environment is highly influential in determining the quality of a child's linguistic development. Children who have many books and records and to whom stories are read frequently, will naturally develop a richer vocabulary and a greater facility with language than will children

[7]Roger Brown and Ursula Bellugi-Klima, "Three Processes in the Child's Acquisition of Syntax," in *Language and Learning, Harvard Educational Review*, 34: 133–51.

[8]David McNeill, "The Creation of Language by Children," in *Child Language*, eds. Aaron Bar-Adon and Werner F. Leopold (Englewood Cliffs, N.J.: Prentice-Hall, 1971), p. 349.

[9]Kornei Chukovsky, *From Two to Five* (Berkeley, Calif.: University of California Press, 1966), p. xv.

[10]Ibid., p. 7.

[11]McNeill, "The Creation of Language by Children," p. 350.

living in homes where books are not part of the life style and the language heard is very limited in quality. Parents can make a conscientious effort to provide varied language experiences, and child-care centers and nursery schools should stress the development of language skills in every way possible.

Picture books for children stimulate the child's thinking and broaden the concepts and experiences to which each child is exposed. ABC books, for example, usually contain pictures of various objects that children can enjoy looking at and name verbally. Children enjoy talking about the pictures, especially if an interested adult or big brother is listening and will join in the commentary.

Reading aloud to children provides them with a richer environment from which to select for their own needs. As stories are repeated, the delighted children will "read" familiar phrases with the adult reader. "You wicked old rascal!" became a favorite for all of us as we read "Little Red Riding Hood," and our daughter knew exactly when that phrase appeared in the sequence of the story.

In the classroom it is important that we provide an environment in which children can continue to learn language as naturally and successfully as they did independently. We mistakenly think we are "teaching language" when we give children duplicated sheets on which to make word choices or ask them to label the parts of a sentence construction. Is this really the way children learn language? We must remind ourselves that children learn language by hearing it and that we can best assist them by seeing that language is heard in the classroom.

Learning English as a Second Language

In almost all classrooms today you will find students who first learned a language other than English—Spanish, Tagalog, Vietnamese, Arabic. These children must now learn English in order to function effectively in the United States; they must become bilingual. At the age of five or older this task is not as simple as learning a first language.

Working with bilingual students is made more complex by the range of language development. A child who has a good command of his or her first language, speaking easily, with a good vocabulary and concept development, will find it relatively easy to learn English. A child who has learned to read fluently in Spanish, for example, will transfer to reading English with ease because the reading process has already been mastered (in a language that has more regular sound–symbol correspondence). On the other hand, children who have not mastered the grammatical constructions of their native language during the early years have little linguistic knowledge to support their learning of a new language. They are linguistically handicapped and will need much special assistance.

Another factor that makes handling a bilingual program complex is the differing philosophy to which educational leaders ascribe. Programs that are truly bilingual have instruction in two languages in approximately equal proportions. English-speaking students could become bilingual by learning a second language through participation in this type of program.

Although referred to as "bilingual," most programs that now exist are teaching English as a second language with the intent of eliminating student use of the native language. Eventually, all instruction will be in English. As Pamela Tiedt points out:

> Language is an important but often neglected part of bilingual education programs. Despite the fact that demands for these programs demonstrate recognition of the importance of language, bilingual education programs take many language related issues for granted. Statements of good intentions are not sufficient. Bilingual programs and program proposals must be evaluated not only by what they claim to provide but in how they carry out their intentions, particularly in the areas directly related to language.[12]

She notes, furthermore, that we need to discuss language-related features and to examine the following: (1) the language of the students, (2) the language of the teachers, (3) the language used in curriculum materials, and (4) the program goals with respect to language.[13]

Helping students who have little knowledge of English is clearly a responsibility of the schools. These children will benefit from working with language arts activities as well as formal English instruction and interaction with other children. Again, we need to remember the most effective way to learn language, through hearing and using it.

Summary

As we analyze the variations among the students who enroll in our classrooms, we need to emphasize the universality of children's needs—self-esteem, acceptance, and growth. Given these universal needs, we can assist children individually to overcome handicaps, to discover their own personal attributes, and to work in a classroom community that is supportive and promotes understanding of others. Language arts instruction can incorporate goals that will encourage children to discover themselves as persons and as successful learners.

MEETING STUDENT NEEDS IN THE CLASSROOM

Our first concern in developing a language arts curriculum should be the needs of the students who enter our classrooms. As we have pointed out in the preceding section, these needs are varied; therefore, the job is not easy. Regimentation, treating all students as if their needs were the same, a teacher-dominated mode of instruction—these solutions are not accept-

---

[12]Pamela Tiedt, "A Linguistic Evaluation of Bilingual Education Programs," in *Multicultural Teaching* by Pamela Tiedt and Iris Tiedt (Boston: Allyn & Bacon, Inc. 1979), pp. 324–335.
[13]Ibid., p. 324.

able if we base the language arts program on research and what we know about how students learn.

Providing Growth for All Children

Learning (and teaching) must begin where the child is. We may choose to defer formal introduction of complex concepts while children develop self-esteem. Time spent on this objective readies the student to achieve successfully.

Objectives that meet the needs of the child directly should be incorporated into the basic curriculum. While you are helping children accept themselves and children of other cultural backgrounds, therefore, you will also be teaching oral language skills, thinking abilities, and moving into reading and writing activities. In this section we will examine methods of reaching the following objectives that meet children's needs within the language arts program:

1.   Children will accept themselves as good persons and will increase their self-esteem. They will develop an "I can" attitude and be motivated to try new learning experiences.
2.   Children will grow continuously to fulfill their greatest potential. Handicapped children will learn to work around their disabilities while the mentally gifted children learn to make the most of the abilities they have.
3.   Children will understand and appreciate each other. They will discuss the concept of diversity and recognize the strengths that diversity has added to the development of our country. They will understand the basic human characteristics and needs that we all share while each individual makes a unique contribution to society.

We can teach toward these objectives through incidental instruction that deals with these concepts implicitly. At other times, however, we will make the concepts explicit as we read aloud to children or introduce discussion topics that touch on a specific understanding.

Individual diagnosis is the key to helping children grow. We need to know the students in each class in order to determine the benchmark from which they begin at this time and to judge their growth against this individual position. Psychological, sociological, physical, mental growth—all are part of the learning process in which children engage. The teacher can gain information from many sources:

1.   *School records.* Cumulative folders are available for children who have been in the school during the previous year. Recorded test scores and teacher observations provide some information with which to begin.
2.   *Informal assessment.* For children who are new to the school or for students about whom you need more information, the teacher can observe performance. Having children read aloud individually from a basic textbook is a quick way of assessing reading ability. Behavior in varied situations provides information about the students' maturation and physical abilities. Informal observation suffices until more formal assessment can be made.

3. *Talking and listening to children.* Individual conferences should be scheduled regularly as part of evaluation procedures. All children need individual attention that is positive and specific to their needs. Some children may require more attention than others, to discuss how comfortable they feel in the classroom. Listen as they tell you how they perceive what is going on or suggest ways that you might help them.

Instructional strategies must provide for individual differences. In the next chapter on instruction we will discuss techniques that facilitate the individualization of language arts learning experiences. Even when you work with the group as a whole, however, you can provide for individual variation by using open-ended topics for discussion or response to a film in writing.

Developing Self-esteem

In order to learn, children need to feel that they can learn. Beginning language arts experiences should be designed for success. Our expectations for what children will achieve must fit their abilities. We must plan activities that allow for the wide range of abilities in any classroom, with the expectation that each child will achieve according to his or her ability. The activities described here are open enough to allow each child to participate successfully. Included are activities that strengthen oral language development and others that help children get to know each other.

Oral language development   The greatest need for children is to develop adequate oral language skills. Suggested activities include the following:

PLAYING GROUP GAMES WHICH INCLUDE SINGING OR CHANTING OF SIMPLE FAMILIAR REFRAINS:

   Young children—"A Tisket-A-Tasket"
                     "Farmer in the Dell"
   Older children—"What's Your Trade? Lemonade!"
                     Jumping rope

ORAL ACTIVITIES WHICH STRESS AUDITORY DISCRIMINATION:

   Which words begin alike? Which one does not?
      bird   baby   teacher
   Which word begins like *horse?*
      hospital   apartment   spoon

ENJOYING A GOOD STORY TOGETHER:

   The teacher reads aloud, showing the illustrations as the story proceeds.

Favorites With Younger Children Include:

   May I Bring a Friend?, Beatrice Schenk de Regniers
   White Snow, Bright Snow, Alvin Tresselt
   The 500 Hats of Bartholomew Cubbins, Dr. Seuss

Older Children Will Enjoy:

Pippi Longstocking, Astrid Lindgren
Homer Price, Robert McCloskey
The House of Wings, Betsy Byars
Robin Hood, Howard Pyle

FILMS AND RECORDS CAN ALSO INTRODUCE EXCELLENT STORIES WHICH PROVIDE
TOPICS FOR DISCUSSION AND ADD TO THE CHILD'S EXPERIENCES:

Weston Woods (Weston, Conn.) has produced films of familiar stories from
children's literature, for example, "The Doughnuts" from *Homer Price* by Robert
McCloskey and *Millions of Cats* by Wanda Gág. Of special interest is *A Snowy Day*,
the film of a young Negro boy's adventures in the snow, and *Crow Boy*, the story
of a boy who felt out of place in the classroom.

One of the most generally effective teaching strategies that can be used
with a group of learners of any age is listening and responding to a story
read by the teacher. Teachers typically read aloud in the primary grades,
but usually the reading is viewed as "frosting on the cake," a pleasant activity
if there is time. Reading aloud is much more than that, however, and it
should be incorporated in the curriculum as part of reading and writing
instruction.

In the first place, reading aloud is a very efficient method of presenting
information to a group of students. In a few minutes the teacher can present
a short story that students will act out or an article that students can discuss.
All students hear the same information, and all are ready at the same time
to begin the followup activity. Although everyone hears the same selection,
each will respond to it individually according to his or her ability. Response
can be oral or written and can be shared immediately. Reading aloud,
moreover, develops a cohesive group feeling and establishes rapport between the teacher and the class. Shared humor, intriguing information, an
emotional experience add to the group's fund of common knowledge. In
addition, reading aloud supports both the reading and writing program
by demonstrating to students what the print media have to offer them, and
it provides an alternative method of providing input for slower readers.

Reading aloud is efficient and effective as a presentation method, but it
has the additional advantage of teaching language arts skills and concepts
in an integrated and enjoyable way. Children are highly motivated to listen
when the teacher reads so that listening skills are emphasized and can be
directly reinforced. New vocabulary is introduced in the context of sentences and paragraphs so that students can understand the meaning; new
concepts are introduced in the same manner. As students listen, they are
hearing new grammatical constructions, kinds of sentences that they might
try writing. They hear the use of language by a skilled author who may
use such figurative devices as simile, metaphor, or personification. They
hear the way a story or article is developed, how a composition is organized,
and they hear the formal "book language" or standard English that we
want them to write and read, language that differs considerably from the

language they usually speak. Reading aloud serves to open books and may invite students to read for information and pleasure independently.

Reading aloud is a successful teaching strategy for students of all ages. Preschoolers and junior high school students respond equally well to the kind of sharing that occurs when the teacher presents a good book. This strategy proves just as efficient and effective across the curriculum in the social studies and science areas. What's more, reading aloud is a very pleasant teaching experience as well.

Getting acquainted   Oral and written language can be used to help students share information about themselves. As they focus on their individual attributes, they also gain self-esteem. In a classroom climate that encourages open presentation of ideas children will enjoy talking about what they know best—themselves. These activities foster a deeper understanding of other students.

Getting acquainted in the fall offers a good opportunity to focus on personal writing. Students can complete the following activity sheets, share them in small groups, and then compile them in a ME BOOK.

Older students might enjoy thinking of a metaphor for themselves much as Jessamyn West did in this example:

Jessamyn West, author of *Cress Delahanty* and *Friendly Persuasion,* drew a picture of herself as an all-seeing eye. As she thinks of herself eyeing the world, she suddenly becomes aware that she is at the same time revealing herself. How does this make her feel?

JESSAMYN WEST

I think I am an eye. Seeing, not seen. If I thought I was seen as well as seeing, I'd be a better turned-out female. Hems where hems ought to be this season; new permanent before the old one has given out; lipstick nicely centered on the mouth. But I'm so busy seeing I forget that that's a two-way street.

The following activity sheet asks students to extend this focus on themselves as they choose an animal metaphor and explain their choices.

Looking at Yourself

How do you see yourself? If, for example, you could suddenly be changed into any animal that you chose, which one of the following twelve animals would you like to be:

Fish	Peacock	Impala	Donkey
Horse	Cat	Butterfly	Lion
Dog	Shellfish	Elephant	Monkey

Write a paragraph explaining why you selected the animal that you did. Talk about these selections with a small group. If you like, read what you have written about your choice.

If you enjoyed this activity, you might like to repeat it by selecting an animal you would hate to be.

Teaching English as a Second Language

The increasing number of students who enter our classrooms knowing little English adds to the responsibility of the elementary school. Part of the language arts program in almost every school provides language instruction for students who have non-English proficiency (NEP) or limited English proficiency (LEP). LEP-NEP students will benefit from special language classes, but they should participate in the full elementary school language arts curriculum as well.

Since the spoken language is the primary form of language, instruction should emphasize speaking, and aural–oral methods of providing information to students should be used to teach English grammatical constructions. The following oral practice techniques, which illustrate varied sentence constructions, will also benefit some primary students whose oral language needs strengthening.[14]

Repetition: Listen and repeat exactly as heard.

Teacher:	I see a dog.
Child:	I see a dog.

Analogy: Repeat exactly with one change.

Teacher:	I am a man.
Anne:	I am a woman.
Fred:	I am a boy.
Sue:	I am a person.

Begin a PROGRESSIVE CONVERSATION so that all members of the group participate in this type of analogical replacement, thus:

Teacher:	I see a dog. What do you see, Jim?
Jim:	I see a cat. What do you see, Janet?
Janet:	I see a mouse. What do you see, Gerri?

Inflection: Change the form of a word.

Teacher:	There is one girl.
Sue:	There are two girls.

[14]Nelson Brooks, *Language and Language Learning* (New York: Harcourt Brace Jovanovich, 1964), pp. 156–61.

> *Teacher:*   There is one house.
>   *Fred:*   There are two houses.

Completion: Finish the statement.

> *Teacher:*   Susan is tall, but . . .
>   *Joan:*   Mary is taller.
> *Teacher:*   John is big, but . . .
>   *Carol:*   Phil is bigger.

Expansion:

> *Teacher:*   Steve is happy.
>   *Chuck:*   Steve is happy because he finished his work.
> *Teacher:*   Milly is happy.
>   *Ann:*   Milly is happy because she has a new dress.

Transformation: Change a given sentence to negative or interrogative form.

> *Teacher:*   Judy is here today.
>   *Carol:*   Judy is not here today.
> *Teacher:*   Judy is here today.
>   *Fred:*   Is Judy here today?

Restoration: Student makes sentences from a group of words.

> *Teacher:*   picture, wall, hanging
>   *Chuck:*   The picture is hanging on the wall.
>   *Phyllis:*   Is the picture hanging on that wall?

Response: Answer or make a rejoinder.

> *Teacher:*   It is chilly in this room.
>   *Mary:*   It feels fine to me.
>   *Jim:*   I think you are right.
>   *Joan:*   Shall I close the door?

In addition to these patterned speaking drills, children who are learning English can begin dictating information to the teacher or an aide who will help the child construct English sentences. The teacher may need to print or write the sentences for the beginning student, who can then read the sentences because he or she spoke them and knows the information. Such language experience approaches that integrate language arts instruction are described in more detail in the chapter on reading.

In the chapters on listening and speaking there are many activities that support language learning. As soon as possible, the students who are learning English as a second language should participate in the language activities of the classroom. The other students will delight in helping them learn English in a supportive classroom situation.

SUMMARY

The language arts curriculum must be student-centered. Listing objectives for language arts instruction will begin, therefore, with aims that meet students' most immediate needs. Understanding how children learn language not only shows us effective methods of instruction but also indicates what children can be expected to know when they come to school. Students who have not attained English language fluency need additional opportunities to work with oral language to support the reading and writing programs. Oral language will remain the primary method of instruction as elementary and junior high school students engage in prewriting and prereading activities and modes of response to various stimuli such as literature in films and books. Oral language activities such as listening to the teacher reading aloud will be used to provide linguistic input from which K–8 students continue to learn English grammar, idiom, and style. Oral language will also be the primary method of developing self-esteem and the understanding of other students in the classroom. A student-centered language arts curriculum will focus on the most important priorities for students as determined through individual diagnosis and carried out through individualized instruction.

CHALLENGE

Engaging in these activities will help you gain understanding of the children you will be teaching.

1. Observe the children in a specific classroom. Describe the group as accurately as possible in terms of:
a. Cultures represented—races, nationalities, language background
b. Mental abilities
c. Physical abilities
d. Behaviors
e. Socioeconomic information—family, income, home
Write a paragraph describing the children in this classroom.

2. Make a collage of children's faces. Write a poem or paragraph about the differences in the children in our schools today.

3. If you were teaching a unit of study on self-identity, how might you plan for the needs of varied students? List at least ten ways that you could adjust instruction to meet an individual's unique needs.

4. Explore the books and other materials available to assist you in helping children understand the cultural backgrounds of Native Americans.

EXPLORING FURTHER

Berry, Mildred F., *Teaching Linguistically Handicapped Children*. Englewood Cliffs, N.J.: Prentice-Hall, Inc., 1980.

Burns, Marilyn, *I Am Not A Short Adult! Getting Good at Being a Kid.* Boston: Little, Brown and Co., 1977.

Canfield, Jack and Harold C. Wells, *100 Ways to Enhance Self-concept in the Classroom.* Englewood Cliffs, N.J.: Prentice-Hall, Inc., 1976.

Cronnell, Bruce, ed., *The Writing Needs of Linguistically Different Students.* Los Alamitos, Calif.: SWRL Educational Research and Development, 1981.

Gantt, Marianne, *Ready for Reading: Classroom Games for Reading Readiness.* Westport, Conn.: Technomic Publishing Co., 1980.

Gerber, Adele and Diane Bryen, *Language and Learning Disabilities.* Baltimore, Md.: University Park Press, 1981.

Johnson, Ferne, ed., *Start Early for an Early Start: You and the Young Child.* Chicago: American Library Association, 1976.

Moffett, James, *Coming on Center: English Education in Evolution.* Montclair, N.J.: Boynton/Cook, 1981.

Moffett, James and Betty Jane Wagner, *Student-centered Language Arts and Reading, K-13.* Boston: Houghton Mifflin Co., 1976.

National Institute of Mental Health, *Children's Play and Social Speech.* NIMH Program Report. Washington, D.C.: U.S. Department of Health, Education, and Welfare, 1976.

Pinnell, Gay Su, ed., *Discovering Language with Children.* Urbana, Ill.: National Council of Teachers of English, 1980.

Rodrigues, Raymond J. and Robert H. White, *Mainstreaming the Non-English Speaking Student.* Theory and Research into Practice Series. Urbana, Ill.: NCTE and ERIC/RCS, 1981.

Tiedt, Iris M., *Exploring Books with Children.* Boston: Houghton Mifflin Co., 1979.

Tiedt, Pamela and Iris M. Tiedt, *Multicultural Teaching. A Handbook of Activities, Information, and Resources.* Boston: Allyn & Bacon, 1979.

Tway, Eileen, ed., *Reading Ladders for Human Relations* (6th ed.). Urbana, Ill.: American Council on Education and the National Council of Teachers of English, 1981.

3

The teacher gives not of his wisdom,
But rather of his faith and lovingness.

Kahlil Gibran, *The Prophet*

PLANNING FOR INSTRUCTION
Designing and Implementing Curriculum

The role of the teacher is complex, but gratifying. Men and women who choose teaching as a career want to improve the world in which they live, and they have selected a helping profession that will enable them to make a difference in children's lives. Teachers deal with the content of many subjects in a self-contained elementary school classroom and work with students who have varied individual needs. In addition, they have administrative, managerial duties as they keep records and plan the year's curriculum. If we were to list all the duties of a language arts instructor, the job of teaching might appear too overwhelming for any person to undertake.

The rewards of teaching are, however, so great that they make the work well worthwhile. The rewards come from watching children grow and knowing that your teaching does make a difference in how they see themselves and their world. The challenge of teaching lies in bringing children and knowledge together in such a manner that learning can take place. As

Rachel Carson notes in *The Sense of Wonder:* "If facts are the seeds that later produce knowledge and wisdom, then the emotions and the impressions of the senses are the fertile soil in which the seeds must grow." The effective teacher integrates the cognitive and the affective aspects of learning so that the classroom becomes a workshop that engages children in activities that move them toward fulfillment of their potential.

BENCHMARK

Begin thinking of yourself as a teacher, a competent person who can direct instruction for elementary school students, design curriculum, confer with parents. Discuss the following questions.

1. Choose a metaphor for teaching, as you see it. Is a teacher, for example, a doctor who cures the ills of his or her patients? If you don't care for the medical metaphor, select one that you consider more appropriate. Write a paragraph describing teaching in terms of the metaphor you choose. Share your ideas with others in your class.

2. Why is discipline such a big problem for teachers? What methods have you seen teachers use effectively in handling discipline problems? How do you think teachers might avoid having discipline problems?

3. Think about the teaching you have observed. Make a list of the things that an effective teacher does that other teachers do not. Compare your list with those made by others in the class. Compile a set of criteria for good teaching, for example:

A good teacher smiles at children in the classroom.

In this chapter we are focusing on the instructional process and the skills involved. We begin by thinking about a philosophy of teaching which is based on specific assumptions about teaching and learning. Then, we consider ways of organizing the language arts curriculum. After examining what research has to tell us about effective teaching we will describe teaching strategies that are recommended for language arts instruction in all grades and across the curriculum as well. After completing this chapter, you should be able to:

- state your own philosophy of teaching
- describe effective instructional methods
- discuss the language arts curriculum and its organization

A POINT OF VIEW

What do you believe about teaching? What is your perception of the teaching–learning process, your philosophy of instruction? The decisions you make about what you will teach and the methods you will employ, even the textbooks you choose, are influenced by how you see teaching.

We need to clarify our thinking, attitudes, and values as we prepare to teach the language arts in the elementary school. A philosophy of instruction is not created overnight but is developed over a period of time as you take in new ideas. Keep your mind open to new ways of looking at student and teacher roles, and be critical of teaching materials that you examine.

Elementary teachers can identify a number of instructional beliefs that most would agree are basic to teaching young children. Read the following credo, which enumerates twelve concepts. Are there any statements with which you disagree? Which beliefs would you consider most important? Are there any that you would eliminate or reword? Can you see how teaching would reflect these underlying assumptions?

Credo for the Language Arts Teacher[1]

The following beliefs are based on our knowledge and training, our sensitivity to problems that influence both teacher and student, and our personal desire to improve English language arts instruction. If you accept these beliefs, then your teaching should reflect them. The statement following each assumption expresses how you might put these ideas into effect in the classroom.

1. The teacher is the key to what happens in the classroom.

   I determine what is taught, and what I do in the classroom reveals my beliefs about teaching. Students will respond to my expectations and my enthusiasm.
2. Much learning takes place before the child enters school.

   I need to assess the child's language abilities and experiential background so that I can build on what the child knows. I will also be better able to plan classroom instruction to meet the individual child's needs.
3. Language skills are not learned in isolation.

   I can help students become aware of the interrelationships among listening, speaking, reading, and writing. I can use the oral language skills to support the more difficult skills of reading and writing.
4. Language development occurs throughout the curriculum.

   I can integrate language arts instruction with that of social studies, science, and other areas of the curriculum. I need to be ready to reinforce language development as opportunities occur in all classroom activities.
5. Students learn by doing.

   I will plan instruction that engages students in actively listening, speaking, reading, and writing. I will try to eliminate classroom time when students are passively disengaged.
6. Children have a natural love of language.

   I will promote this love of language and use it to motivate student language development. I will try to use this positive attitude toward language to stimulate interest in learning more about our language and in improving communication skills.
7. Language learning begins as a self-motivated activity that demonstrates the child's eagerness to learn.

[1]Adapted from "English in the Elementary School: What, How, and Why We Teach," by Iris M. Tiedt, in *English in the 80s* (Washington, D.C.: National Education Association, 1981).

I will capitalize on the child's involvement with language and continue to provide language input from which students can learn.

8. Children need to feel that they are accepted and that they can succeed.

I will use positive reinforcement to help students develop self-esteem, and I will plan instruction so that children can succeed.

9. The needs and abilities of individual children differ.

I can plan individualized diagnosis and instruction so that each child can move toward achieving his or her fullest potential. I will include individual, small group, and large group activities as seems most appropriate to meeting individual needs.

10. The teacher's most appropriate role is to guide and facilitate learning.

I will plan content and devise strategies that will teach students to operate as independently as possible as they work individually, in peer groups, or with the large group. I will think of classroom instruction as being student-centered rather than teacher-dominated.

11. Learning such broad skills as composition and comprehension is more important than the mastery of facts.

I will teach factual information within the context of activities that engage students in developing thinking abilities, for example, composing, synthesizing, and evaluating or understanding, analyzing, and generalizing.

12. Parents can take an active and beneficial role in the schooling of their children.

I will work cooperatively with parents to achieve growth for each individual child.

As teachers, if we accept these basic assumptions as our own, then it follows that the decisions we make about teaching will reflect these beliefs. We may need to refer to these statements as we think about the content we present in the language arts curriculum and the strategies we select for instruction. Several of the statements will be reinforced in the next section as we focus on the organization of the curriculum.

ORGANIZING THE LANGUAGE ARTS CURRICULUM

The language arts is a potpourri of subject areas and skills that focus on the use of language—spelling, handwriting, grammar, composition, literature. Although I advocate integrating the total language arts program, including reading, in actuality language arts has not been taught from a total perspective that relates the information and skills that children need. Language arts have been segmented into separate textbooks and periods of instruction for reading, spelling, handwriting, and English. Because the language arts curriculum has lacked focus, instruction has been inefficient and ineffective.

Recent concern about the teaching of composition (writing) and resulting studies of writing instruction lead me to recommend centering the language arts program on writing. Recognizing the fact that reading will probably always be taught as a separate subject, the components that make up the language arts program can be taught within a composition-centered curriculum that places penmanship, spelling, punctuation, grammar, and literature within the context of a strong composition program that leads to more effective teaching of the language arts.

Focusing on Composition

The foundation of this language arts program (see the model below) is, not unexpectedly, oral language, for children are unable to write (or to read) without a strong oral command of language, vocabulary, and ideas to share. Activities that fit each stage of this model are adapted to individual needs with success built in for each learner, as explained for each step.

STEP 1: ORAL LANGUAGE FACILITY

Listening and speaking activities designed to promote language development, for example: creative drama, reading aloud by the teacher, the voice choir, small group discussion, dictation

STEP 2: WRITING FLUENCY

Beginning writing activities designed for student success and developing positive attitudes toward writing, for example: journal writing, making lists, teacher dictation, short poetry forms, word associations

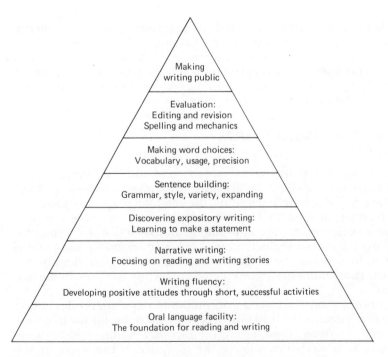

Focusing on Composition: Framework for a Language Arts Curriculum

STEP 3: NARRATIVE WRITING

Telling stories of various kinds, for example, modern fables, retelling a story heard, writing a new ending for a familiar story, telling the same story from a different point of view, writing dialogue with appropriate punctuation

STEP 4: EXPOSITORY WRITING

Learning to make a statement to explain, persuade, or to report, for example: composing a formal paragraph, writing a letter to the editor, reporting the findings of a study

STEP 5: SENTENCE BUILDING

Improving the writing of sentences, the building block of composition, for example: looking at sentence patterns, expanding short sentences, manipulating word order in a sentence, writing sentences of varied length and complexity

STEP 6: WORD CHOICES

Becoming more aware of the words we use, for example: studying the connotations of words, exploring synonyms for overworked words, noting the patterns of English spelling, discussing the use of words and how usage changes the meaning of words

STEP 7: EVALUATION

Deciding on criteria for good and less effective writing, for example: peer evaluation, learning editing skills, learning how to revise writing, checking mechanical errors, a personal spelling guide, preparing writing for publication

STEP 8: MAKING WRITING PUBLIC

Publishing polished writing, for example: displaying poems on the bulletin board, writing a letter to parents about a classroom activity, contributing a story to the class writing book, sending a letter to the local newspaper

As we focus on improving writing, we are developing listening and speaking skills. We use books to stimulate ideas and to provide models of good writing. The development of vocabulary supports all language operations. Focusing on composition, therefore, can lead to a fully integrated language arts program.

Criteria for development in writing   For each step of the curriculum we need means of assessing student growth. Performance criteria can be spelled out for each level of instruction as shown in the following chart, "Criteria for Development in Writing," which was prepared for the Kentfield Elementary School District in Kentfield, California.

HOW CAN WE TEACH MOST EFFECTIVELY?

We know much more about the teaching process and how teaching can be most effective than we realize. Research has suggested clear directions that we do not always choose to follow. In this section we will take a closer look

Criteria for Development in Writing   Grade Level Primary (1-3)

WRITING COMPONENT	WEAK COMPETENCIES THE STUDENT WILL—	TYPICAL COMPETENCIES THE STUDENT WILL—	EXCELLENT COMPETENCIES THE STUDENT WILL—
Oral Language Foundation	*Listen:* Lack interest in hearing teacher read aloud Be unable to discuss story read in any detail *Speak:* Talk very little Be reluctant to answer questions Be unable to discuss topics	*Listen:* Be able to listen for short periods with interest Retell a story covering sequence of events with accuracy *Speak:* Have adequate vocabulary Answer questions Participate in sharing period	*Listen:* Understand reasons for listening Retell a story including some details *Speak:* Have excellent vocabulary Respond to questions fully Respond eagerly to topics
Fluency—Beginning Writing	Be unable to write adequately Operate at oral level generally Begin to write short sentence and word activities Begin to tell stories orally	Print or write adequately Write short sentences using capitals and end punctuation Enjoy reading writing aloud Write wordlists	Handle writing easily Write increasingly longer sentences Contribute ideas verbally Enjoy working with words
Narration—Telling a Story	Give factual statement orally Write simple sentences Retell simple story Dictate stories	Write story sentences Answer questions: who, where, what, when, and why Tell stories; record; act out Write short stories; illustrate	Write short stories Identify components of short stories when read Enjoy sharing writing with classmates Write increasingly longer stories
Exposition—Explanatory Writing	Tell about an object orally Write simple sentences describing something familiar	Write factual statements Give oral report about familiar object or action Write several sentences about familiar object or action	Write short report Complete simple library research Present information orally about selected topic

Sentence—Grammar, Style	Speak simple sentences Read dictated sentences as written by teacher Begin writing short sentences Recognize variety of type of sentence	Write simple sentences correctly Use periods and question marks Capitalize first word in sentence Copy sentences taken from literature as model; imitate model Expand sentences as directed	Write simple sentences Use correct end punctuation Write sentences of increasing length Appreciate writing of skilled authors Try to improve writing
Word Choices—Usage, Vocabulary	Have limited vocabulary Use ungrammatical constructions Repeat same common words	Use a variety of words Recognize correct word order Show interest in new words Use dictionary as taught Play with words orally	Show marked interest in words Unscramble sentences in which words are out of order Explore dictionary independently
Editing—Revision	Read sentences aloud Make corrections with teacher help	Check writing by reading aloud Work with teacher to make revisions Work with peers to find errors in punctuation, capitalization, and spelling	Produce final copy of revised work free from errors Show interest in editing Use dictionary to correct spelling Help other students edit

NOTES:

Criteria for Development in Writing   *Grade Level Intermediate (4–5)*

WRITING COMPONENT	WEAK COMPETENCIES THE STUDENT WILL—	TYPICAL COMPETENCIES THE STUDENT WILL—	EXCELLENT COMPETENCIES THE STUDENT WILL—
Oral Language Foundation	*Listen:* Have some trouble paying attention Retell a story with sketchy coverage of the plot, little detail *Speak:* Have limited vocabulary Answer questions with single words Add little to discussions	*Listen:* Understand reasons for listening Retell a story accurately including main characters and plot *Speak:* Have good vocabulary Answer questions fully Participate in group discussion	*Listen:* Listen with obvious intent Retell a story in detail with personal interpretation *Speak:* Answer questions beyond factual level Lead group discussion
Fluency—Beginning Writing	Have difficulty with physical act of writing Form many letters poorly Write slowly Produce minimal response to stimulus provided Fidget during sharing of writing	Handle handwriting with ease Be motivated to try short writing exercises Enjoy sharing work Benefit from hearing writing of other students	Contribute many ideas to prewriting activities Produce creative responses Adapt ideas Do more than required Write independently
Narration—Telling a Story	Write very short stories Use simple short sentences Include little detail or personal involvement Make numerous mechanical errors	Write a story with a beginning, middle, and end Use varied sentence structures Make few mechanical errors Use some paragraphing Write with some fluency Share writing enthusiastically	Write a story that includes descriptive details Handle mechanics easily Develop characters Include dialogue Write fluently Write independently
Exposition—Explanatory Writing	Write a minimal amount Need much teacher direction Include only meager content Write short choppy sentences Misunderstand directions	Produce a short factual report on a selected topic Write an organized paragraph to explain or persuade Follow directions	Write more than required Enjoy researching chosen topic in varied sources Develop a logical argument Initiate further research

Sentence—Grammar, Style	Punctuate irregularly Use simple, active sentences Include many fragments and run-on sentences Have inaccurate "ear" for English grammar and idiom	Punctuate sentence appropriately Use capitalization as needed Try varied types of sentences Recognize sentences that are nongrammatical and revise Imitate a model sentence as directed	Handle punctuation and capitalization well Use mature sentences Recognize style in writing Try to emulate style Have an accurate "ear" for language
Word Choices—Usage, Vocabulary	Use words imprecisely Use dictionary with help Use few adjectives and adverbs to expand writing Repeat same words often Use ordinary words	Be aware of accepted usage Have good vocabulary Use dictionary as directed Use descriptive adjectives and adverbs Enjoy word play Compose figures of speech as shown	Discuss usage of words Explore new words Use thesaurus independently List and use synonyms for many common words Use words creatively Create original images
Editing—Revision	Read sentences aloud Need much teacher help Copy edited sentences Make errors in revised copy	Read writing aloud to check grammaticality and flow Use proofreader marks as taught Correct mechanical errors Produce final copy relatively free from errors	Work with peers to edit and revise writing Expand, change, rewrite during revision process Enjoy publishing writing Try to improve writing

NOTES:

Criteria for Development in Writing   *Grade Level Middle School (6–8)*

WRITING COMPONENT	WEAK COMPETENCIES THE STUDENT WILL—	TYPICAL COMPETENCIES THE STUDENT WILL—	EXCELLENT COMPETENCIES THE STUDENT WILL—
Oral Language Foundation	*Listen:* Know reasons for listening as a way of learning Retell a story with some detail *Speak:* Respond fully to questions Contribute to discussion	*Listen:* Make an effort to listen for a specific purpose Retell a story with accurate sequence of events *Speak:* Use good vocabulary Ask pertinent questions	*Listen:* Take notes based on listening to content Discuss content of news report on television *Speak:* Lead group discussion Develop argument orally
Fluency—Beginning Writing	Have some difficulty writing specific letters Write rather slowly Make minimal response to writing stimulus provided by teacher	Handle handwriting easily Enjoy trying short writing Compile lists of words Write in journal regularly Enjoy sharing writing in group	Contribute ideas to class prewriting activities Produce a quantity of responses to stimulus Write more than required Continue writing at home
Narration—Telling a Story	Write short choppy sentences Tell stories orally Write short stories about personal experience Make a number of mechanical errors Share writing by reading aloud	Write a story with beginning, middle, and end Use paragraphing Use transitional phrases Make some mechanical errors Share writing enthusiastically	Add descriptive details to setting, characterization, and mood Write dialogue to reveal Handle punctuation and capitalization adequately Desire to publish writing
Exposition—Explanatory Writing	Write factual statements Give an oral report about known object or process Need help following directions Write brief report	Write an organized paragraph to explain or persuade Follow directions explicitly Use cause and effect relations Outline given factual material Write business letter	Develop a logical argument in an essay Outline a selected topic for independent research Write questions about topic Write letter about issues

Sentence—Grammar, Style	Use basic punctuation correctly Write simple, active sentences Lack transition	Use sentence punctuation and capitalization correctly Try varied sentence structures Use some transitional phrases Be aware of need for flow from sentence to sentence	Handle punctuation and capitalization easily Ask about varied sentence structures; notice models Write with increasing maturity Show concern about style
Word Choices—Usage, Vocabulary	Use words imprecisely Limited vocabulary Use dictionary with help Repeat words often	Discuss usage according to situation, appropriateness Use thesaurus for synonyms Play with words Show interest in new words Add words to expand sentences	Discuss dialectology Discuss registers in language Write dialogue showing language variation Keep notebook of new words Work on developing vocabulary
Editing—Revision	Read sentences aloud Need guidance of teacher Recopy edited material	Read writing aloud to check grammaticality and flow Correct most mechanical errors Work with small group to edit Enjoy publishing writing	Expand, change, rewrite, during revision process Serve as class editor Work on improving writing Work independently

NOTES:

at what we have learned about appropriate instructional methods as well as how you can add to your own expertise in the language arts.

The Teacher's Role

Expectations for good teaching are far more complex today than they have ever been. In this age of proficiency testing, mastery teaching, and formative evaluation, the teacher needs to be well-informed in order to plan for effective classroom instruction. The teacher can be identified by a number of different responsibilities, for example:

Diagnostician (Why isn't Sam trying to read?)
Counselor (How can I increase Jan's self-esteem?)
Public relations expert (How do I answer questions about the lack of funds?)
Manager (How can I handle an individualized program?)
Planner (How can I help my new blind student?)
Decision maker (Which textbook will present language arts as I think it should be taught?)

These roles are only a few of those that the elementary teacher is called upon to play. A good teacher must be organized and efficient in order to cope with the varied demands and pressures. At the same time the teacher should recognize the impossibility of being all things to all people. Recognizing the fact that you hold the key to what happens in your classroom, you need to make decisions that will benefit the students you work with—setting priorities, planning learning experiences, engaging directly in the teaching–learning process. You can make a difference in the lives of these students as you convey enthusiasm for learning, sensitivity to the needs of others, a positive *joie de vivre* that is contagious.

Effective Teaching

We are constantly learning more about teaching and specific behaviors that increase student achievement. Bringing research findings and teaching practice together does lead to improved teaching. A six-year study of teaching reports that one of the most significant characteristics of good teaching is Time on Task and that increasing Academic Learning Time (ALT) does promote basic skills learning and achievement of elementary school students.[2] Another relevant study examines competency-based teacher education (CBTE) in an effort to identify teacher behaviors that make a difference.[3] We will examine the ramifications of these two major studies.

Academic learning time. If we want students to learn to write, we must see that they spend time on this task. We readily accept this statement, for

[2]California Commission for Teacher Preparation and Licensing, *Time to Learn*. Beginning Teacher Evaluation Study (Sacramento: State Department of Education, 1980).
[3]Homer Coker et al, "How Valid Are Expert Opinions about Effective Teaching?" *Phi Delta Kappan*, October 1980, pp. 131–4, 149.

we all know that "practice makes perfect." Recent studies, however, are showing us that it is not mere quantity of time that affects achievement; we must also control the quality of the time spent working on the task. This finding has broad implications for instruction in terms of diagnosis, grouping, and evaluation, in fact, the whole teaching process, as spelled out here.

Students must spend more time on the task to be learned, but this time must be in active engagement, involvement, in the process. We need to question some of the activities that we include, for example, in the reading program. We need to ask: "Are students really reading?" Such activities as marking the syllabication of words or using the dictionary to discover the meaning of a long list of vocabulary items should be examined to determine exactly what is being taught. We may be teaching boredom and a negative attitude toward school and learning rather than promoting student reading ability. A strategy, on the other hand, that does engage students in the reading process is Uninterrupted Sustained Silent Reading, a practice that allocates time for reading books, magazines, the newspaper. (USSR is described in more detail in Chapter 7.)

Students must feel successful as they learn. Students' achievement will increase if they spend more than half of their learning time on work at which they can succeed. In order to plan for success, you must first identify the student's "cognitive entry behavior." After you determine what the student knows, you can build from that point, providing an appropriate developmental sequence and learning materials the student can handle. Students who ask for frequent aid and clarification of the task are signalling that the task is still too difficult; their low rate of success is proving frustrating. Telling them to "get back to work" is not the solution. Instead, suggest that they work on a simpler objective that will prepare them to work with the more complex skill.

Students need to interact with others as they learn. As we plan for individual needs, we must be aware that students will achieve much more if they have opportunities to interact with the teacher, parents or cross-level tutors, and their classmates. Having a number of adults or older students in the classroom means that each student will receive more feedback about his or her progress. The training of all aides should include suggestions for providing positive reinforcement as well as helping students solve problems they encounter as they work on a learning task. The level of positive interaction in a classroom correlates highly with student achievement.

Centering on these student needs affects curriculum development and the methods and materials chosen for instruction. This discussion is directly related to the following analysis of the competencies required for effective teaching.

Teacher behaviors. What does the good teacher do that a less skillful teacher does not? Five behaviors have been identified as supportive of student learning and achievement: (1) diagnosis, (2) prescription, (3) presentation, (4) monitoring, and (5) feedback. The successful teacher is able to find out what students know and what they do not know, plan lessons that are appropriate matches for student abilities, present instruction clearly, observe the classroom activities as students engage in learning, and provide information to the student about progress during the learning process. This is a complex process that an experienced teacher may deal with so easily that it looks simple. This book has been prepared to assist you in developing the skills of an effective teacher.

A study designed to identify competencies that could be measured as a way of certifying teachers lists nine competencies that the teachers participating in the project considered important:

1. Gathers and uses information related to individual differences
2. Organizes pupils, resources, and materials for effective instruction
3. Demonstrates ability to communicate effectively with students
4. Assists students in using a variety of relevant communication skills techniques
5. Assists students in dealing with their misconceptions or confusions, using relevant clues and techniques
6. Responds appropriately to coping behavior of students
7. Uses a variety of methods and materials to stimulate and promote pupil learning
8. Promotes self-awareness and positive self-concepts in students
9. Reacts with sensitivity to the needs and feelings of others[4]

As the researchers note, we can make such accepted lists of competencies, but we also need to examine specific behaviors that are incorporated in each. Study of specific behaviors in real classrooms by trained observers reveals a number of behaviors that relate positively to student achievement, as well as a number that are negatively related, for example:

POSITIVE RELATIONSHIP:

2. Selects goals and objectives appropriate to pupil needs
   Involves students in organizing and planning
3. Gives clear, explicit directions
4. Demonstrates proper listening skills
   Respects individual's right to speak
6. Maintains self-control in classroom situations and with students

NEGATIVE RELATIONSHIP:

3. Pauses, elicits and responds to student questions
4. Uses nonverbal communication skills
5. When student not on task, teacher makes contact
8. Provides opportunity for students to have voice in decision making
   Evidence of praise and/or rewards in operation[5]

---

[4]Ibid., p. 132.
[5]Ibid., p. 134.

Can you imagine classroom situations in which "pausing, eliciting, and responding to student questions" might have a negative effect? As you read through the other behaviors that relate negatively with student achievement, consider the possible reasons for the negative effect. Try to put yourself in the student's position.

If you would like to investigate the study of teaching more extensively, you might begin with these articles:

Beginning Teacher Evaluation Study Newsletter, 1979–80. California Commission for Teacher Preparation and Licensing, 1020 "O" Street, Sacramento, Calif. 95814.

"Time on Task, and Off." *Basic Education,* June 1980, pp. 13–14.

"Research into Practice: For Elementary Reading Teachers." Grayce Ransome. *The California Reader,* March/April 1980, pp. 14–19.

"The New Direction in Educational Research: Alterable Variables." Benjamin Bloom. *Phi Delta Kappan.* February 1980, pp. 382–85.

"Effective Instructional Leadership Produces Greater Learning," Gordon Cawelti. *Thrust for Educational Leadership.* January 1980, pp. 8–9.

Studies of effective teaching point up one of the most powerful tools available to a teacher, namely, letting students know what you are trying to do. As students become aware of your intent in diagnosing and prescribing, for example, their self-esteem improves. They become involved in noting their own attending and are interested in ongoing feedback about their progress and that of others in the class.

SELECTING STRATEGIES FOR INSTRUCTION

In light of what we have already discussed about teaching, it is not difficult to describe the characteristics of effective teaching strategies. The effective teacher will select instructional strategies that:

1. Involve students in active, purposeful work
2. Integrate both process and content of the language arts across the curriculum
3. Interest the students
4. Stimulate the student's creative imagination
5. Convey a positive acceptance of each student
6. Emphasize exploration and other open-ended processes
7. Meet the individual needs of students
8. Offer a broad scope and sequence

Not every teaching strategy will meet all of these criteria, but methods that endure and are worth repeating will be sufficiently rich and encompassing so that they do include these characteristics. One such strategy is the learning center approach to individualized instruction. We will discuss recommended teaching methods that you can use immediately that will involve you in the preparation of teaching materials and working directly with students.

Developing Learning Centers

The learning center approach to teaching offers a range of possibilities. A small center can be presented on a poster or tucked into a shoebox. Larger, focused centers can be displayed on a bulletin board or developed in the corner of the classroom. The whole classroom can become a learning center with activities centered around a theme that takes in the whole curriculum. Let us explore the possibilities for each.

Focused skill centers. Small centers focus on one specific objective although others may be developed peripherally. You might, for example, have twenty small centers that stimulate the learning of spelling skills. The sample shown is designed to meet the objective: To learn how to spell common suffixes and other ending spellings. Presented on a large cardboard covered with clear contact paper on which students write with a greased pencil, this word bracket is appropriate for upper elementary grades and junior high school:

H_____Y I_____R S_____O	Word Brackets What word is spelled down the left of this word bracket? Can you see the same word on the right side of the bracket?
T_____T O_____S	Your job is to insert letters on each line that make a word beginning with the letter on the left and ending with the one on the right.
R_____I Y_____H	Your score will be the total number of letters you insert between the brackets. Try to find long words so your score will be high.

Place the learning centers around the room on desks or tables, on the bulletin board, window sill, the chalktray, an easel, a bookshelf. Number the places at each activity, making sure that there are enough spaces for every student in the class. As students complete one activity, they can move to another.

With this type of individualized activity, you might choose to have a learning center day once a week, perhaps on Friday as a change of pace from the daily activities.

Work centers For a focus on teaching writing skills, you could create four or five larger learning centers to accommodate five or six students. In this example, the center is created from the sides of a large cardboard carton mounted on a small table. Directions for making stationery, writing a letter to a classmate who is in the hospital, and composing a business letter requesting free materials from a company are displayed on the sides of the center. All supplies needed are available at the center.

Again, students circulate to the different centers, perhaps working at one each day. Centers like this can be used in conjunction with other learning activities. As students finish an assigned task, they move to the writing center at which they are to work. This is an excellent way to present language arts activities related to the social studies or other subject areas.

Saturating the classroom For an exciting learning experience, convert your whole classroom into an Indian Village or an Ohio farmhouse during the Civil War when the underground railroad was in effect. Students will delight in planning and constructing the props and what structure is needed. A theme offers a wide range of language arts experiences as students make lists, write diaries, dramatize events, and read sources of information about the period being studied. Such a study coordinates learning in the language arts with social studies, art, and music; mathematics and science understandings can be drawn in, too, for a meaningful, realistic enactment that students will remember. This method of saturating the classroom will be discussed in more detail in Chapter 14, Language Arts Across the Curriculum.

Using Literature to Stimulate Learning

Many teachers read books aloud to their students, especially in the elementary school. This pleasant activity is usually done after other work is finished. The reason for stressing this teaching strategy at the beginning of this textbook is to accord it the importance it deserves.

Reading literature aloud to your students is a valuable teaching method that should be employed regularly with specific objectives in mind. You are teaching students the following basic understanding and information:

1. *Literature concepts.* Children are learning about characterization, plot development, and descriptions of settings in time and place. These models will also help them write original narratives.

2. *English grammar.* Children are hearing book language which is not the language
    that they speak. They are learning new grammatical constructions and devel-
    oping an "ear for language" that will facilitate their language growth.
3. *Listening abilities.* A good story motivates student listening as they follow the
    sequence of the action. Afterwards, they can talk about the sequence of events
    and act it out.
4. *Vocabulary development.* Students are hearing words in the context of sentences
    and paragraphs that assist understanding of meaning. Good authors include
    challenging words that add to the interest of the story, for example, Max cries,
    "Let the wild rumpus start!" in *Where the Wild Things Are,* a great book for
    story theater.
5. *Composition skills.* Talking about the author who wrote the book you are reading
    makes writing seem real to students. They will become aware of the skillful
    use of figurative language and will surprise you by personifying an object or
    inserting a fresh simile in their poetry.
6. *Cognitive learnings.* As children follow even the simplest plot, they are called
    upon to interpret, to make inferences, to predict what will happen, to draw
    conclusions. The input their brains receive through listening is preparing them
    to think.

If you haven't read many children's books, you have a wonderful experience before you. Begin with some of the old favorites:

PICTURE BOOKS

Joseph's Yard by Charles Keeping (Oxford)
In the Night Kitchen by Maurice Sendak (Harper)
Crow Boy by Taro Tashima (Viking)
Swimmy by Leo Lionni (Pantheon)

FANTASIES

The Borrowers by Mary Norton (Harcourt)
The Twenty-one Balloons by William Pene de Bois (Viking)
James and the Giant Peach by Roald Dahl (Knopf)
The Phantom Tollbooth by Norton Juster (Random)

REALISM

Last Night I Saw Andromeda by Charlotte Ankers (Lippincott)
Where the Lilies Bloom by Vera and Bill Cleaver (Lippincott)
How to Eat Fried Worms by Thomas Rockwell (Watts)
The Summer of the Swans by Betsy Byars (Viking)

We will talk more about using literature in the classroom in Chapter 12.

Inductive-deductive Methods of Instruction

As we stress process or "doing" language, we usually emphasize inductive
or discovery methods because characteristically, they are more involving
for the student. At times, however, deductive methods may be more efficient as you tell students information rather than having them research it
independently. You will choose the approach that best suits your objectives.

This chart may help clarify the difference between inductive and deductive methods.

Methods of Instruction

INDUCTIVE	DEDUCTIVE
Student oriented	Teacher dominated
Discovery	Lecture
Inquiry	Listening
Investigation	Notetaking
Testing hypotheses	Factual
Problem Solving	Expository
Decision Making	Telling
Active student	Passive student

The inductive method involves the student in learning how to learn. Experimenting or collecting data engages the student in the process of learning. It is more active and therefore, more stimulating. It does require more time for the learning process, and the results are less predictable. It may also be more difficult to evaluate. The effective teacher will use a combination of deductive and inductive methods.

Grouping for Instruction

Gone are the days of desks in rows fastened to the floor. Gone also are the days of limiting instruction to a lecture presentation to the whole class. Concern for the needs of the individual demands that we vary the grouping of students according to the activities planned. Individualized instruction includes experiences in which students work alone, but the individual also needs the experience of interacting with students in small groups, and some activities require the cooperation of the whole group. Let us examine the kinds of activities that fit different kinds of grouping.

THE INDIVIDUAL WORKING ALONE:

Reading a book for pleasure
Recording a story at the listening center
Writing in the student's personal journal

STUDENTS IN DYADS (PAIRS):

Editing each other's writing
Writing a two-character skit
Playing a word game

STUDENTS IN SMALL GROUPS (3–6):

Sharing stories each has written
Brainstorming solutions to a problem
Listening to a record at the listening center
Preparing to act out part of a book read

Choric speaking
Listening to the teacher read a book
Watching a film that will stimulate individual writing

Obviously, it is inefficient to show a film several times when thirty students can view it, discuss the ending, brainstorm vocabulary to write on the board, and then write their personal interpretation of the main character's behavior. It is equally inefficient, on the other hand, to have thirty students listen to classmates reading their original stories one by one. The percentage of actively involved student time is greatly increased by having this sharing done in five small groups so that every child can read to an audience in a matter of twenty minutes. Planning for individualized instruction should take into consideration, too, that children are gregarious and that working with others is stimulating. Plan activities, therefore, that offer a variety ranging from working alone to participating as part of a large group.

A Promising Instructional Strategy: Clustering[6]

The technique of clustering ideas is a versatile strategy that can be used across the curriculum. Use it to assess attitudes, to help students open up an idea, to determine what students know about a concept, or to outline a topic.

Exploring an idea   Clustering provides an amazingly effective device for opening up an idea, a kind of warm-up exercise that prepares students for writing about a subject. It is highly individualized, drawing from each student's personal view of the world.

Introduce clustering by giving the students a word that all understand and can relate to, for example: home, school, happiness, jealousy, Christmas, ugly, friend. Work on the board together to demonstrate the technique. The given word is placed in a circle in the center of the space. Then students free associate with this topic. Place suggested words around the center word. Words that seem to be related are written near each other to form a cluster, thus:

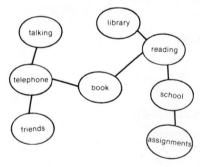

[6]Iris M. Tiedt, *Reading Ideas,* March 1980, p. 11.

Clustering ideas around the word *book* will probably take only 5–10 minutes. When most students have finished, have the class break into small groups of five–six people. Each student can share the associations with *book* orally, explaining the reason for an unusual association. The oral sharing can be followed by having each student write a paragraph focusing on one of the clusters on his or her paper.

Assessing student knowledge   Clustering can be used to find out what students know (or don't know) about any subject. If you plan to introduce a new concept or area of study, have students cluster their ideas related to that concept as a kind of pre-test. You may discover, for instance, that several students already have a surprising store of information that you can tap. Another student may reveal a gross misconception about the subject. This pre-assessment will enable you to teach the unit more effectively.

Clustering can also provide a post-test device. Have students compare the clustering they did before and after the study so that they become aware of the change (learning) that took place. If no change occurred, you might well ask, "What were you doing for the past two weeks?"

Outlining a topic   Clustering provides an effective device for outlining a topic. Each cluster may produce the paragraph of an expository essay. Or, the clusters may be developed into full sections of a longer report.

Beginning student research with the development of one or more clusters will help students assess their own interest in the subject(s) they first thought of. It also points up what they already know and what they need to find out. Beginning, thus, with subjects that interest the students should lead them to sources of information beyond the encyclopedia—more specialized reference books, articles in magazines, interviews, the Yellow Pages of the telephone book, letters.

After students have read a book, clustering will help them outline an oral or written review of the book. The main character may be the focus as in this example based on *Pippi Longstocking* by Astrid Lindgren (Viking).

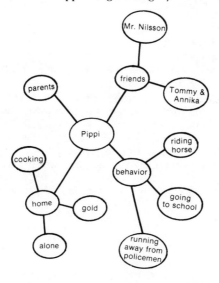

Although it is impossible to own every book that you might like, every teacher collects a number of key books or other resources that he or she sees as particularly helpful. The following basic collection is recommended:

BOOKS:

Student-centered Language Arts and Reading, K–13 by James Moffett and Betty Jane Wagner. Houghton Mifflin, 1976.
Exploring Books with Children by Iris M. Tiedt. Houghton Mifflin, 1979.
Reading without Nonsense by Frank Smith. Teachers College Press, 1979.
Teaching Reading Comprehension by William D. Page and Gay Su Pinell. National Council of Teachers of English, 1979.
Grammar for Teachers: Perspectives and Definitions. National Council of Teachers of English, 1979.
Teaching Writing in K–8 Classrooms by Iris Tiedt et al. Prentice-Hall, 1983.

JOURNALS AND NEWSLETTERS:

Language Arts. The National Council of Teachers of English, 1111 Kenyon Rd., Urbana IL 61801.
The Reading Teacher. International Reading Association, Box 8139, Newark DE 19711.

CHALLENGE

You are a teacher. Try some of the ideas discussed in this chapter as a way of "getting your feet wet." These writing experiments will go in your notebook.

1. Cluster around the word *teaching.* Let your mind consider the perception you have of teaching. Jot down all the associations that come to you. Fill a page with your ideas.

Then, write a short personal essay discussing how you feel about teaching now. You may choose to focus on one or two ideas that stand out in your clustering. Share your writing with others in a small group. Take time to talk about the ideas expressed by members of the group. Share some of these ideas with the whole group.

2. Select a book that you would like to read aloud to a group of students. Share this book with members of your class. Explain your reasons for selecting this book and describe the language arts activities that could be generated through reading the book aloud. (Make a list of at least twenty activities that you might develop as you read the book yourself.)

3. Observe in an elementary classroom. (If you are now teaching, you may analyze your own room.) Look especially at the activities in which students are engaged in terms of the amount of time they are directly involved in learning compared with the time they are "waiting." Observe the classroom to see if there is evidence that language arts are being actively taught. Is instruction teacher-dominated? Is the curriculum student-centered or subject-oriented? (Be discreet in your inquiries, and save notetaking until you leave the classroom.) Share your findings with others in the classroom. What conclusions can you make?

EXPLORING FURTHER

Blake, Howard E., *Creating a Learning-centered Classroom.* New York: A & W Visual Library, 1977.

Britton, James, *Language and Learning.* Coral Gables, Florida: University of Miami, 1970.

Cooper, Charles R., ed., *The Nature and Measurement of Competency in English.* Urbana, Ill.: National Council of Teachers of English, 1981.

Froese, Victor and Stanley B. Straw, *Research in the Language Arts: Language and Schooling.* Baltimore, Md.: University Park Press, 1980.

Gamble, Mildred, "A Classroom Teacher's Crystal Ball for Teaching English in the 80s," in *Education in the 80s: English,* ed. R. Baird Shuman. Washington, D.C.: National Education Association, 1981.

Glatthorn, Allan A., *A Guide for Developing an English Curriculum for the Eighties.* Urbana, Ill.: National Council of Teachers of English, 1980.

Hunkins, Francis P., *Questioning Strategies and Techniques.* Boston: Allyn & Bacon, 1972.

Johnson, Ferne, ed., *Start Early for an Early Start: You and the Young Child.* Chicago: American Library Association, 1976.

Joyce, Bruce, R., *Flexibility in Teaching.* New York: Longman, Inc., 1981.

King, Martha L. et al., eds., *The Language Arts in the Elementary School: A Forum for Focus.* Urbana, Ill.: National Council of Teachers of English, 1973.

May, Jill, P., *Films and Filmstrips for Language Arts.* Urbana, Ill.: National Council of Teachers of English, 1981.

Schrank, Jeffrey, *Teaching Human Beings: 101 Subversive Activities for the Classroom.* Boston: Beacon Press, 1972.

Stanford, Gene, *Developing Effective Classroom Groups.* New York: Hart Publishing Co., 1980.

Tiedt, Sidney W. and Iris M. Tiedt, *Language Arts Activities for the Classroom.* Boston: Allyn & Bacon, 1978.

PART II

A Strong Foundation for Learning

4

"I think; therefore, I am."

René Descartes

THINKING AS A LANGUAGE SKILL

When talking about the language skills, the basic skill of thinking is often overlooked, yet it is the foundation on which all language development is based. Thinking provides the content—the ideas, concepts, and creative connections—that children express through speaking and writing. The child's brain is fed through experiences that include listening and reading as well as other sensory input.

From birth children have an insatiable desire to learn. This thinking–learning process can be fostered by helping students become aware of how they learn. Rather than pouring information into a passive receptacle, educators today advocate that we teach students:

. . . how their recall works during the learning period; how their eyes move when they read; how they can vary the speed of information intake; how to organize thought; how to solve problems; how to think creatively; how to review successfully; how to make adequate notes in brain pattern form—in essence, an education that promotes enthusiasm and enjoyment, rather than foreboding, fear or tedium.[1]

BENCHMARK

As we begin "thinking about thinking," check on your understanding of the concepts in these questions.

1. What is thinking? What do you mean when you use this term?

2. What kinds of classroom activities would promote student thinking? Which activities do not promote student thinking?

3. What relationship does teaching thinking skills have to the teaching of language arts? What relationship does thinking have, for example, to the teaching of writing?

In this chapter we will investigate thinking and the processes involved at various developmental stages. We will also study recent research on functions of the right side of the brain compared with the left side of the brain, and we will review understandings about creativity in children. We will then consider teaching strategies that teach specific thinking skills, with examples of activities suitable for developing intellectual growth. After completing this chapter, you should be able to:

- discuss the nature of creativity in children
- compare right and left brain thinking
- describe methods of teaching thinking skills in the classroom

STUDYING THE THINKING PROCESS

We say, "You're not thinking," and admonish students to "think hard" as we teach. The term "thinking" is used in referring to problem solving or evaluation. We talk about divergent thinking as opposed to convergent thinking, and recognize logical thinking as different from confused or "fuzzy" thinking. The term is used freely, but is not easy to define.

Thinking can be viewed as "the innate ability of the mind to form patterns, mental structures of concepts of objects, events, processes, and relationships." It includes three broad categories of processes: basic operations, integrated operations, and complex strategies.[2] In this section we will examine the early studies of creativity and creative thinking. We will then look at split-brain research that suggests new ways of helping children develop thinking abilities.

---

[1]Tony Buzan, quoted in "Righting the Left-Sided Tilt" by Kathi Martin, *New Realities*, April 1979, p. 29.

[2]Leonard Popp et al., *The Basic Thinking Skills* (St. Catharine's, Ontario: Ontario Institute for the Study of Education, July 1974).

Focus on creative thinking and methods of teaching creativity was part of the concern for affective education that gained momentum in the 1960s. The term "creative" has since been loosely applied to various aspects of teaching, reflecting the difficulty of defining creativity. We can determine a working definition for the word *creativity* by studying research related to thinking.

J. P. Guilford, author of *Personality* and one of the leading authorities in this field of research, was the first to use the term *divergent thinking* as a necessary component of creativity. He states further: "Creative thinking is distinguished by the fact that there is something novel about it."[3] Donald W. MacKinnon, a pioneer in the study of creativity who conducted extensive studies of creative adults, defines creativity as "the ability to make original significant responses to a problem."[4] E. Paul Torrance has studied many aspects of creativity, providing particular insight into the problems of the creative child at the elementary school level. His book, *Guiding Creative Talent,* defines creativity as "the process of sensing problems or gaps in information, forming ideas or hypotheses, testing and modifying these hypotheses and communicating the results."[5]

It is interesting to note that each of the researchers quoted defines creativity in terms of the process rather than the product produced. This is an important distinction, for many misunderstandings arise between those who conceive of creativity in terms of a painting or a novel and those who view it as an ability, a way of thinking or perceiving. For purposes of our discussion we shall define creativity as "the ability to produce something original, to see new relationships, and to use imagination and inventiveness."

It is important to stress the point that *every* person is creative; it is the *degree* of creativity which varies. We are concerned here not only with the highly creative individual but also with the *least creative child.* Our aim is to stimulate creativity in all children, and this aim will influence our methods and even the content we teach. As Torrance notes:

> One of the most revolutionary changes I foresee is a revision of the objectives of education. Today we proclaim that our schools exist for learning. We say that we must get tougher and make pupils learn more. Schools of the future will be designed not only for *learning* but for *thinking.* More and more insistently, today's schools and colleges are being asked to produce men and women who can think, who can make new scientific discoveries, who can find more adequate solutions to impelling world problems, who cannot be brainwashed—men and women

[3]Joy P. Guilford, *Personality* (New York: McGraw-Hill Book Co., 1959), p. 115.

[4]Donald W. MacKinnon, ed., *The Creative Person* (Berkeley: University of California, General Extension, 1962), p. 203.

[5]E. Paul Torrance, *Education and the Creative Potential* (Minneapolis: University of Minnesota Press, 1963); and *Guiding Creative Talent* (Englewood Cliffs, N.J.: Prentice-Hall, Inc., 1962), p. 16.

who can adapt to change and maintain sanity in this age of acceleration. This is the creative challenge to education.[6]

Identifying the Creative Child

A significant problem for the school is identifying creative students. How can the teacher in the classroom recognize the creative individual? What characteristics are typical of the creative person? Can we test for creativity?

Research in creativity   Because identifying creativity is not easy, we often fail to recognize this type of giftedness. The commonly used IQ test, it has been found, does not indicate creativeness. Although most researchers find a positive correlation between intelligence and creativity, the high scorer on the intelligence test may not score high on tests of creativity. Nor is the student who receives the highest grades necessarily the most creative child.

MacKinnon studied more than 500 famous people—writers, architects, composers—who were judged by their peers to be creative. He found that in general these artists had disliked school, did not identify with teachers, and had in many cases dropped out of school.

This study and others which followed resulted in a body of generalizations about the creative person which may prove helpful as we attempt to identify and to understand the creative student. The creative person has been found to possess the following traits:[7]

1.   Nonconformity of ideas, but not necessarily of dress and behavior
2.   Egotism and feelings of destiny
3.   Great curiosity, desire to discover the answer
4.   Sense of humor and playfulness
5.   Perseverance on self-started projects
6.   Intense emotions, sincerity
7.   Tendency to be shy
8.   Lack of rigidity

Victor and Mildred Goertzel studied the childhoods of 400 of this century's best-known men and women. Their book, *Cradles of Eminence*, describes similar findings: (1) most of those people studied did not like school, (2) most of the parents had a love for learning and determination to reach goals, and (3) the creative child was not a contented child.

The latter finding has particular relevance for the classroom, for studies show that the creative student is not always well-liked, agreeable, or conforming; he or she may impress the teacher as a disagreeable, uncooperative child who is mischievous, who daydreams when supposed to be completing assigned work. The suppression of creativity, it is believed, may lead to

[6]E. Paul Torrance, *Education and the Creative Potential* (Minneapolis: University of Minnesota Press, 1963).

[7]Donald W. MacKinnon, ed., *The Creative Person* (Berkeley: University of California Press, 1962).

learning disabilities, behavior problems, and even serious neurotic conflicts, or psychoses.[8]

A Minnesota study of elementary school youngsters identified three characteristics which differentiated the highly creative child from less creative but equally intelligent children:

1.   Reputation for having wild or silly ideas
2.   Work characterized by the production of ideas off the beaten path
3.   Work characterized by humor, playfulness, relative lack of rigidity and relaxation.[9]

Many researchers have observed a decline in imagination as the student advances through the grade levels. Further research indicates an increase in creativity in the primary grades followed by a gradual slump at the fourth-grade level with another at the seventh grade. This finding has significance for those who are designing elementary school curricula.

Guilford, in his research at the University of Southern California, found the creative individual to be:

1.   Sensitive to problems
2.   Fluent in ideas
3.   Mentally flexible
4.   Divergent in thinking[10]

Testing for creativity   Although a variety of tests have been devised for testing creativity, they are largely in experimental stages requiring further development and use to increase reliability and validity. It is interesting, however, to note the types of tests that have been developed.

Guilford developed a variety of tests including word associations, for which the subject is given twenty-five pairs of words which have only remote associations. The task is to provide a third word which relates the pair. Given cat and fish, for example, a person might supply words like animal, food, or pets. The test score is determined by the number of associations made in four minutes. He also used tests for flexible thinking such as listing many uses for a common object (a brick, a tin can) or supplying plot titles for given stories.[11]

Other tests developed by Torrance and colleagues consist of both verbal and nonverbal forms. One verbal form (B) is entitled "Just Suppose—" and consists of six tasks for the student to perform, each of which is a written

[8]Victor Goertzel and Mildred Goertzel, *Cradles of Eminence* (Boston: Little, Brown, & Co., 1962).

[9]E. Paul Torrance, *What Research Says to the Teacher: Creativity* (Washington, D.C.: National Education Assn., 1963).

[10]Joy P. Guilford, *Personality* (New York: McGraw-Hill Book Co., 1959).

[11]Joy P. Guilford, "Creativity: Its Measurement and Development," in *A Source Book for Creative Thinking*, eds. Sidney J. Parnes and Harold H. Harding (New York: Charles Scribner's Sons, 1962), pp. 151–68.

composition based on a picture and an improbable situation as in this example:

> JUST SUPPOSE: Our shadows were to become *real* . . . WHAT WOULD BE THE CONSEQUENCES?

The directions which accompany this test form appear on the front cover, reading as follows:

> INSTRUCTIONS: On the pages which follow are six improbable situations or conditions—at least they don't exist now. This will give you a chance to use your imagination about all of the other exciting things which might happen IF these improbable conditions might come to pass. In your imagination JUST SUPPOSE that each of the situations described were to happen. THEN think of all of the other things that would happen because of it. What would be the consequences? Make as many guesses as you can.
>
> Write your guesses as rapidly as you can in the blank spaces on the page opposite the picture. You will be given five minutes for each of the improbable situations. As soon as time is called, turn the page and proceed immediately to the next situation. Do not worry too much about spelling, grammar, and the like, but try to write so that your ideas can be used.

This type of test is scored on three points: (1) fluency, or the number of responses; (2) originality, or uniqueness; and (3) flexibility, or variety.

Other verbal tests include:

Unusual use: Name all the possible uses for (a tin can).
Improvement: How would you improve (this toy pictured)?
Impossibilities: Name all the impossibilities you can.

Observe the differences between the test of creativity and tests which are more commonly constructed. The student is instructed in the creativity test to (1) write as many different answers as possible and (2) think of answers which no one else will include. The test of creativity gives the high score to the person who can think of answers which are different (divergent thinking). There is no one right answer, for these open-ended questions require the student to think, to invent, to imagine. Getzels and Jackson found, on the other hand, that the IQ test stresses "convergent, retentive, conservative" cognitive processes.[12]

Observing creativity in the classroom   It is admittedly difficult to score tests of creativity. This fact does not, however, prevent classroom teachers from identifying creativity or from teaching *for* creativity.

Awareness of the many facets of creativity will lead to recognition of creative characteristics. A child's possession of one or two of these characteristics may or may not signal creativity. A child who asks many questions

---

[12]Jacob W. Getzels and Philip W. Jackson, *Creativity and Intelligence* (New York: John Wiley & Sons, Inc., 1962).

may need more training in listening skills or merely want attention. Asking probing, discerning questions, on the other hand, is an excellent indication of the creative thinker. Here is a list of characteristics which can be readily observed by the classroom teacher:

1. Probing, discerning questions
2. Avid interest in a specific topic or project
3. Unusual ideas and ways of expressing ideas
4. Great curiosity and a need to explore the answers
5. Playfulness in behavior and in use of words

Brain Research

Related to studies of creativity, right brain–left brain research has clarified our understanding of the interrelated workings of the two hemispheres of the brain. The study of hemisphericity through split-brain research reveals that the left hemisphere tends to work with logical, linear, sequential processes and produces propositional knowledge. The right hemisphere, on the other hand, works best with analogical, multiple, holistic processes. The two sides of the brain are connected by the *corpus callosum* which enables interaction between the two hemispheres and the thinking processes in which the brain engages. When the corpus callosum is damaged or cut surgically, the two sides of the brain continue to function independently. Studies of such brain functions show that although the cerebrum is dual and each side is specialized, there is a limited redundancy in function, as in the handling of emotions. Specialization of the brain is not content-specific; that is, language is processed in both sides of the brain. The hemispheres are specialized in the cognitive processes they can handle.[13] That understanding leads us to the implications for instruction that concern us in this text.

The left hemisphere of the brain processes linear, logical mental thinking that can be easily codified and put in order. Such propositional thinking produces definition, categorization, sequencing, outlining, summarizing, analyzing. The left side of the brain deals, for example, with the rules of syntax, how we string words together to make sentences. It cannot, on the other hand, handle metaphor or synthesis.

The right side of the brain produces appositional thinking—global, holistic processes. Holistic thinking deals with multiple stimuli at the same time. Open to new ideas, new configurations, it goes beyond the literal to deal with inference, association, integration. It is playful and creative in developing structure or restructuring what is given. The structure it seeks is not equated with order, but rather with coherence and wholeness, a unified Gestalt that is created from within.[14]

Without doubt, education has emphasized the linear thinking characteristic of the left brain and has tended to ignore the processes associated

[13]Gabriele Rico, "Metaphor, Cognition, and Clustering," in *Creative Thinking* eds. Stephen Carmean and Burton Grover (The 8th Western Symposium on Learning, 1977).
[14]Ibid

with the right brain. It is clear that we need to rethink instructional practices so that the abilities of both thinking styles are utilized. Samples points out:

> The single most important implication of this research is that in the normal brain, each hemisphere is a complement to the other. Each hemisphere is also an access route to the other. The historical overindulgence in left-hemi-sphere–mode teaching emphases has slighted what can be—and possibly must be—an overwhelming ally in instruction and learning.[15]

The neurophysiologist Karl Pribram recognized the need for a model that explained the functioning of the brain holistically. He perceived the brain as a hologram that could encompass the entirety of an experience that would never be totally lost to either side of the brain. The advantage of this perception of how the brain functions, as Samples explains it, is that we no longer deal with a deficit model if the brain is injured. Instead we encourage the person to focus not on *what has been lost* but *what is still there*. In the same manner, we can emphasize what a child knows as a basis on which to begin instruction. We can put aside the negative connotations of such terms as "learning disabled" and "remedial reading" as we provide broader avenues of learning that "extend experience, rather than reduce it."[16]

Summary

Split-brain research leads us to recognize the importance of teaching to both sides of the brain. This finding substantiates what researchers of creativity and creative thinking recognized at a more intuitive level two decades earlier. Clearly we need both logical, linear thinking as well as creative, holistic thinking in order to function effectively in today's world. Our aim in planning instruction should be to integrate both kinds of thinking in learning activities that challenge students and lead them to extend their knowledge as they also develop more effective ways of processing knowledge and putting it into effect.

TEACHING THINKING SKILLS

In order to teach thinking skills we need to move beyond listing facts and identifying principles. Thinking skills are operations that require students to act on facts and principles, to use this information as they engage in such complex processes as evaluating or analyzing, associating, and synthesizing. Since teaching thinking is an integral part of all learning, teachers need help in grasping the process of thinking and then planning lessons to teach these processes. In this part of the chapter we discuss curriculum

---

[15]Samples, Bob, "Holonomic Knowing: A Challenge for Education in the 80s," in *Education in the Eighties: English,* ed. R. Baird Shuman (Washington, D.C.: National Education Association, 1981), p. 36.

[16]Ibid, 38–41.

development and then describe teaching strategies that involve students in developing their intellectual abilities.

Curriculum Development

Creating a curriculum for developing thinking skills is not unlike establishing a curriculum in any subject area. We need to identify the skills to be taught, determine a sequence for presentation, and select or design instructional methods and materials that will accomplish what we want to achieve.

Identifying and defining the skills to be taught requires knowledge about the thinking processes we want children to learn. The basic operations provide a base from which to begin writing objectives by which to evaluate progress. Notice that the first skills listed are linear thinking skills that are easy to evaluate.

1. OBSERVATION

The student will be able to list objects in a picture.
The student will be able to count the number of pages in a book.

2. CORRESPONDENCE

The student will be able to show how two characters are alike.
The student will be able to describe how his or her life is like that of a child in another country.

3. CLASSIFICATION

The student will be able to sort given words into categories.
The student will be able to list words that fit into a given category.

4. SERIATION (ORDERING)

The student will be able to put a list of words in alphabetical order.
The student will be able to place a series of events in order chronologically.

These basic skills are handled largely by the left brain; they are linear, logical, and deal chiefly with factual information. Each operation can be developed at increasingly difficult or complex levels. They are most effectively taught as part of more intricate processes that require decision making or problem solving. Compare these skills with those that require right brain thinking:

1. ASSOCIATION

The student will be able to list words related to a given theme.
The student will identify the relationships between two objects.

2. ANALOGY

The student will list pairs of words with opposite meanings.
The student will complete word analogies involving varied relationships.

3. JUDGING

The student will be able to establish criteria for evaluating a product.
The student will be able to select poetry for a personal anthology.

4. SYNTHESIS

The student will write a paragraph that supports his or her views on a subject.
The student will roleplay an event from history or a novel.

The first set of thinking skills requires the student to work with given information, while the second requires the student to generate information and ideas. Ideally, classroom activities incorporate both kinds of thinking and have a clear purpose for the student. Consider, for example, the thinking processes required as the student works with problem solving or writes a composition.

Problem solving is a good example of a complex process that involves all the basic operations as well as many of the integrated operations. No matter what the area—academic, personal, physical, political, scientific, or social—the learner usually follows these steps:

Definition of the problem
Search for possible solutions
Generation of ideas, hypotheses
Evaluation of solutions
Repetition of process as needed
Discovery of an adequate solution

The act of writing an expository composition is another complex process that engages the student in varied operations, for example:

Selecting a topic
Researching the subject; taking notes
Sorting and organizing the findings
Planning the presentation
Writing the composition
Judging and revising the work
Final editing and proofreading
Making the writing public

How students are able to handle intellectual operations depends on their mental maturity, and is influenced by individual experience in problem solving or decision making. A third important factor is the teacher's positive attitude and ability to teach thinking skills within a well-structured curriculum.

A Climate That Encourages Thinking

The classroom environment reflects the attitudes, knowledge, and aims of the teacher who establishes that environment. A teacher who values the individual and sincerely aims at helping students grow to their fullest potential will create an atmosphere that stimulates and encourages students to try their wings, to dare to make mistakes, to see the humor of their struggles, and the joy in their creative efforts. A healthy classroom climate will incorporate the ideas described in this section.

Respect unusual questions and ideas   Too often we are busy and hesitate to take time for questions which may appear nonsensical, poorly timed, or not pertinent to the subject under discussion. How do we develop the necessary respect for the questioning attitude both in ourselves and in our students?

1.   Make it plain to the class that good questions have value. A large box can be covered with question marks in which a child can at any time insert a card or sheet of paper on which a puzzling question is written. Each week allocate a time for answering these questions or for discussing them with the class. Those questions which do not produce a ready answer can be researched by volunteers who report their findings at the next question period.
2.   Have students write questions which they might ask about any unknown object, person, or place. About an unknown object, for example, students might ask:
      Is it large or small?
      What color is it?
      Is it a useful object?
      Would it be found in a kitchen?

A sense of worth for individuals and their contributions   The teacher often acts as a buffer between the highly creative child and the peer group, for peers can stifle creativity through ridicule, rigid insistence on the exact truth, and conformity to group standards. The attitude of the students toward imaginative ideas and divergent ways of thinking reflects the attitudes of adults who influence their thinking. How can we promote this sense of the worth of each individual?

1.   Accent the positive in evaluating student work. Some aspect of any student effort can be praised. Circle it, underline it, draw attention to it in some way; under the light of praise it will grow.
2.   When displaying student work, display something by everyone. Must only "perfect" papers be given the limelight? Extract unusual uses of words, effective phrases, new words from student writing to display with the caption, WORD WIZARDRY. When featuring poetry, select a line or poem by every student.

Stimulation of divergent thinking   Aim at stimulating creative thinking rather than memorization of miscellaneous facts. The facts and figures which we teach students today may prove virtually useless, outdated in our fast-moving society. Margaret Mead states this idea thus: "No one will live all his life in the world into which he was born and no one will die in the world in which he worked in his maturity." The ability to think however, will prove worthwhile no matter what the developments of the future. How can the teacher stimulate creative thinking?

1.   Provide the student with many opportunities for problem solving. The problem may actually exist, as, "How can we decrease the noise in our lunchroom?" or

it may be purely hypothetical, "If you were eight feet tall, what problems would you face; how would you solve them?" These problems can be attacked by the group orally in discussion or by the individual through writing.

2. An interesting and rewarding technique for stimulating the imagination is brainstorming (designed by Alex Osborn), which produces a multitude of ideas within a short time. The entire group works on the solution of a problem, the improvement of an object, or the exploration of a topic in a joint effort to suggest solutions, changes, ideas. The rules for brainstorming include:

   a. No criticism or ridicule is allowed.
   b. Any idea is acceptable, no matter how fantastic.
   c. New ideas can be based on previous suggestions.[17]

   Students should be introduced to this technique with the teacher acting as the leader. Later, however, when the technique is more familiar, small groups can brainstorm ideas on specific problems. In beginning a brainstorming session you may have to suggest a few ideas to get the group started. Begin with a problem or topic that is familiar to the entire group, for example, the improvement of the student desk. Suggestions might include: a personal pencil sharpener, a padded seat, a built-in television set.

3. Show short, provocative films designed to stimulate the imagination of young people, for example:

Why Man Creates, 1968, Pyramid Film Producers, 30 min.
The Red Balloon 1956, Brandon Films, 34 min.
Dream of Wild Horses, 1962, Contemporary/McGraw-Hill, 11 min.
Clay, 1964, ACI Productions, 8 min.
The Adventures of an *, 1957, Contemporary/McGraw-Hill, 11 min.
A Chairy Tale, 1957, International Film Bureau, 10 min.
Pigs, 1967, Churchill Films, 11 min.
The Loon's Necklace, 1964, Britannica Films, 11 min.
Up Is Down, 1970, Morton Goldsholl Design Association, Inc., 6 min.
Genius Man, 1970, ACI Productions, 2 min.

Follow up with discussion, writing, or art activities.

4. Many children's books are highly creative in their story content, their illustrations, or their humor. Open books for children by reading aloud, or use some of the ideas presented as the basis for stimulating experiences that encourage children to use their imaginations. After reading *The Wing on a Flea*, for example, children can find other examples of various shapes in the environment around them. *Hailstones and Halibut Bones* often serves to motivate children to write poetry, too, much to the delight of author, Mary O'Neill. Children can paint wild, wonderful fish after reading about those in *McElligott's Pool*. Recommended books include:

Barrett, Peter, and Barrett, Susan. *The Line Sophie Drew*. New York: Scroll Press, 1972.
Borten, Helen. *Do You See What I See?* New York: Abelard-Schuman, 1959.
————. *Do You Hear What I Hear?* New York: Abelard-Schuman, 1960.
Bradfield, Roger. *There's an Elephant in the Bathtub*. Chicago: Albert Whitman, 1964.

[17]Alex F. Osborn, *Applied Imagination* (New York: Charles Scribner's Sons, 1957).

Emberly, Edward. *The Wing on a Flea.* Boston: Little, Brown and Co., 1961.

Fago, Vincent. *Here Comes the Whoosh!* San Marino, Calif.: Golden West Books, 1960.

Garelick, Mary. *Where Does the Butterfly Go When it Rains?* Glenview, Ill.: Scott, Foresman, 1961.

Joslin, Sesyle. *Dear Dragon . . .* New York: Harcourt, Brace, and World, 1962.

———. *What Do You Say, Dear?* New York: Harcourt, Brace, and World, 1962.

Juster, Norton. *The Phantom Tollbooth.* New York: Epstein and Carroll, 1961.

Krauss, Ruth. *A Hole Is to Dig.* New York: Harper and Row, 1952.

Munari, Bruno. *Who's There? Open the Door.* New York: World Publishing Co., 1957.

O'Neill, Mary. *Hailstones and Halibut Bones.* New York: Doubleday, 1961.

Roberts, Cliff. *The Hole.* New York: Franklin Watts, 1963.

Seuss, Dr. *McElligott's Pool.* New York: Random House, 1947.

Waber, Bernard. *How to Go About Laying an Egg.* New York: Houghton Mifflin, 1963.

Wolff, Janet, and Owett, Bernard. *Let's Imagine Thinking up Things.* New York: E. P. Dutton, 1961.

A positive attitude toward failure   When a student makes a mistake or a project fails to produce the expected results, the student should not experience a sense of personal failure. Mistakes should be viewed as stepping stones toward success. How can the teacher develop positive attitudes toward failure?

1. Don't overburden the student with corrections. A composition covered with red pencil marks may prove an insurmountable obstacle to writing anything. Praising wholeheartedly that which is of value has been proved to result in more effective development of writing skills. If a correction needs to be made, concentrate on one or two items which can be readily assimilated at one time by the young writer.

2. Encourage experimentation with the clear understanding that the results are never guaranteed successful. Students should be encouraged to play with words, to invent new forms for poetry, to attempt new effects in their writing without any fear of so-called "failing." These experiments add to the feeling for discovering, exploring, trying the wings of originality.

3. Assume the role of a guide and consultant rather than of one who knows all the answers and stands ready to point out punctuation errors, faulty construction, or misspelling. Teachers need to become admirers of student ideas, accepting them and enjoying them. We should celebrate the achievements of young people.

Acceptance of the nonconformist   As studies have pointed out, the highly creative child has problems functioning as part of a group. For this reason he or she may cause disturbance or refuse to conform to standards of behavior. This may be difficult for the teacher of thirty-five children to condone or understand, and the first inclination may be to chastise the child with the entire class listening. Make a conscious effort to investigate the child's reasons for causing disturbance or for failing to conform. Understanding may lead to rewarding solutions.

Talking to the child privately and discussing the reasons for some measure of conformity in any group situation has proved beneficial. But provision must be made for some outlet for creative abilities and an opportunity to become part of the group. The teacher can assist the child in reducing isolation from peers by letting him or her share results of individual experimentation. James might "teach the class" for fifteen minutes as he explains the project which he is developing.

The class must be helped to understand the creative thinker. As Plato wrote: "What is honored in a country will be cultivated there." The teacher's obvious approval and interest in the activities of the child will make the child's work take on interest and value for peers. Introducing creative activities for the entire class will lead them to understand the need for divergent thinking and the challenge of producing original ideas. Students can discuss creative people of the past, pointing up the fact that their ideas were not always acceptable to people of their times. These approaches may lead to a measure of admiration for the child who formerly was tagged with having "wild ideas."

Parents who understand the concern for creativity   Parents, like teachers, have trouble understanding the nonconforming child. Studies show that the home influence has great effect on the development of creativity; whether creative thinking is stifled or nurtured, therefore, is not the sole responsibility of the school. The school should, however, help parents understand the importance of creativity.

A communique can briefly outline its significance and state the school's concern for encouraging creative thinking in children. This information sheet can draw attention to articles in general magazines or books which parents may be interested in reading.

Ways can also be suggested for parents to encourage creativity in their own children in much the same manner that the school does:

1. Respect questions and ideas
2. Encourage experimentation and exploration
3. Give children time to think and to express ideas
4. Accept children for what they are
5. Help children to understand themselves
6. Recognize and value the talents of creative children
7. Provide materials

Discussion or study groups can also be helpful in promoting understanding of creativity. Speakers can be obtained to present this topic to the group. Parents of unusually creative children should be invited to come to school to discuss the problems of the individual child. The film *Adventures of an* * (McGraw-Hill) is excellent to use with parents, especially with fathers.

THINKING AND THE LANGUAGE ARTS PROGRAM

Teaching the English language arts offers many opportunities to stimulate student thinking. The holistic model presented throughout this textbook stresses the interrelationships of the languaging skills as children learn first that they have something to say, and then how to present their thinking as effectively as possible to others. As teachers, we need

> to recognize that if a person is to make full use of his talents, he should learn to think creatively in a range of situations and on a variety of subjects. The mind, in other words, should be trained to think creatively at the same time that it is trained to think logically.[18]

In many respects English has pioneered specific aspects of creative thinking through creative writing and creative dramatics. Hughes Mearns, writing in 1929, for instance, stated: "Good teaching is not solely the business of instructing; it is also the art of influencing another. Primarily, it is the job of uncovering and enlarging native gifts of insight, feeling, and thinking."[19] The revised edition of his challenging exploration of the creative potential of youth, *Creative Power,* is widely heralded by contemporary writers who are now cognizant of the import of the methods used by Mearns in stimulating creativity. Mearns admonished his young writers in these words:

> You have something to say. Find out what it is. That is the beginning. Once really started, it will carry you through life; for you will be doing for yourself all that education can ever do for anybody, encouraging that deeper and powerful self to rise within you and take possession.[20]

Methods used in the language arts program can encourage creative thinking rather than stifle it. In the past, instruction in English relied chiefly on the authoritarian approach to learning. Studies in science and mathematics have led the way toward the use of questioning, experimenting, exploring, discovering—inductive methods of learning. The following approaches allow for individual development and, therefore, permit the child to operate in a freer environment:

1. Use of open-ended topics which encourage thinking
2. Independent study and research
3. Free selection of topics for speaking and writing
4. Less emphasis on form, more emphasis on ideas expressed
5. Reward of diverse contributions
6. Guidance through individual conference or consultation
7. Tests which emphasize divergent thinking

The writing activities described in *The Language Arts Handbook* are designed to stimulate thinking and to guide students in expressing their ideas fluently and with effect. The teaching strategies described here are representative of those that can be used to encourage children to think.

[18]George F. Kneller, *The Art and Science of Creativity* (New York: Holt, Rinehart & Winston, Inc., 1965), p. 78.

[19]Hughes Mearns, *Creative Power: The Education of Youth in the Creative Arts,* rev. ed. (New York: Dover Publns., Inc., 1958), p. 267.

[20]Ibid, p. 260.

The Venn Diagram

Named after John Venn, an English logician who lived from 1834 to 1923, the Venn diagram uses circles to represent sets and their relationships. This diagram can be employed to compare and contrast any two concepts, ideas, people, events.

In the lesson on the opposite page students are introduced to this method as a way of comparing themselves with a character about whom they have read. Using a combination of left brain and right brain thinking, the students collect and organize information. Notice that some of the information is factual based on the author's description of the character; the student must also analyze his or her own characteristics and then relate them to those of the character described. After collecting and organizing the information, students will be able to write the short essay, as directed. The oral discussion is designed to extend student thinking as they share their conclusions.

Exploring Semantics

It is important that students be introduced to concepts of concreteness and abstraction, for as Hayakawa notes:

> The reason we must concern ourselves with the process of abstracting is that the study of language is all too often regarded as being a matter of examining such things as pronunciation, spelling, vocabulary, grammar, and sentence structure. . . . But as we know from everyday experience, learning language is not simply a matter of learning words; it is a matter of correctly relating our words to the things and happenings for which they stand.[21]

In presenting the concept of abstraction Hayakawa uses the illustration of Bessie, the cow, a familiar animal that can be touched and easily identified. As we move up the abstraction ladder, however, we find that *Bessie* can also be referred to as a member of the *cow* family and as part of the classification *livestock*. She is a *"farm asset"* and, therefore, a general *"asset,"* and still more abstractly, she is *"wealth."*

Trips up and down the abstraction ladder will serve to acquaint young people with these degrees of specificity as they move from the concrete to the abstract or vice versa.

Make a ladder of construction paper or bamboo strips to serve as the abstraction ladder on which students can place cards bearing words which represent levels of abstraction, for example:
  rose, climber, flower, plant, foliage, landscaping
  turkey, poultry, meat, food, farm products
  penny, coin, money, wages, income, wealth

[21]S. I. Hayakawa, *Language and Thought in Action* (New York: Harcourt Brace Jovanovich, Inc., 1972), p. 152.

ALIKE AND DIFFERENT

As you think about the book you have just read, use the form below to help you compare yourself with the character about whom you read. This form is called a Venn diagram, which is used in math to compare two sets. It is adapted here to work with reading and writing.

Title of Book _____

Name of Character _____

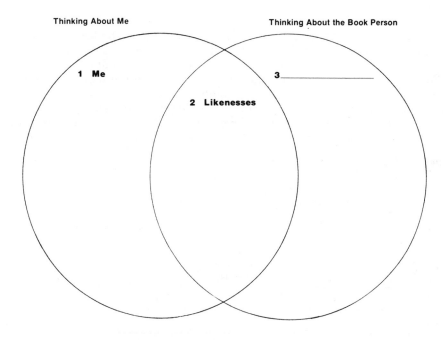

Thinking About Me   **Thinking About the Book Person**

1 Me   3_____

2 Likenesses

Think about how you are like the person you read about. List these ideas in section 2. List characteristics about yourself in section 1 and those about the book person in section 3; these ideas show how you are different.

After you complete the Venn diagram, write 3 paragraphs. In the first one, describe yourself. In the second, describe the book person. In the third, write about how the two of you are alike, what you share in common.

Discuss your essay with others who read the same book. Read your compositions aloud to each other in a small group. How are your papers alike and how are they different? Can you make any conclusions about how all people are alike and how they are different?

In defining words we find that we must narrow the category to include only that which is defined, or the definition has little meaning. How can we define a "bed"?

bed = a piece of furniture (How about a chair?)
bed = furniture in a bedroom (How about a dresser?)
bed = a large flat piece of furniture on which we usually sleep at night (Getting closer.)

In writing we stress the importance of dealing with specific cases rather than high levels of abstraction, for skilled authors hold our interest with the rich detail with which they enliven their writing. We often are impressed by the effective use of detail as in this passage from *John Henry and His Hammer* by Howard W. Felton:

> You're a fine, big boy, John Henry. Mos' a man now. You're as black as the night was that saw you come into this here world. You're as strong as the wind that blowed the trees down low. Your blood is as red as the moon that grew big an' red, an' stopped an' ran backwards. An' the eyes you got sparkle an' shine like the white of a angel's wing, an' your muscles is as powerful an' easy, an' moves strong an' quiet as the river tha turned right 'round in its tracks an' ran uphill.[22]

As we move down the abstraction ladder, we come to the least abstract term, for instance, *rose, turkey* or *penny,* in the examples just cited. As we write, however, we find that we don't mean just any rose, but the red rose in Mrs. Kirk's garden, the one which always blooms in the month of May and perfumes the yards of all her neighbors. We want to become even more specific as we place characters in a setting and describe events. Experiments in language can lead children to become aware of degrees of specificity in this way:

Which of these terms is most specific?
____a lady ____that lady ____Mrs. Wilma Jones
____a Dolly Varden trout ____a gray fish ____a speckled trout
____the dog ____the collie in the street ____the dog in the street

1	2	3	4
girl	a girl in my class	the girl who sits in front of me	Mary Jane Nelson
pet			
house			

Ways of Thinking

The student needs to become aware of fallacious thinking not only to avoid being influenced by the writing of others but also to avoid falling into dangerous ways of thinking. A common error is the *sweeping generalization.* How often do you hear the unqualified generalization in ordinary conversation? "Oh, everyone knows how to dance!" "Teachers are mean!" "Those seniors are so conceited!" We often find ourselves falling into the habit of making unsubstantiated statements which fail to allow for individual cases.

> Display a variety of pictures on the bulletin board. With each picture supply a generalization which students can attack to demonstrate the fallacy of making

[22]Howard W. Felton, *John Henry and His Hammer* (New York: Alfred A. Knopf, Inc., 1950), p. 11.

unsubstantiated generalizations. The generalization, "Every boy should have a dog," for example, might elicit the following arguments:

> My cousin, Tom, is allergic to fur, so a dog is not for him.
> A family that lives in an apartment can't always have a dog.
> I know a boy who is so mean to his dog that he shouldn't have one.

Search the newspaper for examples of generalizations which can be refuted in the same way. Students can also deliberately write generalizations, perhaps ones they have heard, which can be discussed in class. Advertising often supplies good examples of the "glittering generality" which strives to sway opinion or to sell a product.

Another type of thinking which merits attention is the *two-valued attitude* in which matters are decided as either "right" or "wrong" with no thought for gradations of rightness or wrongness. Is a person *bad* or *good,* or is it possible that a person might have one vice mixed with some desirable traits? We have encouraged this type of thinking in students by concocting tests which demand "one right answer" and make no provision for variation. Research in creativity has led to encouragement of divergent thinking through the use of open-ended questions which stimulate thought. How can we assist students in developing more flexible modes of thinking, in breaking the rigid two-valued attitude toward life?

Analyze a character about whom the group is reading. What are the person's good traits? What traits are less desirable? Can we apply a simple adjective "good" or "bad" to a complex being? Guide students to write character sketches which describe a person, real or imaginary, and show that people are both *good* and *bad* at the same time.

The study of antonyms emphasizes this "either-or" thinking. Examine sets of antonyms as you discuss the gradations which are involved in any pair of *opposite* words. Introduce students to the concept of *continuum* as you draw a long line on the board with antonyms at each end, thus:

HOT	warm	cool	COLD

What are the many gradations which lie between HOTNESS and COLDNESS? Fill in all the terms which can be thought of—cool, chilly, warm, sweltering, and so forth. Then try other opposite concepts which represent values—HAPPY–SAD, RIGHT–WRONG. Encourage students to discover examples of two-valued thinking which can be discussed in class.

Of particular importance in writing is the avoidance of *stereotyped thinking,* which is also an example of rigidity of thought. Is every woman over seventy a "sweet little old lady?" Does every Texan wear a ten-gallon hat and ride the range each day? Do all Eskimo families live in igloos? Do all women like to cook? An exciting study of language could focus class attention on ferreting out stereotypes.

Write a description which examplifies a stereotype. Then rewrite the description eliminating the stereotyped thinking. Draw two pictures to illustrate the difference in thought. Use *Sylvester and the Magic Pebble* by William Steig to demonstrate stereotyped ideas.

An important distinction to be made in writing is that between *fact* and *opinion*. *Facts* are statements which can be proved, for example, the fact that a room is thirty feet long can be proved by measurement, and we would all have to agree that the statement is factual. We must recognize the changing quality of factual knowledge, however, for, as we are becoming increasingly aware, the facts of today are not always the facts of tomorrow. Facts, therefore, require constant verification.

Opinions or *judgments* are personal evaluations which reflect attitudes and values; they cannot be verified as facts can. We frequently hear opinions stated authoritatively as though they were facts, and therein lies the fallacy. Opinion has a place in thoughtful writing, but it should be identified as such by introductory words which qualify the statements as a personal judgment—"I think," "It seems to me," "According to the author," and so on. Opinion can be given a measure of validity through substantiation by quoting the opinions of others and by presenting cogent arguments which serve to support the personal judgment. We can provide many classroom experiences in working with fact and opinion.

Debates provide opportunity to support an opinion, with students taking both sides of an issue. It is particularly interesting for students to support the side with which they really do not agree, for they will need to think carefully to support their argument.

Even primary-level children can identify fact as distinguished from opinion. Let them decide which of these statements are fact and which are not by trying to prove each statement.

John's book is red. (We need to clarify our statement. Which boy named John? Which particular book?)

The reading table is in the northeast corner of the room. (This statement can be verified.)

Mr. Popper's Penguins is the best book Mr. Woods ever read to us. (Does everybody agree?)

Another important aspect of thought is the *drawing of inferences,* which we do continually without being conscious of the process. Again, however, we must be careful that the inferences we make are valid according to the facts known, for example:

May is often absent from school. Can we correctly infer that she dislikes school?

Chuck broke a window in the auditorium. Do we infer that he is an incorrigible troublemaker?

We see a little girl on the sidewalk. Can we infer that she is lost?

Wordplay

Recreational linguistics (see pages 157–60) challenges students to think as they use language in varied ways. Avoid the meaningless *hidden word puzzles* as you invite students to be creative as they invent original images or new words that the English language needs. Ideas for challenging students to engage in wordplay are all around us.

Marilyn Fendrick advocates the study of "literary license" as a way to stimulate student intellects. She begins by telling students about a few of the innovative license plates she has seen in California, for example: 10S NE1 (Tennis, anyone?), IAM SEXY, or VIVA YO. She challenges students in the elementary school to decode the messages about children's literature that she has prepared as personalized license plates:

3 OINKS (Three Little Pigs)
AU E LOX (Goldilocks)
111 OSOS (Three Bears)

Then, she introduces license plates that describe the occupation of the driver, thus:

CAR DR (Mechanic)
B FLAT (Musician)
BBBBS (Apiarist)
C BED (Oceanographer)
IADD4U (Accountant)
PET DOC (Veterinarian)

Following this introduction, she invites students to try their ingenuity by designing license plates for different times in their lives, for people they admire, or related to different categories such as sports.[23]

This kind of wordplay encourages students to relate numbers, letters, and ideas in an original way. They are beginning with a base of factual information, but the creative leap must occur to produce a truly humorous or clever personalized message.

Puzzle Challenges

Designate one section of a bulletin board as the PUZZLE OF THE WEEK display. On Monday you can present the weekly challenge to the students. Encourage them to talk about the puzzle you have presented and even to share it with their families. On Friday, discuss the puzzle, see if anyone has found a solution, and disclose the answer or answers.

[23]Marilyn Fendrick, "Literary License(s)," *California English,* March/April 1981, pp. 11, 14.

You might try a spatial puzzle like this one:

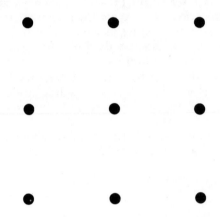

The challenge is to connect all nine dots by drawing only four straight lines. Students must "get out of their boxes" if they are to solve this puzzle. (The answer is on the next page.)

Students will also be intrigued by conundrums like the following:

1. Allow yourself five minutes to rearrange the letters O W D E N A W R to spell a new word. It is not a proper name nor anything foreign or strange. Write it out.
2. Quickly now: How many animals of each species did Adam take aboard the Ark with him? (Notice that the question is not how many pairs, but how many animals.)
3. What unusual characteristic do these six words have in common? (Complete your answer in three minutes.)

> erstwhile   hijack   abcedarian
> defeat   studious   sighing

4. Figure out this problem in diplomatic relations: If an international airliner crashed *exactly* on the United States–Canadian border, where would they be required by international law to bury the survivors? (Remember, this is by *international* law.)
5. If you had only one match and entered a room to start up a kerosene lamp, an oil heater, and a wood-burning stove, which would you light first? Why?

By the time you have presented a few of these tricky questions, your students will begin to catch on to your tomfoolery. (Answers on the next page.) Described elsewhere in this book are many learning activities that promote thinking skills. Especially helpful are the following:

Questioning techniques that probe beneath the surface (p. 73)
Responding to literature (p. 312)
Holistic assessment of writing by peers (p. 174)

SUMMARY

Students need to be aware of the thinking skills they use. They will be challenged to utilize both linear and holistic thinking modes in a classroom where thinking is valued and they know that they can risk failure. Emphasizing thinking ensures that children will have something to say as they speak and write. Learning will be more exciting and effective because students are involved in successful experiences designed to help them develop to their fullest potentials.

Answer to puzzles

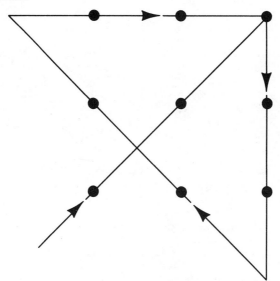

Conundrums

1. A new word. (That's what you were supposed to spell.)
2. Was Adam on the ark?
3. They all have three letters in alphabetical order.
4. I doubt that there would be survivors. If there were, why would you *bury* them?
5. Light the match, of course.

CHALLENGE

Now, try a few stimulating ideas yourself.

1. Use the Venn diagram to compare yourself with a character in a book that you have just read.

2. Read three of the books listed on page 75. Plan how you would use each one in stimulating student thinking.

---

3. In your notebook, begin a collection of word or figure puzzles that you could use with students to challenge their intellect.

4. A teacher who is creative will be more likely to stimulate the creative thinking of children. You might consider your own creative potential by using the following list of creative activities. Which of these experiences have you had during the past month?

_____ 1. Acted in a play.
_____ 2. Wrote a poem.
_____ 3. Kept a diary.
_____ 4. Recorded on a tape recorder.
_____ 5. Made up a recipe.
_____ 6. Wrote a song.
_____ 7. Solved the problem of getting along with my peers.
_____ 8. Wrote a letter to someone in another country.
_____ 9. Made up a game and played it.
_____ 10. Sketched a picture.
_____ 11. Kept a record of my leisure reading.
_____ 12. Cooked a foreign food.
_____ 13. Made jewelry.
_____ 14. Took color photographs.
_____ 15. Collected anything.
_____ 16. Took a walk in the woods.
_____ 17. Drew cartoons.
_____ 18. Helped organize something.
_____ 19. Designed greeting cards or invitations.
_____ 20. Made a toy for a child.
_____ 21. Performed with a group—danced, sang, played an instrument.
_____ 22. Wrote a short story.
_____ 23. Made a play on words.
_____ 24. Wrote a letter to an editor.
_____ 25. Told a child an original story.
_____ 26. Other

EXPLORING FURTHER

Almy, Millie et al., *Young Children's Thinking: Studies of Some Aspects of Piaget's Theory*. New York: Teachers College Press, 1966.

Berthoff, Ann E., *The Making of Meaning*. Montclair, N.J.: Boynton/Cook, 1981.

Bloom, Benjamin, *All Our Children Learning: A Primer for Parents, Teachers, and Other Educators*. New York: McGraw-Hill Book Co., 1981.

Bogen, Joseph E., "The Other Side of the Brain VII: Some Educational Aspects of Hemispheric Specialization," *UCLA Educator*, 1975, 17: 24–32.

PAR Thinking Skills Resource Panel, "Thinking about the Teaching of Thinking." Bloomington, Ind.: Phi Delta Kappa, September 1980. *Practical Applications of Research: Newsletter of Phi Delta Kappa's Center on Evaluation, Development, and Research*, Vol. 3, No. 1.

Parnes, Sidney, J. et al., *Guide to Creative Action*. New York: Charles Scribner's Sons, 1977.

Rico, Gabriele, L., *Metaphor and Knowing: Analysis, Synthesis, Rationale*. Ph.D. dissertation, Stanford University, 1976.

Rico, Gabriele L. et al., *A Metaphor Curriculum in Art*. California: Los Altos High School District, 1976.

Samples, Bob, "Holonomic Knowing: A Challenge for Education in the 80s," in *Education in the 80s: English*, ed. R. Baird Shuman. National Education Association, 1981.

Smith, Frank, *Comprehension and Learning*. New York: Holt, Rinehart and Winston, 1975.

Tarnopol, Lester and Muriel Tarnopol, ed., *Brain Function and Reading Disabilities*. Baltimore, Md.: University Park Press, 1976.

Zepezauer, Frank, "Consciousness Shifting: Intellectual Training in the Schools," *California English*, March–April 1981, pp. 5–6, 10.

5

Listen, my child, and you shall hear.
Henry Wadsworth Longfellow, "Paul Revere's Ride"

LISTENING TO LEARN
LEARNING TO LISTEN

Listening is the language skill with which we all begin the learning process, and which we depend on throughout life. Although listening is basic to all of learning, however, we do not allocate curriculum time for listening instruction as we do spelling and writing. Listening has been, literally, the invisible language art.

Listening is closely tied to speaking since both deal with the oral language. Unlike the productive skill of speaking, however, listening is always dependent on someone else's speaking, their production of speech with all the complexities of rate, pitch, meaning, usage of words, and body language. Listening is also related to reading in that both are receptive skills that depend on language produced by another person. Because listening is widely used in the classroom (about 50% of instructional time), we need to give serious attention to helping students become more effective listeners. We cannot assume that children listen with discrimination and comprehension just because listening is the primary language skill learned.

BENCHMARK

Teacher training often neglects instruction related to listening instruction in the classroom. Take a few minutes here to think about what you know about listening. Answer the following questions in your notebook.

1. How would you define listening? Can you identify different levels of listening?

2. Do you think you listen effectively? What problems do you have while listening? Would you rate yourself as a good, average, or poor listener?

3. What might increase your listening efficiency? List several ideas that might help you as well as the children in your classroom.

Discuss the answers for these questions. Compile a list of the problems you have identified that hinder effective listening. Compile another list of suggestions that might help children listen more efficiently.

This chapter is divided into two sections: (1) The Listening Process and (2) Teaching Listening Skills. The first section discusses theories and background information that will help you understand the complexity of the listening process. The second includes strategies to improve students' listening abilities. Through working with the information presented and trying some of the activities, you should learn:

• different levels of listening
• characteristics of efficient listening
• concepts about listening to share with students
• methods of providing listening practice in the classroom

THE LISTENING PROCESS: BACKGROUND INFORMATION FOR THE TEACHER

As our society becomes increasingly media-oriented, listening becomes more important as a language skill. It is estimated that we comprehend and retain only about 25 percent of what we hear, and furthermore, ideas become distorted by 80 percent of those who try to communicate what they have heard. It is essential that we focus on improving listening literacy.

Training Yourself

In order to become more effective, teachers of listening need to examine the problems inherent in the listening process. We need to develop strategies to help us improve our own listening abilities, because we did not receive this instruction as part of our training. Experiencing this process will enable you to work more realistically with young children in the classroom.

Sylvia Porter, who writes a column "Your Money" which appears on the business page of many local newspapers, emphasizes the economic importance of listening. "The financial toll of poor listening is enormous," she states, and she notes that fewer than 5% of business personnel polled rated themselves as superior or excellent listeners. Her recommended practices for improving job performance and money management skills through listening are worth knowing:

1. DON'T tune out "dry" subjects. Be an opportunist and ask "What's in it for me?" What you don't ask can hurt you in the long run.
2. DON'T judge the speaker's delivery. Instead, pay attention to the content.
3. DON'T be argumentative. Stay quiet until you have completely understood what the speaker is really saying. This will give you time to think of constructive comments and to make a positive impression when you do enter the discussion.
4. DO listen for ideas, not only to facts. If you restrict your attention to facts alone, you may completely miss the point. Not only that, facts can be deceiving.
5. DO keep your mind open. Try not to overreact to emotional words or the emotional impact of certain words. Instead, concentrate on why your speaker is using them.
6. DO capitalize on the fact that thought is four times faster than speech. You can use this time to challenge, anticipate, mentally summarize, and listen between the lines to the speaker's tone of voice as well as to what the speaker is saying.
7. DO, finally, work at listening. The more you exercise your "listening muscles," the more you'll be a step ahead both in your business and in your personal affairs. As a poor listener, you almost surely have been causing havoc in your personal business affairs and having a negative impact on your own work. But vow to yourself: No longer![1]

How many times have you heard your colleagues comment as they left a meeting, "That isn't the way I heard it" or "Did you understand him to say . . . ?" We do have trouble hearing accurately, and we don't always understand what we hear. No wonder messages become distorted! Sylvia Porter's seven steps should help you become a more efficient listener.

Thinking About Listening

"To listen is an effort, and just to hear is no merit. A duck also hears." Thus Igor Stravinsky expressed the importance of moving beyond the mere hearing of sounds. Listening is vital for the musician, but it is also a skill needed by every person every day.

Many sounds are in the air at any one time. Steve hears some of these sounds. Others never reach his level of awareness; he is "tuned out"; he is not listening. There are sounds which he may hear but does not listen to. Still other sounds will cause him to listen but with little attempt to understand or respond. The highest level of listening is reached when the individual listens with purpose and comprehension. This level has been termed

---

[1]Sylvia Porter, "Are You Listening? Really Hearing? Your Money, syndicated column, San Francisco *Chronicle*, November 14, 1979.

"auding" to distinguish the process described from mere hearing or listening without perception.

Compare these levels of listening:

1. *Hearing.* We hear the wind blowing without any conscious response. A mother hears a child talking and may even respond, but could not tell you what the child is saying.
2. *Listening.* A friend listens with obvious attention, but with no particular response. The person is consciously listening without comment.
3. *Auding.* The listener is making an effort to understand, may take notes, or ask questions. There is a high degree of engagement or interaction between listener and speaker.

The listening act consists of four components. First, is the stimulus that attracts the listener's attention. Second is the act of attending, which requires motivation and effort. Third, the listener derives meaning from the stimulus, a personal process based on experience, maturation, and degree of attention. Finally, listening culminates in the storage of information in the memory where it is retained for retrieval when needed.

Wolvin and Coakley point out several questionable views of the listening process, for example:

"Listening may not take place without agreement about what is said." The term *listen* may be used inappropriately in such sentences as: Helen won't listen to what I have to say.

"A person cannot be listening unless he or she responds overtly."

"We must be face-to-face in order to listen effectively." Listening is often done over the telephone or while watching the television or radio. Visual cues do add to the clarity of the speaker's message, aiding the listener.

We need to be aware of such misconceptions as we talk about listening.[2]

We listen for many different purposes. It is important to have a purpose clearly in mind in order to meet our objective, and having a clear objective means that we will listen more effectively.

Purposes of listening include:

GAINING INFORMATION

Listening is a way of obtaining information. We may be listening to a lecture, an excerpt read by the teacher, a report made by an economist. If we are attending by choice, we will try to listen and will reinforce the listening act by taking notes and following up the presentation by discussion with our friends.

APPRECIATION OF A PERFORMANCE

We may listen appreciatively to music, the reading of poetry, or the lines in a drama. Our response and interpretation are highly subjective. We understand according to our ability and background.

---

[2]Andrew Wolvin and Carolyn G. Coakley, *Listening Instruction* (Urbana, Ill.: ERIC and Speech Communication Association, 1977), p. 6.

COMMUNICATION

Listening is an essential part of the communication process. You listen with empathy as a friend expresses grief, and you probably utter words of sympathy and understanding. You try to understand a person's directions so that you can find your way to a committee meeting. And when you speak, you expect the person to whom you speak to listen with equal attentiveness.

Students need to be aware of the varied purposes of listening. Providing time to discuss this purpose before beginning an activity will help students listen more effectively, and prepare them for categorizing information and knowing what kinds of notes they need to take.

Difficulties of Listening Efficiently

Listening is not a facile skill, for many factors impede listening efficiency. The listener, for example, has no control over the rate of speed of the speaker. In *vis-à-vis* conversation it is perfectly permissible to request a friend to speak more slowly, but Mr. Lee addressing a group of 400 has his audience literally at his mercy. He not only may speak rapidly, but may possess speech characteristics which prevent effective listening. As is pointed out in the chapter on speaking, the speaker has a responsibility to those who are listening, but this responsibility is not always recognized and assumed.

The speaker may mispronounce words or place words in odd contexts, causing confusion in the listener's mind. While trying to grasp one point, the listener is no doubt missing the next and is forced to skip ahead mentally with the speaker, hoping that the points missed were not vital to understanding the total message.

The organization of the speaker also influences listening efficiency. A well-organized speech is followed with relative ease, whereas a discussion which flits from topic to topic with no obvious framework may lose many listeners en route to the main point.

The listener usually has no written guide to assist the task of listening. Provision of a script or type of libretto for material to be heard will aid listening efficiency. Reading a play or story which is to be presented on record will greatly aid comprehension when the recording is played for

STUPID! I ASKED YOU TO BRING ME A *FROCK* OR *SHEATH* FROM PARIS!

© King Features Syndicate, Inc. 1973.

the first time. An outline of the material to be heard enables the listener to follow the report of detailed information.

Another factor which impedes comprehension is that there is seldom an opportunity for repetition in the speaking–listening situation. A line that is not "caught" in a play, a television program, or a speech is not likely to be repeated. If time and circumstance permit, a record may be replayed to permit listeners to hear portions of a selection again. The tape recorder has the further advantage of permitting the listener to stop the recording immediately in order to replay lines which he or she would like to hear again.

The group listening experience contains hindrances to effective listening which are not present in an individual listening situation. As a member of a group, Anne may hesitate to request that the speaker repeat a statement or that a portion of the tape be replayed. She may hesitate to expose her failure to understand, or may fear disapproval of her request for repetition. Listening abilities vary as do other abilities, and it is for this reason that we should not expect all students to listen with the same efficiency. Individualized approaches, as in any other area of the curriculum, will also prove effective in teaching listening skills as each child develops abilities according to individual capacity. Listening stations in individual classrooms or in a central library will assist individual development of listening abilities.

Successful listening also depends on the maturation of the listener. A child of five will usually be unable to listen with comprehension to a lecture intended for an adult audience.

The experiential background and the knowledge of the listener are also important factors. An economically disadvantaged child may not be prepared to understand ideas presented with a middle-class child in mind. An urban child who has never seen a cow or pig may be totally unconcerned by a discussion of the farm.

Background or previous knowledge may distort meanings if they cause the listener to conceive of something entirely different from that intended by the speaker. When Father queries, "Where is that pipe?" Terry may begin searching for a pipe her father might smoke, whereas he is preparing to repair the kitchen sink.

Insecurity may prevent a student's listening. The need for attention may be so great a child is actually unable to sit quietly listening while someone else talks.

Listening tasks   We have indicated the large percentage of our time spent directly or indirectly in listening, but just what skills are involved in this complex ability? Incorporated in the broad term of *listening* are the following categories of specific skills: (1) reception, (2) comprehension, and (3) assimilation.

RECEPTION

Hear sounds made externally
Distinguish variety in sounds (auditory discrimination)
Decide to listen or not to listen

COMPREHENSION

Follow words used
Understand ideas expressed
Recognize purpose of listening
    Note details
    Receive new ideas and information

ASSIMILATION

React to ideas expressed
    Disagree
    Ask questions
    Make additions
    Evaluate
Reinforce learning through use
    Follow directions
    Repeat information to another
    Develop given information
    Adapt ideas presented

Each stage of listening development is important to the total listening experience. Receiving sounds is essential, for lack of reception clearly eliminates any possibility for comprehension and assimilation of what is heard. The three tasks of the listener are interdependent and self-generating, for reception leads to comprehension, which in turn leads to assimilation and reaction, and the cycle begins again as the question or commentary is received, comprehended, and reacted to.

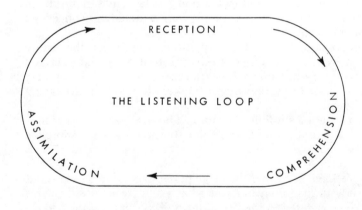

Studies by Ralph B. Nichols and others point out that without training in listening most of us operate at only 25 percent efficiency.[3] Research also indicates that direct instruction in listening does increase listening effec-

[3]Ralph B. Nichols, "What Can Be Done About Listening?" *The Supervisor's Notebook,* Vol. XXII, No. 1 (1960).

tiveness.[4] It is obvious that training in this essential skill should be included at all levels of education.

We find that children actually spend half their school time listening, but at what level of efficiency? Is this a wise use of student time? How might their time be better used? Does the teacher spend too much time talking when students should be more directly involved? Does the fact that only one child speaks while more than thirty listen indicate a low level of direct participation? Does it indicate a need for varied grouping techniques or individualized approaches to learning?

Is listening as practiced a guided, purposeful experience? We say the class is listening; but are the children really auding, or are they merely waiting their turn to participate? Are they literally wasting their time? Could teaching techniques be more exciting, more stimulating, if greater use were made of visual aids—films, filmstrips, pictures, direct observation, experimentation, field excursions? Perhaps some periods of "listening" should be eliminated from the daily schedule.

Relationship of Listening to Thinking

Listening is a vital part of the complex thinking process. As a student participates in listening activities in the classroom, he or she hears words which symbolize meanings. Through practice students learn to abstract meaning from these words and the order in which they are arranged. Through listening they learn to:

Make and substantiate generalizations
Sort ideas, reject or accept
Group into categories
Observe similarities and differences
Make comparisons
Develop or adapt concepts

Children should be exposed to varied types of thinking processes which require careful listening and reaction. After hearing two poems about the same general topic, for example, "P's the Proud Policeman" by Phyllis McGinley and "Bobby Blue" by John Drinkwater, children can compare the treatment of the subject. In the second poem, for instance, the name *policeman* is never mentioned. How do we know that the poet is describing a policeman?

Philip's listening vocabulary is probably the largest of all his vocabularies. He understands many words which he would hesitate to use in speech or be unable to read or write. What factors account for the greater size of the listening vocabulary?

---

[4]Sister Mary Kevin Hollow, "Listening Comprehension at the Intermediate Grade Level," *Elementary School Journal,* December 1955, pp. 158–61.

1. Meaning can be deduced from the general context provided by the speaker.
    The situation was so *ridiculous* that the whole family began laughing.
    (The word *ridiculous* obviously is associated with laughter.)
2. The exact meaning is not necessary to understanding.
    The *cheetah* is the fastest runner in the animal world.
    (The child may not know exactly what the cheetah looks like, but gathers enough meaning to permit discussion.)
3. The burden for introducing the new word lies with the speaker, not the listener; it is the speaker who must be more familiar with the meaning in order to use a word coherently.
4. The speaker's tone of voice implies certain connotations of approval or disapproval.
    The boys were just too *unruly*.

Because the listening vocabulary is so much more extensive than those of speaking, reading, and writing, we must be careful to provide stimulating discussion material for the primary-level classroom as well as for intermediate and upper-grade levels. Discussion must not be limited to the content of controlled vocabulary readers, for instance, for young minds are feasting on more exotic fare via television. We have a tendency to underestimate the abilities of children to understand broad concepts if couched in understandable terms, demonstrated visually, and presented in a stimulating context. This is one strong argument for the teacher's oral reading of books that are too difficult for children to read to themselves, for children can handle ideas orally and visually which may be too difficult for them to read about. First graders will enjoy listening to *Charlotte's Web*, for example, although few would be able to read it enjoyably.

Research indicates that there is a high correlation between reading and ability to listen with comprehension, and there is a corresponding increase in reading ability with increased ability to listen. A strong reading program should provide much listening experience, for the child requires time to develop aural–oral skills which in the long run will add to improved reading abilities. We will find this need recognized more clearly in working with the disadvantaged child and in the teaching of foreign languages, which have long advocated the aural–oral approach to language before composition and reading are taught.

Kellogg and others have found that instruction in listening caused a significant difference in both listening and reading achievement. He worked with first graders and taught listening skills as an integral part of the total language-arts program.[5] Here is an example of instruction that may serve to prevent reading failure as children strengthen their vocabulary, experiential background, and attentiveness to the task at hand.

Help students recognize the relationship between listening and reading, which are both receptive skills. In both, the receiver has to decode a message and similar skills are used, for example, the use of context to comprehend an unknown word. Introduce reading activities through listening first. Read

[5]Ralph E. Kellogg, *A Study of the Effect of a First Grade Listening Instructional Program upon Achievement in Listening and Reading.* Report No. BR–6–8469 (San Diego, Calif.: San Diego County Dept. of Education, 1966).

the following poem aloud to a group of students, for example, or have it available on tape.

CLOUDS

White sheep, white sheep
On a blue hill,
When the wind stops,
You all stand still.
When the wind blows,
You walk away slow.
White sheep, white sheep,
Where do you go?

Follow the reading of the poem by asking several questions about the meaning of the poem, thus:

What is this poem about?
What do the clouds look like?
What makes the clouds move?
What is the blue hill the sheep walk on?

If you tape the poem and questions, allow time for the child to think about the answers to the question. Prepare a sheet for the students that duplicates the lesson in printed form so that they now read what they have heard and write answers that they previously thought or spoke aloud. (See below.) This is an excellent way of integrating learnings in the language arts.

From: *The Elementary Teacher's Ideas and Materials Workshop,* November 1972, p. 15.

CLOUDS

White sheep, white sheep
On a blue hill,
When the wind stops,
You all stand still.

When the wind blows,
You walk away slow.
White sheep, white sheep,
Where do you go?

What is this poem about?
_____
_____

What do the clouds look like?
_____
_____

What makes the clouds move?
_____
_____

What is the blue hill the sheep walk on?
_____
_____

Can you paint a picture of the "white
sheep on a blue hill"?

TEACHING LISTENING SKILLS

Lessons should be planned to meet specific objectives within the range of listening skills that children need to develop. Lundsteen[6] provides a list of skills that you can begin with; as expanded here, the list stresses what the child will be able to do as a result of instruction:

1. Identify significant details accurately.
2. List simple sequences of words and ideas.
3. Follow oral directions for simple procedures.
4. Explain the denotative meanings of words.
5. Explain the meanings of words used in spoken contexts.
6. Answer simple questions asked orally.
7. Paraphrase a spoken message.
8. Discuss the connotative meanings of words.
9. Identify main ideas in an oral delivery.
10. Identify who, what, when, where, and why in a story.
11. Explain the implications of significant details.
12. Make inferences and generalizations based on given oral communication.
13. Respond to the emotions and ideas shared orally by a friend.
14. Discuss the importance of listening and how to improve individual efficiency.
15. Participate in listening exercises designed to improve efficiency.

Our aim in teaching children to listen is to involve them in active listening, what Corinne Geeting terms "assertive listening."

> Skilled assertive listeners practice their particular science (or art, perhaps) by listening in the following ways: *positively,* not negatively; *confidently,* not timidly; *helpfully,* not hostilely; *analytically,* not skeptically; *courageously,* not fearfully; *with concern,* not indifference; *thoughtfully,* not dogmatically; *creatively,* not rigidly; and *actively,* not passively.[7]

Talking with students about these aspects of listening will make them aware of the multifaceted nature of the listening act. They will learn, too, that good listeners are not passive as they engage in communication with others.

Evaluating Present Practices

To improve student listening abilities, take a serious look at what goes on in your classroom. Ask some of these questions:

1. How much time do children spend listening? When they listen, are they performing a specific task? Do they know the purpose of the listening activity?
2. Do you talk too much in the classroom? Could you increase student participation in active learning by using small group activities so that more students are directly involved? Consider how you can avoid dominating the classroom

[6]Sara W. Lundsteen, *Listening, Its Impact on Reading and the Other Language Arts* (Urbana, Ill.: National Council of Teachers of English, 1971), p. 52.

[7]Corinne Geeting, "The Dynamics of Assertive Listening," *The Graduate Woman,* November/December 1980, pp. 16–17.

with your voice. How can you move into a facilitater role, the resource person in the classroom?

In short, to teach students to be better listeners, you should want to teach listening skills, you should examine the practices in your classroom, and you should plan instruction that is designed to meet specific objectives.

Consider, for example, the practice called "show and tell" or "sharing time" which is common in many elementary school classrooms. One teacher wrote, "I hate show and tell," and the reasons were that this method had become so stereotyped that the time was wasted and children were actually being taught poor listening habits.[8] It is essential that we reconsider the value of what we are doing in the classroom and how this basically good idea can be used more constructively. Here are suggestions that may help you make sharing time more worthwhile.

Don't have sharing time every day or always at the same time.
Select a theme for the sharing period—My Best Friend, Was I Scared!, Work Can Be Fun, An Exciting Moment. Announce the theme the day before.
Use an unusual seating arrangement—circle, semicircle, sitting on the floor. Tape the speaking occasionally for evaluation by students.
You listen, too, and comment with interest. (Don't be obviously busy with paperwork.)
If children have something exciting to share, let them, even if sharing is not on your schedule. Take advantage of this show of interest.

Let us turn to listening experiences that are better planned, more purposeful, and therefore more stimulating and effective. Children need specific practice, for example, in critical listening. They need to listen to each other and to combine speaking and listening skills. Positive approaches to listening instruction can be based on provocative material, new ideas, something the child can become excited about; otherwise, slovenly listening habits will be encouraged along with justifiable disinterest, apathy, and boredom with school.

Preparing for Effective Listening

What conditions promote effective listening skills? How can adverse factors be overcome?

Check the physical conditions of the classroom. Is it poorly ventilated, poorly lighted, overheated, or unusually cold? Are some children overdressed for the type of work in which they are engaged? Excess clothing—sweaters, sweatshirts, jackets—should be removed on entering the classroom.

Recommend physical examinations for children who appear to have unusual difficulty hearing. Some children feign hearing difficulties as an excuse for inattentiveness or as a way of gaining the teacher's attention.

---

[8]Pat Timberlake, "I Hate Show and Tell," *Elementary English,* April 1973.

Vary the routines of teaching so that children do not become fatigued or bored. The attention span or the listening attentiveness of the younger child is relatively short. Long periods of uninterrupted listening are less efficient than are short experiences interspersed with more active learning activities.

Plan learning activities to include more speaking by children and less by the teacher. Children who are involved in an activity listen more readily, more attentively, for there is a reason to listen.

Avoid distractions such as noises from the street or activities of other children in the classroom. Listening centers that provide earphones for each child have the advantage of closing out other sounds. Room dividers can prevent visual distraction.

How the teacher listens to children may influence their habits of listening. If you are not sufficiently interested in a child's presentation to listen to it attentively before the class, you cannot expect the class to listen. If you are busy grading papers at the back of the room, what chance has the young speaker of holding the attention of the class?

Discuss the purpose of the listening experience. Are we listening to get the main idea of a story, or are we trying to compare two ways of presenting information? Are we listening especially to notice interesting ways of using words, or are we trying to gain information about a Greek myth?

Characteristics of Good Listening Habits

Talk about good listening practices with students. The identification of desirable habits of listening should lend direction to classroom activities. Student-compiled lists of aids to good listening have been found helpful in motivating individuals to work on specific skills. Nichols[9] published a list of "eight significant listening habits." The good listener:

1. Maintains an awareness of his own motives in listening
   Develops own motives for effective listening
   Analyzes speech and adjusts to motives
2. Shares responsibility for communication
   Considers the different techniques of the speaker
   Assumes half of the responsibility for communication
3. Arranges favorable conditions for listening
   Adjusts for any personal hearing disability or for poor room ventilation or temperature
   Ignores any outside or unnecessary distractions
4. Exercises emotional control during listening
   Postpones personal worries
   Does not permit an immediate dislike for a speech or speaker
5. Structuralizes the presentation
   Recognizes conventional compositional techniques
   Adjusts note-taking to the organizational plan of the speech

[9]Ralph G. Nichols, "The Teaching of Listening," *Chicago Schools Journal*, XXX, 273–78.

6. Strives to grasp the central ideas in the presentation
   Focuses on central ideas and tends to recognize the characteristic language in which they are stated
   Has the ability to discriminate between fact and principle, idea and example, evidence and argument
7. Exploits fully the rate differential between thought and speech
   Demands continuous attention—staying on the track with the speaker
   Mentally anticipates each of the speaker's points; identifies the techniques used in the development of each point; and mentally recapitulates points already developed
8. Seeks frequent experience in listening to difficult expository material

Listeners must assume an active role in developing listening skills, for no other person can listen for them, and no one can force them to listen. The task of listening, therefore, must be approached with a positive attitude which assumes that the listener wants to hear, to find out something. The mind can easily slip to unrelated thoughts without the speaker's noticing.

Listeners should also assume responsibility for the success of the speaking-listening encounter to hear with an open mind. To promote understanding, they keep their eyes on the speaker, make certain that they can both see and hear, and take appropriate notes. The listener may then ask questions, comment on the information discussed, and utilize the acquired knowledge.

Introducing the Study of Listening

Design specific techniques of classroom instruction to increase listening efficiency. Although each focuses on only one aspect of the complex of listening skills, increased efficiency in one task increases overall efficiency.

1. Auditory discrimination between sounds
   Which of these words does *not* begin like BIRD?
   balloon   brother   case
2. Appreciation of oral interpretation of literature
   Play recordings, for example, *Alice in Wonderland* (Caedmon, TC 1097) for enjoyment.
3. Location of central theme or idea
   Read or play recorded passages to provide practice. The student may be asked to state the main idea or several possible themes may be suggested from which a selection is made.
4. Discovery of new word meanings from context
   Talk about words after reading aloud, for example, "Armies in the Fire" by Robert Louis Stevenson.
5. Awareness of the power of words
   Tape passages which propagandize; have students identify examples of slanting, loaded words, or generalities.
6. Discovery of specific details
   In what state did Philip live?
   Where was Linda going?
   How did Mr. Pepper obtain a penguin?

7. Recognition of imagery in writing
    Discuss types of figurative language—simile, metaphor, personification. Try to remember several images or figures of speech while listening to "The Daffodils" by William Wordsworth.
8. Comparison of two or more examples
    Have all students write descriptions of a single item or event. These passages can be recorded, or several may be read by one person. (It is best for this purpose if the writers do not read their own passage.) Discuss the variety of treatment.
9. Recognition of fact and opinion
    After the student talks on assigned topics, discuss the presence of fact and opinion in the speech. Was fact substantiated? Was opinion qualified?
10. Learning needed information
    Provide many opportunities for students to take notes on taped or read passages which explain how to do something. Ability to follow directions may fall in this category.
11. Selection of pertinent data
    Provide experience with passages which include directions for doing something as well as a number of bits of extraneous information. Students record the information necessary to perform a specific operation.
12. Repetition of what has been heard
    Read short stories such as *The Mean Mouse and Other Mean Stories* by Janice Udry (Harper, 1962). After each story ask someone to see if they can retell the story while the class listens to determine which details are omitted.

Present listening as an active process. The students can discuss their roles as listeners, for analysis of the responsibilities of the listener will lead to more active participation in the listening act. Training clearly directed toward increasing listening efficiency can be interesting to the group, as they use themselves as guinea pigs in a scientific bit of research to determine whether their practicing will better their listening abilities.

Why is listening important? This question may lead to a study of time spent each day in listening as each child keeps a listening diary. One fourth-grade boy recorded his daily listening activities, thus:

7:00   When I awoke, birds were singing.
7:15   I watched a TV show.
7:30   Mother called me for breakfast; we talked together.
7:45   My dog barked outside the door for his food.
8:00   Music was playing on the radio.
8:30   The telephone rang.
8:40   On the way to school I heard—
         a horn blowing
         children talking
         cars moving
         the traffic lady's whistle.
8:55   The school bell rang.
9:00   Miss Dell called the roll.
         We talked about spring.
         We read aloud in reading class.
10:10 We played "Flying Dutchman."

> Miss Dell read a chapter of *Chitty-Chitty-Bang-Bang*.
> She explained division and we did mental arithmetic.
> **12:00**   At lunch we whispered; music was playing.
> We played "Dodge Ball."
> **12:45**   Joe read about the mission at Santa Barbara.
> Then we answered questions about the missions.
> We located missions on the map.
> We saw a film about Father Serra.
> Miss Dell asked if we would like to make dioramas.
> **1:30**   We played ball.
> We sang songs and played a new record.
> Sandra reported on her science experiment.
> We talked about a picture and wrote a story about it.
> Some people read their stories.
> **3:00**   Lots of noise on the way home.
> A fire engine passed.
> Mom told me she had two jobs for me.
> Then Jim and I played astronauts.
> **6:30**   We had dinner. Dad talked a lot, mostly to Mom.
> **7:15**   I watched TV until Mom called me.
> **8:30**   Dad talked to me after I was in bed.
> Golly, there's listening in everything.

It is also helpful if students develop simple, specific guides to good listening:

LOOK at the speaker.
CONCENTRATE on what he or she is saying.
THINK about what has been said.
TALK about what has been said.
  Ask questions.
  Add information.

To stimulate the discussion of listening prepare a word crossing puzzle for older students to complete, thus:

— — — — — L — —	What you listen to.
— — — — I — —	Synonym for "get."
— — — — — S —	Reason for listening.
— — T — — —	Concentrate.
— — — E — — — —	To store in your memory.
— — — N — — —	What you understand by listening.

ANSWERS

1. stimulus
2. receive
3. purpose
4. attend
5. remember
6. meaning

You would, of course, not grade the completion of this puzzle. Instead, let students try it individually first and then discuss the words they used to complete the puzzle. Or, work through the puzzle with the group focusing on each item in turn so that the puzzle provides a focus for discussing the listening process with students.

Listening for Specific Purposes

Listening is not an isolated skill to be practiced for fifteen minutes a day and then forgotten. We never know when a message will be directed toward us, for listening is an integral part of life. Because this skill, or complex of skills, permeates all areas of the curriculum, effective methods of listening are better taught in the context of varied subject matters—social science, literature, science, language study, music, art.

We need to establish a sequence of listening abilities to be followed from primary grades through junior high school for only through sequential development of these abilities will true listening efficiency be attained. Young children who have learned to identify similar sounds and to follow simple directions will attack progressively more difficult skills and eventually learn to listen critically to recorded presentations of literary works or to the commentary of news analysts. Described briefly here are varied suggestions for teaching listening to elementary school students.

THE SOUNDS OF SILENCE

Listen to silence! Have everyone be as quiet as possible. Is it really silent? Are there still noises to be heard? Do you think it could ever be completely quiet?

NOW HEAR THIS!

Give a series of short directions with the children following them exactly. NOW HEAR THIS: Walk to the chalkboard; write your last name, and place the chalk on the reading table.
Children will enjoy being the leader. The number of directions can be increased as listening ability develops.

THE TRAVELING TALE

Have one child start telling a story. Children take turns adding a line or two to the story as it travels around the group. Have a number of traveling tales going at one time in smaller groups for greater participation. Each child must listen to the developing story in order to make an appropriate addition when it is his turn.

A LISTENING WALK

Take children for a walk. Have them list all the things they heard after they return. The items can be arranged in a poem in this manner.

LISTEN!
The sound of music—
birds singing,
children calling,
churchbells ringing.

> The sounds of autumn—
> leaves rustling,
> boys and girls on the playground,
> geese honking in a wedge.

You might begin this poem by having students say all the sounds they heard as you list the words and phrases on the board. Stanzas can then be formed as children discover categories of sounds as shown in the example. You might repeat this experience after several weeks to see if perception has improved. You could also compare the kinds of sounds heard, discussing the reasons for hearing different sounds—the time of day, the season, the weather, and so on.

LISTEN FOR THE ANSWER

Before beginning a presentation of information to the class, write a question on the board, for example: "How can we manage our playground?" The student knows what to listen for before the activity begins. As you read a report by the student council, students might take simple notes about what they hear as they prepare to discuss the question presented.

SOUND LANGUAGE

Brainstorm words that we use to express sounds. Write them on the board. Then categorize them as loud sounds (shout, honking, crash, scream, clamor) or soft sounds (whispers, murmuring, tapping, hush, singing, cooing, scraping, humming, buzzing). Have children listen for sound language as stories are read aloud.

SOUND STORIES

Tape a series of interesting sounds—a bell ringing, voices whispering, a motor running. Play this sound story as children tell the story they imagine fits around these sounds. The teacher can print the story so that all can read it. Older children can write their stories, to be combined in a big book of sound stories. Let children make sound stories by taping various combinations of sounds.

I'M ON THE WAY TO ZANZIBAR

Play "I'm Going on a Trip to Zanzibar" in which the first child may say, "I'm going on a trip to Zanzibar, and I'm going to take along a toothbrush." The second child must say, "I'm going on a trip to Zanzibar, and I'm going to take along a toothbrush and a poodle." A third might say, "I'm going on a trip to Zanzibar, and I'm going to take along a toothbrush, a poodle, and a baseball bat." And so it goes, as children listen carefully and concentrate on remembering the sequence of the items listed. Younger children will help each other fill in the items as the list grows longer.

TELL THE STORY

Read a good short story aloud to the class. Have students take turns retelling the story as they think about the sequence of events and the details involved. They should strive to be as accurate as possible, referring to the book, if necessary, to check on specific information. More students can participate if this activity is done in small groups with one student reading aloud while the others listen.

FRIENDLY LISTENING

Have children work in pairs as they listen to each other in turn. The task of the listener is to listen carefully, while the partner talks about what he or she likes to do most of all at home. When the talker's time is up (use a three-minute egg timer), the listener must repeat what has been heard as accurately as possible. Then the tasks are switched as the talker takes a turn listening. Notice that in this task the listener must listen "actively."

Listening is also closely related to memory, for remembering is one of the key components of the listening process. Unless what is heard is assimilated and stored in short- and long-term memory, it is lost; no learning takes place. As we focus on listening, therefore, we must also talk about remembering. Tasks that feature listening development should also improve memory skills.

Examples of listening–memory tasks include:

Twenty words   Tell students that you are going to say twenty words. They are to listen as carefully as possible and try to remember the words. After they hear all twenty, they will see how many they can write from memory without worrying about spelling. After completing the task, follow up thus:

1. Chart the range of words remembered by the whole class. Count the number of students who remembered (a) 1–5 (b) 6–10, (c) 11–15, and (d) 16–20 (probably no one). Beginning with the lower range is psychologically better from the student's point of view.
2. Ask students how they helped themselves remember. They will be aware of relating words in some way—meaning, sound, personal connections. Read the list of words aloud again as you talk about what relationships they can see, now that they are thinking along these lines.
3. Ask students if they think they could listen and remember even better if you repeated this experiment. The gamelike quality of this activity is highly motivating. Use a different list of twenty words this time. Most students will remember more words this time.
4. Repeat this activity about once a week for a while.

Acting out   Read a cumulative tale aloud to the group. Such stories feature the repetition of certain lines and the addition of an action each time. Old favorites that you can find in collections of folktales include:

The House That Jack Built
Three Little Pigs
The Gingerbread Boy

After hearing the story, children can act out or retell the story together.

Helping students become aware of the relationships among listening and other thinking skills will stimulate their desire to work on listening. Activities suggested throughout this chapter will reinforce the same kind of learning in an enjoyable manner.

SUMMARY

You have been listening all your life, but you have probably seldom taken time to think about this process. It seems to take little effort, to be a natural skill, so we tend to ignore listening in terms of instruction. Yet studies show us that we listen very inefficiently. Clearly we need to know more about listening and its role in learning.

We can think about listening in a number of ways. This list summarizes some of the things we know about the listening process:

1. Listening to language, not talking about it, is our source of knowledge about how language works. It is the key process in language acquisition.
2. As Ralph Waldo Emerson wrote: "The hearing ear is always close to the speaking tongue." Speaking and listening are interdependent skills that require the interaction of at least two persons.
3. Aural—oral skills remain an important foundation for learning, throughout life. Everyone needs to continue to receive input orally that feeds the brain and supports reading and writing processes.
4. Listening attentively to other people is important for healthy interpersonal relationships. People also need to be listened to, a supportive act that makes both child and adult feel worthwhile and develops self-esteem.
5. We spend more time listening than we do reading, writing, or speaking. In planning the school curriculum, however, we allocate more time to reading, writing, and speaking in that order, and very little time to listening instruction. That order should be reversed.
6. We can teach more effective listening skills. Such instruction would lead to more efficient use of classroom time and greater achievement in terms of student learning.

This summary will prepare us to move into the next chapter on speaking, for the two skills are inseparable.

CHALLENGE

1. As you plan listening activities for your classroom, compile a list of the kinds available as a reminder. You might begin with the following:
   Brainstorm ideas about a given topic.
   Read a good book aloud to the class as they listen for enjoyment.
   Take listening notes on a selected topic.
Notice that all of these listening activities also involve speaking.

2. Devise a listening test that you could use as a means of evaluating the effectiveness of student listening.

3. Prepare a chart that you could use as an instructional aid in teaching students about the listening process.

4. Choose three listening activities. Plan how you would present these activities at a primary grade level. Then decide how you would adapt the same activities for students in the junior high school. Arrange to teach one of these lessons to both levels. Compare the response of the students and the results in terms of improved listening skills.

EXPLORING FURTHER

Calder, Clarence R. and Eleanor M. Antan, *Techniques and Activities to Stimulate Verbal Learning.* New York: Macmillan Publishing Co., Inc., 1970.

Geeting, Baxter and Corinne Geeting, *How to Listen Assertively.* New York: Monarch/Sovereign, 1978.

Lundsteen, Sara W., *Listening, Its Impact on Reading and the Other Language Arts.* Urbana, Ill.: National Council of Teachers of English, 1971.

Marten, Milton, "Listening in Review," in *Classroom-Relevant Research in the Language Arts* by Harold G. Shane and James Walden, coordinators. Washington, D.C.: Association for Supervision and Curriculum Development, 1978.

Monteith, Mary K., "ERIC/RCS Report: Listening/Speaking Skills—The Art of Interactive Communication," *Language Arts,* January 1979, 56, 1:61–65.

Russell, David H. and Elizabeth Russell, *Listening Aids Through the Grades.* New York. Teachers College Press, 1959.

Taylor, Stanford E., *Listening. What Research Says to the Teacher, No. 29.* Department of Classroom Teachers, American Educational Research Association. Washington, D.C.: National Education Association, 1964.

Tiedt, Sidney W. and Iris M. Tiedt, "Learning through Listening," in *Language Arts Activities for the Classroom.* Boston: Allyn & Bacon, Inc., 1978.

———, "Focus on Speaking and Listening," in *Elementary Teacher's Complete Ideas Handbook.* Englewood Cliffs, N.J.: Prentice-Hall, Inc., PEP Books Edition, 1980.

Tutolo, Daniel, "Attention: Necessary Aspect of Listening," *Language Arts,* January 1979, 56, 1:34–37.

Wagner, Guy et al., *Listening Games.* Darien, Conn.: Teacher Publications, 1962.

Wolvin, Andrew and Carolyn G. Coakley, *Listening Instruction.* Theory into Practice Series. Urbana, Ill.: ERIC and Speech Communication Association, 1979.

Word, Barbara S., *Development of Functional Communication Competencies: Pre-K–Grade 6.* Urbana, Ill.: ERIC and Speech Communication Association, 1977.

6

"The time has come," the Walrus said, "To talk of many things . . ."

Lewis Carroll, *Through the Looking Glass*

SPEAKING TO COMMUNICATE

"Children who talk will develop a command of the English language which is lacking to those who do not talk," writes Robert Pooley.[1] Speaking is a way of learning as children develop language abilities and express their ideas. Oral language development provides the foundation on which reading and writing are built. We need, therefore, to place a much stronger emphasis on oral language instruction that will encourage children to talk as they discover what they think and how to express their thoughts.

Like listening, the ability to speak may be taken for granted. While most children learn to speak, not all people speak with equal effect. The most highly educated person, even a skillful writer, may be a boring conversationalist or an amazingly dull speaker. Our verbal society demands that successful participants be able to communicate orally as they interact face to face, on the telephone, or through such media as radio and television.

[1]Robert C. Pooley, "Foreword" to *Talk in the Language Arts Classroom* by Marvin Klein (Urbana, Ill.: National Council of Teachers of English, 1977).

Teaching children to speak coherently for varied purposes will provide them with an invaluable tool as they grow up in today's world.

For some students we need to begin with the basic concepts of English as a foreign language, while for native speakers of English, continuous language input enables students to develop vocabulary and more mature constructions. The speaking component of the language arts curriculum will include varied speaking experiences from conversation and discussion to drama and the more formal speeches or panel presentations.

BENCHMARK

What part does speaking play in your life? How do you feel about speaking to a large group? Your own attitudes toward the value of talking may affect how much time you allocate to oral language activities. Jot down answers to these questions before discussing them in the class.

1. Discuss the following proverb: Children should be seen and not heard.

2. Brainstorm a list of topics, situations, or other stimuli that would interest elementary school children and motivate discussion.

3. What value do such dramatic activities as role playing or acting out a television script have for children?

After reading this chapter and trying suggested activities, you will be able to:

- present an argument for increasing the amount of student talking in classrooms
- list objectives for an oral language program in the elementary school
- demonstrate techniques for stimulating speech in classrooms

INCLUDING SPEAKING IN THE CURRICULUM

On entering school, most children have an extensive speaking vocabulary. They have been practicing talking for four to five years; many have earned the label "chatterbox" because they love to talk so much.

The extent to which their oral language ability has developed depends on the child's home environment. The development of language at the preschool stage determines how ready a child is to begin reading and writing, for the child must know words in order to read them with meaning or to use them in composing. Early language development also familiarizes children with grammar, how we string words together to make sentences. The child in kindergarten should be able, for example, to tell a teacher which of these spoken groups of words constitutes a sentence, which one "sounds right."

Phil patted the tiny kitten.
Patted Phil the tiny kitten.

The child has learned language "by ear," and we should teach children to rely on this intuitive sense of rightness. It is linguistically valid for children to say sentences aloud as they test whether a sentence sounds "right." We can also teach them to speak a sentence aloud before writing it as a way of constructing grammatical sentences.

Speaking should be included in the elementary school curriculum, but it is often ignored because it is not as easy for the teacher to present. It usually requires more teacher time because students cannot always work alone in speaking activities. Oral activities can, however, be exciting and engage students in learning in a way that independent reading and writing activities do not. In this section we will consider the objectives for elementary speech activities. We will also discuss background information that teachers may find helpful.

Setting Up Objectives

In planning a speech program in the elementary school, we need to consider our objectives. What proficiencies are we trying to develop as children move through the grades? The aim is clearly not to prepare each child to be an entertainer, a performer, a public speaker. However, having a command of the English language and being able to express one's ideas orally in varied situations is a definite asset. The spoken language, moreover, is foundational to all learning. Our objectives for children might be grouped in four categories to be introduced and developed at all levels: (1) acquiring verbal fluency, (2) extending the speaking vocabulary, (3) learning about the elements of speech, and (4) experiencing varied forms and styles of speaking. Under each of these categories, we can list a number of specific topics or activities that will aid children in developing a command of spoken English.

1. Acquiring verbal fluency (ability to speak with little hesitation)
   Experiential background (information about which to talk)
   Frequency of opportunities to speak (practice)
   Self-esteem (self-confidence)
2. Extending the speaking vocabulary (greater knowledge of words)
   Meanings of words; hearing words in context
   Use of words orally; pronunciation
   Knowledge of language appropriate to specific situations
3. Learning about the elements of speech
   The science of the speech mechanism
   Discussing the voice; effective use
   Interrelationships between speaking and listening
   Aspects of spoken language—dialectology, idiom
4. Experiencing varied forms and styles of speaking
   Informal talking—discussion, conversation
   Formal speaking—an oral report, performing orally

In order to promote the development of effective speaking abilities, the elementary school teacher must recognize the importance of planning activities designed to meet these objectives. Oral activities can be used to introduce reading and writing lessons. They should become a regular mode of working with social science or science concepts. Oral language should be perceived as the backbone of the language arts curriculum, and be given top priority at the planning stage.

Teaching to Support Speech Development

How can we teach students to speak effectively? Classroom instruction in oral language skills must be directed toward providing many opportunities for speaking, stimulating the child to want to speak, and providing a supportive atmosphere. In this section we shall explore strategies to be used in the elementary school classroom to achieve these goals.

Small group work   It is imperative that students work individually or in small groups (5–6) as they engage in activities designed specifically to develop speech abilities. This small group approach is especially well suited to a classroom with learning centers about the room. The advantages of the small group include:

1. A sense of security for students who are uncertain about language abilities
2. Greater opportunity for each individual to speak
3. A better diagnostic situation as the teacher strives to guide individual development

Unless a child is particularly aggressive (and the child who needs help with language is far from aggressive), he or she can be lost even in a group of twenty-five. As noted in the preceding chapter, more than half of student time is spent in listening activities.

Increased focus on oral language   Linguistics has pointed the way toward an emphasis on oral language in the elementary school. It has become evident that success in school depends on linguistic fluency and the development of an extensive vocabulary, and that speech development is related to later development in reading and writing.

Why have teachers not stressed oral activities previously? A major deterrent is the unstructured nature of oral instruction and the fact that the teacher has had few materials to assist in developing oral abilities. There has been confusion about the aims of instruction in oral language, with emphasis being placed largely on "correct usage." As in other aspects of elementary school English, there has been no sequential program for speech development.

Use of the tape recorder   The tape recorder or cassette player is invaluable in speech development. Although all classrooms will not be equipped with language laboratory facilities, each can and should have a listening and speaking center which is planned around a tape recorder fitted with earphones and microphones for listening and recording. In this way language development can be accomplished individually as children work with teacher-prepared tapes or those available commercially.

Oral language activities across the curriculum   To teach concepts in history or music, mathematics or art, composition or science, such oral activities as the following are effective:

Guided discussion in small groups
    Planning a skit to honor Martin Luther King's birthday
Creative drama
    Dramatizing the discovery of the electric light
Reader's theater
    Presenting several of the Roman myths
Storytelling
    Retelling folktales from Africa
Reporting
    Giving information about an artist and his or her work
Explaining
    Explaining a mathematical process
    Demonstrating a scientific experiment
Reading aloud
    Reading original compositions to a small group
Singing
    Learning the words of "America, the Beautiful"
Ensemble speaking
    Reciting poetry together

Oral language can also introduce new topics and provide warm-up activities as students brainstorm ideas. You can quickly have students give sample answers to a question or compose a list of words related to a theme. Writing a class composition orally or talking about a topic is an excellent prewriting activity. These activities can motivate student interest and prepare them to succeed at the learning task they are to undertake.

Concepts from Linguistics

There is more to speaking than making sounds and forming words. Linguists have identified several aspects of intonation that we use to add to the meaning of the language we speak: namely, stress, pitch, and juncture, which children have learned to use as they have learned to speak English. The following explanation suggests how you might introduce this topic in the classroom.

Stress: accent or loudness
    Which word would you stress in the following sentences? Try stressing each word in turn.
    What are you planning to do?
    I'm not ready to go.
    Who does he think he is!

Pitch: highness or lowness of tones
   Which part of this sentence has the highest tone?
      My name is Irene. (Can the pitch vary?)
Juncture: pauses (clues to punctuation in composition)
   Can juncture change meaning? Explore the pauses in these sentences.
      That lady is a queer bird.
      Where did they find Joe's will?
      Help somebody please.

Actually, linguists note four degrees of stress which can be marked in all speech, four degrees or levels of pitch, and four types of juncture according to the length of the pause. For our present purposes, however, it is sufficient to note the effect that each of these features of intonation has on meaning of the spoken language. We quickly notice the variation in meaning obtained by stressing different words in a sentence. There is truth in the statement: It isn't *what* you say, but *how* you say it, that matters. Students will enjoy experimenting with spoken language as they explore these concepts.

- Tape several samples of student speech in the classroom. Analyze these samples sentence by sentence to note pitch which is recorded, thus:

                 2   1   1   4   3   3
       What are you doing here, Jim? (4 is high; 1 is low)

- Work with several sentences on the board first so that disagreements can be discussed and the tape replayed to check points made. Then students can experiment with analyzing other sentences.
- Compare the different variations of pitch and stress possible in a simple interjection or phrase.
   All right. (Say it with anger, annoyance, agreement, reluctance)
   Please.
   Go ahead and take it!
   Yes.
   No.
- Compare the manner of speaking the same word in two different contexts. Is it exactly the same?
   What present did you give her?
   Were you present when they arrived?
- Heteronyms provide provocative material for comparison of stress or accent as in these examples:
   Did you present Mrs. Smithson with a present?
   Should a rebel rebel?
   Are you content with the content of his remark?
   That magician standing in the entrance may entrance you.
- How does changing juncture change meaning? The results are often amusing. In what situation might the following have been appropriate?
   "I will not hit any, Mother," she said sweetly.
   "I will not hit any mother," she said sweetly.
   "How will you help me?" he asked.
   "How! Will you help me?" he asked.

Discussion of these aspects of language are inherently interesting to students. You are talking about something they all know, language, and how they produce it. The experiments described here will help motivate further study of how language works as you move into the structure of sentences (grammar) and the way we use letter symbols to represent the sounds we make (spelling).

DEVELOPING ORAL LANGUAGE SKILLS

Classroom speaking experiences should range from informal to formal. Informal speaking activities include responding to questions and interacting with other students. Although unstructured, this type of speaking is an important part of functioning in the world. More formal speaking experiences assist the student in learning to participate at different levels of responsibility. At the same time, however, expectations of the child's performance should be realistic. Positive reinforcement and sensitivity to the needs of children will help you to guide their development as speakers. In this section we will explore a variety of activities that are recommended for the elementary school classroom.

Forms of Speaking

A wide variety of speech activities are suitable for the elementary school classroom. As children participate in discussions, they learn how to state their opinions and how to evaluate the contributions of others. More formal speaking experiences before the class will introduce young students to the skills of preparing a presentation. Such activities as choric speaking and storytelling support the literature program as well as developing speaking abilities. All forms of speaking can be coordinated with learning experiences across the curriculum.

Discussion   Perhaps the most familiar speaking activity in the classroom is discussion of a common topic, which often arises from studies or activities undertaken by the class. These discussions may focus on:

- Answering questions to which there is no specific answer.
  Why did people move westward in the United States?
- Giving opinions about current issues.
  Should we continue spending money on space exploration?
- Solving a problem.
  How can our class raise enough money to go to science camp?
- Talking about ideas and feelings.
  What makes you happy?
  Would you like to live the life of Pippi Longstocking?
  What makes you feel uncomfortable?
- Talking about *what if*.
  What if pets could talk?
  What if I were invisible?

Ability to participate successfully in discussions is important. Students can think of ways to improve skill in discussion, for example:

- A feeling of responsibility for contributing to a group discussion
- Ability to ask intelligent, pertinent questions
- Willingness to listen to contributions of others
- Ability to wait one's turn before speaking

Assigned speaking   Assigned speeches in the elementary school should never be long, and the topics should allow for individual interests. Schedule delivery of speeches so there are never too many delivered at one time, for the whole class will lose enthusiasm if forced to listen to other students speaking for more than twenty minutes. Vary assigned speaking experiences, thus:

Explanation: How to do something.
  How to make scrambled eggs
  How to make money
  How to make an impression
  How to write a news story
Argument: Why I hold this opinion.
  Girls are awful. (Boys are terrible.)
  A woman should be President of the United States.
  We should reform our spelling system.
  Everyone should know how to type.
  No one should have to attend school unless he or she wants to.
  No one should smoke cigarettes.
Humor: How these words came to be spoken.
  "George, you are the cat's meow!"
  "I got that story straight from the horse's mouth."
  "Cross my heart and hope to die."

Impromptu speaking   The extemporaneous speech is presented without time for extensive planning and should be regarded as a "speech experiment." Any aspect of the experiment which turns out well should be praised. Sets of 3 × 5 file cards can be developed with student assistance to provide stimulating topics for the short unrehearsed speech.

- *Quotations by famous people[2]*—Why I agree or disagree.
    You must look *into* people as well as at them.—*Lord Chesterfield*
    Behavior is a mirror, in which everyone shows his image.—*Johann von Goethe*
    No man is an Island, entire of itself.—*John Donne*
    To be of use in the world is the only way to be happy.—*Hans Christian Andersen*
- *Sequence pictures*—Tell the story as it is pictured. Students can create sequences like the ones illustrated here.
- *Small pictures*—how an illustration fits in a story
- *Two words*—how two words are related

[2]For additional quotations see *Quotes for Teaching* by Sidney W. Tiedt (San Jose, Calif.: Contemporary Press, 1964).

- *Questions*—answer the question.
  Have you ever been afraid?
  What is the funniest thing you have ever seen?
  What was the most exciting moment in your life?
- *Introductions*—Pretend you are asked to introduce a famous speaker. What would you say as you introduce:
  Mark Twain
  The President of the United States
  Theodor Geisel (Dr. Seuss)
  The Governor of your state
- *What do you do now?*—A card presents an improbable situation which the speaker reads aloud, concluding with his or her action. Motivate this speaking experience

by reading from Sesyle Joslin's *What Do You Say, Dear?* (Harcourt). Cards can be written as a writing experiment after reading this book.

* *It's a Joke*—Read the joke on the card, and then tell it to the group without aid of the card.
* *Extra! Extra!*—Cut unusual headlines from old newspapers. Students may create "enchanting examples" by cutting out single words from the paper as needed. The speaker uses the headline as the topic for a speech.

Sharing books Let's talk about books, use books, enjoy books together, for explorations in children's literature add to growth in reading, writing, general information, thinking, as well as speaking and listening. The following suggestions contribute to literature learning as well as oral language development.

READING TOGETHER: Small groups of students can form reading circles which meet at a specified time to read a book together. Each child takes a turn reading aloud, passing the book on when tired of reading. Emphasis is on enjoyment of the book in a group situation which brings readers together according to interests rather than abilities, for there is a need to learn to work with persons of mixed abilities. Time is spent on talking about points of interest as the story progresses.

WORDLESS BOOKS: Using a wordless book the child creates a story orally, usually in an impromptu approach. A teacher can prepare a paperback booklet titled THE WORDLESS BOOK, or other titles may suggest a story on a specific theme:

Tom's Adventures at the Beach
Camping in the Deep Woods

At a learning center display such wordless books as Mercer Mayer's *A Boy, A Dog, and a Frog.* Provide paper for writing the story (of course, there can be more than one version) or tape cassettes for telling the story. Following is a selected list of wordless books that illustrate stories children can tell.

Bobo's Dream by Martha Alexander. Dial Press, 1970.
Look What I Can Do by Jose Aruego. Charles Scribner's Sons, 1971.
What Whiskers Did by Ruth Carroll. Henry Z. Walck, 1965.
Shrewbettina's Birthday by John Goodall. Harcourt, Brace, 1971.
Look Again! by Tina Hoban. The Macmillan Co., 1971.
Making Friends by Eleanor Schick. The Macmillan Co., 1969.[3]

Storytelling "Everyone is a potential storyteller," writes Ruth Sawyer, and she notes also that, whether conscious of it or not, "everyone has been telling stories since he learned to talk."[4] We all tell stories of things that have happened to us or our friends, often embroidering them a bit to add zest! Encourage students to tell stories in the classroom with enthusiasm and effect by providing opportunities and helping them find good material. Students will grow in self-esteem by sharing their own experiences.

[3]For a more complete list of wordless books see: *Exploring Books With Children* by Iris M. Tiedt (Boston: Houghton Mifflin, 1979), 73–76.

[4]Ruth Sawyer *"How To Tell a Story"* (New York: Compton's, n.d.), 3–4. Reprint from *Compton's Pictured Encyclopedia.*

RIDDLES AND JOKES: A first step in beginning storytelling might be the telling of riddles which have some story element. The joke contains a little more story content and requires much the same skill as the telling of a longer story. In each case practice is required, and close attention must be paid to the conclusion, the "punch line."

FAMILIAR STORIES: Young children will develop skill in following the sequence of a story as they tell stories cooperatively. "The Little Red Hen found a grain of wheat. What did she say then, Neil?" Each child contributes to the telling of this story, which may then be retold as the contributors stand in order before the class, each telling a line or two at the appropriate time. Legends, folktales, stories of mythology, fairy tales—all provide excellent storytelling material for the elementary school.

THE STORYTELLERS: A club can be formed of students who have special interest and ability in storytelling. This group can use varied approaches to storytelling, both individual and group, depending on the material. At times they can present samplings of their repertoire to an appreciative audience.

For students in the elementary school, storytelling is wisely directed toward short stories, verses, myths, folklore. Humor, surprise endings, and audience participation add to the effectiveness and the enjoyment of both performer and audience. The values of storytelling experiences include:

1. Attention to voice quality—pitch, tempo, enunciation
2. Investigation of literature suitable for presentation, an interesting research project for able students
3. A pleasurable combination of literature and language experiences, delight in words and their use
4. Appreciation of literature—What makes a good story?

Almost all children's books can be used as storytelling material. Those which contain many illustrations can be used in storytelling before the child learns to read, for after hearing the story, he or she can retell it by following the illustrations. Bruno Munari's enchanting book, *Who's There? Open the Door* (World) is a favorite as is Albert Lamorisse's *The Red Balloon* (Doubleday). Children of all ages will enjoy retelling stories they have read and enjoyed. In addition, use selected collections of short stories which provide excellent sources of storytelling material:

Anderson, Hans C., *Fairy Tales* (Walck).
Arbuthnot, May H., *The Arbuthnot Anthology* (Scott, Foresman).
Bacmeister, Rhoda, *Stories to Begin On* (Dutton).
De la Mare, Walter, *Tales Told Again* (Knopf).
Fenner, Phyllis, ed., *Giants and Witches and a Dragon or Two* (Knopf).
Hamilton, Edith, *Mythology* (Little, Brown).
Huber, Miriam B., *Story and Verse for Children* (Macmillan).
Kipling, Rudyard, *Just So Stories* (Doubleday).
Lang, Andrew, ed., *The Blue Fairy Book* (Longmans).
Leodhas, Sorchie, *Gaelic Ghosts* (Holt).
Sandburg, Carl, *Rootabaga Stories* (Harcourt).
Thorne-Thomsen, Gudren, ed., *East o' the Sun and West o' the Moon* (Harper).

Children can make up different endings to old favorites and tell them aloud; or, after hearing a good story read aloud, a group can do an add-on story. One student starts the story; then each participant in turn adds a few sentences.

Choric speaking   Group recital of selections from literature, both poetry and prose, is an excellent technique for enriching the oral language program and for encouraging all children to speak. A wealth of material is appropriate for this purpose.

Poems are made for saying or reading aloud, for only through an oral approach to poetry do we get the full effect of its rhythm. This approach permits a group to share appreciation of the poet's work. In the chapter devoted to poetry we explore the use of a voice choir, but there is such a wide range of poetry available that we can add a few suggestions here.

- Short humorous verse appeals to young children as well as to students in the intermediate grades. Stress clarity of enunciation, and a long questioning pause of the comma, when speaking this anonymous poem:

> ### A SLEEPER FROM THE AMAZON
>
>   A sleeper from the Amazon
>   Put nighties of his gra'mason—
>   The reason, that
>   He was too fat
>   To get his own pajamason.

- An occasional tongue twister adds spice to speaking and adds to the child's awareness of wordplay:

>   I saw Esau sawing wood [pause]
>   And Esau saw I saw him; [quickly]
>   Though Esau saw I saw him saw [pause]
>   Still Esau went on sawing.
>
>   A tutor who tooted the flute
>   Tried to tutor two tooters to toot.
>   Said the two to the tutor,
>   "Is it harder to toot, or
>   To tutor two tooters to toot?"

- Verses known to children, for example, rope-jumping songs, provide good rhythmical chants:

>   Not last night but the night before,
>   Twenty-four burglars at my door.
>   I went downstairs to let them in;
>   They hit me over the head
>   With a rolling pin!

- Combine actions with speaking a poem as in this selection from *Mother Goose:*

> The noble Duke of York [majestically]
>   He had ten thousand men.
> He marched them up a very high hill; [last words quickly]
>   Then he marched them down again.
> And when he was up, he was up; [quickly]
>   And when he was down, he was down; [quickly]
> And when he was only halfway up
>   He was neither *up nor down!* [distinctly]

- A poem that tells a story lends itself to clear enunciation and varied intonation:

THE SECRET
Unknown

> We have a secret, just we three,
> The robin, and I, and the sweet cherry-tree;
> The bird told the tree, and the tree told me,
> And nobody knows it but just we three.
>
> But of course the robin knows it best,
> Because she built the—I shan't tell the rest;
> And laid the four little—something in it
> I'm afraid I shall tell it every minute.
>
> But if the tree and the robin don't peep,
> I'll try my best the secret to keep;
> Though I know when the little birds fly about
> Then the whole secret will be out.

- Repetition adds interest to a poem for younger children, and also makes it easier to learn:

SING OUT!
Iris M. Tiedt

> Sing, sing sing;
>   Racing to the swing.
>
> Hum, hum, hum;
>   Spring at last has come!
>
> Call, call, call;
>   The grass is growing tall.
>
> Shout, shout, shout;
>   School will soon be out!

- Older children will enjoy the humor and the actions of this delightful poem by William Makepeace Thackeray:

A TRAGIC STORY

There lived a sage in days of yore,
And he a handsome pigtail wore;
But wondered much and sorrowed more,
   Because it hung behind him.

He mused upon this curious case,
And swore he'd change the pigtail's place,
And have it hanging at his face,
   Not dangling there behind him.

Said he, "The mystery I've found—
I'll turn me round"—and he turned him round,
   But still it hung behind him.

Then round and round, and out and in,
All day the puzzled sage did spin;
In vain—it mattered not a pin—
   The pigtail hung behind him.

And right and left, and roundabout,
And up and down and in and out
He turned; but still the pigtail stout
   Hung steadily behind him.

And though his efforts never slack,
And though he twist, and twirl, and tack,
Alas! still faithful to his back,
   The pigtail hangs behind him.

Prose should not be ignored as a source of excellent material for speaking together. Explore the literature of the social sciences or combine storytelling techniques with choric speaking.

- Enrich a social studies experience by teaching children the Gettysburg Address or passages from the work of Martin Luther King.
- Combine the arts of storytelling and choric speaking as children tell a story, for example, Wanda Gág's *Millions of Cats,* with a chorus coming in on the repeated words which add so much to the story:
    Hundreds of Cats, thousands of Cats, millions and billions and trillions of cats . . .

Dramatization   Speaking is also stimulated through dramatization. The source of ideas for dramatization is endless, and variation in the form of dramatization is sufficiently wide to provide for all interests and abilities. As Winifred Ward explains:

The term "creative dramatics" includes all forms of *improvised* drama—drama created by the children themselves and played with spontaneous dialogue and action. It begins with imaginative play of the young child, which mirrors life as the child sees and feels it, and is followed by simple story dramatizations. It also includes: creative plays based on ideas and on literature, dramatizations of incidents from the social studies, original dance, pantomimes, creative work with puppets and shadow plays, and integrated projects in which many of the subjects in the school program contribute to an adventurous play which the children create from a book or a story. . . .[5]

A major advantage of creative dramatics is that participants do not learn set parts or lines. For this reason they literally cannot "make a mistake." Varying from simple actions and dialogue to the dramatization of a lengthy story, this form of dramatics permits children to interpret roles freely. Geraldine Siks observes:

> This freedom of imagination that characterizes child-thought is both the envy and terror of the adult. . . . Children in their own way are highly creative because of their innate freedom of imagination. . . . Creative dramatics utilizes and challenges the imagination of the child.[6]

Emphasis in creative dramatics is not on preparing a drama to be presented before an audience, but on providing opportunity for children to express themselves freely. All children participate in the acting when space and the type of dramatization permit, for there need be no audience at all. At other times one portion of the class, perhaps a third or a half, will participate while the others observe and await their own turns. An effective classroom arrangement for creative drama is the THEATER IN THE ROUND, with chairs forming a circle from which observers can readily view the action.

The advantages of dramatization as a way of developing language abilities include the following:

1. Pleasure is combined with learning.
2. Physical and social abilities are developed.
3. Freedom of action encourages the child's expression.
4. Preparatory discussion extends vocabulary and interests.

Language development can be encouraged through enjoyable creative activities, as described here:

Pantomime   Pantomime is a good dramatic activity to begin with, although the mime in performance uses no language.

Pantomime does include language, of course, as the children think, plan, talk about the mime's role, or try to guess what act is being mimed. Activities like these introduce children to creative dramatics.

> GUESS WHAT I'M DOING: An interesting way to initiate experiments in pantomime is to ask students to mime an activity as others try to identify the activity depicted. Favorites are:

[5]Winifred Ward, *Creative Dramatics* (Washington, D.C.: Association for Childhood Education, 1961), 3.

[6]Geraldine B. Siks, *Children's Literature for Dramatization* (New York: Harper & Row Pubs., Inc., 1964), 1–3.

Peeling a banana and eating it
Unwrapping gum and chewing it, blowing bubbles
Opening an umbrella as it suddenly begins to rain
Being bothered by a mosquito or fly
Petting a cat
Making a sandwich
Combing hair before a mirror

Variation: Bring a "magic bag" to class. Students take turns reaching in and pulling out whatever they wish—perhaps an ice cream cone, which they proceed to eat in pantomime, or a comb, or a tiny butterfly which they watch fly away. The first child to guess what is in the bag is the next to find another treasure in it.

INTERPRETING SITUATIONS: Briefly sketch a situation for pantomime. Have several groups try the same topic to see how the interpretation develops. Students enjoy suggesting *interesting* situations, for example:

Showing a bad report card to Mother and Dad
Teenage girls talking on the telephone
Father giving son first driving lesson
Two children watching puppies in a pet store window

Finger play activities   An oral activity that is particularly suitable for work with primary children is the finger play story which may aim at teaching some concept such as the difference between *left* and *right* or the order of the numerals in addition to encouraging young children to speak.

A favorite finger play is "Eency Weency Spider," a song that has appeal for children. Children can also invent finger plays to accompany familiar songs, for example, "Three Blind Mice."

A wonderful story to motivate finger play activities after children have developed some familiarity with this technique is *A Handful of Surprises* by Anne Heather and Esteban Francés (Harcourt) which presents five puppets, named Mac, Marc, Tink, Tarc, and O'Tooley, who fight constantly but always stay together because each is a finger on the hand of Fleek, the clown. The story tells of their troubles and how they finally learn to get along together.

Puppetry   A form of dramatization which delights people of all ages is puppetry. Puppetry as a means of encouraging students to speak has many advantages, one of which is hiding the shy person who can then feel free to play a role with enthusiasm.

Puppets should be kept simple so that emphasis remains on use rather than construction. Simple but effective puppet heads can be made from:

Faces cut from magazines mounted on cardboard for stiffness
Styrofoam balls with features and hair pinned on
Toe of a sock stuffed with cotton or small rags
Layers of paper glued and dried over an orange or ball
Plasticine covered by white cloth
Papier-mâché strips glued around a small balloon

They are all hitched to the same hand!

Encourage children to invent different kinds of original puppets. Clever puppets can be fashioned from almost any kind of scrap material:

Bottle caps (bugs with legs)
Dixie cups stuck on popsicle sticks (add faces)
Peanuts in shells (animals with tails, ears, legs added)
Potatoes and other vegetables (animals suggested by shapes)
Wooden spoons (faces painted on back of spoon)
Paper plates (glued to sticks; add hair, features)
Squares of cloth (tie knots for head and two hands)[7]

Dramatization of poetry   Many narrative poems suggest a skit, pantomime, or creative dramatization. "Jonathan Bing" contains humor and a story that children can take turns portraying. Have several children be Jonathan at

[7]Sidney W. Tiedt and Iris M. Tiedt, *The Elementary Teacher's Complete Ideas Handbook* (Englewood Cliffs, N.J.: Prentice-Hall, 1965), 228.

the same time while another group acts the part of the narrator who reminds Jonathan, "You can't go to court in pajamas, you know," sadly shaking their heads at the very thought.

Robert Louis Stevenson's "My Shadow" is another delightful poem to combine with dramatic play or choreography. A few children move according to the poem followed by "shadows" who imitate their behavior until the final verse when the shadow is left at home in bed.

MY SHADOW

I have a little shadow that goes in and out with me,
And what can be the use of him is more than I can see.
He is very, very like me from the heels up to the head;
And I see him jump before me, when I jump into my bed.

The funniest thing about him is the way he likes to grow—
Not at all like proper children, which is always very slow:
For he sometimes shoots up taller like an India-rubber ball,
And he sometimes gets so little that there's none of him at all.

He hasn't got a notion of how children ought to play,
And can only make a fool of me in every sort of way.
He stays so close beside me, he's a coward you can see;
I'd think shame to stick to nursie as that shadow sticks to me!

One morning, very early, before the sun was up,
I rose and found the shining dew on every buttercup;
But my lazy little shadow, like an arrant sleepyhead,
Had stayed at home behind me and was fast asleep in bed.

Multimedia to Motivate Speech

Using varied media is helpful in motivating children's speech. Records, tapes, films, filmstrips, slides, transparencies, the flannel board, pictures, bulletin board displays, and exhibits—all add variety and stimulus to the elementary school speech program.

Films   Many fine films are being developed. Some present a title from children's literature visually, which extends the child's vocabulary and provides a source of discussion topics. Films of excellent books and stories are available from Weston Woods, among them *The Sorcerer's Apprentice, A Snowy Day,* and *The Doughnut Machine* (from *Homer Price*).

Another type of film which presents interesting possibilities to motivate both speech and writing is the "wordless" film. A beautiful example is *Rainshower* (Churchill Films), a 15-minute film in color. The expert photography focuses on the effects of rain in the country compared with the effects in the city—the mother runs to get washing from the line, the geese move ponderously toward the poultry yard, the parched ground soaks up the first drops—and only natural sounds are heard.

A short filmed story without sound is *The Hunter in the Forest* (Encyclopaedia Britannica). The hunter bags a game bird and sights a family of deer. Does he shoot? This moment is an effective stopping place for writing or discussion after which the remainder of the film is shown.

Flannel board   A device for assisting language development is the flannel board, a device much used by primary teachers but less commonly employed in intermediate grades. It has distinct advantages for instruction at all levels, for the flannel board:

1.   Provides the shy speaker with a "prop"
2.   Guides students through a sequence
3.   Motivates student interest
4.   Combines visual and oral activities

Figures prepared by students guide the class in retelling stories, finger play activities, choric speaking of poetry, and singing songs which have many verses. Figures can be cut from flannel, felt, or construction paper backed with sandpaper, but perhaps most satisfactory is *pellon,* a synthetic interlining material sold in any fabric store.

Children in the primary grades will enjoy a guided recitation of "This Is the House That Jack Built."

THE HOUSE THAT JACK BUILT

This is the house that Jack built.

This is the malt
That lay in the house that Jack built.

This is the rat,
That ate the malt
That lay in the house that Jack built.

This is the cat,
That killed the rat,
That ate the malt
That lay in the house that Jack built.

This is the dog,
That worried the cat,
That killed the rat,
That ate the malt
That lay in the house that Jack built.

Other songs and stories for this purpose are: "Old MacDonald Had a Farm," "The Farmer in the Dell," "The Mulberry Bush," *Goldilocks and the Three Bears, Three Little Pigs,* and *The Little Red Hen.*

Suitable for presentation on the flannel board by older students are such poems as "Poor Old Woman," and "Jonathan Bing," as well as songs, "I Gave My Love a Cherry," and "The Frog Went A-Courtin'." Students enjoy the repetitive song, "Green Grass Grows All Around," for which we have provided the words and music.

Old Folk Song

1 All in a hole, there grows a tree, the fin-est tree
2 And on the tree, there grows a limb, the fin-est limb
3 And on this limb, there grows a branch, etc.

you e-ver did see (go to Refrain) 2 Oh the limb is on the tree
you e-ver did see   And the tree is in the hole
4-nest 5-egg 6-yolk   (Keep adding a line with each verse)
7-bird 8-wing 9-feather

Refrain

And the green grass grows all a-round, all a-round,

and the green grass grows all a-round!

Tape a class-created poem or story with suitable musical background. Using 16mm leader the students can create a film to go with the tape for a multimedia experience. Each student draws with permanent ink on a three-foot section of the film leader. If desired, the film can be drawn first and the poem created orally by the class while viewing it, then read aloud by the class as a choral poem and recorded.

Records Recorded stories supply stimulating materials for discussion and for developing vocabulary. A fairy tale is featured, for example, in *Emperor's Nightingale* (Folkways/Scholastic Records).

I highly recommend the recording of *Ruth Sawyer, Storyteller,* who captures the listener from the moment she says, in the traditional Spanish manner, "Once there was and was not . . . ." Two records by this author and storyteller are available from Weston Woods.

Tapes The tape recorder has a fascination of its own whether individuals are recording or the teacher records the whole group. Once children become accustomed to it through frequent use, they lose any fear of being recorded. The flexibility of recording devices and the availability of inexpensive tape make this medium invaluable in working with speech development.

- Older children can tape stories for use in Listening Centers in primary grades. Primary teachers can request specific titles for which uppergrade students volunteer, for practice is required to produce a well-read recording.
- Record materials for blind students, an excellent project for a student speaker's club.
- Tape speeches made by students so each can hear his/her own speech for purposes of evaluation. Tape a class discussion to determine ways of improving discussion techniques. A conversation or interview might also be taped.
- Record poetry to accompany a group of illustrative slides from parent or teacher collections. Advanced students who have access to a camera might develop a series of slides specifically for use with certain titles which they enjoy.
- Use a teacher-prepared recording to assist LEP/NEP students in developing sentence patterns. The child repeats patterned sentences spoken first by the teacher, thus:

    Jimmy has a dog.
    Jimmy has_____. (Child supplies "a dog.")
    Jimmy has a black dog.
    Jimmy has_____.
    Jimmy has a big black dog.
    Jimmy has_____.
    Jimmy has a big black dog. Can you say the whole sentence?

Patterns can be developed to focus student learning on any aspect of language development—phonology, vocabulary development, sentence structure.

Evaluating Speaking

As in all language experience, evaluation should be the responsibility of both student and teacher, and it should always be constructive in nature. Speaking should never become a traumatic experience. Evaluation should be directed toward helping the student improve, a goal which will most readily be achieved with the elementary school student through positive reinforcement rather than the shocked "No, no" equivalent of the red pencil. Speaking should be evaluated immediately, for the effectiveness of the evaluation diminishes considerably with time unless the speech is recorded. The following techniques of evaluation have been helpful in working with young students:

Note from teacher to speaker   After hearing the student deliver a "speech," write a short note to the individual who spoke, saying perhaps:

Dear Brian,
You spoke clearly, and the class enjoyed your story.
I liked your description of Onion John.

Mrs. K.

Taped replay   The teacher (or a student) tapes the speeches given at one time. Later Laura has an opportunity to "hear herself as others hear her." Ask her to make *one* specific suggestion which will help her improve her next speech.

Oral Presentation Evaluation

POINTS	POSSIBLE	ACHIEVEMENT	COMMENTS
Interest Enthusiasm of speaker	5		
Audience response	5		
Expression of voice	5		
Gesture, movement of hands	5		
Friendly attitude	5		
Total	25		
Voice Enunciation, clearness	5		
Pronouncing words	5		
Volume	5		
Use of words (meaning)	5		
Pace	5		
Total	25		
Organization Introduction, effect	5		
Organized points	5		
Knowledge of material	5		
Conclusion	5		
Total	20		
Bearing Rising to speak	5		
Eye contact	5		
Posture	5		
Movement of body	5		
Total	20		

Student evaluation This technique must be used with care, for students can be brutal. The whole class should, therefore, be taught the purposes of "criticism," and they should be encouraged to use positive criticism when evaluating a fellow student's speaking. The following suggestions may serve to guide student evaluation in a more positive direction.

Have only three students (rotate positions) evaluate any speaker. These three serve as the critics, and the remainder of the class observes not only the speaker's abilities but also the abilities of the critics.

Have one group of five students complete evaluation forms for the speech delivered. An evaluation form similar to that illustrated can be developed by the class.

Focus on one aspect of speech As in the evaluation of writing, speaking is more accurately evaluated if students are told in advance that they are to focus attention on the introduction, the use of gestures, the use of humor, or another specific component of the speech. All other aspects of the delivery except that specified are then ignored in evaluation.

Test the results For specific types of speeches the effectiveness of the speaking can be tested by noting the results. In telling a joke, for example, the effectiveness can be judged by the audience response, laughter. When the student is assigned to explain how to do something, the successful speaker will be the student who explains so clearly that listeners can follow the explanation and produce what is described.

CHALLENGE

In order to use the ideas described in this chapter it is helpful to try them out. Work on one of the following activities with a small group of your classmates.

1. Select a poem that you enjoy. Present it to the class as a choric speaking. You might consider:

"Jonathan Bing" by Beatrice Curtis Brown

"Pop Goes the Weasel!" Anonymous

"Texas Trains and Trails" by Mary Austin

(These poems are found in The Sound of Poetry by Mary C. Austin and Queenie B. Mills, Allyn & Bacon, Inc.)

2. Conduct a model lesson with your fourth-grade students, for example: Introduce the students to a diagram of the vocal tract. Then try some of the activities.

3. Choose a folktale that you would like to know. Follow the directions for developing a story to tell on pages 118–119. Practice with other classmates who are interested in storytelling. When you are prepared, perform for the entire class.

EXPLORING FURTHER

Anastasiow, Nicholas, *Oral Language: Expression of Thought* (2nd ed.), International Reading Association, 1979.

DeStefano, Johanna S., "Enhancing Children's Growing Ability to Communicate," Research Update. *Language Arts,* October 1980, 57, 7:807–12.

———, *Language, The Learner and the School.* New York: John Wiley and Sons, Inc., 1978.

Ehrlich, Harriet W., ed., *Creative Dramatics Handbook* (rev. ed.), The School District of Philadelphia. Distributed by the National Council of Teachers of English, 1974.

Gallo, Donald R., ed., *The Heard Word.* Urbana, Ill.: National Council of Teachers of English, 1979.

Klein, Marvin, L., *Talk in the Language Arts Classroom.* Urbana, Ill.: National Council of Teachers of English, 1977.

Stanford, Gene, *Developing Effective Classroom Groups.* New York: A & W Visual Library, 1980.

Stibbs, Andrew, *Assessing Children's Language.* London: Ward, Lock Ltd., 1979. Distributed by the National Council of Teachers of English.

Tiedt, Pamela and Iris M. Tiedt, "Focusing on Language" in *Multicultural Teaching.* Boston: Allyn & Bacon, 1979, pp. 59–115.

Tiedt, Sidney W. and Iris M. Tiedt, "Focusing on Speaking and Listening" in *The Elementary Teacher's Complete Ideas Handbook.* Englewood Cliffs, N.J.: Prentice-Hall, Inc., 1980.

Wood, Barbara S., ed., *Development of Functional Communication Competencies, Pre-K–Grade 6.* Urbana, Ill.: ERIC, 1977.

7

Don't put all your eggs—in the microwave.
All's fair—in hockey.
People who live in glass houses—better not take off their clothes.
He who laughs last—didn't understand the joke.
　　First graders in Texas, quoted by The Honorable Shirley
　　M. Hufstedler, United States Secretary of Education*

USING THE ENGLISH LANGUAGE

The English language is a broad subject encompassing content and process that belongs at the heart of a language arts program. Inherently fascinating to children who are discovering the intricacies of using language, this study touches on:

Body language (kinesics)
Dialectology (regional and social dialects; standard English)
History of language; history of English
Grammar (how language is structured to convey meaning)
Lexicography (dictionaries)
Semantics (the meaning of language)
Usage (acceptable use of language)
Recreational linguistics (wordplay)

*Hufstedler, Shirley M., "Viewpoints," *Language Arts*, 58, 1:11–13 (January 1981).

Selecting topics that are appropriate for study in elementary classrooms is limited only by your own interest in language. First graders can create new endings for old proverbs like those quoted above. Fourth graders can talk about how body language reveals feelings. Sixth-grade students can conduct a study of how students in your school pronounce specific words. As students delve into the study of English, they will raise interesting questions that may lead to further investigation, for example:

Why doesn't *champagne* sound like *chain* when they begin with the same letters?
How did a word like *trip* get such different meanings—to stumble and a journey?
How does a word get in the dictionary?
What does a "holy stone" have to do with a ship?
Why do people say that "ain't" is a bad word when Lord Peter Whimsey uses it on television? (BBC dramatizations of Dorothy Sayers' novels)
Do you know the longest word in the English language?
  (SMILES—there is a mile between the first and last letters)

Such questions can open the door to an exciting investigation that will demonstrate to students that our English language is a treasury that will never cease to delight and amaze them. In order to guide student explorations, however, you need to know something of the lore of language yourself.

BENCHMARK

As a benchmark from which to begin your study of the English language and strategies for presenting relevant information in your classroom, write your answers to the following questions:

1. How would you explain to a parent what grammar is and how you are presenting it in the classroom?

2. From which language were the following words borrowed?
   Ballet
   Mosquito
   Piano
   Sauerkraut
   Alcohol
   Smorgasbord

3. To which European language is English most closely related?

4. How many different language backgrounds are represented in your county?

Discuss these questions and the answers you gave. With which questions did you have difficulty?

In this chapter you will find an overview of concepts you will be presenting to students in your classroom. For a more in-depth study, however, you should refer to the books listed at the end of the chapter. Through reading and trying some of the activities in this chapter, you should learn:

- the difference between grammar and usage so that you can use the terms accurately
- ways to help children appreciate the diversity of language in the United States
- information you can share about the history of the English language
- the importance of accepting a child's personal language as one aspect of self-esteem
- strategies for making the study of language enjoyable as well as informative

LINGUISTIC FOUNDATIONS FOR TEACHERS

The study of English, as well as the many other languages of the world, continues. With increased knowledge of language systems and how they work, scholars have learned how to describe languages more accurately; the descriptions they write are called "grammars." Not only are they concerned with describing the grammar or system a language follows, but they are also interested in how people use language, the psychological and sociological factors that influence linguistic change and the attitudes of people toward language. The range of their studies is wide and intriguing. In this section we will examine some of the findings that have particular interest to us as we work with students.

The Development of Linguistics

What is linguistics? There still remains much confusion about linguistics as a field of study. The term has been variously used as textbook writers, for instance, sought to identify their materials with the "new English." "Linguistic readers" and "linguistic approaches" to teaching everything appeared. Use of these terms meant just as much or as little as saying that these readers used language because the adjective *linguistic* simply means: *belonging or pertaining to language.* The word originates in the Latin word for tongue, *lingua.*

What then is linguistics? According to the college edition of the *Random House Dictionary of the English Language,* linguistics is: "The science of language, including phonetics, phonology, morphology, and syntax, and often divided into historical linguistics and descriptive linguistics." This field has been further defined as: ". . . the study, according to rigorously defined methods or principles, *of language as a system.* The linguist is concerned, not with the listing of miscellaneous items, as in a dictionary, but with the recurrent patterns and characteristic relationships."[1]

Linguistics has contributed the following concepts of language and language study which have influenced English instruction:

1.   Language constantly changes.
2.   Change is normal.
3.   The spoken language *is* the language.

---

[1]Hans P. Guth, *English Today and Tomorrow* (Englewood Cliffs, N.J.: PrenticeHall, Inc., 1964), p. 25.

4.   Correctness rests upon usage.
5.   All usage is relative.[2]

Areas of linguistic study   Within the broad area of linguistic science sub-areas focus on specific aspects of language structure, for example, historical linguistics, psycholinguistics, comparative linguistics, sociolinguistics, geo-linguistics, and descriptive linguistics. It is within descriptive linguistics that the examination of the structure of the English language developed, bearing with it changed perspectives of our supposedly "familiar" language.

One of the prime movers of this development was Charles C. Fries, author of *The Structure of English,* who has been both praised and blamed for his attention to English structure and the resulting questioning of traditional grammar. Some preceded his work—Otto Jespersen, Edward Sapir, and Leonard Bloomfield—and others have followed his lead in developing this study of the structure of English, but Fries is credited with establishing important basic concepts such as the well-researched fact that there exist *social levels* of language usage rather than "right" and "wrong" usage. His chief contribution has been a more realistic approach to the study of language and the teaching of English.

Emphasis in linguistics is clearly on the scientific approach to language. Ignoring existing concepts or *mis*conceptions, the linguist sets to work to examine the language as it is in operation. Subsequent statements about language are not derived from intuitive prescriptions for what language "ought to be" but are based firmly on direct observation of the language as it is used by the people. The study of English includes, therefore, direct research of this language as it is used by widely differing socioeconomic groups within the United States as well as Great Britain, and Africa, India, and other parts of the world.

To provide some insight into the significance of linguistic study, we can cite an interesting field project undertaken by a group of international linguists in the spring of 1966 when they met to create a new alphabet for the Mandingo languages which include, for example, Bambara (spoken in Mali), Malinké (Mali, Guinea, and western Senegal), Songhay–Jerma (Mali and Niger), Tamashek (Tuareg), Hausa (Nigeria and Niger), Kanuri (Nigeria and Niger) and Fulani (scattered from Senegal to northern Cameroon). As is true of many languages, these tongues existed primarily in spoken form, for efforts to write the languages had been unorganized and conflicting.

With contemporary emphasis on education, publication, and mass communication came the need for a written language. The assembled linguists were convened by UNESCO for the purpose of:

1.   Proposing for these languages a common alphabet for all the consonants they share
2.   Creating an alphabet simple enough to avoid technical and economic problems disadvantageous to educational systems and publishing ventures

[2]Commission on the English Curriculum, National Council of Teachers of English, *The English Language Arts* (New York: Appleton-Century-Crofts, 1952), pp. 274–77.

What seems an impossible task was accomplished in one busy week, for the linguistic scholars developed a practical alphabet which encompasses the sounds of these six languages and deviates only slightly from the systems of most European languages. The creation of this alphabet will enable these African peoples to work more effectively toward mass education. As the UNESCO report states, "Six linguistic groups spread over seven nations now have alphabets that should enable them to start on the more and more urgent task of transcribing an immense heritage of oral literature."[3]

New terminology   One aspect of linguistics that has proved confusing for those new to the field is the introduction of new terms. In many cases, familiar terminology has been redefined. Let us examine some of the linguistic terms that you need to be able to use.

Phoneme (fo' anēm) The smallest unit of sound that makes a difference in meaning. Linguists can identify all the phonemes used in any language; for example, in English there are about forty phonemes, depending on the dialect examined. The sounds heard at the beginning of the words *fan* and *tan* represent two phonemes because the meaning of each word depends on the particular phoneme used. The single sound change represents a change in meaning. Phonemes are written within slashes, thus: /f/ /t/. The phonemes in English and the symbols we use to write them are discussed in detail in Chapter 9.

Grapheme (gra' fēm) The writing of a phoneme according to English spellings. One phoneme might, for instance, be represented by ten or more graphemes, whereas some sounds are spelled in only a few alternate ways. The phoneme /f/ might commonly be spelled *f, ph, ff,* or *gh.* The vowel phoneme /ey/, the long *a,* might be spelled in many different ways: pl*ay,* th*ey,* r*ai*n, fl*a*me, br*ea*k, n*eigh,* and so on. The relationships between phonemes and graphemes are explored in Chapter 11 because they are related to teaching reading and spelling.

Morpheme (mor' fēm) The smallest unit of meaning in the language. A morpheme is not necessarily a word although it might be. Notice the morphemes in these English words.

One morpheme: words such as *dog* or *book,* past tense (as in walk*ed*), plurality (as in cat*s*)
Two morphemes: *dogs, walked, playful, piglet*
Three morphemes: *girls', unspeakable*

Can you identify the meaningful elements in each word?

Linguists have often used the term *free* to identify those morphemes that can stand alone as words—for example, *turn* or *light.* Morphemes that are part of a longer word and cannot stand alone are called *bound morphemes,* as *de* or *ful* in the word *delightful,* which contains three morphemes; or as *re* in the word *return,* which contains two morphemes. The study of morphemes is called *morphology.*

[3]Adapted from *UNESCO Features* No. 477, p. 1.

Grammar The terms *grammar* and *usage* have been clearly differentiated by the modern linguist. *Grammar* is defined as the study of the syntax of the sentence, the structure of the language. Traditional or Latin-based grammars were prescriptive in that people were told how language ought to be used. Prescriptive grammar was replaced by descriptive grammar that literally described how language is really used and allowed for linguistic change.

Usage Grammar had long been considered a study of how to use words and the learning of "proper" or "correct" English. When the definition of *grammar* was clarified as the study of syntax, usage was more accurately defined as "the choice of appropriate words." We began to recognize that we use language in different ways according to the situation and that the formal language of an academic lecture would be inappropriate in the bowling alley.

The changed concepts of grammar and usage caused great consternation in English classrooms, and many chose to continue teaching prescriptive rules for usage under the title of grammar. Fortunately, most English teachers now realize it is more important to use language in speaking and writing than it is to keep on teaching artificial rules which never helped anyone learn to use language effectively. Grammar and usage are such important topics that we will explore them more thoroughly in the following pages.

English Grammar and Usage

The change brought about by linguistic studies which has probably caused the greatest controversy for teachers is that of modern approaches to grammar. The only grammar which teachers had been taught was the so-called "traditional" grammar which linguistics revealed as an inaccurate representation of English sentence structure. Naturally it was disconcerting to find that this knowledge was no longer useful, and there was resistance to change, as noted by W. Nelson Francis in 1954:

> The definitive grammar of English is yet to be written, but the results so far achieved are spectacular. It is now as unrealistic to teach "traditional" grammar of English as it is to teach "traditional" (pre-Darwinian) biology or "traditional" (four-element) chemistry. Yet nearly all certified teachers of English on all levels are doing so. Here is a cultural lag of major proportions.[4]

Although numerous grammars have been developed for the English language, three have directly influenced classroom instruction: (1) traditional, (2) structural, and (3) generative or transformational.[5] Other grammars are being developed, for with new perceptive minds come new perceptions of the structure of English; and too, the flexibility of our changing

[4]W. Nelson Francis, "Revolution in Grammar," *Quarterly Journal of Speech*, October 1954, pp. 229–312.

[5]Owen Thomas, "Grammatici Certant," *English Journal* (May 1963). Reprinted in *Linguistics in the Classroom* (Champaign, Ill.: National Council of Teachers of English), p. 6.

language creates a need for new descriptions. Each grammar has made its contribution as we will note in the following discussion.

Traditional grammar Traditional or Latin-based grammar has its roots in the eighteenth-century work of Joseph Priestley, Robert Lowth, George Campbell, and Lindley Murray, who based their precise rules on Latin, which they viewed as a perfect language, and on their own concepts of linguistic "correctness." The work of these early scholars is still evident in many English texts today as we observe the emphasis on "correct usage" and definitions of parts of speech—for example, "A noun is the name of a person, place, or thing."

Structural grammar Structural grammar is a descriptive grammar which began with the work of Leonard Bloomfield in the first half of the twentieth century. He attempted to separate structure of language from its meaning, distinguishing between the study of syntax and that of semantics. The purely descriptive approach employed by the structural linguist caused panic among traditionalists who deplored the structural grammarian's failure to judge "correctness" of usage. Linguists Charles C. Fries, James Sledd, H. A. Gleason Jr., Archibald Hill, and many others attempt to present language as it really exists.

Studies of the structure of English identified new concepts of (1) phonemes (the sounds of English, which number about forty), (2) morphemes (meaningful units of language), and (3) phrase structure. The structuralist also devised a new system of classifying the words in a language. Unlike the traditional grammarian, the structuralist bases definitions on syntax or function rather than meaning. Researchers discovered, for example, that all nouns are distinctive from other words in that a noun can be made plural and possessive. This is not true of any other group of words—verbs, adjectives, adverbs. Here, then, we have a clear test for identifying nouns. Can all of the following words be classified as nouns? Might any of them also be included in other categories?

mother	winning	footstep	drive
pupil	score	telephone	parking
English	publishing	pencil	spelling

Compare this approach to classifying words with that of traditional grammar, which bases definitions on the meanings of words. Are there words in this group which could not be identified as the "name of a person, place, or thing"?

Transformational–generative grammar Another influential grammar is based chiefly on the work of Noam Chomsky, whose work appeared in 1957 and 1960. Transformational–generative grammar extends the concepts of structural grammar, which was concerned with syntax devoid of meaning, to include the semantics of language. It seeks to:

1. Identify kernel sentences—simple, declarative, active sentences with no elaboration; for example, Joe has a dog.

2.   Supply rules for transforming kernel sentences.
     Judy ate a big hamburger.
     Is Judy eating a hamburger?
     Judy is not eating a hamburger.
     What is Judy eating?
3.   Identify obligatory transformations and optional transformations.
     An obligatory transformation: agreement of subject and verb.
       Mary is tall. (We cannot use *are* in this sentence.)
     An optional transformation: any elaboration of a kernel.
       The teacher is working. (We may add *tired* to describe teacher or *in her room* to designate the place, but these additions are optional.)

Transformational–generative grammar has developed very exact rules for transforming sentences, and these rules are usually stated in a formula. The changing of a kernel (simple, active, declarative) sentence into the passive form is stated in this formula:

Passive = Second noun phrase (+ auxiliary) + *be* + past participle + by + first noun phrase

Thus, the kernel sentence—Mrs. Parker called Joe—is made passive by applying the formula.

Joe (NP₂) was (form of *be*) called (past participle) by Mrs. Parker (NP₁).

Questions about grammar

1. What is grammar? The definition of grammar is somewhat difficult, for there are many conceptions of what grammar is, and far too many of these conceptions have been proved to be *mis*conceptions. We can begin defining grammar by pointing out, therefore, what grammar *is not*.

Grammar is not "usage." For many English instructors the problems of using "shall" or "will" or distinguishing between the use of "I" and "me" means the teaching of grammar. The linguist observes, however, that knowledge of this nature pertains to the manner in which English is used, to the selection of words according to appropriateness, not to the study of the structure of the English sentence, for grammar and usage are separate studies.

Grammar is not "good English." The placing of emphasis on the "correctness" and "incorrectness" is related to the study of usage. As we will point out in the discussion of usage, these concepts are relative depending on our personal values and the situation in which speech takes place.

Grammar is not "parts of speech." Some teachers have assumed they were teaching grammar as they drilled students on the identification of eight parts of speech. In the first place, linguists quickly teach us that there are more than eight categories of words in English, and that mere identification of each word as belonging to a certain category does not take note of the structural meaning of the sentence. We soon see, too, that many words fall into more than one category, for example:

His *running* of the race was unexpected.
The *running* water was cold.
John was *running* toward the school.

Jim hit a *home* run.
They were at *home*.
The family headed *home*.

Grammar is not "the mechanics of composition." Another interpretation of grammar has been the knowledge of punctuation, capitalization, and spelling—skills of composition. Although it is true that knowledge of juncture (the pauses in spoken language) has relevance for the study of grammar as well as for the use of punctuation, the study of punctuation is not the study of grammar.

How, then, shall we define *grammar* in accordance with modern linguistic concepts? One definition is "grammar is a study of the way a language works encompassing morphology (meaningful forms), syntax (sentence structure), and phonology (sounds)."[6]

It will be some time, however, before these definitions are assimilated by the teaching profession and even longer until the public understands, for example, that there is a distinction between grammar and usage. When critics of education advocate a return to the teaching of grammar to improve composition skills they really want the classroom teacher to stress the teaching of "correct usage."

2. Does knowledge of grammar improve ability to speak and write?
Research indicates that skills of composition are learned through composing, not through learning to identify classes of words, rules of grammar, and so forth.

> In view of the widespread agreement of research studies based upon many types of students and teachers, the conclusion can be stated in strong and unqualified terms: The teaching of formal grammar has a negligible, or, because it usually displaces some instruction and practice in actual comparison, even a harmful effect on the improvement of writing.[7]

Paul Roberts, who authored a set of language books which feature transformational grammar for elementary students,[8] asserted:

> It is not to be expected that study of the grammar, no matter how good a grammar it is or how carefully it is taught, will effect any enormous improvement in writing. Probably the improvement will be small and hard to demonstrate and for the large number of students who lack the motivation or the capacity to learn to write, it will be nonexistent.[9]

[6]Mary E. Fowler, *Teaching Language, Composition, and Literature* (New York: McGraw-Hill Book Co., 1965), p. 183.

[7]Richard Braddock et al., *Research in Written Composition* (Champaign, Ill.: National Council of Teachers of English, 1963), 37–38.

[8]*The Roberts English Series* (New York: Harcourt Brace Jovanovich, Inc., 1966).

[9]Paul Roberts, "Linguistics and the Teaching of Composition," *English Journal,* May 1963.

Researchers note the need for more extensive studies of composition, and this would certainly be true of the effects of instruction along the lines of structural and generative grammars which have only recently found their ways into the schools. It is our own observation that work in expanding basic sentences does increase student flexibility in writing by suggesting possiblities for more effective original sentences. Mere knowledge of terminology or ability to classify English words does not improve composition skills, but moving beyond that basic information to manipulation of words, phrases, clauses, that is, to composing, does improve ability to write.

3. Why is traditional grammar no longer considered satisfactory? Linguistic studies have pointed out that, as can be readily proved, traditional grammar does not describe the English language. The following criticisms of traditional grammar have been made:

a. Prescriptive rules based on Latin, a dead language, had little effect on changing usage of a living language.
b. Traditional grammar did not recognize the changing nature of language.
c. Its definitions of word classes were based on meaning, which changes for a word in varied contexts; the definitions were ambiguous.

The emphasis on learning sterile rules made the study of English boring and distasteful and actually inhibited learning. As Marckwardt observes, students tended to adopt a "classroom dialect, a sapless and super-correct form of the language employed only within the hearing of the English teacher and in written work subject to her scrutiny, and for the most part, dropped like a hot-cake as soon as the hour was over."[10] It is probable that an excessive amount of time was spent on repetitious drill in usage when time might more wisely have been allocated for writing.

4. Does modern grammar offer something more effective than traditional grammar? Modern grammar (based on structural linguistics and transformational–generative grammar) emphasizes learning about grammar by engaging in the work of the linguist, that is, examining the language itself. The student can discover word classes inductively, for example, through learning processes advocated by Bruner.[11] He or she can also discover sentence patterns and methods of expanding them as we will discuss in more detail later in this chapter. The advantages of modern grammar include the following:

a. Description of the structure of English is based on a study of this unique language as it is actually used.
b. Grammar is differentiated from usage.
c. The student acquires a more realistic attitude toward language and language study.

---

[10]Albert H. Marckwardt, "Grammar and Linguistics in the Teaching of English," *Illinois English Bulletin,* October 1956, p. 3.
[11]Ibid.

d.   Emphasis on creating original sentences after study of sentence structure patterns suggests a beneficial relationship between grammar study and composition.

Questions about usage   More flexible concepts of language based on realistic descriptions of language use have altered attitudes toward usage, which is now viewed as changing along with the changing language.

1. What is the difference between grammar and usage? Grammar, as has been explained, is the structure of English sentences, the language as it operates, the syntax. Grammar does not consider the meaning of individual words.

The grammar of a language tells us that, for example, the subject and the verb must agree in number. We say, therefore, "Tom and Sammy are going." Grammatically, we cannot say, "Tom and Sammy is going." We could, on the other hand, change our selection of words in other respects without changing the syntax, for example:

> Tom and Sammy are running.
> Thomas and Sam are walking.
> Tom and Sam are playing.

Our choice of words may change the meaning, but it does not change the syntax or grammar.

2. What shall we teach about usage? Linguists recommend that we teach the concept of varied levels of usage. Usage that is acceptable in an informal social situation may not be acceptable in a written composition and vice versa. We recognize, but don't condemn, the presence of varied social dialects among which *standard* English is only one, and even this dialect may vary regionally.

We teach, therefore, educated forms of standard English without undue stress on minor points. Pooley recommends that we forget, for example, a number of specific items of usage which were formerly taught:

Any distinction between *shall* and *will*
Any reference to the split infinitive
Elimination of *like* as a conjunction
Objection to the phrase "different than"
Objection to "He is one of those boys who *is*"
Objection to "the reason . . . is because . . ."
Objection to *myself* as a polite substitution for *me* as in "I understand you will meet Mrs. Jones and myself at the station."
Insistence on the possessive case standing before a gerund[12] [Note that there is an example in this item.]

[12]Robert C. Pooley, "Dare Schools Set a Standard in Usage?" *The English Journal*, March 1960, p. 180.

3. What is "good" English? The definition of good English written by Robert C. Pooley in 1933 has been widely quoted and remains a valid statement today:

> Good English is that form of speech which is appropriate to the purpose of the speaker, true to the language as it is, and comfortable to speaker and listener.[13]

Notice that there is no mention in this definition of "correctness" or of knowledge of rules of grammar.

4. Does memorization of rules improve usage? Meckel reports that "Improvement of usage appears to be most effectively achieved through practice of desirable forms than through memorization of rules."[14]

The child learns through hearing language from infancy; many language patterns and much knowledge of English usage are formed before the child comes to school. Both home and peer group are highly influential in determining usage. Changes will be brought about only when the student discovers a reason for changing speech, and learning of rules does not provide sufficient motivation.

5. Is slang "bad"? Here again we must rethink our concepts of correctness and usage. Slang is a vernacular which has a high interest value and often provides a means for snaring the interests of students in language study. Termed in French "*la langue verte*," slang represents the growth, the aliveness, of our language. Have students list as many slang words as they can. The words can be defined, categorized into word classes, used in sentence patterns, and compiled by several "lexicographers" into a dictionary of SLANGUAGE. Entries might include:

Run that by me again. (Repeat what you said.)
That's the pits! (That's the worst thing possible.)
soap opera
going bananas
cold shoulder
a ball park figure
make a comeback
rapping

The teacher does not teach slang, but aims students toward standard English without authoritatively condemning slang. Students are taught the concept of varied levels of usage. Sometimes words which originate as slang become elevated to a higher level of acceptability, and on rare occasions a slang word becomes acceptable as standard English.

Although we have made suggestions about classroom instruction

---

[13]Robert C. Pooley, *Grammar and Usage in Textbooks on English*, Bureau of Educational Research Bulletin No. 14 (Madison: University of Wisconsin, August, 1933), p. 155.

[14]Henry C. Meckel, "Research on Teaching Composition and Literature," in *Handbook of Research on Teaching*, American Educational Research Assn., ed. N. L. Gage. (Chicago: Rand McNally & Co., 1963), p. 981.

throughout this section, it is important to stress that grammar and usage should be taught as students use language. Avoid preparing drill sheets that focus on choosing between *is* and *are* or *had did* and *had done*. Such artificial tasks can have only negative effects. Instead, talk with students about the grammaticality of sentences they write as they ask, "Does it sound right?" Teach grammar and usage in the context of speaking and writing activities, as described in more detail in the next section.

LANGUAGE STUDY ACROSS THE CURRICULUM

"Perhaps of all the creations of man, language is the most astonishing," wrote Giles Lytton Strachey in *Words and Poetry*. As you lead students to discover what J. Donald Adams has called "the magic and mystery of words," your students will experience some of this feeling for the English language. They may be intrigued by their ability to manipulate language, to achieve surprising results, to create beautiful arrangements. Your enthusiasm will be contagious as you involve students in investigations and guide them to observe the language that flows around them every day.

In this section we will first consider the characteristics of a good approach to language study in the elementary school. Then we will examine possible content and strategies to use as in working with various aspects of language across the curriculum.

Planning the Language Component

The content we have already discussed suggests a multitude of concepts that could be presented in K-8 classrooms. The following summary suggests content around which to develop lessons:

1. History and development of the English language
   a. English is part of the Indo-European language family.
   b. Changes in spelling and pronunciation influence contemporary spelling and pronunciation; changing nature of language.
   c. Origins of English words; continuing growth of English.
   d. Comparison of American and British English.
   e. English is part of the world culture.
2. Structure of the English language, grammar
   a. Specific sounds (phonemes) can be identified for the English language; corresponding graphemes can be identified.
   b. English words can be grouped according to their function in sentences; some words may belong to more than one group.
   c. Word order helps to signal meaning.
   d. English sentences are based on distinct patterns.
   e. Basic sentence patterns can be elaborated through specific techniques.
3. Usage of American English
   a. There are varied levels of acceptable usage or varied degrees of appropriateness of usage.
   b. Usage concerns the selection of specific words to be used in any given speech situation.

    c.   Usage is not "right" or "wrong," for the choice is up to the individual. Usage may be judged on the basis of suitability to the context, whether it be a social context or a composition context.

    d.   Speech dialects differ according to region and social class. Even standard English allows for variety of acceptable speech.

    e.   We should develop sensitivity to language habits as we do to habits of eating and dress.

4.   Oral and written composition in English

    a.   The purpose of using language is to communicate ideas and feelings.

    b.   The success of composition is evaluated on the basis of success in communicating.

    c.   Skills associated with written composition, for example, spelling, punctuation, and handwriting, facilitate communication.

    d.   In order to communicate one must first have an idea, or thoughts.

    e.   We increase effectiveness in communication through practice in composing varied types of messages.

    f.   The study of other authors' attempts to communicate (literary models) can aid growth in ability to compose and communicate.

5.   English semantics

    a.   Semantics deals with the meanings of words.

    b.   Words vary from the concrete to the highly abstract.

    c.   The connotation of a word may be more significant than its denotation.

    d.   Meaning is carried not only by words but by intonation, body language, and so forth.

    e.   A special dictionary that deals with synonyms of words is the thesaurus.

6.   Dialectology in American English

    a.   American and British English differ widely in many respects, yet the grammar is basically the same.

    b.   The study of dialectology includes both social and regional variation in language.

    c.   Language varies more widely in pronunciation than it does in syntax.

    d.   Many people in our country are bidialectal.

    e.   Each person speaks at least one dialect.

7.   Folklore in our language

    a.   All of us are the folk who create the lore of language.

    b.   Proverbs and sayings are often the same in many cultures.

    c.   Folklore is reflected in children's literature: Brer Rabbit tales, Anansi the spider, Paul Bunyan.

    d.   The jokes we tell are part of our folk literature: Knock-knock jokes, Elephant jokes, Tom Swifties.

    e.   We expand language and lore around subjects that are important in our culture.

An exciting method for teaching students about their own language is through inductive activities or discovery techniques. In general children enjoy language and feel that it is something they know about. Let them examine their own language. They can make a study of the dialects represented in their own classroom.

A national committee for evaluating curriculum guidelines recommends that the language component of a language arts program:

- suggest that the content of language study often comes from real life
- provide for study of conventional areas of linguistics
- suggest study of unique customs of specific language areas; for example, advertising, politics, or education
- provide for frequent imaginative use of language in student-created and student-moderated groups
- reflect knowledge of current or recent developments in modern language theory
- suggest activities that help students learn the difference between grammar and usage
- recognize that analysis of language, as in grammar study, does not necessarily improve performance in composing
- recognize the assets of bidialectal, bilingual, and non-English-speaking children in exploring language concepts
- suggest activities that help students acquire or expand their facility to understand and use the English language
- recognize the importance of children's accepting their "home-rooted" language, as well as that of others.[15]

Vocabulary Development

The study of words provides a basic foundation for both reading and writing growth. Introduce new words through reading aloud, and pick up on words that are mentioned incidentally in the classroom. Encourage students to share interesting words they encounter.

The study of word origins described earlier in this chapter will stimulate the student's investigation of words. Another language study that will lead to vocabulary development is the classification of parts of speech, as spelled out in the following pages.

Tell the students that linguists can identify different groupings of words according to how they are used in sentences. (Do not limit yourself to the eight traditional parts of speech. We have included the more commonly used groupings.) Discuss one group at a time, explaining the characteristics of each group as presented below. As part of each presentation, have students expand their knowledge of words by making lists according to a different focus each time. You might, for example, have students create an ABC of nouns or a long list of synonyms for the overworked verb *said*. Think about such activities as you read through the descriptions of the classifications.

Main word classes The four main word classes—noun, verb, adjective, and adverb—are open classes to which an unlimited number of words can be added.

Noun A noun is a word that can be made plural or possessive and may follow the words *the, a,* or *an.* A noun fits in patterns like these:

---

[15]Winkeljohann, Rosemary, Associate Chair, ed. *Recommended English Language Arts Curriculum Guides K-12 and Criteria for Planning and Evaluation* (Urbana, Ill.: National Council of Teachers of English, Committee to Evaluate Curriculum Guidelines, 1979), pp. 18–19.

She has a _____ (book, ball, pencil, dress, headache).
He looked at the _____ (house, car, boy, dog, spot, movie).

Verb A verb is a word that can be changed from past to present and usually (except for forms of *to be*) adds *s* when patterned after *it, she, he.* The morpheme *ing* may be added to a verb. A verb fits in patterns like these:

The boy _____. (runs, plays, speaks, shouts, ran, played).
They _____ it. (found, chased, wanted, like, have, want).
What are you _____? (saying, doing, missing, singing).

Adjective An adjective patterns with the word *very,* as *very lovely girl, very soft music, very small boy,* and the adjective can follow a linking verb.

She is very _____. (happy, pretty, nice, healthy).
The very _____ boy arrived. (tired, tall, unhappy, first).

Adverb Adverbs pattern like *often, up,* or *sadly.* They modify verbs or adjectives.

Mary sings _____. (well, clearly, often, sweetly).
The baby climbs _____. (up, eagerly, down, quickly).

Notice that many words may be placed in more than one word class according to their function in the sentence. Consider, for example, the various meanings and functions for these words:

check	book	trip
looking	walk	sound
leap	plane	root

Function words The other word categories are called *function* words or *structure* words. Included are: prepositions, conjunctions, subordinators, auxiliaries, intensifiers, pronouns, and determiners. These groupings are relatively limited in number, for only infrequently is a new word added to any of these structure categories.

Determiners The determiner signals that a noun follows. Included in this class are *the, a, an, every, each, this, that, these, those, my, one, two, three, four, most, more, either, neither, our, your, their, his, her, its, no, both, some, much, all, any, several, few.*

_____ cat chased _____ dog.
_____ boys played with _____ ball.

Pronouns *Pronouns* (like proper nouns) do not pattern with determiners, but they substitute for nouns or proper nouns.

The boy is tall.   *Bruce* is tall.   *He* is tall.

A special group of pronouns also function as determiners when followed by a noun, thus:

These boys are helpful.   *These* are helpful.
That man is Mr. Sutter.   *That* is Mr. Sutter.

Intensifers Intensifiers *(very, quite, somewhat, rather)* pattern with adjectives and adverbs, thus:

Jim was *very* talkative.   Jim walked *very* slowly.
He was *somewhat* uncertain.   He was *rather* uncertain.

Auxiliaries The auxiliary signals that a verb follows. Some auxiliaries *(do, be, have, can)* may also serve as independent verbs, and only two *(be, have)* pattern with the past form of verbs.

I *can* go.   He *did* help the teacher.
He *has played*.   She *was* helping.

Subordinators Subordinators are connecting words that join subordinate subject–predicate word groups (clauses) with independent subject–predicate word groups (clauses). Included are *who, when, until, unless, that, since, if, what, which, whenever, while, although, as, because, whatever, whichever, whoever, how, before, whether, as if, unless, until.*

> Their house is the yellow one *which* faces the park.
> She is the person *who* called you.
> *When* you return home, send me a copy of that book.

Conjunctions Conjunctions are linking words which join equal words or groups of words. Included in this group are *and, but, for, either . . . or, neither . . . nor, not only . . . but also, or, yet.*

> *Either* David *or* I will come.
> Her name is Joanna, *but* everyone calls her Jo.

Prepositions Prepositions signal that a noun follows, usually in a prepositional phrase which serves an adjective or adverb function. Common prepositions include *about, above, across, after, among, around, at, before, by, in, for, from, in, into, of, off, on, over, since, through, to, under, up, upon, with, within.*

> The cat jumped *over* the box.
> *At* noon we stopped working.
> Walk *to* the corner *with* me.

What techniques can we use in the classroom to introduce students to these parts of speech? One of the most effective ways is the inductive approach, through which students make linguistic discoveries for themselves. A class is asked, for example, to see how many words they can name in five to ten minutes as recorders write the words on chalkboards. The students then examine the group of unsorted words to determine how these words can be sorted or classified. Varied methods may be explored—alphabetical order, length of words, meaning (animals, feelings, etc.—not all words will fit semantic groups), and so on.

Discoveries can be guided by the teacher who might ask, for example, after varied methods have been tried, whether any of the words can be made plural. After this identification of the noun class other groupings can be gradually introduced.

Additional practice in identifying words can be effected through these activities:

- Nouns and determiners:
  The _____ and the _____ followed the _____.
  _____ mice are in _____ cage eating _____ cheese.
  I want to buy a _____ and two _____.
- Can you unite these sentences?
  Sheryl is pretty. She is popular. She studies hard.
  The siren shrieked. The car pulled over. The driver got out.
  This boy is the winner. He has long legs. He is in fifth grade.
- What word would you choose?
  We walked _____ the hill.
  _____ the assembly we returned _____ class.
  He sat _____ the table.
  The child was climbing _____ the box.
- Why is the meaning of these words uncertain?
  Plan moves ahead.
  City shelters poor.
  Ship sails today.
- Grammar activity sheet on next page.

Composing Well-structured Sentences

The sentence merits considerable attention in the study of language and in developing composition skills. It is through study of the sentence that students can be made aware of grammar, for there is little justification in teaching grammar as an isolated subject. Grammar is not just a set of terms and rules to be learned; it is a study of the relationships of words and groups of words in the context of a sentence. These ideas should be taught, therefore, as students learn to write, to manipulate words and phrases, to create interesting, varied sentences.

Focusing attention on the sentence also provides an opportunity to talk about style. Encourage students to consider varied ways of saying the same thing as they strive for clarity and more precise use of words. Discussion of ways to make writing more effective helps students grow. We can guide students in examining model sentences from literature and experimenting with sentence combining techniques as ways of promoting their development as young writers.

WHO DID WHAT?

Can you read this familiar poem even though some of the words have been omitted?

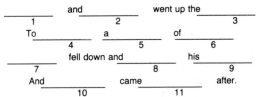

Can you explain how you knew this poem? How did the printed words help you read the poem?

Now complete the following exercise.

1. A man's name_____
2. A woman's name_____
3. The name of a place_____
4. An active verb_____
5. A container (noun)_____

6. Something in a container_____
7. A man's name_____
8. Verb (past tense)_____
9. Part of the body_____
10. A woman's name_____
11. Verb (-ing form)_____

Now read the poem again. This time insert the words you wrote beside each number. Share what you wrote with other people in the class. Have a good laugh.

If you enjoyed this activity, do the same thing with another short nursery rhyme. First make a frame with blanks as shown above. Then make a wordlist. Have fun!

Exploring sentence patterns Structural linguistics introduced the concept of the sentence pattern, of which there are many. In the elementary school, however, we usually work with only five basic patterns. After introducing one pattern—for example, the simplest of all, noun–verb, let the students play with the pattern as they modify it in many ways. At any time, of course, they can still identify the basic pattern. Challenge class members to create a long sentence beginning with only two words, perhaps: *Horses run.* Compare the results.

The following five sentence patterns can be explored as you try experiments both orally and as written exercises. Students will enjoy developing the sentences according to specific directions. You can invent games based on working with these patterns—for example, HOW MANY SENTENCES CAN YOU WRITE IN FIVE MINUTES? Composing sentences is also a good activity for small groups, as students brainstorm sentences and develop them along specific lines together. Notice that terminology is taught and reinforced through use. The child who works with nouns and verbs begins to generalize what a noun is and what a verb is. Later the class might talk about nouns and how we know a word is a noun in a sentence.

N–V (SUBJECT–PREDICATE)

EXPERIMENTS:
Girls *giggle.* Girls *run.* Girls *sing.* (Analogical changes)
Boys *shout.* Boys *fight.* Boys *race.* Boys _____
Cows *moo.* Cows *eat.* Cows *walk.* Cows _____

The girls giggle. (Expansion—determiner)
Boys shout *loudly*. (Adverb)
In the morning cows moo. (Prepositional phrase)
The *amused* girls were giggling. (Adjective)

N–V–N (SUBJECT–PREDICATE–OBJECT)

EXPERIMENTS:
Boys run races. *Girls* run races. *Horses* run races.
Jane eats *ice cream*. Jane eats *sandwiches*. Jane eats *everything*.
Mrs. Barker *reads* books. Mrs. Barker *buys* books. Mrs. Barker *enjoys* books.

Boys and girls run races. (Expansion—compounding)
Jane eats *ice cream and cake* (Compounding)
Mrs. Barker reads books *about Africa*. (Modification)
A *world traveler*, Mrs. Barker reads books about Africa. (Apposition)

N–LV–N (SUBJECT–LINKING VERB PREDICATE–NOUN COMPLEMENT)

EXPERIMENTS:
This dog is a terrier. This dog is a collie.
My mother is a tall woman. My mother is a good driver.
Henry was a teacher. Henry was a barber.

This dog *which is lost* is a terrier. (Subordinate clause)
Although my mother is a tall woman, she is thin. (Subordination)
Henry was a teacher *in a small college*. (Prepositional phrase)

N–LV–ADJ (SUBJECT–LINKING VERB PREDICATE–ADJECTIVE COMPLEMENT)

EXPERIMENTS:
Nancy is pretty. Nancy is intelligent.
Carnations are sweet. Roses are sweet.
Karl appears old. Karl appears unhappy.

Nancy and Susan are pretty. (Compounding)
Carnations and roses are sweet. (Compounding)
Although Nancy is pretty, Susan is more intelligent. (Subordination)
Carnations are sweet, *but roses are lovelier*. (Coordination)

N–V–N–N (SUBJECT–PREDICATE–DIRECT OBJECT–INDIRECT OBJECT)

EXPERIMENTS:
Daddy gave me the book. (to me)
She read Peter a story. (to Peter)
The teacher told Larry the assignment. (to Larry)

Daddy gave me the _____. (book, money, permission)
Daddy gave _____ the book. (Mother, the neighbor)
_____ gave me the book. (Milly, A friend, My teacher)

Complete the formula:
    $Noun_1$ Verb $Noun_2$ $Noun_3$

Other methods of categorizing sentences   In addition to the identification
of sentence patterns such as those described, you may wish to talk about
sentences according to the purpose of the speaker. In the following chart,

INTENT OF THE SPEAKER		PUNCTUATION USED	
Statement	Declarative	Period	.
Question	Interrogative	Question mark	?
Command	Imperative	Period	.
Exclamation	Exclamatory	Exclamation mark	!

the terms in the first column are relatively simple to understand compared with those in the second column, which could be introduced as a part of vocabulary growth. Notice that these categories are related to the punctuation marks we use.

The intonation or tone of voice is revealing as we speak sentences belonging to these categories. Have students compose sentences and speak them orally as others identify the kind of sentence and appropriate punctuation mark to be used. Help students make generalizations, for example:

You can tell a person is asking a question because the voice goes up at the end.
When a person makes a plain statement, the voice is flat, not excited, and goes down a little at the end.
A command is like a statement, but the form of the verb changes. The speaker is saying, "Do something."

When students are having trouble with punctuation as they write, remind them to say their sentence aloud to determine the kind of punctuation needed. Have them observe that we use punctuation marks to assist the reader.

Another method of categorizing sentences that you might discuss with older students is based on sentence structure as we compare simple sen-

The Structure of Sentences

SIMPLE (1 INDEPENDENT CLAUSE)
  Examples: The horse ran away.
                Jim and Bob took the books to the library.
                Will you ask Jerry to arrive on time?
COMPLEX (1 INDEPENDENT CLAUSE PLUS 1 OR MORE DEPENDENT OR SUBORDINATE
           CLAUSES)
  Examples: When Jill left the barn, the horse ran away.
                While the teacher was busy, Jim and Bob took the books to the library.
                If it's convenient, will you ask Jerry to arrive on time?
COMPOUND (2 OR MORE INDEPENDENT CLAUSES)
  Examples: The horse ran away, but his rider soon had him under control.
                Jim and Bob took the books to the library, and the rest of the class began rehearsing the play.
                Will you ask Jerry to arrive on time or we may miss the train?
COMPOUND–COMPLEX (2 OR MORE INDEPENDENT CLAUSES PLUS AT LEAST 1 DEPENDENT
                   CLAUSE)
  Examples: If you don't hold the reins, the horse may run away, and you may not be able to control it.
                While the teacher was busy, Jim and Bob took the books to the library, and the rest of the class began rehearsing the play.

tences with more complex ones. This discussion might be helpful in working with punctuation.

After presenting each type of sentence described, have students try to find examples in books available in the classroom. Write examples on the board or on an overhead transparency as you point out the punctuation used. Students will probably find examples that include the semicolon, which is used to assist the reader in reading a more complicated sentence. Note the use of the semicolon in these sentences.

Independent clauses without a conjunction:
  At first no one was in the room; then all the people arrived.
  Tomás sang the song; the whole class joined in the chorus.
Compound-complex sentence that is complicated:
  When Tomás sang the song, the whole class joined in the chorus; and everyone agreed that the singing would be a great ending for the assembly.

Although a brief discussion of these more involved sentences is helpful as students develop their abilities to write, it is not recommended that you spend time on having them identify the correct label for lists of these sentences. Elementary students are not likely to compose compound–complex sentences that require the semicolon; if they should, you can help them with punctuation. It is better to spend classroom time on having students write rather than discussing rules that remain abstract until needed in the context of the student's own writing.

Sentence-combining practices   An approach to helping students improve their writing that has received much attention is the use of sentence-combining exercises designed to demonstrate methods of producing more effective sentences. By showing students more complex structures than they are accustomed to using, you may move them toward writing with greater maturity and, it is assumed, greater effect. James Mellon and Frank O'Hare are credited with developing the first sentence-combining exercises and conducting research that revealed growth by students who practiced using such exercises as the following:

Night came. (WHEN)
We sat huddled in blankets.
The blankets were *thick* and *wooly*.
It was time to turn in for the night.
(LONG BEFORE)[16]

The words in parentheses are cues that the student learns to use in creating a combined sentence that reads as follows:

  When night came, we sat huddled in thick, woolly blankets long before it was time to turn in for the night.

[16]O'Hare, Frank, *Sentence-combining: Improving Student Writing without Formal Instruction.* Research Report No. 15. (Urbana, Ill.: National Council of Teachers of English, 1973), p. 96.

Used as an instructional strategy that supplements the students' independent writing, these exercises can serve to expand the student's ability to write fluently. The lesson below is an example of the kind of work sixth-grade students might be expected to do.

A Sentence-Combining Activity Sheet

SENTENCE-COMBINING EXPERIMENTS

Sometimes combining short sentences is a way of making your writing more interesting. Notice the words that are repeated in these four sentences.

The hound came running toward the house.
The hound was *panting*.
The hound lifted its head. (,)
The hound sniffed the ground like a metal detector. (, and)

We can combine these sentences by using the cues in ( ) and leaving out the repeated words. Remember that the cues are placed before the sentence they follow. An underlined word is simply placed where it fits in the sentence. Read the combined sentence aloud.

The panting hound came running toward the house, lifted its head, and sniffed the ground like a metal detector.

Now see if you can follow the cues in these examples. Write only the combined sentence each time. Read the example again if you are confused.

EXPERIMENT 1:
The cougar charged over the fence before us.
The cougar was *frightened*.
The cougar hesitated. (,)
Then the cougar turned back toward the jungle. (, and)

EXPERIMENT 2:
A hummingbird hovered near the feeder.
The hummingbird was *tiny*.
The hummingbird sipped the sweetened water. (,)
Then the hummingbird darted off. (, and)

EXPERIMENT 3:
The kitten played with a catnip mouse.
The kitten was funny.
The kitten rolled on the carpet.
Then the kitten curled up to sleep in the sun.

You can find additional information about sentence-combining in these articles or books:

Combs, Warren E., "Sentence-combining Practice Aids Reading Comprehension," *Reading Teacher*, 21:18–24. 1977.

Cooper, Charles R., "An Outline for Writing Sentence-combining Problems," *English Journal*, 62:96–108, 1973.

Hunt, Kelly, *Grammatical Structures Written at Three Grade Levels*. Research Report No. 3. Urbana, Ill.: National Council of Teachers of English, 1965.

Mellon, James C., *Transformational Sentence-combining: A Method for Enhancing the Development of Syntactic Fluency in English Composition*. Research Report No. 10. Urbana, Ill.: National Council of Teachers of English, 1969.

Perron, Jack, "Beginning Writing: It's All in the Mind," *Language Arts*, 53:652–657, 1976.

Creating original sentences The chief purpose of examining the structure of English sentences and experimenting with methods of expansion should be, as we have previously noted, the development of student ability to create, to compose, to generate original sentences. Experiments with sentence patterns and methods of expanding basic patterns should lead, furthermore, to greater skill and confidence in creating sentences that are not only interesting and effective but also written with style, a style that is distinctive for each individual. There should be many opportunities for students to compose and discuss sentences.

Expanding a basic pattern can help students acquire flexibility in producing interesting original sentences. After students have explored the possibilities of expansion, they can inductively discover certain methods which can be repeated. You can then supply the common terminology for these methods to provide the vocabulary for discussing sentence development.

MODIFICATION

Basic sentence—The boy went home.
   The tired, but happy, boy went home. (Development of noun cluster)
   The boy went home after school. (Prepositional phrase)
   The boy immediately went home. (Adverb)
   Having completed his work, the boy went home. (Participial phrase)
Combination: Having completed his work, the tired but happy boy immediately went home after school.

COMPOUNDING

Basic sentence—Debbie lives on Oak Street.
   Debbie and Karen live on Oak Street. (Subject)
   Debbie lives on Oak Street and goes to Maynard School. (Predicate)
   Debbie lives on Oak Street, and she attends Maynard School. (Whole sentence)

APPOSITION

Basic sentence—Mr. Hadmon is an interesting person.
   Mr. Hadmon, *our sixth-grade teacher,* is an interesting person.
   Our sixth-grade teacher, *Mr. Hadmon,* is an interesting person.
   An interesting person is our sixth-grade teacher, *Mr. Hadmon.*
   Mr. Hadmon, *well-read and informed,* is an interesting person.

SUBORDINATION

Basic sentence—Joe likes to play ball.
   Joe, *who is in eighth grade,* likes to play ball. (Modifying subject)
   Joe likes to play ball *whenever he has a chance.* (Modifying predicate)
   Although Joe likes to play ball, he also studies hard.
   Because Joe likes to play ball, he practices each Saturday.

If you present the study of language as a discovery process that is related to daily life, your students will catch your enthusiasm, and they will respond eagerly. Present information about word origins, interesting new words, conventions of spelling, and the folklore in language in the context of writing and reading assignments.

Recreational Linguistics

One of the most important aspects of language study is what you might call "recreational linguistics." Having fun with words, using language to provoke laughter, or just observing the amazing things we have done with language breaks down any negative attitudes students may have acquired. From recreational linguistics you can branch out to explore any number of language topics.

- Scavenger hunt—This variety of word quiz, and others, can be prepared by students who often display real skill in writing provocative types of word activities. The students' dictionaries are needed for these discoveries:
  What is the word following murder? _____
  Find two birds. _____
- Yes or No—Dictionaries are needed to determine the right answer.
  Is a bird fond of eating limericks? _____
  Is a lion carnivorous? _____
  Might a lady be garrulous? _____
- Introduce students to Spoonerisms, speech slips of the type named for the Reverend W. A. Spooner of Oxford University. Have students invent these slips and create situations around them for fun with words and writing. Here are two remarks supposedly made by this illustrious gentleman:
  "Is the bean dizzy?"
  When a parishioner complained, "Someone is occupewing my pie," he rejoined, "I'm very sorry, Madam. I'll sew you to another sheet."
- Add an A to the following words to produce a new word. Each student should try to find additional examples.

  rod—road
  pry—pray
  red—read
  fir—fair
  slam—salaam (2 A's)
  bird—baird
  bred—bread, bared
  shred—shared

- The interest of this type of puzzle depends on its form, DIAMOND O. Definitions will usually need to accompany the unsolved example.

```
                        c   o   t
                    s   n   o   w   y
                u   n   d   o   i   n   g
            r   e   s   t   o   r   i   n   g
        s   u   b   f   l   o   o   r   i   n   g
            d   e   p   l   o   r   i   n   g
                s   p   r   o   u   t   s
                    p   r   o   u   d
                        t   o   n
```

- Many commercial games found in most toy and stationery stores can be well put to use in a language arts interest center. These would certainly include Scrabble, Spill 'N' Spell, and Password.

A student teacher[17] in a third-grade classroom used a number of word activities with the children. Then she encouraged each child to construct an activity. Geoff produced a group of scrambled words:

MAKE WORDS OF THESE

1. sdnuo—noise   s _____
2. npduo—hit   p _____
3. inur—to wreck   r _____
4. urn—flee   r _____
5. israya—fee   s _____
6. yco—shy   c _____
7. mjup—pep   j _____
8. stsasi—help   a _____

Michelle developed a group of antonyms with the instructions: "Draw lines to their antonyms."

dog	glad
white	sea
mad	south
happy	cat
land	girl
north	sad
west	stand
boy	black
sit	east
father	work
sister	out
in	brother
play	mother

• Double tactics—Two students can play a word-forming game on a frame as in the illustration. As the players alternate turns, each tries to form a word by adding only one letter at a time. Each word formed scores one point.

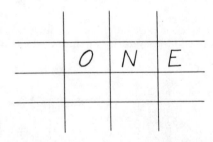

Encourage students to keep notes about their word discoveries. They can share intriguing words as a way of increasing interest in vocabulary development.

---

[17]Mrs. Bonnie Manley teaching with Mrs. Young, Booksin School, San Jose, California.

FUNNY PHRASES

①
sgge
sgeg
gegs

②
Your nose
right

③
once
2:30

④
don't
eat

⑤
ME
AL

⑥
he art

⑦
y y y men

⑧
La w Yer

Answers:

① scrambled eggs
③ once upon a time
⑤ square meal
⑦ 3 wise men

② right under your nose
④ don't over eat
⑥ broken heart
⑧ crooked lawyer

159

CHALLENGE

1. Browse through a book for adults on wordplay. Play with some of the ideas, and note ones that might be useful with your students. Look for such titles as:

The Play of Words by F. Allen Briggs (Harcourt)

Words on Vacation by Dmitri Bjornsted (Knopf)

2. Read three or more of the books listed in the student's language library on page 155. Plan three lessons based on information presented in the books you read.

3. Prepare activity sheets like those on pages 151 and 155 that you could use with students in fifth grade (or another level that you may be teaching).

EXPLORING FURTHER

Dietrich, Daniel, ed., *Teaching about Doublespeak.* Urbana, Ill.: National Council of Teachers of English, 1976.

Eisenhardt, Catheryn, *Applying Linguistics in the Teaching of Reading and the Language Arts.* Columbus, Ohio: Charles E. Merrill Publishing Co., 1972.

Fries, Charles C., *Linguistics: The Study of Language.* New York: Holt, Rinehart and Winston, Inc., 1964.

Hall, Edward T., *The Silent Language.* New York: Fawcett World Library, 1969.

Hayes, Curtis et al., *The ABC's of Languages and Linguistics: A Practical Primer to Language Science in Today's World.* Silver Spring, Md.: Institute of Modern Languages, 1977.

Laird, Charlton, *The Miracle of Language.* New York: World, 1953. Excellent history of the English language; paperback edition, Premier Press.

Malmstrom, Jean, *Grammar Basics: A Reading/Writing Approach.* Rochelle Park, N.J.: Hayden Book Co., Inc., 1977.

Milosh, Joseph E., Jr., *Teaching the History of the English Language in the Secondary Classroom.* Urbana, Ill.: National Council of Teachers of English/ERIC, 1972.

Nilsen, Don L. F. and Alleen Pace Nilsen, *Language Play: An Introduction to Linguistics.* Rowley, Mass.: Newbury House Pubs., 1978.

Minteer, Catherine et al., *Teachers Guide to General Semantics.* San Francisco: International Society for General Semantics, 1968.

Opie, Iona and Peter Opie, *The Lore and Language of Schoolchildren.* New York: Oxford Univ. Press, 1967.

Pooley, Robert C., *The Teaching of English Usage* (2nd ed.). Urbana, Ill.: National Council of Teachers of English, 1974.

Read, Charles, "What Children Know About Language: Three Examples," *Language Arts,* February 1980, 57: 145–48.

Reed, Carroll, E., *Dialects of American English.* New York: World, 1967.

Tollefson, Stephen K. and Kimberly S. Davis, *Reading and Writing About Language.* Belmont, Calif.: Wadsworth Publishing Co., Inc., 1980.

Tiedt, Pamela and Iris M. Tiedt, *Multicultural Teaching.* Boston: Allyn & Bacon, 1979. See Chapter 3: "Focusing on Language."

Weaver, Constance, *Grammar for Teachers: Perspectives and Definitions.* Urbana, Ill.: National Council of Teachers of English, 1979. Excellent overview.

PART III

Commanding
the Written Language

8

To say that my books were written for children is not exactly true. In one sense they were written for myself, out of happy and unhappy memories and a personal need. But all of them lie in the emotional area that children share with adults. . . . If children like your book they respond for a long time, by thousands of letters. It is this response, this concern and act of friendship, that for me makes the task of writing worth the doing.

Scott O'Dell, *Island of the Blue Dolphins*

WRITING
AS SELF-EXPRESSION
AND COMMUNICATION

Writing is a productive skill, a means of expressing oneself and communicating to others. An accepting classroom climate makes it possible for children of all ages and abilities to express their ideas, even the most personally revealing. Growing confidence in their ability to handle writing skills enables students to make statements about their beliefs and to argue a position. Writing reflects individual growth and supports the development of self-esteem.

We learn to write by writing. Learning activities provide purposes for writing—lists, questions, journals, stories, letters, reports, poetry. An integrated approach focused on a theme involves students in listening and speaking as they clarify their thinking and leads them directly into reading and writing as they search for information and respond to the literature they encounter. Writing records a child's knowing.

In this chapter we will focus on the teaching of writing as a way of integrating the language arts program. After reading the chapter and working through the activities described, you should be able to:

- describe a sound writing program
- discuss the teaching of the mechanics (conventions) of writing in the context of composition
- explain various methods for engaging students in writing both narrative and expository prose
- compare different ways of grading and evaluating student writing

TALKING ABOUT WRITING

Concern about improving student writing ability has led to a nationwide effort to clarify goals and objectives for writing programs and to provide staff development for teachers who have not learned how to teach writing effectively. This section of the chapter examines the assumptions underlying a strong writing program and outlines the sequential development of writing ability.

Establishing Goals for Writing Instruction

In developing a writing curriculum, basic understandings of the writing process determine decisions about the methods and materials used to teach composition. The following assumptions drawn from research and teacher experience provide the basis for establishing goals for writing instruction:

1. *Students learn to write by writing.* Students need to write frequently; teachers cannot "correct" or even read everything their students write on this basis. Alternative and more effective ways of improving student writing, for example, peer editing, should be used.
2. *Students need to develop oral language fluency before they can be expected to write.* Oral language activities such as reading aloud by teachers should become an integral part of the writing/reading program. Writing activities should always be preceded by oral warm-up discussion, and students should be encouraged to "speak a sentence" before writing.
3. *Students need to feel successful if they are to continue trying to write.* Positive evaluation will encourage student efforts and teachers should be as helpful as possible,

for example, writing words on the chalkboard during a prewriting discussion or brainstorming session.

4. *Writing is the most difficult of the language arts.* Beginning tasks should be short and they should be planned so that every student can succeed.

5. *Writing is an individualized process.* Students responding to the same stimulus will select different aspects of the subject about which to write, and they will write according to their individual abilities. Their achievement should be measured accordingly.

6. *Writing cannot be taught in isolation.* Ability to write is supported by development in listening, speaking, and reading skills. Writing should always be related to the other language skills, including thinking.

7. *Students need to write for audiences other than teachers.* Sharing in small groups with their peers should always be scheduled as part of the writing lesson. This approach facilitates editing. Peer evaluation is more effective than teacher evaluation in motivating students to improve their writing.

8. *The writing process is a continuum that begins in the preschool years and continues into adulthood.* Young writers are not expected to produce publishable literature. Rather, writing should be seen as a means for personal growth and the communication of ideas with other students. Student writing is a first draft that should not be graded. Periodically, however, students should be given a purpose for revising their writing and making it public.[1]

Goals for a strong writing program should reflect these assumptions. Goals must be realistic, and they must recognize students' varying abilities and interests. Motivation, instruction, and evaluation should demonstrate the teacher's awareness of sound theory. Basic goals for writing instruction can be stated thus:

STUDENTS WILL—

Write frequently to express and record ideas.
Observe the relationship between speaking and writing.
Use literature models to extend writing abilities.
Write for varied purposes and to varied audiences.
Experiment with varied genres and content.
Learn how to use the conventions of writing.
Edit their own work and that of others.
Enjoy and take pride in their writing.

Specific instructional practices enable the teacher to move toward achieving one or more of these goals. Reading aloud to students, for example, helps them recognize the relationship between the spoken word and writing as well as providing models that can be emulated. Responding to literature involves students with varied content and may suggest writing different genres such as a personal essay, poetry, or a short play. The effective teacher can incorporate most of these goals in any planned writing experience as students move through the stages of prewriting, writing, and editing.

[1]Iris M. Tiedt, "A Model for Teaching Writing Holistically," *California English*, May/June 1980, pp. 8–9.

Sequential Development in Writing

One of the problems in the English curriculum is the need for established sequences of learning based on the needs and abilities of children as well as on the nature of the content to be introduced. The following experiences could be included in a developmental sequence in composition.

PRIMARY (KG, 1–2)

Storytelling and dramatization
Dictation of stories—individually and as groups
Extension of vocabulary, experimental backgrounds
Writing of sentences and phrases, paragraph stories
Introduction to four basic sentence patterns and noun and verb classes
Experiments in expanding patterns through compounding and modification
Composing poetry—free verse, couplet, triplet, cinquain
Increased awareness of words through word play, discovery, experimenting
Skills of punctuation—period, question mark
Spelling integrated with composition and reading

INTERMEDIATE (3, 4, 5,)

Many experiments in writing for varied purposes
Poetry—free verse, haiku, limerick, quatrain
Review and extension of basic sentence patterns
Expanding through compounding, modification, and subordination
Identification of word classes—noun, verb, adjective, adverb
Introduction to the function words and their uses
Vocabulary development, use of dictionary, synonyms, connotation
Use of literary models in writing
Focus on writing the sentence and paragraph
Developing concepts of imagery—simile, metaphor
Word study—homonyms, synonyms, antonyms, heteronyms, affixes
Word play to extend vocabulary development, word usage
Writing skills emphasized in all subject areas
Beginning research techniques—outlining, note taking, library tools
Punctuation skills—comma, quotation marks

ADVANCED (6, 7, 8)

Increased coordination of composition and literature study
Writing the short story—beginning, setting, dialogue, characterization
Writing of nonfiction—articles, reviews, reports
Continued use of expansion techniques with basic sentence patterns—compounding, subordination, modification, apposition
Review of word classes and function words
Poetry appreciation and composition—free verse, quatrain, ballad, triplet, invented forms
Study of imagery in writing—simile, metaphor, symbolism
Use of irony, satire, personification, alliteration, onomatopoeia
Experiments with words—word play, use of thesaurus, discovery
Advanced research techniques—library tools, bibliography, conducting a short research study, writing a report
Punctuation marks—colon, comma, semicolon, quotation marks

Beginning writers at all levels need supportive activities. Oral prewriting activities help students sort out their thoughts and warm up to the topic. Students prepare for writing through discussion, brainstorming, and group composing of a model that students will try individually. Teachers of the primary grades often feel that writing has little to offer them. It is surprising, however, how much can be accomplished.

During kindergarten and the beginning months of first grade, writing activities can be oral, for oral language leads directly to written language. The activities described in this chapter for motivating writing can be adapted to oral approaches as children learn to think, and *writing readiness* is developed. A good atmosphere for writing is created naturally as children learn language skills. Beginning writers will benefit from the following kinds of activities.

Dictation   An activity which lends itself to language development is the dictated sentence, story, or poem which can be handled in a number of different ways. One way to begin is to encourage students to share personal experiences. One morning, for instance, children may contribute ideas like these which the teacher prints directly on the chalkboard or on a large sheet of tagboard mounted on an easel:

Today is Tuesday, November 11 . . .
Julie has a new baby brother, David.
Steve lost a tooth this morning.
Jill is wearing her birthday dress today.

What are the advantages of this type of group dictation? The children are learning to use words to express ideas. They are learning to make simple sentences, and they are becoming oriented to words in print reading from left to right. As the teacher prints their sentences, they soon notice, too, the use of capital letters and marks of punctuation.

Later children learn to copy and to read this type of group dictation. After the class has taken a field trip to the fire station, the experience might read like this:

Yesterday we went to the fire station.
The fire station is close to our school.
We saw the hook and ladder wagon.
We saw the firemen's dog, Flame.
We heard the fire bell ring.

Another variety of group dictation is the short story or poem which the group composes orally. The teacher records this story as it develops sentence by sentence. You might begin by asking the class what animal they would like to write about, and someone might suggest a cat or dog, or sometimes there is a more adventurous suggestion of a tiger, an elephant, or a bear. The teacher's conversation with the class, as they prepare to "write," might proceed thus:

All right, we will write a story about a dog. I'll need your help. Are you all ready to write with me? (They will nod enthusiastically or answer aloud.) Now what shall we name this dog? (Jock) Good, Jock's a fine name for a dog. Let's imagine what Jock looks like, so we all have a picture in our minds of the dog in our story. What color is Jock? (black) How big is he? (About two feet high and a yard long demonstrated by a volunteer.)

Can you all picture Jock now—a black dog, about so big . . . ? What is Jock doing today? (Jock is playing with a little girl, Susan.) Fine, that's a good place to begin our story. Who would like to make the first sentence? (One day Jock was playing with Susan.) What might happen next?

So the story grows with the help and encouragement of the teacher who sees that each student gets a chance to participate in some way. The story is then typed for inclusion in the class storybook, or it may be printed with a felt pen on a large sheet for use in reading activities.

A variation of group dictation is individual dictation, which is an excellent device but requires more teacher time or the assistance of a parent, or an older child. Each student is given an opportunity to sit on the story chair beside a primary typewriter. Ed tells his story while the typist records it. Individually dictated stories can be duplicated for use as reading material, or they may be stapled in book form with an attractive cover decorated by the author. Eddie is eager to read his story to his parents, and because he *wrote* the story himself, he reads it easily. This activity aids in developing orientation to the format of the book, left-to-right movement of reading and writing, and adds to the individual's feeling of personal potency. *He* can tell a story which is important enough to be typed, to be recorded, so that all can read it.

A modification of this idea is the use of the cassette tape recorder. Stories can be dictated into the recorder, and transcribed at a later date. Dictation benefits any student who needs additional support in beginning to write and read.

Writing independently   As soon as students learn the rudiments of printing, they are intrigued by printing words, many of which they soon learn to spell. Very quickly they can compose a sentence or two expressing the ideas which they have depicted in a painting. They can also compose several sentences based on a topic introduced on the chalkboard by the teacher such as these:

* What do you do on *Sunday?*
  Students are directed to begin the first sentence thus:
  On Sunday I . . .
     go to the park.
     visit my grandmother.
     go shopping.
     play ball.
* What do you *like* best *to play?* (I like to play . . .)
* What *is* your *favorite food?* (My favorite food is . . .)

Help can be given with spelling by printing requested words on the chalkboard or on the student's paper, although many teachers prefer to encourage spelling by sound so that writing is not inhibited by the need to make every word letter-perfect. There is little doubt that concern with spelling slows the child in recording ideas; spelling will improve as children add to their knowledge of words.

Once students have learned a simple writing vocabulary, they are ready to write creatively, for writing is an area that allows each child to progress and to produce at his or her own level of ability. The more able child may write six good sentences, while a slow child writes only one simple idea. Each is progressing, however, and can continue to progress through adulthood.

Rethinking the Teaching of Writing

The teacher's attitude toward writing influences how writing is taught in the classroom. A teacher who is enthusiastic about language and is responsive to student efforts will have students who enjoy writing, students who produce interesting compositions. Evidence that writing is important in that classroom will be noticeable to the person entering the room for the first time.

The effective teacher of writing knows how to:

1. Teach students to edit their own work rather than doing it for them
2. Put grammar and usage instruction in proper perspective so they do not interfere with the writing process
3. Use evaluation techniques as part of the learning process and not as a punitive measure

These three understandings remove obstacles that hinder the teaching of writing and have caused students to dislike their English classes.

Editing as part of the writing process   Many teachers have avoided teaching writing because they dreaded correcting stacks of student papers. The solution is to teach students to edit their own papers, for editing is part of the writing process.

Editing is more than proofreading or correcting spelling and punctuation errors. It includes revision, rewriting, and final proofreading. Since not all student papers will be made public (published), not all of the compositions that students write need to be edited. That fact reduces the paperload and makes the task much more realistic. The student who writes daily selects a composition periodically that he or she wants to edit. This gives purpose to the process. Editing may consist of self-editing, peer-editing, or teacher-student editing.

Self-editing involves the student in reading his or her own writing to see if communication is clear. All students should be taught to begin the editing task by reading the selection aloud quietly to answer such questions as:

Does each sentence sound like an English sentence? (grammar, idiom)
Does the writing flow? (sentence variety, transition)
Have I used dead language? (there is, are; some; get; nice)

Have students compose a checklist of specific questions that will help them catch fragments and run-on sentences, vague phrases, or repetition. Self-editing may involve crossing out words, phrases, or whole sentences. Revision means "seeing again"; the first draft should be reworked with visible changes. When students turn in a completely edited paper, ask them to include each draft or revision.

The second draft might receive peer editing as students work in pairs or small groups of three to five. Students should talk about the qualities that make some writing more effective than others. Even the young writer can discuss the characteristics of a good story. These characteristics then serve as guidelines for the editor as well as for the writer who produced the work. They can examine the work of a peer to see if the writer has:

Included dialogue between characters
Answered the questions: who, when, where, what, why?
Written a beginning, middle and end to the story

Elementary students can list specific aspects of writing that they want to achieve or avoid. Sixth or seventh graders who have been exposed to this approach to writing instruction could list the following:

What are we trying to achieve?
  Writing that indicates thought
  Use of exciting words which create effects
  Completeness, conciseness, and clarity
  Variety of content, words, sentence patterns
What are we trying to avoid?
  Passive, inactive verbs
  Overworked phrases, clichés
  Misplaced modifiers
  Wordiness, repetition
  Vague references
  Sweeping generalizations

Introduction of the terminology of composition gives the young writer a vocabulary with which to discuss writing. Note, too, that the skills and concepts of composition discussed here represent ways of thinking as well as of writing. Students can be exposed to these concepts at their levels of ability.

I can't write five words but that I change seven.

Dorothy Parker

The teacher and students can also work together during the editing process. Projecting selected papers (with student names removed) on the overhead projector enables the whole class to examine a piece of writing as they discuss the strong qualities of the writing and then suggest ways of improving paragraph development, sentence structure, or word choices. Working together in this manner teaches students how to respond to a piece of writing. All kinds of writing problems can be presented in the context of real students' original compositions.

The teacher can also work with individual students in the role of consulting editor through student-teacher conferences. While students are writing independently, individuals are called to a table where the teacher reviews their writing with them and suggests areas for improvement. It is much easier to explain orally the suggestions about sentence structure or the development of a character, and the teacher can make sure the student understands by having her or him make the changes orally. Individual attention is also rewarding to the student. The conference offers teachers a way of getting better acquainted with more reticent students.

One or two conferences can be scheduled each day so that each student has about one individual conference per month. Since writing is so individualized, students may be working on different projects as they complete specific writing experiments. They should be permitted to select the writing to discuss with the teacher. If, each week, the conference schedule for the coming week is announced, students will have time to complete or prepare a selection for examination.

Proofreading is a special aspect of the editing process that occurs when writing is prepared for publication. "Reading proof" involves an editor in checking writing that has been typeset (in the student's case, carefully written or typed). Proofreader's marks are used to tell the typesetter which corrections to make before the work is published. Proofreading is often inaccurately used in classrooms as part of the revision of a student's first draft. Editing of the first draft should be more comprehensive following the revision procedures just described, while proofreading is reserved for the final check for incorrect spelling, accurate use of punctuation, or omitted words, before the writing is made public on the bulletin board, in a newsletter that is going home, or in the school writing magazine.

Teaching students how to edit their work teaches them how to write. It is an integral part of the writing process that is often ignored. Although only a few of each student's writings will be fully revised and published, providing a purpose for fully editing a selection periodically can help students mature in their writing abilities.

Grammar in the context of composition   For many teachers grammar instruction is synonymous with teaching writing. This misperception causes teachers to focus on identifying word functions and sentence parts rather than using valuable student time for writing. Students use grammar intuitively as they speak sentences and then write them, but they do not have to be able to define terms or to label the parts of speech. As students mature in their writing ability, they will benefit from such practices as sentence expansion or sentence combining.

Many educators have mistakenly conceived of the teaching of grammar as consisting of drill along these lines:

Choose the right word:
  Gwen has (gone—went) to school.
  Where have Billy and Brian (gone—went)?
  They (gone—went) home already.

Sentences of this nature emphasize specific points of usage (not grammar), and there remains much doubt about the transfer of the supposedly acquired knowledge to writing or to speaking.

How do we learn usage and grammar? We learn through our ears, and it may be that certain usage patterns which "sound right" to us may not "sound right" to others because of exposure to different language backgrounds. This is an example of levels of usage and the acceptability of specific usage in varied situations.

As outlined in Chapter 7 children can learn to recognize basic sentence patterns and to identify word classes. This information, however interesting, does little to increase writing fluency.

Writing is learned by using words to communicate ideas. The expansion of basic sentence patterns through modification, compounding, subordination, and apposition enables more mature, varied ways of expressing ideas to be developed. The following example shows the simplest of patterns, containing only a noun and a verb, expanded as noted.

Karen swam. (Pattern I, N–V)
Karen *swam and sunbathed.* (Compounding)
Karen swam and sunbathed *at the beach.* (Modification)
Karen, *the tall girl,* swam and sunbathed at the beach. (Apposition)
When she was on vacation, Karen, the tall girl, swam and sunbathed at the beach. (Subordination)

The development of writing ability which can be assisted through practice of this nature has little to do with identification of word classes. It is not necessary that children know that they are *compounding the predicate* when they use two verbs, "swam and sunbathed." We can just as effectively extend an idea being expressed by asking pertinent questions, thus:

What else did Karen do besides *swim?*
Where did she swim and sunbathe?
How can we describe Karen?
When did she swim?

The student learns to extend ideas, not just add *a prepositional phrase, a clause,* or *an apposition,* for we are concerned with communicating ideas rather than with the terminology of these structural features.

A second approach to sentence development that has been found helpful for younger writers is the sentence-combining exercise. Projecting such exercises as the following on an overhead projector facilitates discussion of this technique:

1. Mary read a book.
    The book was 210 pages long. (THAT)
    Combined: Mary read a book that
    was 210 pages long.
2. The police caught the thief.
    The thief robbed a bank. (WHO)
    Combined: The police caught the thief
    who robbed a bank.
3. The boys are selling greeting cards.
    The boys are *busy*.
    The cards are for *Christmas*.
    Combined: The busy boys are selling
    Christmas greeting cards.
4. The sheep ate grass.
    There were *six* sheep.
    The sheep were *wooly*.
    The sheep were *black*.
    Combined: The six wooly black sheep
    ate grass.

Sentence-combining or expansion activities indicate how to avoid short, choppy sentences. Discussing writing styles exemplified by excellent writers (for example, in *The Slave Dancer* by Paula Fox) also demonstrates how the writer manipulates the structure of sentences. This approach to the study of grammar has real meaning for the student who is involved in writing.

Evaluating student writing Evaluation is a broader term than "grading." Evaluating a student's writing means establishing its value or worth, and all writing has value. It is important to share an appreciation of what is valuable in each student's writing and to assist him or her in increasing the value of that selection. Grading, on the other hand, ranks work in comparison with other student writing, according to criteria that are often unclear and subjective. Evaluation processes, rather than grading, should be stressed in learning to write.

Methods of guiding and evaluating writing must reflect the philosophy stated in our objectives of teaching children. Student endeavors should not be discouraged by authoritarian approaches to evaluation. (This is not to say that student writing is never to be reworked.) The teacher cannot tear a story to shreds and retain the student's sense of personal worth or an atmosphere conducive to free expression. Strickland[2] emphasizes the importance of security, interest, and constructive attitudes for the young writer. She terms the grading of papers and assigning of marks as inap-

---

[2]Ruth Strickland, "The Language of Elementary School Children," *Bulletin of the School of Education,* Indiana University, July 1962, pp. 1–131.

propriate for beginning stages of language development. It is for these reasons that we recommend the following general rules:

Praise sincerely in public.
Make corrections and suggestions in private.

Many teachers feel that they must read everything that a student writes (and some school districts enforce this approach). If students write every day in school and at home, it is impossible for the teacher to mark every error. This task alone may have accounted for the failure to encourage students to write daily.

The answer is obvious although not always acceptable to teachers who resist changes in philosophy. The teacher *should make no attempt to read everything the students write.* Maize's study[3] of remedial students points up the validity of this approach.

Reading only representative selections each week has proved just as effective in guiding development. All writing can be placed in the student's writing folder, and one day each week designated for reviewing a selection chosen and edited by the student.

Evaluation should be formative as well as summative. Peer evaluation or editing is formative in that it is part of the developmental learning process. Teacher conferences offer opportunities for formative evaluation that is aimed at shaping the student's growth, supporting efforts through positive reinforcement, suggesting development. Summative evaluation can take the form of publishing student work.

Two forms of evaluation are widely used for the assessment of student writing abilities: holistic and analytic. In each case a writing sample is taken for a group of students, a class, a school, or a whole school district. Holistic assessment is a quick way of determining which students fall below a minimum proficiency level and should, therefore, have beginning-level instruction in writing. Holistic assessment also determines the ranking of students using a scale of 1–4 or 1–9 points and a set of predetermined criteria or standards (sometimes called a rubric). Analytic assessment takes much more time per paper, but it provides specific information about an individual writer's ability to handle language and is therefore an excellent diagnostic tool and a guide for instruction.

Pretesting a group of students before beginning instruction in the fall and post-testing at the end of the year provides feedback about the effectiveness of instruction. Conducting a holistic assessment is efficient and is recommended for large groups:

1. Select a topic or stimulus (sometimes called a "prompt"). The topic must be of general interest so that all students can respond to it. It should also be simple and straightforward so that students are not penalized because they don't cover the topic assigned. Two useful writing topics are:

[3]Ray C. Maize, "A Study of Two Methods of Teaching English Composition to Retarded College Freshmen," Ph.D. dissertation, Purdue University, 1952

     a. If you could be any animal that you want, which animal would you choose? Explain why you chose that animal.

     b. Think about a friend or relative who is really important to you. Describe this person.

2. Select a writing day so that all students write on the same day. Specific instructions about introducing the topic, amount of time for discussion, and amount of time for writing must be agreed on if more than one teacher is participating in the assessment. Instructions usually include:

     a. Discussion and brainstorming orally for 20 minutes before writing

     b. Writing for 30 minutes with no assistance from the teacher. (The topic should be printed on a sheet as well as read aloud.)

     c. Collection of student papers immediately by a designated person to be held until a scoring date. Student papers are identified by a code number; e.g., telephone number

3. Holistic assessment by teachers can be conducted on any day when teachers are free, for example, Saturday or a released day. All teachers whose students participate in the assessment should serve as readers for scoring papers, but teachers should not read the papers of their own students. A training session precedes the reading of papers. Teachers will be amazed to see how closely their assessments of papers matches that of other teachers on the team. Each paper is read quickly as a whole and given a score based on established performance criteria. At least two persons read each paper, scoring it independently. The following set of criteria was prepared for use with personal narrative written by students in grades 5–12:

Holistic Scoring Criteria

Use of this rubric assumes that writing samples will be read by at least two readers and that papers will be read as a whole without analysis. Even numbers may be used when papers seem to fall between the scores listed here.

SCORE	CHARACTERISTICS OF THE WRITING

---

1   The writer lacks understanding of the topic.
      a. Little communication with the reader
      b. Confused sense of audience
      c. General lack of coherence or evidence of purpose
      d. Weak grasp of spelling, punctuation, and syntax
      e. No sense of paragraphing

3   The writer understands the topic and writes relatively clearly.
      a. Lacks singleness of purpose
      b. Contains some irrelevancies
      c. Some attempt at organizing the materials coherently
      d. Some knowledge of spelling, punctuation, and syntax
      e. Frequent mechanical errors

5   The writer presents a fairly competent discussion of the topic.
      a. Uses examples and/or details
      b. Reasonably clear purpose
      c. Evidence of adequate organization with few irrelevancies
      d. Some attempt at paragraphing
      e. A clear sense of conclusion
      f. Occasional mechanical errors do not interfere with clarity
      g. Syntax generally adequate with some fragments or run-ons

7   The writer presents a full discussion of the topic with well-chosen examples and details for support.
      a. Some elaboration and refinement of ideas

Holistic Scoring Criteria (Cont.)

SCORE	CHARACTERISTICS OF THE WRITING
	b. A clear beginning, middle, and end
	c. A clear sense of purpose and audience
	d. Generally competent mechanically
	e. Few run-ons or fragments
	f. Some variety in sentence structure
9	The writer presents unusually complete and/or imaginative development of the topic.
	a. Striking use of evidence, examples, details, or reasoning
	b. Tightly or imaginatively organized with an effective opening and conclusion
	c. Clear sense of writer control of voice, purpose, and audience
	d. Mature sense of sentence structure
	e. Free from mechanical errors

Iris M. Tiedt (San Jose State University: South Bay Writing Project, 1980).

Assessment scores are recorded so that comparisons can be made at the end of the instruction period. This efficient method provides a benchmark with which to compare student writing at any time. A set of coded papers for your classroom is valuable, too, in conferring with parents. You can show parents how students write at this stage of development and how the writing of their child compares with that of others in the class.

Analytical scoring of the same set of papers may be helpful to diagnose an individual student's writing problems and indicate the kind of instruction needed. Papers should be read by a knowledgeable person who can identify the kinds of miscues made in the student's writing. A checklist like the following is needed:

The Tiedt Analytical Checklist for Composition

This test of writing abilities is designed to be used in conjunction with the collection of a writing sample. It is intended to be used as a guide to instruction for individual students.

AREA A: FLUENCY (EASE)
1. Handwriting   10   5   0
     (clear) (legible) (illegible)
       —
2. Total number of words written   —
3. Total number of sentences indicated   —

AREA B: FLEXIBILITY (VARIETY)
4. Average length of S/P units (in 1st ten lines)   —
5. Number of complex/compound sentence patterns (anything other than simple sentence)   —

AREA C: ELABORATION (DETAIL)
6. Number of adjectives/adjectival constructions   —
7. Number of adverbs/adverbial constructions   —
8. Number of figures of speech   —

AREA D: ORIGINALITY (UNIQUENESS)
9. Number of unique images used   —
10. Comparative imaginative quality
     10   5   0
     (unique) (ordinary) (dull)   —

AREA E: FORM (STRUCTURE)
11. Organization
     10   5
     (intro & conclusion) (1 missing)
          0
         (neither)   —
12. Paragraphing
     10   5   0
     (well handled) (adequate) (poor)   —
13. Title
     5   0
     (present) (not present)   —

AREA F: WRITING CONVENTIONS (MECHANICS)				SCORING TABULATION		
					Raw Score	Percentile
14. Spelling				1.	_____	_____
10	5	0		2.	_____	_____
(0 errors)	(few)	(many)	_____	3.	_____	_____
15. Punctuation				4.	_____	_____
10	5	0		5.	_____	_____
(0 errors)	(few)	(many)	_____	6.	_____	_____
16. Capitalization				7.	_____	_____
10	5	0		8.	_____	_____
(0 errors)	(few)	(many)	_____	9.	_____	_____
17. Usage (word choice)				10.	_____	_____
10	5	0		11.	_____	_____
(0 errors)	(few)	(many)	_____	12.	_____	_____
18. Grammar (syntax)				13.	_____	_____
10	5	0		14.	_____	_____
(0 errors)	(few)	(many)	_____	15.	_____	_____
				16.	_____	_____
				17.	_____	_____
				18.	_____	_____

Teaching writing is more than just assigning a topic and letting students write. The effective teacher of writing assumes responsibility for motivating, planning writing experiences, developing rapport with the group to facilitate editing and evaluation, extending experiential backgrounds to supply content for writing activities, and perhaps most important, appreciating the results of student efforts. In the next section we will explore ways of involving students in writing.

PLANNING FOR WRITING

Planning for writing experiences is essential if this part of the language arts program is to be effectively carried out. Without careful attention to planning it is easy to lose sight of long-range goals. We shall examine three aspects of planning for writing which frequently perplex the teacher: (1) time for writing, (2) sources of new ideas, and (3) lesson plans.

Time for Writing

One of the aims of the writing program is frequent opportunity to write, but classroom teachers sometimes complain that they do not have any time for writing. Admittedly the elementary school schedule is a crowded one, but writing can be included without excluding other subjects.

1. Scheduled writing periods
   Example: Several thirty- to forty-five-minute periods are scheduled each week for introducing new writing tasks. This amount of time is usually allotted by the course of study.

177

2.   Relating writing to other subjects

Example: Writing an adventure set in Brazil which utilizes knowledge of the geography and history of that country; writing a diary of a founding father or an early pioneer.

3.   Writing before school

Example: Designate the five or ten minutes before the bell rings as the writers' workshop, when each student writes a daily entry in his or her personal journal.

4.   Writing at home.

Example: Encourage able students to continue writing activities at home. Writing done at home is placed in the writing folder and can be the subject of an individual conference.

5.   Writing clubs meeting after school

Example: Those students who are especially interested in writing can form a club called PEN POINTERS or WRITERS, INC. They can meet once or twice a week to write, discuss their writing, or learn about writing. With a chairman, the club can be student-managed.

6.   Writing when other work is completed

Example: Writing is an excellent individualized activity which can be pursued independently by a student who has completed assigned work. The student can get a writing folder at any time. Tom might, for example, be publishing a collection of poems at the publishing center at the back of the room.

"Imagination is like any muscle, it improves with use."

William Faulkner

Creating a Climate for Writing

The classroom should provide an atmosphere conducive to writing freely without fear of criticism. Two components are vital to the success of this concept: teacher attitude and student attitude.

If we truly value writing as a means to learning and self-expression, we must operate on the theory that there is *worth in the writing of every child.*

As a teacher, what would be your comment after reading the following short composition written by a second-grade girl?

Judy

My dog is blak.
He is a good dog.
We play ball after
skool.

Judy was eager to share this story with "Teacher," who would surely like it. Her teacher might have made any number of remarks:

1. "Your story is not very long. Why not add more to it?"
2. "I see two words that are misspelled. See if you can find them."
3. "Why, Judy, I didn't know you had a dog. I'd like to hear more about him."

The first two statements are certainly justifiable and are not unkind, but the third would be made by a teacher who understood, a teacher who was concerned for the development of a child. The focus remains on the child and her ideas, not on her mistakes, and carries a warmth and interest in the child as well as the writing. The use of the student's name is also an excellent device for adding to her security in the classroom situation. The teacher's desire to know more about Judy's dog suggests that Judy write more while at the same time approving subject matter which is familiar to the child. This type of enthusiasm and understanding stimulates the child to write freely.

In order for children to write effectively, creatively, they must feel *a sense of freedom*. By freedom we do not, however, mean license. Robert Frost defined this type of freedom as: "feeling easy in the harness." The child functions well in the harness, in this case the controlled situation of the classroom, but also needs a feeling of being at ease, of being free to experiment with language, of daring to disagree or to try something different. The student must know that originality or difference will not be ridiculed by peers.

There should also be some assurance that intimate emotional revelations will not be tacked on the bulletin board for all to read. Some teachers tell students early in the year that anything they write which is not for reading aloud may be marked NOT TO BE READ or PERSONAL. A child's writing folder can be clearly designated as Personal Property, with the understanding that no writing *has* to be shown to anyone else, even to the teacher.

The writing center can add to the importance of writing, encouraging writing and providing a place where students can work undisturbed and undisturbing. Equipment and materials which add to the writing center are:

Table and chairs to accommodate about six students
Paper supplies, pencils, erasers
Dictionaries suitable to grade level
File of individual writing folders
Typewriter (a motivating addition if available)

Sometimes the writing center becomes a publishing center. The student is encouraged not only to write but also to publish work in simple form with an attractive cover. The publication may consist of a leaflet with appropriate illustrations by the author. The more ambitious, prolific author may produce a book which can be properly stitched and bound. Publishing lends an additional note of value to the writing of each child. Published works of individual children make excellent gifts for parents and provide a good way to let the public know what the school is doing.

Writing must be *an integral part of the child's learning activities*. A regularly scheduled daily writing period provides time for the development of language abilities. A student who completes assigned writing tasks is then free to develop any writing project in the writing folder, which may include the following:

A story that the student wants to develop from a previous writing period
A topic which has been noted for exploring
A long story or book written independently
Checking definitions for words accumulated in a class word book
Revising a selection to discuss during individual conferences
Preparing a final draft of writing to be published or displayed

Prewriting Warm-up

There is little likelihood that students will be stimulated to write interesting, creative stories if the teacher passes each student a clean sheet of composition paper and says, "Now I want each of you to write an interesting story." The situation will be little remedied even if you state, "I want each of you to write an interesting story about a cat."

The writing experience can, however, be rescued if the teacher allots just a few minutes for warming up before the students have a sheet of paper before them. Using the suggested topic of cats, the teacher might begin something like this:

"How many of you have a cat at your house? What kind of cat do you have, John?" (Students name the species, color, size of their house pets.)

"Are there other types of cats than those which have already been described?" (She elicits the naming of wild animals in the cat family—tiger, lion, jaguar—which are listed on the board as named.)

"Where would you see cats like these?" (Jungle, circus, zoo—pictures can be shown.)

By beginning the writing period with this type of discussion, students become involved with the topic. Each one has begun to think of some sort of cat in a specific situation. A wide variety of possibilities have been opened up by the discussion. Each child is ready when the teacher continues:

"Today I want each of you to write a description of a cat, any kind of cat that interests you. While I pass paper to you, you can begin thinking of the cat you will describe. Where is this cat? What does it look like? What is its name? What is it doing? Is it with a human being or another animal?"

Some of the resulting descriptions may be incorporated in stories. They may be about the common feline, but others will describe leopards, panthers, or Bengal tigers. Some will be based on real experiences whereas other young authors may stretch their imaginations as they track the jungles of Kenya or sail down the Ganges. At any rate each student will produce a story, long or short, which can be included in a class book of CAT TALES.

Another important aspect of preparing for writing is the *development of the student's self-image as a writer*. It is infrequent that the home environment provides students with the image of themselves as writers, for parents may regard any type of writing as an undesirable task. Although it is true that the objective in teaching students to write is not that they produce writing of commercial quality, we wish to promote the concept that writing, like reading, is a desirable occupation whether one earns a living through writing or merely writes for personal enjoyment.

One good method for strengthening the desirability of writing is the knowledge that the teacher writes. Students are greatly impressed if Mr. West can share personal writing experiences of any nature with the class; they will respect him not only as a teacher but also as a writer who really knows what writing is all about. Teachers should also write with students frequently and share their writing, too.

Another effective device is to acquaint students with published authors. Local authors can be invited to visit the school to talk with the class about writing; or books and films can be found which tell about an author's view of writing. In *Writers at Work,* edited by Malcolm Cowley (Viking), Joyce Cary, Dorothy Parker, James Thurber, William Faulkner, and many other authors describe their writing experiences and their feelings toward writing. Biographical information and pictures are included, as well as a sample sheet of manuscript with the writer's corrections and changes.

Even the young child will be interested in hearing Frank O'Connor, who recommends, "Get black on white . . . I don't give a hoot what the writing's like. I write any sort of rubbish which will cover the main outlines of the story, then I can begin to see it."[4] It would be interesting to play O'Connor's recording of one of his best stories, "My Oedipus Complex" (Caedmon, TC 1036) which appeals to both child and adult. His pleasant Irish voice reads the humorous story of five-year-old Larry, who resents the return of his father from war.

You might locate copies of the following books about writing and writers for the elementary school student:

Books Are by People and *More Books by More People.* Edited by Lee Bennett Hopkins. Citation, 1969; 1974.
You Can Be a Writer: A Career and Leisure Guide by Clifford L. Alderman. Messner, 1981.
Gifts of Writing by Susan and Stephen Judy. Oxford, 1981.

Lesson Plans for Writing

The lesson is sure to be more effective if the teacher is certain of the motivational device to be used, the method for its introduction, and follow-up activities. It is also helpful if suggestions are noted after the activity has been completed. A simple lesson plan form like the one illustrated for Traveling Tales provides the necessary guidelines for a successful writing activity. This form aids the teacher in thinking through the activity from start to finish, clarifying the development of the teaching technique.

---

[4]Malcolm Cowley, ed., *Writers at Work* (New York: Viking Press, Inc., 1964), p. 167.

LESSON PLAN FOR CREATIVE WRITING

Title: *Traveling Tales*

Time: *45 minutes*

Technique:

Questions:
"Have you ever traveled?"
"Have you ever heard of a Traveling Tale?"
"What does this kind of tale mean?" (write on board)
"What would a traveling tale be?"

Directions:
Today we are going to write Traveling Tales, stories that move from place to place. Each one of us is going to begin a story. When I say TRAVEL TIME, you will pass your story to the person behind you. Then each of you will read what is on the paper and add what you think would happen next. We'll have our stories travel several times so that each of you will work on several different stories. Then we'll read the stories to see how they grew as they traveled.

Tips:
Stop writing soon enough so a number of students can read their tales.
At each passing allow enough time for passing as well as for writing.
Each child can finish one of the stories next day.
Compile stories in a book Traveling Tales

Notice that the activity has been given a title. Students respond more readily to an activity which bears an intriguing name. Students may apply an apt name to the activity which can be adopted for future use.

The amount of time required for this activity may appear to be too long. Experience will prove, however, that an effective warm-up period requires perhaps ten minutes, that students need about twenty minutes to write using this technique, and that fifteen minutes is not too long a time to allow for reading some of the results. Other activities may not require as long a period of time; certainly forty-five minutes will usually be the longest writing period needed. The second day of this activity, for example, does not require as much motivation because students do not have to read new material as it is passed to them. Thirty minutes would suffice. With practice, the teacher will be better able to judge the amount of time required for varied activities.

Under the heading "Procedures" should be included the exact words that will be said to the class as the writing project is introduced. You may begin with a question, by showing the class an object of interest, writing something on the board, or pinning words or a picture on the bulletin board. The objective of the introductory procedures is to immediately arouse the interest of the class.

In asking "Have you ever traveled?" the teacher is sure to get a positive response that will involve the entire class. "Have you ever heard of a Traveling Tale?" may mystify the class of third graders. The teacher may then write the word *tale* on the board, asking someone to identify the homonym *tale* as a story, leading them to identify a traveling tale as a "story which moves around or goes from place to place." The teacher can then read the directions.

If the children have not written much before this experience, they may be assisted in getting started by supplying one or two first lines which can be used by anyone who needs help:

I ran happily down the beach, but stopped suddenly when I saw . . .
It was eleven o'clock one evening when the telephone rang.

Sufficient time is allowed for the children to write a few sentences before calling "travel time." If you walk around the room during the writing period, you can easily ascertain when most students have written enough. The time allowed must be progressively longer, for the growing story requires more time to read. Time must also be allotted for some of the stories to be read aloud before the writing project is put aside for the day. The reading of these efforts shows the class the wide variety of possibilities for developing stories. It also points up the value placed on their work as all enjoy it together. (If one child from each row or group is called to read, probably something written by almost every child will be read.)

On the following day each child may be given one of the partially completed stories with the instructions to read the story, make any changes desired, and complete it. Again some stories can be read. The entire group of stories can be compiled (by one or two students) in a book entitled TRAVELING TALES. Other students can illustrate the volume. If the stories are especially good, ten to fifteen copies can be made on ditto, collated, and combined by students to create "readers." This set can be given or loaned to other classes later on.

Perhaps the most important single aspect leading to successful writing experiences is the motivation of the student. The child who lacks motivation may find the writing period a chore and a bore, and it is unlikely that the writing will be creative.

There is a great need for research regarding the techniques of motivating writing. Many people question, for instance, whether writing can be motivated effectively. Through questionnaire, interview, and observation in forty elementary schools, Smith compiled a list of ten factors that motivate writing.[5]

1. Providing attractive classrooms rich in materials
2. Encouraging pupils to write from their own interests and needs
3. Providing rich experiences about which children can express themselves
4. Developing sensitivity to good writing, which in turn helps children improve
5. Using real needs and interests of children or helping them to develop new interests
6. Providing freedom from fear and helping pupils gain confidence in their ability to write
7. Providing abundant time and opportunity for writing in many areas and in many forms
8. Developing skill in mechanics without sacrificing spontaneity
9. Sharing the end products of writing
10. Evaluating the writing in terms of the total growth of the child

More recent research on motivation stresses the importance of prewriting experiences, which prepare students to write successfully. Planned activities engage students in thinking and talking together as they brainstorm ideas so they are ready to write. Studies show that the language arts teacher stimulates writing most effectively through (1) creating a climate for writing, (2) providing a warm-up period before writing, and (3) using varied techniques for motivation.[6] In the following section we will describe a number of beginning writing activities.

INVOLVING STUDENTS IN WRITING

The beginning stages of writing are the most important, for it is at this time that student attitudes are established. Students must feel successful from the very first moment they begin writing. Beginning experiences should, therefore, be short activities which all students can participate in according to their varied abilities. Our aim is to move students toward fluency with the written language, a feeling of being at ease with writing much as they are with oral language. Beginning activities may include:

[5]Ethel Smith, *Procedures for Encouraging Creative Writing in the Elementary School,* Ph.D. dissertation, Northwestern University, 1944.

[6]Charles R. Cooper and Lee Odell, eds., *Research on Composition: Points of Departure* (Urbana, Ill.: National Council of Teachers of English, 1978).

Listing
Copying
Transcribing
Taking dictation
Completing patterns
Recording observations

A Potpourri of Stimuli

Keeping a personal journal is a highly recommended beginning activity as students discover what writing has to offer them. The journal is free writing done for a specific length of time, perhaps ten to fifteen minutes daily over a period of several weeks. Students should keep their journals at school so they are ready to write with the whole class, even the teacher. Journals are not evaluated although teachers usually read them periodically and respond to the content presented. Students need to know that journals are private; if they do not want the teacher to read a particular page, they can simply fold it down. Journal writing encourages students to write about what they know best, themselves. To aid writers who have difficulty thinking of something about which to write, you may wish to suggest a daily topic, for example:

What is your favorite color? What does this color mean to you?
I get angry when . . .
When I grow up, I want to be . . .
The funniest thing that ever happened to me

The other beginning activities described in this section are also designed to stimulate students to write. Representing various kinds of writing, they allow for individual writing abilities.

"An experience isn't finished until it's written."

Ann Morrow Lindbergh

WORDS

A single word or a group of words can provide a stimulus for writing.

- Write the word HAPPINESS on the board, ask the class to identify the word, and question the meaning of this word for them. Each class member then writes on the meaning of happiness. This idea originated with the publication of *Happiness Is a Warm Puppy* by Charles Schulz (San Francisco: Determined Press, 1963), which can be used to stimulate discussion. Other abstract ideas can also be explored in this manner—LIBERTY, LONELINESS, LOVE, TEACHER, SCHOOL, MISERY, SUMMER.
- Write a group of words on the chalkboard or print them on cards around a picture displayed on the bulletin board. The words focus on one theme—*ship, ocean, suitcases, vacation, porthole, exploration, engine trouble*—to motivate student thinking about a possible story.

TITLES

The title (or several titles) can be provided by the teacher or written by the class.

- Ask each student to write two titles at the top of a paper. Each student then passes the paper to another person, or the papers are collected and redistributed. As students receive a paper, they select one of the two titles and write a story based on that title.
- Write three provocative titles on the chalkboard (it is best to use a limited number). Each student may then select one title about which to write. Titles should allow for many possibilities:

Do You Know What I Saw?   What I Like to Do Best
Early in the Morning   It Happened at Six O'Clock
I Couldn't Believe My Eyes!   Was I Embarrassed!

SENTENCES OR PHRASES

Either first or last lines can be suggested by the teachers or students.

- Write a sentence on the board. After a discussion about the possibilities for story material based on that beginning sentence, each student is directed to write the sentence on a paper and to create a story situation. A comparison of results is especially effective when all begin with the same line, for it demonstrates the many approaches to one topic and also the differences in individual thinking.

  When I heard the door open, I turned around quickly.
  What could be the meaning of the words I had just heard?
  "Tell me where it is," he begged.

- The last line for the story can be supplied in the same manner. Each student writes a story so the given line will be an appropriate ending.

  Was I ever relieved to see Mom and Dad!
  I had no desire to enter that house again.
  That was the last time I ever saw the big dog.

PARAGRAPHS

A short paragraph can be the stimulus for the development of a story.

- Duplicate a descriptive setting. Each student then writes a story using that paragraph to set the action.

  It was dark in the woods at eight even though it was July. We walked slowly along the path guided by the light of Jim's flashlight. The tall trees grew thick along the narrow stream, but the path was wide. As we approached a familiar outcropping of rock, we knew we were almost to our camping spot.

STORIES

Stories that are read by students often supply ideas which motivate writing.

- Read aloud a story that is unfamiliar to the class. Stop at a crucial point in the story, asking, "What happened next?" Each student writes a conclusion for that particular story. Student endings can be read and later that of the original author, not to set the author's work as a model, but again to demonstrate differences in thinking. Try these short stories or chapters:

  Lindgren, Astrid. *Pippi Longstocking* (Viking).
  McCloskey, Robert. *Centerburg Tales* (Viking).

- Often students express the desire for a story to continue. After reading a story together, tbe class may write stories based on the same characters telling of further adventures. These adventure stories can be compiled as a class book.
- Students can write their own story starters. These can be put in a box at the writing center, and others can use them for starters.

BOOKS

The ideas and illustrations of books are often highly provocative. Described here are several books that are especially effective in motivating student writing.

- Young children are fascinated by *The Hole* by Cliff Roberts (Watts), which explores the many possibilities of a single shape, the crescent. A large crescent-shaped hole is cut from cover to cover in this book forming part of each illustration—a piece of watermelon, the body of a crane, and so on. Children can expand this idea by drawing pictures based on other given shapes—cone, triangle, cylinder. After the drawings have been completed, each child can write a story to accompany the picture.
- Another charming book is *Here comes the WHOOSH!* by Vincent Fago (Golden Press). "Here it comes . . . WHOOSH . . . there it goes and in such a hurry, no one could see it . . ." and the reader never does see the mysterious creature, whatever it is. We are introduced, however, to many other interesting animals— the pigadoon, the snakearoo, and a whole family of be-whiskers. This book leads to the invention of many unusual animals as children describe their habitats, appearances, and behavior.
- Both of the above books are picture books, but they are used successfully with older children who appreciate the imaginative humor of these modern authors. Others recommended for use in similar fashion include:

YOUNGER IDEAS:

Borten, Helen. *Do You See What I See?* (Abelard-Schuman).
Borten, Helen. *Do You Hear What I Hear?* (Abelard-Schuman).
Joslin, Sesyle. *What Do You Say, Dear?* (Harcourt).
Krauss, Ruth. *A Hole Is to Dig* (Harper).
Munari, Bruno. *Who's There? Open the Door* (World).

MORE MATURE IDEAS:

Piatti, Celestino. *The Happy Owls* (Atheneum).
Rand, Ann. *Umbrellas, Hats and Wheels* (Harcourt).
Reid, Alastair. *Supposing* (Little, Brown).

Straight, Dorothy. *How the World Began* (Pantheon).
Wolff, J., and B. Owett, *Let's Imagine Thinking Up Things* (Dutton).
Viorst, Judith. *Alexander's Terrible, Horrible, No-Good, Very Bad Day* (Atheneum).

PICTURES

Pictures and drawings represent one of the most often used techniques in motivating writing. Pictures, both large and small, should be collected by the teacher and students so that a good collection is always available. Parents will contribute magazines for classroom use.

- Excellent sources of pictures that encourage writing are Sierra Club books such as *The Gentle Wilderness* or *Time* and *The River Flowing*.
- One large picture can be displayed before the class, which discusses the action depicted, suggesting names for characters, possiblities for the setting, and so forth. The use of a large picture is a good beginning activity in writing as it provides excellent stimulation of ideas and an opportunity for the teacher to observe with the class the author's right to name the characters, to have events develop as he or she chooses, that is, the possibilities for original, divergent thinking.
- Distribute smaller pictures to students for use as illustrations for stories. Each student writes about one picture, mounting the story and picture on one large sheet. The next writing is based on another picture which again is mounted on a large sheet together with a story. After this activity has been repeated several times, the sheets can be stapled together with an attractive cover to form individual story collections.
- Some questions that help generate ideas about a picture are: How many things can you see? What is happening now? What happened in the past? What will happen in the future? What does the picture make you think of? How does it make you feel? Ask students to imagine that they are part of the picture.
- A more advanced type of motivation is an incomplete drawing which requires students to complete a picture based on several given lines or shapes. They then write about the completed drawing. Inkblots are used in this manner also, with students interpreting what they see in the blot or what the shape brings to mind.
- A picture collection can be filed in a box that becomes the focus of a learning center. At specified times or during free time, students can go through the file

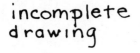

incomplete
drawing

inkblot

of pictures and choose an appealing picture creating a paragraph or story around it.

Bring in a small Oriental rug (3′ × 5′ or smaller) or carpet scrap—a magic carpet. Discuss where you might fly with it. Write the names of the cities, countries, imaginary places on the board. When the enthusiasm is high, pass out paper and encourage the children to pick the place they'd most like to go on the magic carpet and tell all about the trip.

OBJECTS

Both familiar and unfamiliar objects lend themselves to use as stimuli in writing.

- A delightful exercise is hiding an object in a large paper bag. Each child in turn feels the unfamiliar object without seeing it and then writes about it. It is interesting to compare results and then to display the object for all to see—a coconut in the hull, an eggplant, an empty plastic bottle, a wooden animal, pumpkin seeds, and so on.
- Another somewhat unusual device which elicits a good response from students is the use of an old bottle which has a cork or cap. Inside this bottle the teacher places a note. The bottle containing the note is shown to the class as the teacher excitedly explains that the bottle was found on a local beach (or sent by a friend). The class speculates on the contents of the note, its origin, etc. in writing. That night the teacher "breaks" the bottle and the next day reads the note to the class.
- An inanimate object can be given life with each student playing the role of a chair, a pencil, a book, or, to be more imaginative, a picture frame, a traffic light, a crown, a building in the city. The student imagines the feelings of the chosen object, describing the activities of the day, reactions to the behavior of people, and so on.

  A good way to start thinking about making inanimate objects come alive would be to use the film, *A Chairy Tale*, available from the International Film Bureau. Harper & Row's *Making It Strange* series of workbooks also has many good ideas for becoming an inanimate object, including a series on being a bullet in the gun of a trigger-happy outlaw or in a policeman's holster. Exploring being inanimate objects can add great variety and sensitivity.

  This idea fits well with science units on ecology—for instance, practice being a redwood tree about to be cut down, or standing majestic in the forest; or try being a waterfall or a dam, a smokestack, or a building built too close to its neighbors. Besides encouraging writing these ideas can help develop insight.

RECORDED MATERIALS

Both recorded music and recorded sound add real variety to the writing experience. Tapes can be prepared by students or the teacher to fit specific needs of the class.

- The playing of recorded music for the class is often used as a stimulus to writing. The mood of the music may suggest settings for stories or the music may actually suggest action. Several effective musical selections are:

Danse Macabre, Saint-Saëns
The Moldau, Smetana
Flight of the Bumblebee, Rimsky-Korsakov
Capriccio Italien, Tchaikovsky

• Recordings of stories can also be utilized in stimulating writing. Rudyard Kipling's *Just So Stories* (Caedmon) will interest young writers in producing original stories which explain how animals came to be made as they are following Kipling's explanation of "How the Camel Got His Hump." This writer's wonderful imagination and his way of playing with words serve to inspire students.
• The tape recorder, too, offers a way of motivating. Taping "sound situations" is an interesting experience for teacher or students. A combination of several intriguing sounds—a clock ticking, footsteps, a door slamming—can suggest a situation, the basis for a story.

FILMS

Slides, filmstrips, and movies challenge the imagination in a visual manner and serve to vary the more routine approach.

• Eight films for motivating writing are listed here. Show the short film; discuss; then write.

Hunter and the Forest, 1955, Encyclopedia Britannica, 8 min.
Rainshowers, 1965, Churchill Films, 14 min.
Leaf, 1962, Pyramid Films, 7 min.
Concrete Poetry, 1970, Pyramid Films, 15 min.
Cosmic Zoom, 1969, McGraw-Hill, 8 min.
Neighbors, 1952, International Film Bureau, 9 min.
Pigs, 1967, Churchill Films, 11 min.
Story of a Book, 1962, Churchill Films, 11 min.

• Filmstrips of stories such as *Alice in Wonderland* and *Bambi* (Encyclopaedia Britannica Films) also offer introductory material for imaginative writing. Students can write more adventures about the same characters, or they can imagine changes in the action—"What would have happened if . . . ?"
• Use your personal collection of colored slides to inspire writing. A group of pictures on varied topics can be shown while students rapidly suggest titles for each picture. Two or three related pictures can be shown to furnish material for a class discussion which leads to writing. The picture of an old house will lead students to imagining the past of this house, the people it has known, and so on.

STUDENTS AS AUTHORS

The writing of other students can be motivating.

Joseph, Stephen M., ed., *The Me Nobody Knows.* New York: Avon Books, 1969. Children's voices from the ghetto.
Kohl, Herbert. *36 Children.* New York: The New American Library, 1968. Illustrations by Robert George Jackson, III. A young teacher's account of his revolutionary, unforgettable year in a ghetto classroom; includes children's writings.
Lewis, Richard, *Journeys.* New York: Simon and Schuster, Inc., 1969. Prose by children of the English-speaking world.

Mirthes, Caroline, *Can't You Hear Me Talking to You?* New York: Bantam Books, Inc., 1971. Writing from and about children from the ghetto.

Narrative Writing

Students move naturally into telling stories orally and in writing stories as they develop skills and confidence. You can begin teaching them more about how narratives are created and the vocabulary that we use in discussing a story. Talk first about such familiar kinds of stories as jokes or folktales. Then progress to original creations based on personal memories and students' imaginations.

Beginning Orally

As you read aloud to students, discuss the events in the story, the way the author writes, or the development of a particular character. Make sure that students are aware of the author as a human being who writes much as they do.

Focus on storytelling in small groups as preparation for writing stories. Suggest that students begin telling very short stories that they know, jokes or an experience they remember. They can retell stories they have heard— fairytales, fables, or a story you have read aloud. Help them improve their storytelling ability by having them memorize the first and last lines, a line that is repeated throughout the story, or special wording that adds interest to the story.

As students begin telling original stories, point out the need for a beginning, middle, and end for each story. After they have told stories orally, they will find it easier to record the stories in writing.

Introducing Literature Terms

Students need appropriate vocabulary to enable them to discuss narratives they read and write. Develop a story chart that is based on the question words students know.

A Story Chart

QUESTIONS	LITERATURE CONCEPTS	RELATED IDEAS
Who?	Characters	People, animals
		Protagonist, Antagonist
		Dialogue
Where?	Setting	Place
		Mood
When?	Setting	Time
What?	Plot	Point of view
Why?		Sequence
		Problem
		Foreshadowing
How?	Conclusion	Solution

Students can apply these questions to any story you are discussing as they identify the characters and setting. As they begin to write, they will find the questions help them tell a fully developed story.

A Sample Lesson: Point of View

Provide opportunities for students to write stories. Each time you plan a lesson schedule time for the three essential elements of a good writing experience: prewriting, writing, and postwriting. This sample lesson demonstrates how you might introduce writing from a specific point of view.

Prewriting Select a human interest story from the newspaper that contains varied factual information. Often such stories are about animals and children as in the following example:

DOG FALLS 14 STORIES, HITS, INJURES WOMAN

JOHANNESBURG—A small lapdog, apparently thrown from a 14-story building into the street below, struck and seriously injured a woman passerby, a spokesman for the Johannesburg General Hospital said Tuesday.

The dog was a miniature Pomeranian named Blackie.

The injured woman, Mrs. Rose Hurst, 54, underwent an emergency operation but was still reported in serious condition. The animal struck her on the head, knocking her to the ground unconscious.

Blackie was the pet of Adele Looden, 10, who had been playing with him on the roof of the 14-story apartment building in the heart of Johannesburg's densely populated high-rise apartment district. The girl left her pet alone for a short while and when she returned he was gone.

Tell the students you are going to read a newspaper story aloud to them. They are to listen and try to remember the facts in the story. Read the story aloud slowly and clearly. Include the headlines and dateline.

Then ask the students to list the facts they remember as you write the key words on the words, thus:

dog struck woman
14-story apartment building
Pomeranian named Blackie
Adele Looden, 10
Rose Hurst, 54
emergency operation
Johannesburg General Hospital

Then, ask students who told the story (a reporter). Ask them who else might tell this story. Write the suggestions on the board: the dog, Adele, Mrs. Hurst, a passerby, the hospital surgeon, the ambulance driver, a lawyer, and so on.

Tell them to choose one point of view and to retell the story from that point of view. Leave the lists of facts and points of view on the board to help students write as easily as possible.

Writing Have students write about twenty minutes. All will begin a story, and some will probably be able to finish the story in that length of time. The prewriting activity prepared them well, supplying the ideas and giving help with spelling.

Postwriting Have students break into small response groups of five to six students each. Each student is to read his or her story to the group completing it orally as needed. Instruct the groups to choose the best one in each group to share with the whole class.

This first draft would not be graded in any way. In this case, the story would be placed in students' folders. Individual students might choose to complete the story and revise it for the selection to be discussed in a conference with the teacher.

In developing this lesson observe that the actual writing is less important than prewriting activities that prepare students to write. A carefully planned prewriting session ensures that each student has something to say and that obstacles to successful writing have been eliminated as much as possible. Postwriting activities provide an opportunity to share with an audience and to hear the writing of other students, important components of the writing process. We need to plan prewriting and postwriting experiences and to schedule time for them if we want students to write successfully.

Expository Writing

Expository writing makes a statement. It explains, argues, persuades. Students can use expository writing in reports of factual information and in statements of their own opinions.

Although narrative and expository writing have much in common, there are basic distinctions. The chief difference between the two kinds of writing lies in the handling of the paragraph. Students should be made aware of the meaning of "paragraphing" as a convention of indenting. In dialogue one word may be indented as different people speak, but we could scarcely call that word a paragraph. The expository paragraph by contrast, is a fully developed set of sentences following a prescribed formula.

The formula paragraph Even young children can follow the simple basic formula for an expository paragraph once you show them how. The basic formula is:

Paragraph = 1 Topic Sentence + 3 Supporting Sentences +
1 Concluding Sentence
P = 1 TS + 3 SS + 1 CS

Example I really like to eat. One of my favorite foods is a hamburger. I also enjoy a goopy fudge sundae. Another food I love is popcorn with lots of butter and salt. Eating is one thing I never mind doing.

A Sample Lesson: The Expository Paragraph

Prewriting   Read *Alexander's Terrible, Horrible, No Good, Very Bad Day* by Judith Viorst (Atheneum) aloud to the class.

After reading this humorous story as students listen, ask students to list all the terrible things that happened to Alexander. Write the key words on the board, thus:

seat by the window
lima beans
best friend
fighting, getting muddy
cavity in tooth
father's office

Writing   Dictate the following sentence to students: Alexander had a terrible, horrible, no good, very bad day. Ask students what punctuation is needed. Discuss commas in a series and identify these words as a series of adjectives.

Then, direct the students to write three sentences that tell unpleasant things that happened to Alexander. The list on the board makes it easy for them to write these sentences. As most students complete this task, direct them to add a fifth sentence that concludes or pulls the ideas together.

Postwriting   As students complete their paragraphs, have them work in pairs to make sure they followed directions exactly. Point out the elements of the formula paragraph. Have students read some of the completed paragraphs aloud.

Student paragraphs can be displayed around the cover of this book on the bulletin board.

Follow this same procedure with another book that you read aloud. Have students suggest topic sentences, supporting sentences, and concluding sentences orally. Then, have students write a paragraph independently.

Later, use this form for writing responses to books that students read independently. Students can write such paragraphs to describe processes, to compare two items, and to state their opinions. Expository paragraphs can be written in all areas of the curriculum.

Longer Expository Forms

The expository paragraph is used in combination for longer forms of writing.

The Business Letter   Have students bring in examples of business letters and identify purposes for writing such letters. They can examine letters to the editor in the local newspaper. Students can write a formal letter, preferably one that they will really mail—a letter of inquiry, complaint about a product, or expressing an opinion.

Formula Paragraph	*Five-paragraph Essay*
Topic Sentence	Introductory paragraph (The formula paragraph)
Supporting sentence 1	Expansion of SS 1
Supporting sentence 2	Expansion of SS 2
Supporting sentence 3	Expansion of SS 3
Concluding sentence	Concluding paragraph

The Five-paragraph Essay This formal essay or theme simply expands the basic five-sentence paragraph. A formula paragraph serves as the introductory paragraph of the essay. Show students how the two forms are related.

The I-Search Paper Instead of formal research papers I recommend the I-Search paper that engages students in going beyond library books for information. Because the student decides on the topic to be studied, he or she does not waste time copying paragraphs from the encyclopedia. The use of interviews, telephone calls, or letters engages the students in varied methods of finding the information they need. The student writes a report that contains all the elements of formal research as described in the following student activity sheet. Each step of the process should be discussed in class. Class periods may be used for writing each of the four parts of the report. (See page 196.)

Teaching the Conventions of Writing

The conventions of writing include punctuation, capitalization, and spelling as well as such practices as indentation of paragraphs and dialogue. Notice that some of these conventions differ from language to language so that it is interesting for students to observe a book printed in Spanish or Asian languages. Conventions are somewhat arbitrary decisions that writers have agreed on, and naturally, they should be taught as needed within the context of student writing.

An excellent discovery method for teaching various conventions uses literature models. Simply duplicate a page of dialogue, for example, from a book you are reading to the class. Let the students observe how quotation marks are used and then make a list of generalizations about the punctuation and capitalization of dialogue. This literature-oriented method of teaching is much more effective than a duplicated activity sheet that you might devise to teach the use of quotation marks.

Punctuation, like spelling, has been overemphasized as an aspect of composition. Again, we stress the importance of placing primary emphasis in composition on the ideas expressed rather than on the mechanics of recording the ideas. On the other hand, knowledge and use of punctuation does facilitate communication, as Charlton Laird illustrates:

STEP 1: IDENTIFYING THE PROBLEM
You are going to investigate something that you would really like to know about. First, you need to decide what you want to know, so complete these lines:
  I would like to know _____
  I would like to know _____
  I would like to know _____

STEP 2: LOCATING INFORMATION
Now choose one of these three subjects to investigate. Think about how you can find information. Then begin searching for information and write notes about what you find.
Go to the library and look for:
  The *Reader's Guide*
  Almanacs
  Atlases
  Encyclopedias
  Books about your subject
Talk to people by using:
  Yellow pages of the phone book
  Interviews with family and friends
  Visits to businesses
Write to:
  The state capital
  The U.S. government
  City officials

STEP 3: PREPARING A REPORT
Then, your report is ready to be written. Include these four parts:
  Part I.   *Statement of the Problem*—What did you decide to investigate?
  Part II.   *Procedures*—Describe how you went about your search.
  Part III. *Findings*—What did you find out? You may outline the information or prepare graphs. Use any method to present your information.
  Part IV: *Conclusions*—What will you do now? Tell how you will use the information you discovered.

STEP 4: SHARING THE INFORMATION
Present your I-Search paper to the class. Share the information you discovered and show the group any objects or material you may have obtained. Be prepared to answer any questions from the group.

Dr. Iris M. Tiedt, *Elementary Teacher's Ideas and Materials Workshop*. West Nyack, New York: Parker Publishing Co.

    icertainlyshallnotkeepthisuplongitevenlooksrepulsive
    if you made anything of that you have the key to make something of this too but i shall not keep this one going very long either
    These samples represent an attempt/ to write modern english in ways that suggest writing in earlier days/ when there was no punctuation/ or when punctuation was not standardized as it is now/ this particular style is one used by the first english printer William Caxton/ who used a period to mark a paragraph.
    th's 's ' st'll "rl"r 'n' 's'd d'r'ng ' t'm' wh'n 'v'n v'w'ls w'r' 'nd'c't'd b' p'nct"t"n[7]

We can also observe humorous, and sometimes disastrous effects of punctuation either misused or omitted as in these examples:

Don't! Stop!
Don't stop.

[7]Charlton Laird, *A Writer's Handbook* (Boston: Ginn & Co., 1964), p. 358.

No help is coming.
No, help is coming.

Seventy-nine and thirty are the winning numbers.
Seventy, nine, and thirty are the winning numbers.

"Shift!" he cried.
"Shift?" he cried.

How might we punctuate these words?
　　What are you giving him dope
　　She bought a car coat and riding boots
　　Paula Marie Susan and Kathy were absent

Skill in using punctuation can be greatly assisted by knowledge of the intonation patterns of our speech. As we listen to a sentence, we can usually hear the pauses, the *juncture,* which may require punctuation to aid the reader in correctly interpreting what has been written. The falling pitch and full pause, for example, tell us clearly that a period is needed, whereas a slight pause may indicate a comma. Speak these sentences, noting the type of punctuation indicated by the juncture.

John will go with us
Is John going with us
My friend John Brownton will go with us
Although he doesn't like to ride John will go
John Brownton although he doesn't like to ride will go with us

Punctuation taught to students in the elementary school should be functional, that is, it should be punctuation needed by the student as he or she writes. It is easy to become so entangled in minute points of punctuation that we lose sight of the aims of teaching composition. Beginning from the first stages of writing, therefore, let us teach these skills as they are needed:

1.　Period:
　　At the end of a declarative sentence. *He went home.*
　　After abbreviations. *Mr. Andrew R. Cooper*
2.　Comma:
　　To separate parts of a series. *We ate corn, peas, and hot dogs.*
　　With an apposition. *Molly, my best friend, is here.*
　　After an introductory clause. *When I get there, I'll tell you.*
　　To separate a quotation from the speaker. *He said, "How are you?"*
　　After yes and no. *Yes, I will be here.*
　　With direct address. *Jimmy, do you know?*
3.　Question marks:
　　At the end of an interrogative sentence. *Who is it?*
4.　Quotation marks:
　　Around quoted speech. *Mark called, "I can go!"*
　　Around a title of a short work—poem, article, short story. *We read "The Doughnut Machine."*

5. Exclamation mark:
    After a word or words showing excitement. *Help me!*
6. Apostrophe:
    To show possession. *This is Sid's pencil.*
    In contractions. *Don't you know better?*

The INTERABANG

The first innovation in punctuation since the seventeenth century, the interabang is a combination of the exclamation point and the question mark. Examples of how it might be used are:
"How do you like that   "
"What do you know   "

An occasional touch of humor helps the teaching of almost any content. Here are ways of providing practice in using punctuation.

Provide a paragraph or two which contains no punctuation at all. Have students compare their punctuation of the given paragraph with one you prepare on a transparency. Use a joke, thus:

miserly Sam went to the dentist because he had a terrible toothache as dr fixem reached into sams mouth to pull out the aching tooth sam cried out doctor if it costs $4.00 to pull the tooth how much will it cost to loosen it a little

Cartoon figures can be used to assist students in learning to identify the portion of a sentence to be set off by quotation marks:

Jane said, "I'm delighted to see you."

Although it is true that ideas expressed are more important than the mechanics of composition, frequent misspellings and illegible handwriting do confuse and prejudice the reader. The written words replace the winsome personality of the writer; the writing stands exposed to the rude view of the critic. How far, for example, will the student advance who writes this sentence in sixth grade?

We hopt to Get Good grades on those importent examunoshuns.

Admittedly a certain snobbery is related to correct spelling, and those who spell English easily do "look down their noses" at those who never learned the intricacies of English spelling. Spelling, in this case, becomes an outward sign of education or intelligence in the eyes of the public, although only low correlation has been found between spelling ability and the intelligence quotient.

On the other hand, poor writing and misspelling can totally confuse the reader, as in these sentences:

1. He could not be *hear*. (Does the writer mean *here* or *heard*, perhaps?)
2. Mary Jane was hopping. (Was she? It could be that she was hoping.)
3. *You owe me $ 5 4.* (He may get cheated.)
4. *They brought in the cot.* (Does it meow?)

We can see that illegible handwriting or confused spelling can impede communication. The wrong message may be conveyed. As pointed out in the following chapters, spelling and handwriting are important aspects of communication.

SUMMARY

The teaching of writing can be very exciting as students discover the ideas they have to share. Emphasis throughout writing instruction should be on positive reinforcement as we recognize the complexities of skills involved in writing, the most difficult of the language arts. We need to provide as much support as possible as students learn to write and to select beginning writing experiences that they can perform with creditable success. Teaching students to edit their own writing helps them grow as writers, and it reduces the paperload that has overwhelmed many teachers. As students express themselves in writing, they find that other students enjoy reading what they have written, and it is then that they begin to think of themselves as writers who have something to say. Therein lies the excitement of teaching writing.

CHALLENGE

To prepare yourself for teaching writing it is important that you try writing yourself. The following activities are designed to help you experience what your student writers experience.

1. Begin keeping a personal journal. Continue writing daily about whatever is important to you for at least a month. Such personal writing is therapeutic; you may wish to make journal writing an integral part of your self-growth efforts.

2. Write a paragraph in response to this quotation from a teacher–consultant:

The child's pleasure in writing can be destroyed by making writing into drudgery or punishment. Students can fear writing if the teacher is overzealous in analyzing and correcting the student's errors. Larry Brandt, South Bay Writing Project, 1981

3. Select a title from the list of Newbery award winners in Chapter 12. As you read the book, observe the writing and think how you could use this piece of literature to teach students to write. Plan three specific lessons for fifth-grade students based on the book you selected.

4. Follow the directions for the sample lessons on pages 192 and 194. Write examples for these lessons. Use the lessons with elementary school students.

EXPLORING FURTHER

Adler, Richard, *Back to the Basics: Composition.* Urbana, Ill.: National Council of Teachers of English, SLATE Committee, 1976.

Britton, James et al., *The Development of Writing Abilities (11-18).* University of London Institute of Education, Schools Council Research Studies, 1975.

Burrows, Alvina et al., *They All Want to Write.* New York: Holt, Rinehart and Winston, 1961.

Calkins, Lucy M., "Children Discover What Writers Know," *Learning Magazine,* April 1978, pp. 34–37.

Carlson, Ruth, *Writing Aids Through the Grades.* New York: Teachers College, 1970.

Deen, Beverly and Frank Deen, *Writing Ideas.* San Jose, Calif.: Contemporary Press, 1976.

Cooper, Charles R. and Lee Odell, *Research on Composing: Points of Departure.* Urbana, Ill.: National Council of Teachers of English, 1978.

Gunter, Deborah et al., *Writing: A Sourcebook of Exercises and Assignments.* Belmont, Calif.: Addison-Wesley Publishing Co., Inc., 1978.

Graves, Donald H., *Balance the Basics. Let Them Write.* New York: Ford Foundation, 1978.

Haley-James, Shirley, ed., *Perspectives on Writing in Grades 1-8.* NCTE Committee on Written Composition in Elementary School. Urbana, Ill.: National Council of Teachers of English, 1981.

Hennings, Dorothy G. and Barbara M. Grant, *Content and Craft.* Englewood Cliffs, N.J.: Prentice-Hall, Inc., 1973.

Judy, Stephen, *Explorations in the Teaching of English.* New York: Dodd, Mead & Co., 1981.

Maxwell, Rhoda and Stephen Judy, *Composing.* Lansing, Mich.: The Michigan Council of Teachers of English, 1979.

Neman, Beth, *Teaching Students to Write.* Columbus, Ohio: Charles E. Merrill Publishing Co., 1980.

Petty, Walter T. and Mary E. Bowen, *Slithery Snakes and Other Aids to Children's Writing.* New York: Meredith, 1967.

Shaughnessy, Mina P., *Errors & Expectations: A Guide for the Teacher of Basic Writing.* New York: Oxford Univ. Press, 1977.

Tiedt, Iris M. et al, *Teaching Writing in Grades K-8.* Englewood Cliffs, N.J.: Prentice-Hall, Inc., 1983.

———, "A Model for Teaching Writing Holistically," *California English,* May/June 1980, pp. 8–9.

——— and Sidney W. Tiedt, *Language Arts Activities for the Classroom.* Boston: Allyn & Bacon, 1978.

Tway, Eileen, "Teacher Responses to Children's Writing," *Language Arts,* October 1980, 57, 7:763–72.

Writing Committee, Santa Clara County, California, *Students Can Write.* San Jose, Calif.: Office of the Supt. of Santa Clara County Schools, 1977.

9

Wants pawn term dare worsted ladle gull hoe lift wetter murder inner ladle cordage honor itch offer lodge dock florist. Disc ladle gull orphan worry ladle cluck wetter putty ladle rat hut, end fur disc raisin pimple caulder ladle rat rotten hut.

Howard Chace[1]

SPELLING ENGLISH WORDS

The ability to spell words correctly has a high value in our society. And while it is often seen as the mark of an educated person, many well-educated people cannot spell accurately. Clearly, teaching students to spell is not as easy as it might seem.

Spelling is a writing skill. Learning and using the conventions of spelling English words adds to the complexity of communicating through writing. Spelling is also related to oral language, for students must hear words accurately and be able to discriminate between sounds in order to relate sounds and symbols as they write. In addition, spelling is related to the reading process, for the student must deal with the same patterns of spelling in both decoding and encoding activities. Effective teaching of spelling,

[1]Don L. F. Nilsen and Alleen Pace Nilsen, Version of "Little Red Riding Hood" quoted in *Language Play: An Introduction to Linguistics* (Rowley, Massachusetts: Newbury House Pubs., 1978), p. 129.

therefore, will incorporate thinking, listening, speaking, reading and writing processes.

Spelling is also a visual skill. In order to spell easily students need to see patterns of English spelling. Spelling, therefore, is closely correlated with ability to read, for only good readers become good spellers. We find, on the other hand, that many good readers remain inaccurate spellers, for they do not perceive words and the spelling patterns in the same way that other readers do. We need to help students to become aware of spelling patterns.

Learning to spell can be more effectively taught if we stress the interrelated processes of hearing and saying words, thinking about acceptable patterns in English spelling, and noticing similar concepts in reading and spelling words. Learning to spell can be enjoyable if students discover word play and games that reinforce knowledge about how the English spelling system works. Certainly we have a responsibility to examine both the efficiency and the effectiveness of present instructional practices and their results.

BENCHMARK

Think about the part spelling plays in your own life. Jot down comments in your notebook about the following:

1. Are you a good speller? If so, how did you learn to spell words correctly with relative ease? If you are not a good speller, can you explain your not learning to spell effectively?

2. Students will often argue that we don't really need to know how to spell. Secretaries or computers will handle that skill. How would you respond to this argument?

3. List ten words that you find difficult to spell. Take the spelling test below with the class. Talk about the words misspelled.

acclimate	ascension	physique
sincerely	truly	loveliest
anxiety	fiery	guarantee
technique	subtle	receiving
comprehension	advisable	grammar
circuit	subscription	accommodate
symbolism	definitely	approximately

In this chapter we explore the linguistic background of the English spelling system, discuss the teacher's role in working with spelling in the classroom, and suggest strategies for motivating student interest in spelling and in teaching basic understandings. Spelling is considered as part of both writing and reading processes. After reading the chapter and trying some of the activities, you can expect to:

• have a better understanding of the characteristics of English spelling
• be able to outline plans for an effective spelling program

- know specific activities that teach basic concepts about the spelling of English words to children at all age levels
- be able to differentiate between spelling as part of the writing process and the relationship of spelling to reading

Notice that the chief emphasis of this chapter is on teaching children how to spell words as part of the writing process. Because it is important, we do discuss the interrelationships between reading and writing and the advisability of integrating instruction. As with listening and speaking, you cannot deal with writing and reading apart from each other. Refer also to Chapter 11, where we discuss decoding skills that are related to spelling instruction.

BACKGROUND INFORMATION
FOR THE TEACHER

Spelling involves working with the written language. In order to write words children must learn to relate the sounds they use in saying words to the letters or groups of letters that we have come to use in representing these sounds in written form, the conventions of spelling.

From the beginning of a writing program children must learn the most regular correspondences among sounds and letters, for example, the spelling of bat, tin, and pig. As students mature and have the need to spell more sophisticated words, they learn the graphemes used in such words as psychology, grotesque, or technique. Throughout instruction we stress awareness of the relationship between sound and symbol (phoneme and grapheme).

Knowledge about the spelling of English words is basic to the reading process. As children learn to decode unfamiliar words during the initial stages of learning to read, they must recognize the written symbols, relate each grapheme to a corresponding phoneme, and say (or think) the word. As students become fluent readers, they learn to leap quickly from the visual impression to meaning without the intermediary step of decoding. Although the process is done quickly, however, gaining meaning from written symbols (reading) ultimately does depend on recognition of spelling patterns and the phoneme–grapheme relationship. As Hanna notes:

> The use of all writing systems . . . necessitates the user's acquiring two closely related processes: (1) the mastery of the graphic symbols needed to set forth speech in writing (encoding or spelling) and (2) the ability to translate written or printed graphemes into the oral forms they represent (decoding or reading).[2]

This section of the chapter investigates the phoneme–grapheme relationship in English. Then we will discuss various aspects of developing a spelling curriculum.

[2]Paul R. Hanna et al., *Spelling: Structure and Strategies* (Boston: Houghton Mifflin Co., 1971), pp. 25–26.

Using Symbols to Represent Sounds: Spelling

The study of sounds made in the English language (phonology) is important in developing the ability to spell, pronounce, or read a word. Although researchers have pointed out that (1) regional pronunciations differ, (2) English sounds are frequently spelled in several ways, and (3) more than half of our words contain "silent" letters, others have found that the spelling of a large percentage of English words is highly regular. For this group of regular words, phonology will prove especially helpful.

The study of the sounds of English introduces several terms related to phonology: *phonics, phonetics,* and *phonemics.* These terms, confusing to those beginning a study of reading and writing instruction, can be defined as follows:

Phonics—determining the sound or meaning that is represented by a set of given symbols, usually associated with reading
   Example: *tion*—usually pronounced /šən/
Phonetics—analysis of sound production in scientific detail developed in a code called the International Phonetic Alphabet, so that all linguists can identify the sounds
Phonemics—identification of the sounds of a specific language such as English, which has about forty phonemes (sounds that change meaning)
   Examples: The phonemes that begin these two words are different; the words mean something different.
   /fin/   /pin/
   The phonemes that begin these two words are the same although they are spelled differently in English.
   phone /fōn/   fun /fʃn/

Many critics have pointed with ridicule to the peculiarities of English spelling and to the fact that spelling and pronunciation are not consistent. George Bernard Shaw, one of the more literate critics, gibed: "How do you pronounce GHOTI, if the letters are pronounced as follows: *gh* as in *rough, o* as in *women,* and *ti* as in *nation*?"[3]

Since the days of Chaucer, spelling and pronunciation have grown ever farther apart, with pronunciation tending to change more than spelling. This tendency continues today. An anonymous poet records many oddities of English spelling ending with the conclusion that "sounds and letters disagree."

OUR QUEER LANGUAGE

When the English tongue we speak,
Why is "break" not rhymed with "freak"?
Will you tell me why it's true
We say "sew" but likewise "few";
And the maker of a verse
Cannot cap his "horse" with "worse"?
"Beard" sounds not the same as "heard";

---

[3]The answer is FISH!

"Cord" is different from "word";
Cow is "cow," but low is "low";
"Shoe" is never rhymed with "foe."
Think of "hose" and "dose" and "lose";
And think of "goose" and yet of "choose."
Think of "comb" and "tomb" and "bomb";
"Doll" and "roll" and "home" and "some."
And since "pay" is rhymed with "say,"
Why not "paid" with "said," I pray?
We have "blood" and "food" and "good";
"Mould" is not pronounced like "could."
Wherefore "done" but "gone" and "lone"?
Is there any reason known?

> And, in short, it seems to me,
> Sounds and letters disagree.

Although it is undeniably true that English contains many unusual and often inexplicable oddities, today's researchers are focusing attention on the fact that approximately 85 percent of English words have been found to follow regular patterns of spelling.[4] Few linguists claim that English spelling is easy, but it is not entirely without reason. There are many relatively consistent rules which bear teaching, and many concepts in phonics will assist students in attacking the large body of consistent spellings as they learn to read and write.

The consonant sounds and spellings Linguists have identified twenty-four consonant sounds in spoken English. We teach the consonants first because they are more easily identifiable in the common initial position than vowels which, usually surrounded by consonant sounds, are more difficult to distinguish. Consonants also serve to provide visual structure in printed words. Notice, for example, how easily you can read these words even though the vowels are completely eliminated:

g __ __ gr __ph __
b __rthd __
c __ns __n __nt
ph __n __l __g __

The more consonants that appear in the word, of course, the easier it is to identify. We recognize, at the same time, that we need vowel sounds because we can't pronounce the consonants without adding a vowel. This accounts for the fact that every syllable contains one vowel sound.

In an integrated language arts approach, it is essential that you understand the relationship between the sounds of English and the various spellings that represent these sounds in written form. The outline of consonant sounds includes numerous alternate spellings for many of the sounds. Obviously, we could not work with all sound-spelling relationships at one

[4]Hanna, Paul et al., Ibid.

time, so we teach the simpler and more common spellings for each sound first. To assist the teacher I have sorted the various spellings into three levels of difficulty. Those listed under Level 3 might not be taught until the upper elementary grades; in a few cases, these spellings might not be taught at all in elementary school.

The position in which the various spellings occur are also important to observe. There are certain spellings, for example, that never occur in the initial position. The *gh* spelling of /f/, for instance, never appears initially. The *gh* spelling in the initial position is an alternate way of writing /g/. Children can be helped to recognize this kind of generalization after they have been exposed to many English words.

As you read throught the charts on pages 208-211, identify each consonant sound by pronouncing the words listed under the initial position column. Then notice the variety of possible alternate spellings. Which sound-symbol relationships would be easiest to teach?

The vowel sounds and spellings   The vowel sounds are more difficult to identify because they are commonly hidden in the middle of a word. Also there is much variation in regional dialects regarding the pronunciation of the vowel sounds. It is interesting to aid children in hearing varied ways of saying the same word—for example, *dog*. Be cautious, however, about evaluating the "correctness" of pronunciation. Your own speech represents only one speech sample in the classroom, and it may differ widely from the speech of children in the classroom.

Because the vowel sounds are usually internal or medial in position, they are not grouped on the chart according to position or difficulty level. They are divided, however, according to simple sounds and complex sounds called *diphthongs* (combinations of more than one vowel sound to make a clearly identifiable new phoneme). Refer to the chart on p. 211.

Although many of us might say there are five vowels in English, linguists identify at least sixteen different vowel sounds in spoken English. We need to clarify our thinking about vowel sounds (not five letters of the alphabet) and learn to identify these sounds when we hear them. We will find, for example, that there is wide variation in the pronunciation of the vowel sounds used in specific words. For example, are the words *Mary, merry,* and *marry* homonyms for you? Do you pronounce them exactly the same? As you check with others, you will find that for some people, each of these words is pronounced differently; it is the vowel sound that varies.

We need to be aware of varied dialects as we teach, for we should not expect the speech of all children in the classroom to be the same. This can be a problem in dictating to children or pronouncing spelling words. Studies of dialectology can be helpful with children of all ages as they learn to observe these variations with interest. Dialectal variations are not labeled as "wrong," however, nor should children be made to change their pronunciations to match the teacher's. We aim instead at awareness of variation in our own speech as well as that of children. See p. 212.

Observe the sixteen vowel sounds and their alternate spellings as outlined

CONSONANTS

PHONEMES	GRAPHEMES					
	Difficulty Level			Examples		
	1	2	3	Initial	Medial	Final
/b/	b			bill	tuber	cab
		bb			rubber	ebb
/d/	d			dill	coding	hard
		ed				pulled
		dd			sudden	Fudd
		ld				could
/f/	f			fill	fifer	loaf
		ph		phone	telephone	
		gh			roughing	cough
		ff			ruffle	off
			v			Chekhov
			pf (Ger.)	pfennig		
/g/	g			gill	tiger	bug
		gu		guest		
		gh		ghost		
		gg			logging	
			gue			catalogue
/h/	h			hill	unhappy	
		wh		who		
			j	Jose'		
/j/	j			jam		
		g		giant	imagine	wage
		dg			judger	judge
			di		soldier	
			du		graduate	
			de		grandeur	
/k/	k			kill	raking	look
		ke				lake
		c		cat	act	
		qu (1)*		quit	equinox	
		qu (2)*			liquor	
		ck			lacking	pick
		cc			accost	
		x			fix	
			cu		biscuit	
			cch		bacchanal	
			ch	chorus		

*In the initial position the grapheme qu(1) spells the blended phonemes /kw/; in other positions qu(2) is usually an alternate spelling for /k/.

CONSONANTS

PHONEMES	GRAPHEMES					
	Difficulty Level			Examples		
	1	2	3	Initial	Medial	Final
/k/ (Cont.)			kh	khaki		
			cqu		acquit	
			que (1)		barbeque	
			que (2)			plaque
/l/	l			like	failing	fatal
		ll (1)**	ll (2)**	llama	calling	doll
/m/	m			mill	timer	ham
		me				come
		mm			simmer	
		mb			climbing	lamb
			mn			hymn
/n/	n			no	lining	fun
		ne				line
		kn		knot		
		gn		gnat		feign
		nn			runner	
			pn	pneumonia		
/p/	p			pill	caper	top
		pp			copper	Lapp
/r/	r			rose	caring	fair
		rr			carry	Carr
		wr		write		
			rh	rhyme		
/s/	s			so		thus
		c		cell	receive	
		sc		scent		
		ss			classes	toss
		x				fox
			ps	pseudo		
/t/	t			to	later	hit
		tt			hotter	mutt
		bt			debtor	debt
		ed				licked
			pt	ptomaine		receipt
			dt			veldt
			th	Thomas		

**The grapheme ll (2) is very rare in the initial position. For that reason it is considered a difficult spelling while the ll (1) grapheme is rather common.

CONSONANTS

PHONEMES	Difficulty Level			Examples		
	1	2	3	Initial	Medial	Final
/v/	v			very	cover	
		f				of
		ve				weave
			ph		Stephen	
			vv		flivver	
/w/	w			will	slower	how
		one		one		
		wh		while	awhile	
			qu (kw)		quit	
			ui		suite	
			oui	ouija		
/y/	y			yes	lawyer	
			j		hallelujah	
			io		onion	
			ll		bouillon	
/z/	z			zoo	dozing	whiz
		s (e)			miser	lose, is
		zz			dazzle	buzz
		ss			Missouri	
			sc		discern	
			x	xylophone		
			cz	czar		
/č/	ch			child		much
		tch			matches	hutch
			c	cello		
			cz	Czech		
			eou		righteous	
			t		nature	
/š/	sh			shoe	worship	rush
		s		sugar		
		ch		champagne		
			sch	schist		
			ce		ocean	
			si		mansion	
			ss		mission	
			sci		luscious	
			ti		patient	
			xi		anxious	
			chs		fuchsia	

CONSONANTS

PHONEMES	GRAPHEMES					
	Difficulty Level			Examples		
	1	2	3	Initial	Medial	Final
/ž/		g		gendarme (Fr)	adagio	garage
		s (i)			pleasure, Asia	
		z (i)			brazier	
			j	jejeune		
/θ/	th			thimble	ether	loathe
/δ/	th			the	either	breath
/η/	ng				ringer	wing
	nk				think	
			ngue			tongue

on the chart. Say each word aloud as you listen carefully to the vowel sound your voice is making.

Compare your pronunciation of these words with that of other members of your class:

house	Mary	child	park
merry	garage	here	bath
log	idea	because	fire
were	right	of	Harvard

DIPHTHONGS

PHONEMES	GRAPHEMES
/iy/ (long e)	see, sea, me, deceive, believe, carbine, ski, gladly, Aesop, people, quay, key, suite, equator, Phoenix
/ey/ (long a)	bay, rain, gate, they, gauge, break, neigh, rein, straight, care
/ay/ (long i)	kite, right, I, by, cries, find, buy, height, eye, stein, aisle, dye, aye, lyre, iodine
/ow/ (long o)	lone, road, foe, slow, dough, beau, sew, yeoman, whoa, odor, oh, solo, soul, brooch
/yuw/ (long u)	use, few, view, beautiful, queue
/oy/	toy, moist
/aw/	now, out, bough
/uw/	too, blew, tune, suit, lose, flu, do, canoe, through, tomb, blue, group, prove, maneuver

SIMPLE VOWELS

PHONEMES	GRAPHEMES	
/i/	give, pit, myth, quilt, busy, women, England, sieve, been	
/e/	red, said, breath, friend, any, leopard (leisure), says, aesthetics, their, foetid	
/æ/	had, have, laugh, plaid	Unaccented Syllables
/ə/	nut, flood, rough, son, of, dove, was, does	cattle ahead fountain parliament
/a/	ah, halt, hot, mirage, cart, heart, fault, sergeant	moment happily burgeon porpoise
/u/	good, full, put, wolf, could	
/ɔ/	caught, jaw, talk, fought, daughter, watch, broad, toss, otter, Utah	
/ɨ/	her, sir, fur, work, satyr, journey, heard, grammar	

Listen to the record *Our Changing Language* by Evelyn Gott and Raven I. McDavid, Jr. (New York: McGraw-Hill Book Co.) for further comparisons of speech samples across the country.

Developing a Spelling Program

Spelling is probably one of the most regularly taught studies in the elementary school English curriculum. Literature may be discussed only spasmodically; writing may be totally ignored; but a daily spelling period is included in most classroom schedules.

The most obvious reason for this is that the subject matter to be taught is familiar to every teacher. It is also relatively easy to present to students, and it is easily evaluated. The teacher feels secure with the content as it is usually taught. The routine nature typical of spelling instruction provides a comfortable niche in the curriculum.

Spelling instruction provides few uncertainties and few excitements. As Horn reports, "Weekly time allotments are still much larger than can be justified either by the relative value and difficulty of spelling as compared with other subjects or by the results obtained."[5]

The task at hand, therefore, is to investigate the objectives for teaching spelling and to determine efficient and effective ways of reaching these objectives. Spelling is a tool, a skill that is closely allied with composition, or the writing of words. The prime objective in teaching spelling is, therefore, to teach children to spell words which they now need in order to write, or which they will need as adults.

[5]Ernest Horn, "Spelling," in *Encyclopedia of Educational Research,* 3rd ed., ed. Chester Harris (New York: Macmillan Publishing Co., Inc., 1960), p. 1346.

Selecting words for study   What words shall we teach? On what basis should they be selected? How many words should be taught each week? Published wordlists, that is, series of spelling books each of which contains a portion of the total list, vary widely. Betts found, for example, when studying twenty-five spelling series, that the total number of words included was about 10,000.[6] Since each series usually presents about 4000 words, the variation was obviously great.

All lists include a nucleus of words which are used repeatedly in everyone's individual writing, for it has been estimated that approximately 50 percent of our writing consists of only 100 words used in varied combinations. Three thousand words comprise approximately 98 percent of those words most commonly used.

Students could conduct an enlightening study of papers written over a period of time to determine what group of words is most commonly used. Their study would motivate student interest in learning these needed words, for the list would be composed of words which they themselves have discovered that *they* need to know.

How do we decide which words shall be taught at any grade level? Although it was once thought that the difficulty of spelling a word was a superior method of placing it for study by grade level, more recent studies find that, though a word may be difficult, the child's early need of the word may warrant its inclusion at a lower grade level. Horn cites the word *receive* as one which is consistently difficult for adults to spell, but which is presented in the elementary school because young children use the word widely. Words are selected for placement at specific grade levels usually on a basis of:

1.   Permanent value
2.   Difficulty of spelling
3.   Use by children
4.   Type of logical grouping[7]

Causes of spelling difficulty   In order to teach spelling effectively you might examine the causes of deficiency in spelling. Why do some students require little teaching of spelling, while other children have repeated difficulty in mastering spelling skills? Following is a list of deficiencies compiled from several sources:[8]

---

[6]E. A. Betts, *Spelling Vocabulary Study: Grade Placement in Seventeen Spellers* (New York: American, 1940), p. 143; and *Grade Placement of Words in Eight Recent Spellers* (American, 1949).

[7]James A. Fitzgerald, *A Basic Life Spelling Vocabulary* (Milwaukee, Wis.: Bruce, 1951).

[8]James A. Fitzgerald, *The Teaching of Spelling* (Milwaukee, Wis.: Bruce, 1951), p. 193. See also: Ernest Horn, "Spelling," in *Encyclopedia of Educational Research*, 3rd ed., ed. Chester W. Harris (New York: Macmillan Publishing Co., Inc., 1960), pp. 1347–49.

Lack of interest Noted frequently as the most influential factor in learning spelling skills, the interest factor can provide a point of attack for the teacher. See the discussion of motivation of student interest.

Physical defects Disability of the eye or ear can make a child unable to perceive the word visually or aurally. Either handicap results in misconceptions about the spelling of a word.

Intelligence Although a high intelligence quotient does not guarantee ability to spell, the child with a low IQ is handicapped in learning any skill, including spelling. He or she brings less ability to the task at hand and therefore cannot be expected to achieve at the same level as the more able child.

Poor memory ability We need to focus attention on memory abilities as the child learns to perceive the word in varied ways. Memory will be assisted by the development of other skills: listening, speaking, knowledge of phonology, and so on.

Speaking and listening skills How do we hear a word? How do we speak a word? Both skills are essential to correct spelling. Improved speaking and listening abilities will aid auditory discrimination, which is an essential aspect of correct spelling.

Poor study habits How is spelling presented? How is the child directed to study? Is he or she assisted in any way with the study of spelling? Most of the time spent studying spelling is in the classroom, and therefore study habits can be directed by the teacher. The poor speller needs special attention and may work better in a small group situation.

Developing positive attitudes The chief responsibility of the teacher is to establish positive attitudes toward spelling. Presented as a problem for investigation about which you are obviously knowledgeable and enthusiastic, spelling can be incorporated in a rewarding study of the English language. (See Chapter 7 for more ideas.)

Research indicates that the classroom teacher frequently dislikes teaching spelling, an attitude which is inevitably projected to the student. If the techniques used become routinized and uninteresting to the teacher, it is unlikely that children will display any genuine liking for this study. You should analyze methods employed to determine their effectiveness. Explore the following questions:

1. Are the words studied of interest to my students?
2. Are able spellers being held down to a low level of achievement?
3. Am I spending too much time on spelling activities?
4. Are poor spellers receiving help as needed?
5. Am I reinforcing spelling learning through use of composition?
6. Do I vary techniques of teaching spelling? Is spelling "dull"? Are student attitudes positive?
7. Am I really "teaching" spelling?
8. Do I permit spelling to inhibit creative writing?
9. Are techniques of teaching spelling based on the findings of research?
10. Are spelling and reading skills introduced together so children see the relationships?

Knowledge of the development of the English language, and American English in particular, will enable you to include information about changes in spelling, the origins of words, variations in British and American spellings, and so on.

Concepts of correctness should not be rigid. We must allow for differences in spelling (for example, ax–axe, fulfill–fulfil, catalog–catalogue).

In teaching, there is rarely *only one right answer*. The discovery of differences in spelling can add interest to the spelling lesson, and the child who discovers variations in spelling should be praised. The teacher who is aware of spelling variations will not be disconcerted by the child's questioning attitude nor will the questions be regarded as threatening teacher authority.

If you feel guilty about permitting a child to use the shorter spelling of such words as *dialog,* perhaps an examination of your attitude is in order. Why do you object? Is it that you had to learn the longer, older (and, therefore, more respectable) spelling? Is there something inherently better in one of the two variations? Don't they both communicate? Discussions of this nature can prove highly stimulating.

Methods of study   Most of the words in a spelling list are already present in the child's speaking or reading vocabulary. Only occasionally is it necessary to present detailed information about the meanings of words presented. When presenting a new list of words, on the other hand, interesting characteristics can be noted. What aspects of this list might the teacher use to add interest to spelling?

coal	goal	foal	hole	whole	mole
bowl	pole	role	roll	soul	roll

An inductive approach to this lesson will lead the children to identify several spellings for the sound ōl: *oal, ole, owl, oll, oul.* This list has been grouped according to a common sound with only the initial sound changing in each word. Extend learning by having children experiment with changing the vowel or the ending sound; for example, "If you know how to spell *coal,* what other word might you spell?" (coat, cool) What will be noticed about the pairs of words: *hole* and *whole, roll* and *role?*

An assorted group of words might be presented to a group of fourth graders.

huge	rather	spoken	hopeful	crimson
bicycle	control	present	examine	complete

We might begin with the first word by asking, "Who recognizes this word?" "Who knows what it means?" There would follow a discussion of other synonyms for *big.* What sound does the *g* make in this word? If we removed the *e,* what word would we have? Why is the *e* there? (To keep the *g* soft; to make the *u* long.) The word bicycle might initiate a discussion of the prefix *bi*, and *control* would warrant a comment on the prefix *con*. The word *present* is a heteronym which can lead to an interesting discussion (Who will present the present?).

Pretesting As noted previously, many spellings are learned incidentally, therefore before any study takes place the teacher should dictate each word to the group as a test, having each student attempt to spell the words correctly. The purpose is simply to determine which words are already known by each individual student. This test is marked (not graded) by the teacher or students, who may circle the part of each word which has been incorrectly spelled. The student can then compare the incorrect spellings with the list in the spelling book or on the board. This test–study–test method has been found more effective than study followed by testing without a pretest.

The student who already knows the spellings of the words presented can spend the time with some other profitable activity.

When marking student papers, accent the positive by noting the number right rather than always marking those wrong.

Inductive or discovery methods An effective technique of teaching understanding about spelling is through the inductive method, in which the student is led to make the discovery. Have older students name, for example, words which end with the common suffix, *tion*/šen/. As the words are named, write them on the board: *nation, convention, impression, examination, vacation, fission, confession, relation, aggravation, completion*. After twenty or more words have been named, ask the class what they notice about these words (that is, about the spellings of this sound in English). Have them form generalizations about the spelling of this suffix. One might expect a class to suggest statements similar to these:

1.   The suffix which sounds like SHUN is spelled SION or TION.
2.   -TION occurs after A.
3.   -SION occurs after the letter *s* which is then double.

Record the findings of this particular study on a chart to which additional findings can be added. The generalizations may be revised as new findings are noted; for example, someone may discover the group of deceptive words which terminate in SION which sounds /žən/ as in DECISION and REVISION. Also watch for the word COERCION.

Generalizations may be made after exploring the spelling of other commonly used affixes or phoneme groups. Have students examine these examples in the manner described:

1.   boner, honor, sulfur, grammar, recorder, splendor (How about martyr?)
2.   ease, marry, teens, piece, detour, sardine, pique, rainy, wee, fear
3.   mended, scored, shocked, crooked, hoped, spelled

Study steps Almost every set of spelling texts includes a list of steps for learning to spell a word. The steps usually are something like these:

1. Look at the word.
2. Say the word.
3. Say the parts of the word.
4. Try to write the word without looking at it.
5. Compare your spelling with that in the book.

These steps would undoubtedly be helpful if they were applied, but it has been found that the child studying spelling independently does not follow the prescribed steps—either because of their complexity or perhaps of sheer boredom.

Teaching concepts about spelling   It should be remembered that spelling is not taught in isolation. Encoding skills must be related to decoding skills so that children learn to read and write English words at the same time. They need to understand that these skills are related. We must keep pointing out these relationships as children write and read.

Spelling is the only standardized form of the English language. Oral speech is widely varied as people speak dialects according to the region of the country they live in. It is likely in any classroom that you will have children who have lived in different areas of the country. They will be aware of different ways of pronouncing such common words as *dog, house,* or *fire.* This variation in speech is perfectly acceptable. As we pronounce words in dictation exercises, for example, we are pronouncing words according to our own dialect. The variation is largely in vowel sounds, but a few consonant sounds such as /r/ are dropped by some speakers or added by others.

Written English, therefore, represents a form of the language to which all of us must learn to relate our speech. As you talk about spelling with students, you might discuss questions like these:

1. How did spelling become standardized?
2. How might not knowing how to spell be harmful to you?
3. Why is it easier to make spelling standardized than it is to standardize speech?
4. What is an advantage of having standardized spelling?
5. Do you think we overemphasize correct spelling?

STRATEGIES FOR INDIVIDUALIZING SPELLING

The spelling of English words opens up a fascinating study that will add to children's love of language as well as their ability to work more easily with the written language. Awareness of the patterns of spelling, the legitimate combinations of letters, and the relative frequency with which certain letters appear in English words are concepts that are acquired gradually by many, but not all, good readers. Guiding children to make such generalizations at an earlier stage through specific instruction will ensure that all children are exposed to such basic concepts and will provide a foundation for a well-developed spelling program that is essentially individualized. As Moffett and Wagner observe:

> Whether composing or transcribing, the continual groping to put words onto paper causes students eventually to find out how those words are spelled—to generalize, to memorize, to ask others, to consult the dictionary, and so on. The conditions for success are that they care about what they are saying and that they not feel penalized for misspelling what they are trying to say.[9]

What is individualized spelling? No single approach has been determined, although most authorities agree that the practice of teaching for individual needs and allowing for individual differences is highly desirable. Because the subject matter of a spelling program is more structured, it is easier to organize for individualized instruction than are other areas of the elementary school curriculum. A recommended approach includes diagnosis of spelling ability, teaching spelling as part of the writing program, and management by the teacher.

Diagnosing Individual Needs

Before we begin any instruction, we need to know what each child knows already. We also need to identify the miscues the child makes, indicating that instruction should provide specific information. The most reliable way to conduct this diagnostic analysis is through examining each child's individual writing. The writing to be examined can be free writing or a personal essay written about a given topic, for example: A Day That I Remember. A more structured analysis will be obtained through use of dictated sentences that are adapted to the general level of ability of students in your classroom.

Plan to dictate three sets of five sentences so that you have fifteen sentences for each student. You can compose your own sentences or select suitable ones from a reading book. Aim the difficulty level at the average or above-average student so that only a few students are likely to make no errors. Tell the students you are having them write so that you will know how to plan spelling lessons for them and that you don't, therefore, expect them to be able to spell all of the words correctly. Here is a set of sentences used in a fourth-grade classroom:

1. Mr. Johnson asked if he could help solve the mystery.
2. The policeman said, "I'd be happy if someone knew the answer."
3. "Where haven't you searched?" inquired interested neighbors.
4. "We've looked through the house, but not the yard," answered the detective.
5. Soon everyone was poking behind the bushes hunting vainly for the missing jewelry.

---

[9]James Moffett and Betty Jane Wagner, *Student-centered Language Arts and Reading, K-13* (Boston: Houghton Mifflin Co., 1976), p. 228.

Through dictation of selected sentences you can obtain a great deal of information. In addition to the spelling of specific words, you will learn how much a student knows about punctuation and capitalization. In this particular set of sentences quotation marks are featured, and several contractions appear. As you examine each student's writing, note errors made on a sheet which is designed for recording additional analyses at later dates:

Analysis of Writing Errors   Student_____

SPELLING: joolery havn't solvd
              mysterys intesested naybus

PUNCTUATION: ((((?
                  .

CAPITALIZATION: Detective
                     ≅

OTHER:
                                              Date: _____

SPELLING:

PUNCTUATION:

CAPITALIZATION:

OTHER:
                                              Date: _____

After conducting this analysis, arrange to have individual conferences with students to talk with them about planning an attack on their spelling problems. You might discuss the following topics:

1. What kind of help does the student think he or she needs?
2. How does the student feel about spelling?
3. Have the student read certain words to see whether pronunciation is affecting spelling.
4. See if the student can spell a word correctly after you say it, carefully emphasizing the syllables in the word.

Further analysis can focus on auditory discrimination. Test the whole class on their ability to identify the beginning consonants in given words, the consonant blends with which words begin, prefixes, suffixes, and so on. Focus on any grouping in the developmental sequence beginning on page 286. Space such tests over a period of several months so that instruction can follow each focus.

Keeping a Spelling Notebook

In a section of their writing notebook, have students collect interesting information about words. They can include their personal dictionary in this section, using one sheet for each of the common letters, perhaps placing two or three of the less common ones on the same page. Introduce students to word activities that will help them learn to spell more effectively and encourage them to share the results. Try some of the following:

• Name acrostics—Each child can make an acrostic based on the letters of his or her name. Some names are difficult, so allow plenty of leeway.

Carol might write: Coughs
                     Are
                     Really
                     Old
                     Laughs

Students can use the letters in their names to suggest adjectives that describe themselves, for example:

James Teel might write:

Joyful	Talkative
Ambitious	Effective
Massive	Efficient
Evasive	Lover
Saving	

• Tom Swifties—The Tom Swifty was a twentieth-century contribution to word play. Small books quickly appeared illustrating the use of adverbs especially appropriate to the quotation in a sentence as in these examples:

"I'll have seafood salad," she muttered crabbily.
"What a beautiful piece of wood," he remarked craftily.
"My, I'm terribly hoarse today," she whinnied.
"That song is too long," he announced curtly.

Students can invent Tom Swifties and portray a situation in which someone is making this remark. The humorous illustrations can be displayed for enjoyment by all and later compiled in an entertaining book.

Spelling in the Context of Writing

We need to spell only when we are writing, so it makes sense to teach spelling as a writing skill. Although it should not be allowed to impede the student's writing, the following suggestions will help students handle spelling as they write:

1. When you are writing, your ideas are more important than spelling every word correctly. If you don't know a word, you might use one of these methods:

    Leave a big space or draw a line where the word should go, and then go on writing.

Write as much of the word as you can without struggling, and then go on writing.

2. After you have finished your writing, read what you have written. Find out how to spell the words that you didn't know. Use one of these methods:

If you know the beginning letters, look in a dictionary. See how quickly you can find the word and write the correct spelling in place. Look at the word carefully to see how it is spelled and what part you didn't know. Try spelling it without looking so you won't be stuck on that word again.

If you can't think of the beginning, ask for help. The neighbor or the teacher will tell you how to spell a word if it is really hard, but don't wear out your welcome!

3. Write the words that stumped you in your personal dictionary. Study these words before you write again. Have another student test you on the words in your dictionary at least twice a month. Cross out words as you think you have mastered them.

4. Learn or create mnemonic devices that will help you remember spellings that are consistently difficult for you. Murray Suid lists eight basic links that can assist students:
    a. The build-in word link
       Example: *Forty* soldiers stormed the *fort*.
    b. The definitional link
       Example: A *beach* is land by the *sea*.
    c. The analagous pattern link
       Example: We will go *all together* or *all separately*.
    d. The story link
       Example: Use both *i's* (eyes) in skiing.
    e. The acronym link
       Example: Arithmetic—A rat in the house might eat the ice cream.
    f. The pronunciation link
       Example: Say Wed-*nes*-day
    g. The etymological link
       Example: If you have mus*c*les, you're mus*c*ular.
    h. The descriptive link
       Example: There's no *x* in ecstasy.[10]

Teaching with Word Games

Word games add to the fascination and enjoyment of learning to spell. We need to evaluate these game activities, however, to see that they really do teach spelling skills. Here are a number of pleasurable activities that do teach spelling concepts.

Word brackets[11]   Here is a game that helps to emphasize the patterns of English spelling. Choose a word that is interesting or related to a topic the class is studying. Print that word vertically on the board or a sheet of paper. To form the other side of the bracket, simply reverse the letters as shown:

---

[10]Murray Suid, *Demonic Mnemonics* (Belmont, Calif.: Fearon Pubs., Inc., 1981).

[11]Iris M. Tiedt, *Spelling Strategies* (San Jose, Calif.: Contemporary Press, 1975), p. 14.

M	erril	Y	S	cathingl	Y
O	bo	E	H	ustle	D
N	ec	K	A	caci	A
K	ee	N	D	evilis	H
E	ch	O	Y	earling	S
Y	a	M			

Score: 14   Score: 30

The score is the total of all letters within the brackets. The bracket letters themselves do not count. The object, obviously, is to find long words that increase your score. This game will send students to the dictionary as they search for words; naturally they scan through many possibilities during the search.

To adapt this game for younger children, permit them to extend words beyond the brackets. Only the letters that are within the brackets, however, count toward the score.

Help students make generalizations about English spelling after they have played word brackets a few times. This game particularly points up the ending patterns of English words. For example, whenever children see the letter *y*, they should remember that the word can end in the suffix *ly*. Knowing this immediately makes finding a long word easier. They soon learn that a final *s* makes it a cinch, because many words can be made into plurals or an *s* can be added to a verb. The letter *d* guarantees the use of *ed* to form a past tense of many verbs. The letter *h* signals the suffix *ish* which is frequently useful. *R* will appear in the common suffix *er* while *c* is in *ic*. *G*, of course, is especially easy because so many words end with *ing*. Students will learn at the same time that English words don't commonly end with vowels or such letters as *v* or *f*, and never with *q*.

Challenge students to make additional sets of word brackets to work on. Mount them on a bulletin board so other students can try to get bigger scores.

Focus on a phoneme[12]   The puzzle on page 223 focuses attention on the phoneme /g/ and the alternate ways of spelling that phoneme in English.

Phonograms[13]   Phonograms are groupings of letters that form consistent patterns in English spelling. We learn to spell and read them easily because of their familiarity. Here is a basic list although there are many more you might add:

all	an	ad	eat	eam
at	ang	ack	ean	en
ate	ap	ad	eed	eg
ail	ape	ell	eet	each
ain	ag	ed	end	eck
ait	age	et	ent	een

[12]Ibid., p. 25.
[13]Ibid., p. 29.

Across

1—someone staying in your home
4—opening
7—young woman
8—Russian girl's name
9—does go
10—score
11—game of catch
13—something to chew
14—old cloth
16—horrible
18—weight in metric system
19—obtain
21—sticky liquid
22—in the past

Down

1—an unreal being
2—in a bird's nest
3—male deer
4—jobs for a musician
5—bad disease
12—fruit
15—used ore
17—city in Holland
18—man's name
20—small stick

ill	ick	oat	oom	ule
it	iss	oar	ock	up
in	ite	ore	ood	ure
ip	ice	on	ull	um
id	ig	one	un	uss
ing	ike	ong	ung	ut
ind	oll	ort	ub	ute
ine	ot	oon	ug	uck
int	ote	ool	unt	ud

An interesting way to help students become more aware of phonograms is through developing rhyme lists. Give pairs of students a phonogram or two to develop as fully as possible. As students prepare rhyme lists, they will find that there may be several ways of spelling one set of phonemes, as in this example:

/eyn/

feign	gain	bane	sein(e)
deign	Cain	cane	vein
reign	lain	Dane	skein
	main	Jane	
	rain	Kane	
	vain	lane	
	brain	mane	
	chain	pane	
	(re)frain	sane	
	grain	vane	
	plain	wane	
	train	Zane	
	slain	crane	
	Spain	plane	
	strain		
	sprain		
	twain		

Dictionary games[14] Until children are ready to use a dictionary, alphabetical order has little use. Focus attention on letter order by displaying the alphabet cards around the room. Play games like these:

- *Beginning, middle, or end?* Say a word aloud as students open the dictionary to the approximate position. Don't worry about finding the exact word, but simply give a student a point if he or she opens the book to the right letter section.
- *Treasure hunt.* Students will enjoy a scavenger hunt that takes them into the dictionary. Each person must find the following:

  an animal
  a bird
  a word containing more than twelve letters
  a place
  a word that begins with a capital letter

  Let students suggest additional items to include in the search. Students write only the word found and the page number on which the word is located.
- *Catty words.* Initiate a search for words that contain the word *cat* in some fashion, for instance:

  catapult
  tomcat
  catch
  scatter

[14]Ibid., p. 31.

Display these words on a bulletin board decorated with pictures of many kinds of *cats.*

- *Getting at the root of things.* Help students develop vocabulary facility by giving each small group a root to investigate. How many words can you find that are based on each of these root words?

curro (run): current, course
onyma (name): synonym, antonym
phone (sound): microphone, phonology
malus (bad): malady, malpractice
capio (seize): capture, capacity

Managing an Individualized Spelling Program

A diagnostic report can be completed periodically, indicating clearly how each student is progressing. Keeping an individual record enables you to make comparisons and to determine the specific errors that are made, the quantity of errors compared with others in the same class, and whether the same errors are repeated.

Scheduling individual conferences about once a month maintains personal contact with each student. While discussion can focus on the needs of that student, the most important characteristic of the conference is positive reinforcement. You can flip through the student's personal dictionary to see that words are being entered and that some have been crossed out. You might want to ask the student to spell a few of the words that are crossed out.

Diagnosis will guide instruction. If you note that two or more students seem to have the same difficulty, invite them to meet with you at a table near the chalkboard. Discuss the spelling problem and have the students work together as they focus attention on the phoneme–grapheme relationship, the capitalization of proper nouns, or the spelling of such words as there–their–they're.

As you prepare new dictation exercises, include words that were missed in previous sentences or ones with which students have been having difficulty. After analyzing the sentences to record the errors, return the sentences to the students. Have individuals write each sentence in turn on the board. Discuss errors made as everyone corrects those on their own paper. The next day you could dictate the same sentences again as you challenge the entire class to try to "beat the teacher" by writing the sentences without errors. Have an able student dictate the sentences again, if you wish, to give more students a chance to write the sentences perfectly.

Motivating Student Interest

The most important task of the spelling instructor is to develop student interest and concern for spelling. What are the reasons for learning to spell words? It is beneficial to discuss this topic at the beginning of a school year. A list of reasons contributed by students is often more influential in affecting student opinion than a teacher-prepared list, although both lists might include the same points:

1. People can understand what you have written.
2. You make a better impression on those reading your work.
3. You make better grades in school on written work.
4. There is personal satisfaction in doing something well.

Why do we need standardized spelling? Why not permit everyone to spell as he chooses? This sentence written on the board will bring laughter, but should make your point:

Noo Girzee lize ahn thu koste.

The next problem in motivating interest is to select techniques which are stimulating rather than routine. Many spelling games are of little real value—for example, the spelling bee's emphasis on oral spelling does not teach the written skill of spelling, and too few children are actively involved at one time.

- BEWARE OF THE SILENT LETTER is the caption of a display featuring words (contributed by students) that contain silent letters printed in contrasting colors, for example:
  gnat   knob   debt   cupboard   column   slide
- Practice spelling words which are not known. Even the longest word can be spelled readily if it follows regular phonic patterns. Familiarity with common prefixes and suffixes is also helpful. Pronounce words carefully as children write them and build confidence through success. Aren't these words easy?

plantation	equitable	surrounding
fantastic	explanatory	blameless
convention	discovery	alliteration
insistent	reputation	equation

How would this exercise assist children in composition skill? Would you grade these words? What would you say if a child left out one L in alliteration?
- Unusual characteristics of words lend interest to the study of spelling as they do to the study of words (see Chapter 7). This poem can be read aloud, although each person should be looking at a copy, as an introduction to a study of homonyms:

> *A TAIL OF WHOA*
> (Two bee red allowed)
> Iris M. Tiedt
> Eye stood before the window pain
> To stair out on the stormy seen.
> The wind it blue
> With grown and mown
> As rein pored threw the lain.

Eye razed my head to view the cite
And new my hart wood brake
    Four rested from hour would
    Were awl the furs sew tall and grate
Know more too waive the see.

Aisle ne'er forget that dreadful knight—
A quire of desolation maid
    Buy hale and creek of bows—
    Yet still no paws or lesson.
The whether it was fowl!

Then shown at last the mourning son.
The heir now boar the fare suite cent
    Of rows and hair belle whet.
    At piece the wind; knot sew my sole,
Fore their the land lei waist.

- To give practice in using capital letters with names of cities and states, conduct an alphabet search as each person tries to find a city beginning with *A* (Akron, Ohio), then *B* (Baltimore, Maryland), and so on.
- WHAT WORD IS THIS? might be the title of these riddles which focus attention on the spelling of specific words as in this example:

I like green but I don't like purple.	(G)
I like house but not mouse.	(H)
I like autos but not cars.	(O)
I like sheet but not blanket.	(S)
I like night but not nigh.	(T)

(GHOST: one letter indicated by each line. Each letter is within the first word but not the second.)

- This humorous poem by an unknown poet may interest students in discovering examples of plurals which follow a similar pattern and those which deviate.

AN ENGLISH TEST

We'll begin with box, the plural is boxes,
But the plural of ox should be oxen, not oxes.
One fowl is a goose, but two are called geese,
Yet the plural of mouse is never meese.
You may find a lone mouse, or a whole nest of mice,
But the plural of house is houses, not hice.
If the plural of man is always men,
Why shouldn't the plural of pan be called pen?
The cow in the plural may be called cows or kine,
But a bow, if repeated, is never called bine;
And the plural of vow is vows, not vine.
If I speak of a foot and you show me two feet,
And I give you a boot, would a pair be called beet?

> If one is a tooth and a whole set are teeth,
> Why shouldn't the plural of booth be called beeth?
> If the singular's this, and the plural these,
> Should the plural of kiss ever be written keese?
> We speak of a brother, and also of brethren,
> But though we say mother, we never say mothren.
> Then the masculine pronouns are he, his, and him,
> But imagine the feminine, she, shis, and shim!
> So the English, I think you all will agree,
> Is the funniest language you ever did see.

• Teach any of these skills and spelling itself through the technique of dictation. Compose (or have students compose) sentences which illustrate the use of capitalization, plurals, contractions, and possessive forms, thus:

Mary's mother said, "Please, Mary, set the table."
Your three cats won't stay out of Mr. Handy's garden.
Harry's coming home for his grandfather's birthday.

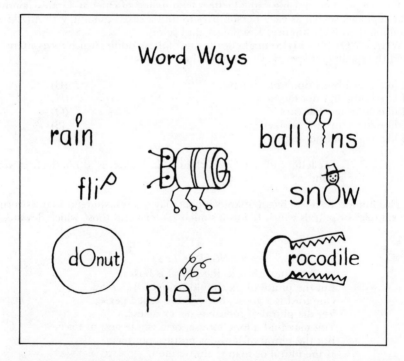

• *Word Play.* What is the value of this type of word play? Is time spent in this manner justified? The chief argument for presenting word play activities in the classroom is that these activities promote a feeling for words, a liking and respect for words. Words should never frighten or be considered dull, dutiful responsibilities. Rather they should intrigue and fascinate, inviting the young writer to play with them, to manipulate them. Intrigued by words met in this fashion, the child reaches out to discover other words.

SUMMARY

Spelling has been overemphasized as a writing skill to the extent that fear of misspelling words has impeded the student's free expression of ideas. Spelling should be viewed as a means to communicating accurately in writing. When students write first drafts, they are encouraged not to worry unduly about accuracy. Spelling can be corrected as part of the editing process. Improved methods of teaching students to spell by observing patterns and relating the sounds of English to specific graphemes will help make students aware of correct spellings. Students who play word games that stress spelling will learn much about the patterns of English spelling through enjoyable practice. Spelling should be taught as one aspect of the history and development of the English language.

CHALLENGE

Once you become aware of the intricacies of English spelling, spelling becomes a fascinating study to share with students. It can have much more depth and interest if you combine the focus of learning to spell with the study of language (See Chapter 7). Prepare for this approach to teaching through the following activities.

1. Prepare 3 activity sheets for students using ideas from this chapter. On the back of the sheet print the objective(s) you are trying to meet.

2. Outline a spelling program that you could follow at a specific grade level. Consider the basic needs of students at that level as well as the individual needs of each student.

3. Review the content of Chapter 7. Plan a series of lessons that relate language study and spelling instruction.

EXPLORING FURTHER

Allred, Ruel A., *Spelling: The Application of Research Findings.* National Education Association, 1977.

Barnitz, John G., "Linguistic and Cultural Perspectives on Spelling Irregularity," *Journal of Reading,* January 1980, 23:320–6.

Barnitz, John G., "Interrelationship of Orthography and Phonological Structure in Learning to Read," *Technical Report No. 57.* Urbana, Ill.: Center for the Study of Reading, University of Illinois, January 1978.

Chomsky, Carol, "Reading, Writing and Phonology," *Harvard Educational Review,* May 1970, 40, 2:278–309.

Dickerson, Wayne B., "English Orthography: A Guide to Word Stress and Vowel Quality," *International Review of Applied Linguistics in Language Teaching,* May 1978, 16, 2:127–47.

Goodman, Kenneth S., "Reading: A Psycholinguistic Guessing Game," *Journal of the Reading Specialist,* March 1967, 6, 3:126–35.

Graves, Donald H., "Research Update: What Children Show Us About Revision," *Journal of the Reading Specialist,* March 1979, 56, 3:312–19.

Hanna, Paul R. et al., *Spelling: Structure and Strategies.* Boston: Houghton Mifflin, 1971.

Hodges, Richard E., *Spelling: A New Approach.* Urbana, Ill.: National Council of Teachers of English, 1981.

Marino, Jacqueline L., "What Makes a Good Speller," *Language Arts,* February 1980, 57, 2:173–7.

—————, *Children's Use of Phonetic, Graphemic and Morphophonemic Cues in a Spelling Task.* Ph.D. dissertation, State University of New York at Albany, December 1978.

Smith, Frank, *Psycholinguistics and Reading.* New York: Holt, Rinehart and Winston, Inc., 1973.

Steinburg, Daniel D., "Phonology, Reading, and Chomsky and Halle's Optimal Orthography," *Journal of Psycholinguistic Research,* July 1973, 2, 3:239–58.

Venezky, Richard L., "English Orthography: Its Graphical Structure and Its Relation to Sound," *Reading Research Quarterly,* Spring 1967, 2, 3:75–105.

Wade, Barrie and Klaus Wedell, *Spelling: Task and Learner, Education Review.* Birmingham, England: Birmingham, 1974.

10

Handwriting allows the student to see his own spirit in action.

Charles Lehman[1]

HANDWRITING:
Communication and Art

Handwriting, writing by hand, has a long history dating back to the centuries before the birth of Christ. The Romans wrote in large capital letters that seem awkward compared with the flowing cursive we use today. Styles of penmanship and attitudes toward writing reflect the society in which they developed.

Handwriting, or penmanship, is a communication skill. Students need to learn the writing skills that enable them to communicate clearly in writing that is legible and comprehensible to the reader. Handwriting is also an art form that is beautiful, from a fine Spencerian hand to stylized calligraphy. Students can learn to write to communicate, but they can also learn to write beautifully to enhance their original compositions.

---

[1]Charles Lehman, *Handwriting Models for Schools* (Portland, Oregon: Alcuin Press, 1976).

BENCHMARK

Consider the following questions as you begin this study of handwriting:

1. Why do students need handwriting instruction?

2. Take a sample of your own handwriting. Are there certain letters that you make poorly? Is your writing legible to other people? How might you improve your writing?

3. How does handwriting instruction fit into the total language arts program? What is its relationship to the teaching of composition?

In this chapter we will explore the historical development of handwriting and outline procedures for teaching students to write. We will experiment with calligraphy as an art form that you can share with students to add stimulus to the language arts program. After completing this chapter, you should be able to:

- discuss the various styles of handwriting and the development of handwriting instruction
- demonstrate the manuscript alphabet
- know methods of presenting beginning calligraphy techniques
- write legibly with a cursive style
- use italic calligraphy as an art form
- list problems that students have with handwriting
- suggest ways of motivating interest in improving handwriting

LOOKING AT HANDWRITING INSTRUCTION

Despite the presence of typewriters and word processors, people do write. Handwriting is a skill that students need to learn as a way of communicating with the world. Children may begin writing before they enter school, but the primary-grade teacher is responsible for seeing that all students are introduced to the writing of letters during the first years of formal schooling.

There is some controversy about the teaching of handwriting. Should children learn to print or should they begin using a cursive style immediately? Which style of cursive writing should be used in the schools? How shall we deal with the lefthanded writer?

In this section of the chapter we will examine the historical development of handwriting and consider the state of handwriting instruction today. We will also discuss some of the issues related to handwriting instruction such as "handedness" and working with students who have disabilities.

How Handwriting Has Changed Historically

The history of handwriting is interesting information that can be shared with students of any age. The following chart summarizes the changing styles of cursive writing, the kind of writing that people have used both

λbcδefgHiKlMᶰ

EARLY ROMAN CURSIVE, 3rd C., B.C. to 3rd C., A.D.

Late Roman Cursive sample

LATE ROMAN CURSIVE, 4th C., A.D. to 8th C.

Lady Elizabeth by

SECRETARY, 13th C. to 19th C.

l'altro e' acuto et sotti

ITALIC (Chancery Cursive), 15th C. to 16th C.

Consolarrui fello mio nella uastra pouerta

ITALIAN HAND, 17th C. to 19th C.

ABCDEF abbcddefo

ENGLISH ROUNDHAND, 18th C. to date

Opportunity Opportunity

AMERICAN BUSINESS HANDS, 19th C. to date

Aa Bb Cc Dd   Aa Bb Cc

COMMERCIAL CURSIVE—MANUSCRIPT, 19-20th C. to date

Italic handwriting

ITALIC, 20th C. to date

The Development of Cursive Writing

formally and informally to record messages. All of us learned one of these styles as we began to write.

Lehman outlines the history of handwriting instruction in the United States by noting the major influences chronologically.[2] He credits Benjamin Franklin with one of the early efforts to create an instruction manual. Major influences between 1776 and 1976 include:

[2]Charles Lehman, *Handwriting Models for Schools* (Portland, Oregon: Alcuin Press, 1976), pp. 17–58.

JOHN JENKINS

This 36-year-old American published *The Art of Writing* in 1791. He simplified the formation of letters into six foundational strokes. Although his approach was highly mechanical, it served to standardize handwriting in a practical manner.

MUSCULAR MOVEMENT

Following Jenkins came such educators as Benjamin Franklin Foster who stressed motion of the fingers and the forearm. Described in *Practical Penmanship* (1830), Foster and others devised a wrist/finger strap that mechanized the writer in order to produce greater speed to meet the needs of industry.

COMMERCIAL PUBLICATIONS

As the need for writing increased in business, publications such as Platt Roger Spencer's *Business Penmanship* in 1848 appeared. Spencerian writing is characterized by a very fine line achieved with a steel pen. Others who entered the publishing of handwriting materials at this time included Charles Zaner and Austin Palmer, who began producing instructional materials for elementary school children around 1900. Handwriting styles taught in the classroom today still reflect the simplified forms and the stress on ease, speed, and legibility initiated at this time.

VERTICAL WRITING

At the turn of the century cursive writing was judged physically harmful to students, who were directed to face their desks straight forward and to write without slanting the letters. Although vertical writing did not last long, it did lead to more scientific research of handwriting. In 1904 Edward Thorndike introduced handwriting scales by which student writing could be judged.

MANUSCRIPT WRITING

At the beginning of the twentieth century revived interest in arts and crafts led to examination of handwriting and renewed interest in calligraphy. Marjorie Wise, a graduate student in education, who studied in London and in New York, devised manuscript writing as her thesis at Columbia University in 1924. Manuscript quickly became popular because of the simplicity of the forms and the attractiveness of the writing, which children mastered readily. Manuscript was intended to be used for all writing without the use of cursive.

The manuscript alphabet is used today for beginning writing instruction in most American elementary schools. The letters are formed much as they were in 1930:

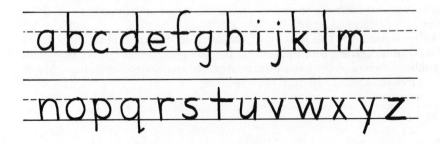

Emphasis on the speed of writing, however, still mandated the introduction of joined letters, cursive, usually in the second or third grade. The purchase of published instructional workbooks often dictates the particular letter style that is taught. According to research, however, none of the current cursive alphabets is better than another. The emphasis should be on writing comfortably and legibly rather than conforming to a specific alphabet form.

A trend that developed in the 1970s is the use of an alphabet for beginning writing instruction that is based on italic writing as performed by calligraphers. Similar to the manuscript, the beginning printing in italic materials adds the strokes that will later adapt into the joining of consecutive letters as students write cursively. The following italic alphabet is typical.

abcdefghijklmnopqrstuvwxyz

Italic printing and writing seem to make sense for handwriting instruction except for a few oddities such as the joining of the lowercase *e,* as shown here:

Do not join into letters that go up high.

Renewed concern about the total writing process has brought about a reconsideration of handwriting instruction. In general, emphasis is placed on mastery of the physical act of handwriting to facilitate the communication of ideas. Handwriting is a means to an end, not the end itself. Taught in conjunction with students' composition efforts, handwriting has purpose, namely, communication with the reader, the writer's audience.

Introducing Handwriting in the Classroom

When students enter school, they should be observed to see if their coordination and language development is appropriate to the introduction of writing. A few students in kindergarten will be ready to begin manuscript printing, but handwriting is more commonly introduced in first grade.

Manuscript printing   In most schools children learn a simple printing form before learning cursive writing. Manuscript printing is thought to be easier for the child to master because the forms are combinations of straight lines and circles and there are no joinings. The transition to cursive writing is relatively easy.

For manuscript printing the student sits with feet squarely on the floor. The paper is placed in front of the writer without slanting. Students should be introduced to letters in groupings that involve similar forms, for example:

Elementary teacher Sophie Gale describes the formation of the lowercase letters thus:

straight lines   l i t

circles   o c

circles and straight lines   a e d p

variations of a curve   u n m h

others   g j q f k r s v w x y z

> The general principle is that each letter has a left and a right side. Strokes on the left are made first. All circles are made to the left except *b* and *p*. Straight lines are generally made from top to bottom and from left to right. Touch students on their left or right shoulder, if necessary, to clarify left and right. Keep the pencil on the paper whenever possible, and establish a rhythm as soon as the students can form the letters.
>
> Begin writing by practicing sticks and circles. Tall sticks go from the top line to the bottom (base) line. Short sticks go from the dotted line on composition paper to the base line. Large circles start at the top line and go to the left. Do not allow students to repeat strokes as this slows the writing process.[3]

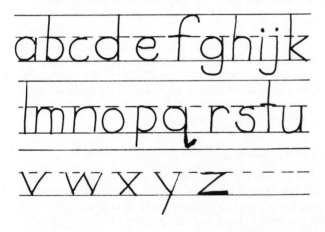

Cursive writing   After students have worked with manuscript, they will be able to make the transition easily by slanting their paper to the right or left. The corner of the page should point to the student's chest. The student sits straight facing the desk.

[3]Sophie Gale, "Manuscript and Cursive Handwriting," *The Elementary Teacher's Ideas and Materials Workshop,* March 1981.

Letters are grouped for instruction, thus:

Introduce one letter at a time. Students will slant the letter and add up-strokes at the end to facilitate joining. Demonstrate the difference between manuscript and cursive writing on the board to help students see the additions needed in cursive. The capital letters will be learned after students have been introduced to all of the lowercase letters. The capital letters are quite different from the lowercase, so require considerable practice.

Problems Students Have with Handwriting

Handwriting is sometimes ignored, particularly in the upper grades, but students do need help with this manual skill. Putting words on paper requires dexterity if students are to approach composition with any degree of success. The child who has problems with handwriting will not feel positive about writing and is not likely to become an effective writer, for the physical act of handwriting will continue to get in the way. It is important, therefore, that we assess the student's handwriting to determine if the student needs help. We should check the following:

1. Formation of specific letters, both lowercase and uppercase
2. General legibility
3. Speed of writing
4. Hand position, management of pencil and paper
5. Spacing and slant

Notice that being lefthanded is not viewed as a problem. The same attitude is true of physical disabilities that require individual consideration. These aspects of writing instruction will be discussed in another section.

Formation of letters Certain letters or combinations of letters have been identified as consistently causing difficulty, for example, the letter *f* in cursive writing. Although each child will differ in the types of problems they have with formation of letters, the following often require special attention: *b, d, f, g, h, k, q, r, v, w, x, y, z.* Notice that many of these letters have ascending or descending parts. Very few of the capital letters are written with ease so that we might list the few that appear to be relatively easy for most chidlren, for example: C, M, N, O

Legibility Formation of letters will, of course, affect legibility. Usually, the problem lies in confusing one letter with another, as follows:

a made like *u* or *o*
c made like *e* or *i*
d made like *cl*
l made like uncrossed *t*
m made like *w*
n made like *u* or *v*
o made like *a*
r made like *i* or *n*

Poor letter formation often occurs in the process of joining letters, for example: *r* following *b, o,* or *w.* Children consistently have trouble with joining *o* to any letter because they fail to keep the arm of the *o* up as in: corn, top, road, and how.[4]

Speed of writing Students for whom writing is difficult frequently are very slow. They write painfully, laboriously. It is often clear that they have not mastered the formation of many letters so that they are uncertain about making the letters needed. Testing students to determine the number of words they write per minute demonstrates to the students one reason for learning how to form letters more easily; it provides them with an incentive to practice writing to gain fluency. Having students copy from a page of a textbook that everyone has will enable them to compare their work with norms for handwriting speed like these:

MANUSCRIPT

	Grades 1	25 words per minute
	2	30

CURSIVE

	Grades 3	45
	4	50
	5	60
	6	67
	7	74[5]

[4]Edward R. Lewis and Hilda P. Lewis, "An Analysis of Errors in the Formation of Manuscript Letters by First-grade Children," *American Education Research Journal,* 2:25–35, 1965.
[5]*Guiding Growth in Handwriting: Evaluation Scale* (Columbus, Ohio: Zaner-Blosser, Inc., 1966.)

Repeat this speed test periodically for students who wish to improve their score. Help students analyze their problems individually so that they know how to focus their practice. The game nature of this approach to handwriting practice is motivating to students who can challenge themselves to get a better score.

Managing paper and pencil   Two ways of holding a pencil or pen seem to be equally comfortable and, therefore, equally effective. The traditional hold rests the pencil against the middle finger supported and guided by the index finger and the thumb. The shaft of the pencil extends between the index finger and the thumb. An alternate hold places the pencil between the middle and index fingers while the thumb supports the pencil below. Let children try both methods; eventually they will select the one that is most comfortable.

Paper is usually slanted on the desk to the left for a righthanded writer and toward the right for a lefthanded writer. The position of the paper should facilitate writing as comfortably, rapidly, and legibly as possible. Discussing the position of writing paper with students will lead to their discovering a comfortable slant for paper as they write.

Spacing and slant   Spacing involves both space between letters and between words and also the spacing of letters between the writing lines, the size of the letters. Attention to spacing should focus on legibility. If letters run together, the reader has difficulty discerning meaning. Letters that are unduly small are also difficult to read. Writing on the chalkboard will aid students in examining the spacing in their writing. Have students work in pairs as they critique their handwriting together and then practice to correct the spacing on the board.

The position of the hand, the way the pencil is held, and the slanted position of the writing paper determine the slant of the writing. The main point to make with students is that slant should be consistent. Writing in which the letters slant first one way and then another is unattractive and more difficult to read. Students can readily observe the slant of their writing by holding the paper toward the light and looking at the back of the sheet. Show students how to avoid changing hand position as they write. They can observe each other in pairs, helping each other diagnose the problems and taking turns writing slowly with the proper slant. Positive reinforcement will stimulate students to practice until they feel the proper position for maintaining an attractive slant.

All of these problems with handwriting are best attacked as soon as possible, for correcting a thoroughly ingrained habit is much harder than preventing it in the first place. Attention to these problem areas as children are introduced to handwriting will alleviate many of them. The cause of the problem may be due to the student's attitude or physical characteristics. Or it may be due to instructional practices, for example, forced early instruction or lack of assistance from the teacher. Recognizing the handwriting problem, finding its cause, and providing appropriate learning activities is the responsibility of the language arts teacher.

Special Considerations in Handwriting

As in all instruction, we need to be aware of individual student needs in handwriting. In each classroom there are likely to be a few lefthanded students; instruction must be adapted to recognize their needs. A few students will have other needs because of physical or learning disabilities. Students who don't happen to approach handwriting in the same way should feel comfortable in the classroom. All students need help in accepting and understanding students who may differ from them in any way.

Lefthanded students   Although only about 5 percent of our population is lefthanded, being lefthanded is not a disability. For some time educators tried to force the lefthanded student to change to writing with the right hand, but this practice has been discredited. Instead, we assist the lefthanded student to work with handwriting much as the righthanded student does, simply reversing the hand and paper positions.

Hand dominance is usually established before the child enters school. If there is any uncertainty, a child can be tested to determine if the left hand is dominant. A small percentage of persons may be ambidextrous. If the dominance of the left hand is found to be weak or wavering, the child may be encouraged to use the right hand because it makes living simpler in a righthanded world.

The sensitive teacher might compare lefthandedness to difference in eye color, interesting and distinctive, but not a matter to cause concern. A lefthanded person can be expected to perform no differently than one who is righthanded. Howell notes the use of the term "sinistrals" for lefthanded people, a word derived from the same Latin root as sinister, demonstrating the negative connotations we have associated wtih lefthandedness. This same attitude is reflected in phrases: lefthanded compliment, two left feet, out in left field. She concludes that we need to provide individualized help for lefthanded students.[6]

Disabled students   Disabled students who are mainstreamed into the regular classroom need individual consideration to determine their approach to handwriting. The deaf student, for example, will have no particular difficulty with handwriting. The blind student, on the other hand, will need special equipment and will not perform in the same manner as the sighted child. Students for whom handwriting is physically difficult or impossible should be aided in recording their thoughts in varied ways, for example:

1.   *Recording.* Students can record their thoughts on a cassette player, perhaps after special help in developing thoughts before recording them. Recording also requires a different approach to editing, revising, and improving the initial recording. One way of assisting the development of a composition is to transcribe the recording to provide a typed or printed copy that the student can edit and then record again.

[6]Helen Howell, "Write On, You Sinistrals!" *Language Arts,* 55, 7:852–56 (October 1978).

2. *Dictation*. Dictation can be directed to the microphone, like recording. It can also be done directly, with an aide or another student writing what the disabled student dictates so that a printed copy is produced immediately. Taking dictation is a beneficial experience for students who need more practice in developing writing fluency; assisting a disabled student can be a beneficial learning experience for students who may not be as orally fluent.

We need to recognize that physical disability does not equal mental disability. The physically disabled student may work with language readily with increasing sophistication and should be enabled to express thoughts orally. The mentally disabled student will have linguistic problems and may not be able to structure complex thoughts or to coordinate hand movement as necessary to produce legible handwriting. Each individual must be diagnosed to determine the most effective way of helping him or her grow to the fullest possible potential.

Today we recognize that handwriting instruction should not be ignored. We need to plan a handwriting program that begins when the student enters school and continues throughout the school years as part of composition instruction. As Peck states:

> In an age of technical and mechanized communication media, from response-equipped cable television to computerized personal letters, it is pleasing to witness a continuing concern with handwriting. Although seemingly almost an archaic tool, handwriting remains one means of individualized expression.[7]

In the next section we will examine instructional practices that stimulate students to practice handwriting skills and encourage them to improve their ability to write well.

HANDWRITING AS A COMMUNICATION SKILL

As Donald Graves observes: "Handwriting is for writing. It does not exist to make rows of circles, establish habits of cleanliness, copy epigrammatic statements, or involve the students in independent activity during the reading period. It is not an end in itself."[8] With the contemporary focus on composition instruction has come the need to reexamine the physical act of writing, handwriting or penmanship. Studies that revealed the poor quality of college freshman's composition abilities also revealed the poor quality of their handwriting. Mina Shaughnessy notes:

> . . . it is not unusual to find among freshman essays a handwriting that belies the maturity of the student, reminding the reader instead of the labored cursive style of children. Often, but not always, the content that is carried in such writing

[7]Michaeleen Peck et al. "Another Decade of Research in Handwriting: Progress and Prospect in the 1970s," *Journal of Educational Research*, 73:283–97, 1980, p. 297.

[8]Donald H. Graves, "Handwriting Is for Writing," *Language Arts*, 55:393–99 (March 1978), 399.

is short and bare, reinforcing the impression of the reader that the writer is "slow" or intellectually immature. Yet the same student might be a spirited, cogent talker in class. His problem is that he has no access to his thoughts or personal style through the medium of writing and must appear, whenever he writes, as a child.[9]

Handwriting is a skill, a tool to be used to facilitate communication. Visible immediately to the eye of the reader, the quality of a person's handwriting makes the first impression; illegible, messy writing is an obstacle and may establish a negative set in the reader's mind which is difficult to overcome.

In this section we will examine methods of teaching students to communicate more effectively through improved handwriting. Activities suggested should be incorporated in the teaching of composition. Many ideas will fit with the teaching of editing skills.

Seeing Personal Handwriting Realistically

Shaughnessy points out that "handwriting styles become extensions of ourselves and are therefore difficult to see, let alone change. Yet it is this 'seeing' of the handwriting through other eyes that is the most important experience for the student."[10] We need to provide experiences that help students see their own handwriting realistically. The following activities will aid students in evaluating their handwriting more objectively:

> Turn the page of writing upside down in order to view the writing without being distracted by the meaning. Students can observe the ease with which they write or the clearly laborious manner in which they form letters. Smooth curves, compared with angular, jagged lines, indicate writing that is easy, comfortable. To develop this fluency students who write in a cramped uncomfortable way may need exercises that loosen up the hand and arm muscles, for example, writing in the air with large swooping letter forms.
>
> Have students work in pairs as they examine each other's writing and discuss it together. Let them diagnose the problems and construct plans for helping each other improve the ease and legibility of letter formations. This approach is recommended for older students particularly.

Discuss the following topic with the whole class:

Everyone has one thing they can usually do better than anyone else: read their own handwriting!
We recognize this when we say: "I can't read my own handwriting!"

Graphology is a topic that can interest students in handwriting. Although it is not considered a scientific study, handwriting does represent the individual who performed the writing, and it may reveal subconscious per-

---

[9]Mina P. Shaughnessy, *Errors and Expectations* (New York: Oxford Univ. Press, 1977), p. 15.
[10]Ibid., p. 15.

sonality traits. The graphologist looks at margins, spacing between words, the pressure placed on the writing instrument, slanting, and size of letters, in addition to numerous specific aspects of writing such as the dotting of *i* and crossing of *t*. Having a guest speaker discuss handwriting analysis with your students opens up intriguing ideas and provides a new perspective for looking at writing. One recommendation that is supported by psychology as well as graphology is that we not force students to rigidly imitate a given style of writing. Experimenting with flourishes, for example, reveals a healthy creative attitude that supports the use of writing to communicate.

Research has also explored graphotherapy to determine whether handwriting analysis and instruction can change or improve self-concept. Stoller[11] worked with an experimental group of fourth graders who were taught certain handwriting strokes considered indicative of positive concepts of self while a control group received only conventional penmanship instruction. At the end of six weeks students in the experimental group showed significant gains in self-esteem as well as substantial improvement in handwriting skills while the control group made only minimal gain in handwriting ability and displayed a loss of self-esteem.

Talking about handwriting with students and helping them view their own writing realistically is a first step toward improving individual handwriting. Possibly, too, handwriting instruction can boost the students' self-concepts as they are made aware of the characteristics of handwriting done by strong personalities. The student who becomes interested in his or her own writing is likely to improve both legibility and attractiveness.

Relating Handwriting to Other Writing Skills

Graves considers research on handwriting to be in its infancy in terms of the interrelationships among spelling, handwriting, and composing processes.[12] Obviously, the student who writes laboriously and illegibly is not likely to enjoy writing and will not be motivated to write independently. This student will not, therefore, become a good writer if we operate on the assumption that students learn to write by writing. Improving the physical act of handwriting can be included with objectives for a composition-centered language arts program presented within the context of the whole writing process, thus:

Discuss the nature of handwriting as a physical act that is used to communicate in written form. Have students demonstrate and critique writing positions—body, feet, hands, way of holding pencil, paper position. Talk about the reasons for using one position compared with another.
Demonstrate ways that handwriting can affect spelling, for example, in forming the letters *o* and *a* or making an *i* that looks like an *e*. Have students compose sentences in which such spelling variation would confuse communication in humorous ways.

[11]Richard J. Stoller, *Can Self-concept Be Improved in a Group of Children by Changing Certain Handwriting Strokes in Their Writing?* (Urbana, Ill.: ERIC, 1973).
[12]Graves, p. 393.

Speed writing focuses on helping students write more easily and more quickly so that they can compose an essay or write answers to questions in a test more readily. Have students copy sentences from a textbook that everyone has. Time them for three minutes as they write as quickly, yet legibly, as they can. At the end of the three minutes students should count the number of words they copied and divide by three. Prepare an analysis of the varied rates of words per minute, thus:

90-99	‖‖	40-49	‖
80-89	ℍℍ ‖‖	30-39	‖
70-79	ℍℍ ℍℍ ‖	20-29	
60-69	‖‖	10-19	
50-59	‖	0-9	

Students who write fewer than fifty words per minute should analyze their handwriting to determine what keeps them from writing easily. After practicing on difficult letters for a week, give them a speed test again. Repeat this practice and testing periodically, as needed. Help students see this exercise, not as competition, but as a way of improving individual skill with performing a physical task; use the analogy of learning to ride a bike or a horse.

In England, the following sentence is used by typing students:
Have students compose sentences that contain every letter of the alphabet. Identify each letter of the alphabet in this example that is frequently used by typists for practice:

> The quick brown fox jumped over the lazy dog.

In England, the following sentence is used by typing students:
> The junior office clerks were quite amazed at the extra reward
> given by their generous employer.

Copying the original sentences students compose provides interesting practice. Challenge students in the class to devise innovative ways to write the alphabet, for example:

1. Print each letter in manuscript.
2. Write each letter in cursive writing.
3. Write the capital letters.
4. Write the small letters, but join them as you write, thus:

abcdefghijklmnopqrstuvwxyz

Combine writing with art activities, for example, make a design by writing one letter across a page vertically as well as horizontally, as shown:

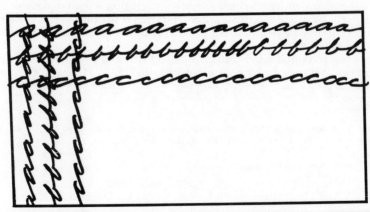

Show students examples of letters written by early statesmen. Have them emulate this elaborate writing style as they communicate with someone who lived at that time. For a variation, two students might write letters to each other assuming the roles of two historical figures.

Show students how handwriting varies in different countries. Bring in examples of published materials used for teaching handwriting in other countries such as Mexico. For example, in this page from a Russian copybook, students can observe the use of a different alphabet in print and in cursive.

Если указательный палец легко поднимается, отделяется от ручки, то это показывает, что ручка свободно держится

Пальцы должны быть лишь слегка согнутыми и не сжимать сильно ручку.

Положение ручки при письме

Так надо сидеть во время письма

Учись писать

грамотно,

чисто

и красиво!

Reproduction of beginning instructions in Russian handwriting copybook, published in 1963, Moscow.

The chalkboard can be used to stimulate interest in writing. Students can use small slates or the large chalkboard for practicing the formation of letters that they find difficult. Being able to erase and rewrite is a distinct advantage. Provide challenges to stimulate practice, for example:

Print several new vocabulary words on the board with space below where students can write the word to meet the challenge: Who can write this word most beautifully?

tortuous   ravenous   serendipity

tortuous

ravenous

serendipity

Write a quotation on the board that all students can use for handwriting practice, for example:

   Never leave until tomorrow what you can do today.—Benjamin Franklin
   Fear always springs from ignorance.—Ralph Waldo Emerson

Then, have students choose a quotation to present on the chalkboard. Individual students can take turns presenting a new one each day. Students will enjoy poring over books of quotations.

As a special incentive, let students use colored chalk.

   If we want students to become better writers, we need to plan activities that engage them in writing for clear purposes. Activities should be designed to teach specific skills, but they should also be creative and enjoyable.

Research and Handwriting

As we focus attention on improving composition skills of students at all levels, we are also becoming more aware of the importance of handwriting and its relationship to the total writing process. Although we have operated on certain implicit assumptions, it is important that we clarify our knowledge about handwriting and make findings of research explicit. The types of questions that research might address include:

1.   What is the effect of handwriting speed on composition? How does speed affect the content of student writing?
2.   How does physical development affect handwriting? How do children for example, change in their use of the thumb and forefinger?
3.   How does the amount of writing affect handwriting? How does the continuousness of writing change?
4.   How does the use of writing space change with practice and a developing sense of audience?
5.   How does involving students in self-diagnosis and planning for self-improvement affect handwriting development?
6.   How do specific practices in the teaching of writing affect student handwriting?

   Classroom research by teachers is badly needed. Through diagnosis of student problems followed by the use of specific instructional strategies you can contribute to knowledge in this field and improve your own instruction. The steps in conducting classroom studies are relatively simple:

STEP 1:

Assess student writing by taking a sample of handwriting in as clearly defined a way as possible. For example:

Have all students copy this sentence from the board (a farpoint model in sentence form that includes all letters of the alphabet):
The quick brown fox jumps over the lazy dog.
Ask students to copy the sentence three times in their very best handwriting. They select the best copy to be used as their benchmark. These sentences are analyzed to determine what the student can and cannot do.
Items to be evaluated may include:
Formation of letters
General legibility
Spacing of letters
Spacing between words
Relative speed of writing

STEP 2:

Use classroom instruction to improve student handwriting as needed.
Define the procedures to be used as specifically as possible, for example:
1. Students will be given a copy of the lowercase letters of the alphabet. Those with which individuals had difficulty will be underlined. Discuss how student writing was evaluated—formation of letters, legibility, spacing, speed. Write test sentence on board.
2. Students will trace any letters that are underlined and write those letters correctly five times each. All students will write the assessment sentence (see step one) two times, trying to form each letter correctly. This practice will be repeated on Tuesday and Thursday for one month (four weeks).

STEP 3:

Assess students' handwriting again using the same method as in the pretest. Compare results to determine if student handwriting has improved.
Further information about conducting research in handwriting and improving instruction can be found in these publications:

Andersen, Dan, *Handwriting Research: Movement and Quality.* National Council of Teachers of English, 1966.

Brown, Gerald R., *Handwriting: A State of the Art Research Paper.* ERIC, National Council of Teachers of English, 1977.

Graves, Donald H. "Handwriting Is for Writing." *Language Arts,* 55:393–9, March 1978.

Peck, Michaeleen et al., "Another Decade of Research in Handwriting," *The Journal of Educational Research,* 73, 5:283–299.

Towle, Maxine, "Assessment and Remediation of Handwriting Deficits for Children with Learning Disabilities," *Journal of Learning Disabilities,* 11:370–77, June/July 1978.

HANDWRITING AS AN ART

Recently interest in calligraphy has been renewed. Numerous classes offer adults the opportunity to learn italic styles which are fairly easy to master and to move on to other styles of writing as an art form. These same techniques can be introduced to students as a way of adding interest to the study of handwriting and improving their own handwriting. Calligraphy also offers a marvelous way to present short original student writing or to enhance collections of student writing.

In this section we explore ways of working with calligraphy in the classroom. Included are the basic techniques of printing with the italic alphabet. Activities that involve students in using calligraphy will extend their interest and ability in forming the letters as well as spacing the material to be presented and coordinating the writing with other art. Some classroom activities will integrate language arts instruction with other areas of the curriculum.

Introducing the Italic Alphabet

The italic alphabet is similar to manuscript printing, which most students already know. They will have little difficulty with the italic forms and with practice will produce them adequately, deriving great satisfaction from the result. This sense of achievement motivates students to practice without pressure from the instructor or the feeling that the task is something they "have to do." Calligraphy provides a new impetus to working with handwriting.

The italic alphabet reproduced below and on page 251 consists of a basic lowercase (miniscule) and uppercase (majuscule) set of letters. Variations of these forms will be found in reference books such as:

Eager, Fred, *The Italic Way to Beautiful Handwriting: Cursive and Calligraphic.* New York: Collier Macmillan.
Johnston, Edward, *Writing & Illuminating & Lettering.* New York: Pentalic Corp.
Reynolds, Lloyd J., *Italic Calligraphy and Handwriting.* New York: Pentalic Corp.
Svaren, Jacqueline, *Written Letters: 22 Alphabets for Calligraphers.* Freeport, Maine: Bond Wheelwright Co.

As in any kind of instruction, it is imperative that you experiment with calligraphy before attempting to share the techniques with students. Although you do not have to be an expert, you do need to know how to hold a pen and to be aware of the characteristics of each letter. Taking a class in calligraphy is highly recommended, but you could learn independently by using the book by Eager cited above.

a b c d e f g h i j k l m n o

p q r s t u v w x y z

As you plan to introduce calligraphy, collect the supplies that you need. Students can begin with pencils, crayons, or felt pens, but they will soon be able to use ink for more authentic and satisfying effects. The following basic materials will provide for beginning experiences:

MUSIC LINER

A useful tool that holds five pieces of chalk for producing a staff for writing music on the chalkboard. Use with three pieces of chalk to make wide lines on which to print letters as models for student work.

LINED PAPER FOR STUDENTS

You can purchase this paper or make it yourself by copying a sheet on a duplicating master. The center line should be marked as shown here:

PENS

Inexpensive dip pens can be purchased for use with replaceable points (nibs). Such pens are recommended for use with class groups. Convenient fountain pen sets are available in art supply stores. Because they do not require constant dipping for new ink, these pens eliminate the need for open bottles of ink in the classroom, but are more expensive.

INK

Standard fountain pen ink is the least expensive kind of ink recommended for student use. India ink may be used for special projects. Tempera paint may be used for larger poster printing with a brush or special pen.

PAPER FOR FINISHED PRODUCTS

A variety of paper should be available for printing after students have attained a certain degree of proficiency with printing the letters. If pens are used for printing, the paper should have a smooth surface.

Steps for instruction with students can begin with pencil or crayon on newsprint that students line themselves. Older students can move quickly into working with ink on lined paper that you provide. Begin instruction with ink as outlined by teacher Kathleen Watanabe:

STEP 1:

Have students focus on holding the pen at a 45° angle to the paper as they practice making lines as in this exercise:

STEP 2:

Introduce sets of related letters. Students should complete a full line of each letter after you demonstrate the formation on the board.

Set A: *itl*

Set B: *hnm*

Set C: *bp*

Set D: *rk*

Set E: *audgqc*

Set F: *oe*

Set G: *fjs*

Set H: *vwy*

STEP 3:

Practice words using various combinations of the lowercase letters, for example:

breadth among mammal had piquantly

A quick brown fox jumps over the lazy dog

STEP 4:

Introduce the capital letters one by one as students make a line of each letter for practice. Use the following groupings:

Key strokes used in other formations: *IO*

Wide letters: *AVHNTZKXY*

Medium widths: *BPRLEFJS*

Widest letters: *MW*

Elliptical letters: *OQ CGUD*

Students have been introduced to all of the lowercase and uppercase letters so they are ready to write sentences, their names, quotations, or short poems. As with any skill, the way to learn how to be a good calligrapher is to practice. Before students work more extensively, you might discuss the following points with them:

1. A calligrapher would never write a whole name or word in all capital italic printing.
2. Spacing between words should be even. It is measured by the size of the letter *o* and is, therefore, called an *o*-space.
3. Students can forget to join letters entirely as they enjoy presenting writing artfully. Later, if you want to show them how to join letters, point out the following:
   a. Three basic joins:
      strokes that swing up: *i, u, s, o, e, j, p, t*
      strokes that curve into the next letter: *n, r, m*
      crossbars: *f, t*
   b. Letters that are not joined: *k, g, q, b, v, w, x, y, z*[13]

[13]Kathleen Watanabe, "The Art of Beautiful Writing." Unpublished monograph, San Jose, California.

Activities Using Calligraphy

The language arts studies will be much enhanced by the use of calligraphy. Calligraphy can be used in a variety of ways, for example:

Titles of student-made books—When students complete a written report in any subject area, they can prepare an attractive cover page.

Attractive posters for the library give students the opportunity to experiment with different kinds of printing.

Favorite short poems—haiku, cinquains, couplets—can be presented in calligraphy. Students can experiment with the layout of the page including both art work and printing.

Have students print their own names. They may make nameplates for their desks for an open house when parents will visit the classroom, thus:

Teach students the vocabulary of lettering, for example:

Encourage students to collect meaningful quotations that they would like to present in calligraphy. Students will enjoy browsing through books of quotations as they select quotations such as:

Go and catch a falling star.—John Donne
To err is human, to forgive divine.—Alexander Pope
Nothing happens unless first a dream.—Carl Sandburg
Science belongs to no one country.—Louis Pasteur

Have students design an artful presentation of their favorite quotation as a holiday gift for a friend or relative. The example below demonstrates a varied lettering style.

Paper bound books of quotations can be purchased in any bookstore. A good assortment for teachers is: *Quotes for Teaching* by S. Tiedt (Contemporary Press, Box 1524, San Jose, Calif. 95109, $2.50 including postage):

*The first time
I read
an excellent book,
it is to me just as if
I had gained
a new friend.*

— Oliver Goldsmith

Students will discover many uses for calligraphy. Encourage them to add interest to their writing by adding an artful touch to monographs, brochures, flyers, party invitations, and family trees. Students can decorate their own stationery and make greeting cards for members of their families. Calligraphy helps to make their writing efforts special.

SUMMARY

Handwriting should be taught as an integral part of the writing process, for skill in performing the physical act of writing affects the student's ability to communicate through writing. Students should discuss the importance of being able to write comfortably and easily as they become aware of their own writing and how it affects their communication with the world.

Handwriting should be viewed primarily as a means of communicating. It also can be enjoyed as an art form as students experiment with calligraphy, using penmanship to enhance language arts activities. Open, imaginative approaches to the teaching of handwriting will increase student interest in improving their ability to write legibly and attractively.

CHALLENGE

As you think about handwriting instruction, try the following activities that can be used with students in the classroom.

1. Create your own personal alphabet chart for manuscript or cursive handwriting. Add art to decorate the chart as you like.

2. Collect samples of varied handwriting to share with students. Duplicate copies of writing done by various people in the early days of our country's history to add reality to social studies.

3. Work through the instructions for introducing italic printing to students. Use a book on calligraphy if you need more suggestions. Create samples that you can use in the classroom as models for ways that students might use calligraphy.

EXPLORING FURTHER

Askov Eunice et al., "A Decade of Research in Handwriting: Progress and Prospect," *Journal of Educational Research* 64:100–111, 1970.

Herrick, Virgil E., ed., *New Horizons for Research in Handwriting*. Madison: University of Wisconsin Press, 1963.

Lehman, Charles, *Italic Handwriting & Calligraphy*. Portland, Oregon: Alcuin Press, 1973.

Lehman, Charles L. *Handwriting Models for Schools*. Portland, Oregon: Alcuin Press, 1976.

Metzger, Louise and Rutheda R. Lehotsky, *Functional Handwriting Manual*. ERIC, National Council of Teachers of English, 1977.

Peck, Michaeleen et al., "Another Decade of Research in Handwriting: Progress and Prospect in the 1970s," *Journal of Educational Research*, 73:283–298, 1980.

Sloan, Charles A. and DeWayne Triplett, *Parents and Teachers: Perceptions of Handwriting*. Urbana, Ill.: ERIC, 1977.

PART IV

Opening Doors
to Reading Literature

11

Being able to read is one of the best things in everybody's life.

Charlotte Zolotow[1]

READING AS A
LANGUAGE ART
Oral Language, Print,
Comprehension

Reading is not a single skill that can be taught in isolation from other areas of the curriculum and the child's development. It is a complex process that is interrelated to thinking and all language growth, and reading instruction overlaps the other subjects that comprise the total elementary school curriculum. In this chapter, therefore, we will discuss reading as a language art that is best taught within the context of a well-integrated language arts program.

Children begin learning to read when they begin learning language long before they enter a formal classroom. As Page and Pinnell note:

When children approach the complex task of trying to make sense out of printed language, they rely on all their background, particularly on what they

[1]Charlotte Zolotow, quoted in: *Books I Read When I Was Young: The Favorite Books of Famous People* ed. Bernice Cullinan and Jerry Weiss (Urbana, Ill.: National Council of Teachers of English, 1980).

have learned about language. By the time they are asked to comprehend printed symbols in school, they have already learned an extraordinary amount of language.[2]

As we have pointed out in preceding chapters, the child's way of learning to speak provides a model for reading instruction. Assuming a close relationship between oral language and the printed word will support the child's early efforts to read.

BENCHMARK

To be a good teacher you do not have to be a linguist. You do need, however, to think about the relationship of reading to language learning and to consider how children can learn to read with efficiency and enjoyment. Discuss the following questions.

1. Review your thinking about how young children acquire language. List the characteristics of this learning process.

2. Discuss ways that teachers might facilitate the child's learning to read in a manner similar to that used when learning language. Jot down your conclusions for reference at a later time.

3. What role does reading play in your life? Can you remember experiences involved with learning to read? Write a paragraph about reading in your life.

4. What are appropriate goals for a reading program today? What should children learn through reading?

In this chapter we will focus on helping children learn to read. We will examine the sound–symbol system that children are learning to relate. We will also look at varied perceptions of reading and their implications for teaching. In the second half of the chapter we will explore strategies that assist children in learning to read, methods that fit an integrated approach to language arts instruction. The following chapters on children's literature and poetry will augment this presentation of ways to teach reading, for a good reading program must incorporate the best of children's literature, including that special genre, poetry, as students learn to gain meaning from reading. After reading this chapter, you should be able to:

- describe a strong reading program that meets the needs of students
- compare several approaches to the teaching of reading
- discuss ways of helping children relate print to the language they know
- compare the way children learn speech and ways of learning to read
- define reading as gaining meaning or comprehension
- explain the importance of moving children into reading literature

[2]William D. Page and Gay Su Pinnell, *Teaching Reading Comprehension* (Urbana, Ill.: ERIC/ National Council of Teachers of English, 1979), p. 21.

UNDERSTANDING READING

What is reading? How can we best help the child to read? These are essential questions to be considered in the 1980s as new insights from research in psycholinguistics, brain studies, and new perceptions of literacy as liberation, empowerment for the student, suggest alternative approaches to reading instruction.

A student-centered approach to reading will "respond to what the child is trying to do," as Frank Smith suggests, for "the motivation and the direction of learning to read can only come from the child, and he must look for the knowledge and skills that he needs only in the process of reading. Learning to read is a problem for the child to solve."[3] This perception of reading calls for greater emphasis on reading as a way of learning and integrated language arts activities that provide purposes for reading.

Studies of the child's acquisition of language demonstrate the child's ability to abstract the complex rules of English grammar from speech that is heard. No one tells the child the rules for constructing a sentence; no one tells the child how language works. Goodman and Smith believe that this is the way children should approach reading:

> The child is already programmed to learn to read. He needs written language that is both interesting and comprehensible, and teachers who understand language learning and who appreciate his competence as a language learner.[4]

Operating from these ground rules, we will begin exploring the reading process and strategies that will bring children to reading in as natural a manner as possible.

Reading in the United States

Reading has been a major focus for education since the beginning of our country. The rationale for teaching reading, however, has changed radically. The *New England Primer* includes this incentive for learning to read in the 1600s:

GOOD BOYS AT THEIR BOOKS

He who ne'er learns his A, B, C,
Forever will a Blockhead be;
But he who to his Books inclin'd
Will soon a golden Treasure find.

The treasure is, of course, religious enlightenment, exemplified by the "Assembly of Divines and Mr. Cotton's Catechism, Spiritual Wisdom Drawn

---

[3]Frank Smith, "Twelve Easy Ways to Make Learning to Read Difficult," in *Psycholinguistics and Reading*, ed. Frank Smith (New York: Holt, Rinehart & Winston, Inc., 1973), p. 195.

[4]Kenneth Goodman and Frank Smith, Ibid., p. 180.

from the Breasts of Both Testaments" contained at the back of the primer.

The purposes for teaching reading have changed, and so has the method of instruction. This outline records the major directions through the years.[5,6]

Prior to 1900	Spelling and alphabet approach to reading
	Moralistic reading materials; *The Bible*
	The New England Primer, 1683
	The American Spelling Book, 1790
	McGuffey Readers, 1836
1900–1910	Reading-focused curriculum
	Emphasis on oral reading
1910–1920	Scientific analysis applied to reading achievement
	Standardized tests of reading
	Beginnings of silent reading
1920–1930	Many research studies
	Concept of individual differences
	Remediation in reading
1930–1940	Reading as part of the activity program
	Reading readiness concept
1940–1950	Focus on adult literacy
	Mass media influence
	Interrelationships of language arts
1950–1960	Public criticism of reading instruction
	Influence of television
	Individualized instruction
1960–1970	Innovation in beginning reading instruction
	Concern for education of "disadvantaged" child
	Influence of linguistics on study of reading
	Technology in reading instruction
	Stress on literature in reading and English programs
1970–1980	Studies of child acquisition of language
	Psycholinguistic analysis of reading process
	Description of Black English; writing of BE primers
	Concern for affective as well as cognitive learnings
	Studies of sexism in literature and textbooks
	Right to Read effort at the national level
	Emphasis on reading in secondary schools
1980–	Focus on gaining meaning from reading, comprehension[7]
	Reading across the curriculum
	Studies of right-brain and left-brain thinking processes
	Learning to read by reading
	Concern for instruction of minority students
	Bilingual programs and ESL instruction
	Multicultural education within basic instruction
	Literacy for liberation, empowerment of the student

[5]Nila B. Smith, "What Have We Accomplished in Reading?—A Review of the Past Fifty Years," *Elementary English*, March 1961, pp. 141–50.

[6]Charles C. Fries, *Linguistics and Reading* (New York: Holt, Rinehart & Winston, Inc., 1962), pp. 1–34.

[7]Stephen N. Judy, *The ABCs of Literacy*. (New York: Oxford Univ. Press, 1980).

Currently, emphasis lies on a student-centered approach to reading for the purpose of freeing the child or the adult. A definition that reflects this emphasis stresses the social significance of reading and writing literacy:

> Literacy is that demonstrated competence in communications skills which enables the individual to function, appropriate to his age, independently of his society and with a potential for movement in society.[8]

Methods for Teaching Reading

The teaching of reading is "big business," and publishers have produced quantities of textbook series, packaged reading kits, and programs for print or computerized presentation. Behind each of these sets of teaching materials lies a philosophy or theory of how children can best learn to read. The theory varies according to the author's perception and knowledge of the reading process. The theory mandates how the reading process is presented to the learner, the types of teaching materials used, and the expectations for student performance. In this section we will examine a number of systems for organizing and presenting a reading program in the elementary school.

The basal reader   The method of instruction most widely used in reading is the "basal reader," or "controlled vocabulary," approach. Almost every textbook company has a series of reading books for grades one through eight, usually with two or more titles prepared for each grade level. This highly structured method of teaching reading is based on student texts, workbooks, and teacher's editions which provide detailed guidance for the teacher. The basal reader series has the following attributes:

1. It represents an early attempt to provide for the sequential development of reading instruction.
2. It assists the beginning teacher who is uncertain about the teaching of reading.
3. It provides the poorly trained teacher with an acceptable approach to reading.

As new approaches to reading have been explored, the basal reader approach has received much critical attention. Slavish adherence to the "system" has sometimes resulted in attitudes like that of the principal who stated: "I don't care how well Ann reads. She is to go through the basic reader like any other fourth grader. And I don't want to find her in the library again doing special work."[9] The following questions have been raised:

1. Can any *one* system provide for individual needs of students?
2. Is the material read in this reading program of highest literary quality?
3. Is the basal reader program monopolizing the reading program to the exclusion of the teaching of literature in the elementary school?

[8]Robert Hillerich, "Toward an Assessable Definition of Literacy," *The English Journal,* 65:50–55 (February 1976).

[9]Cynthia Parsons, education editor, *The Christian Science Monitor,* January 22, 1965.

4. Are teachers using the program to its fullest potential, or is it used as a "crutch"?
5. Are teachers, especially at upper grade levels, really *teaching* reading?
6. Are children motivated to read each story, or are reading experiences assigned routinely, with workbook pages used as *busy work?*
7. Has the basal reader program been successful in producing a citizenry that reads?

Simplifying phoneme–grapheme correspondence Consisting of an augmented Roman alphabet of forty letters, the Initial Teaching Alphabet, commonly known by the acronym ITA, represents one attempt to provide a one-to-one correspondence between the sounds of English and the letters we use to signal each sound. To avoid confusion, no special uppercase letters are used. This alphabet is reproduced on the following page.

The contribution of Sir James Pitman, ITA was introduced in England in 1959 and has been used in both England and the United States. The Early to Read Series consists of seven books using the Initial Teaching Alphabet; the last book of the series is aimed at assisting the transition to traditional orthography. Both the reading texts and titles from children's literature are available.

An experimental program in the Fremont Unified School District, California, found the following advantages in the use of ITA:

1. First-grade children learned to write creatively at the middle of the year.
2. Interest level of ITA materials was considered higher, with less repetition and with vocabulary similar to that used by the child.
3. With the sound symbols, the child could attack any word.
4. Parents were favorably impressed.

Disadvantages noted were:

1. Difficulties when children transferred to other schools.
2. Expense of the program (texts were not state-adopted).
3. Substitute teachers were unable to teach this alphabet.[10]

Although modified alphabets seem to have promise and are still recommended by some researchers, ITA has not been adopted to any great extent. It may have some use as a remedial technique with students who have been "turned off" to reading.

Programmed instruction Programmed materials can be especially helpful at varied levels of reading development ranging from visual discrimination to the study of affixes to exploration of literature concepts. Books have been prepared, for example, by Sullivan Associates which guide the beginning reader step by step through the acquisition of reading skills. Programmed materials include not only books and workbooks but also com-

æ	b	c	d	ee
f__ace__	__b__ed	__c__at	__d__og	ke__y__

f	g	h	ɨe	j	k
__f__eet	le__g__	__h__at	fl__y__	__j__ug	__k__ey

l	m	n	œ	p	ɼ
__l__etter	__m__an	__n__est	__o__ver	__p__en	g__ir__l

r	s	t	uɐ	v	w
__r__ed	__s__poon	__t__ree	__u__se	__v__oice	__w__indow

y	z	ʒ	wh	ch
__y__es	__z__ebra	dai__s__y	__wh__en	__ch__air

th	th	∫h	ʒ	ŋ
__th__ree	__th__e	__sh__op	televi__s__ion	ri__ng__

a	au	a	e	i	o
f__a__ther	b__all__	c__a__p	__e__gg	m__i__lk	b__o__x

u	ω	ɷ	ɷu	ɔi
__u__p	b__oo__k	sp__oo__n	__ou__t	__oi__l

263

puters which immediately indicate whether the student's answer is correct. An interesting study was made of instruction in reading with a computer-assisted instructional system at Stanford University where first-grade children were taught to read.[11]

The advantages of programmed instruction are several:

1. Programs can be used individually with little aid from the teacher, and students work at their own rate.
2. The response is immediately checked against the right answer; there is no waiting period for correction of papers.
3. A carefully designed sequence will cover all points in a developmental program.
4. Programs are planned in such small learning units that children are able to succeed.
5. The teacher is freed for *teaching;* drill type tasks, for example, spelling, identification of letters, can be programmed.

Disadvantages of the programmed approach lie in the following:

1. Teachers sometimes resist the idea of a "teaching machine."
2. It is limited to factual knowledge, fixed learnings.
3. Slow students are less motivated to work independently.

Realizing the limitations of the programmed approach, elementary school teachers and reading experts are discovering the possibilities of programmed materials used in conjunction with other approaches to reading.

The phonemic (or linguistic) approach Linguistic scholars, as we note in other chapters, have contributed much to our understanding of the English language and its functioning. The application of these concepts of language has revolutionized the teaching of language and approaches to composition. It is not surprising that linguists have also attempted to apply linguistic concepts to reading instruction. Thus far, however, the results are disappointing, for the "linguistic" approach, almost solely a phonemic–graphemic presentation, has produced material like this:

had	can	cat	bag
lad	Dan	fat	nag
pad	man	hat	rag
sad	pan	rat	tag

Dan had a bat.
Has Ann a bag?
Ann had a bag.
Nat had a nag.
A fat cat had a rat.
A man had a hat.
Pat had a nap.[12]

---

[11]Richard C. Atkinson, project director, *Progress Report: A Reading Curriculum for a Computer-Assisted Instructional System: The Stanford Project* (Stanford, Calif.: Stanford University, 1966.)

[12]Leonard Bloomfield and Clarence L. Barnhart, *Let's Read, A Linguistic Approach* (Detroit: Wayne State University, 1961), p. 2.

The linguist's approach to reading is essentially based on the presentation of words by phonemic and graphemic groups. As in the linguistic approaches to spelling, the child is introduced to a family of words, for example, *look, book, cook, took, hook.* Those advocating this linguistic approach to beginning reading point out that children can learn groups of words rather than single words. While learning *eat,* the child might just as well learn *beat, heat, meat, neat, seat,* and so on. It is a simple step also to branch out to related phonograms as in the linguistic relationship diagram below.

Although this approach has validity for the teaching of spelling, as an answer to beginning reading instruction, it leaves much to be desired. What is it that linguists are ignoring in approaching reading?—children's interests, their previously acquired large vocabulary, their knowledge of language patterns. Critics of the basal reader approach to reading instruction have long decried the "Dick and Jane" content of basal readers which relied on sight recognition of words which were repeated *ad nauseam* to enable the child to learn the words.

Are the linguists offering a more stimulating content when they suggest reading matter like that advocated by Fries //Pat a fat cat// //Pat a fat

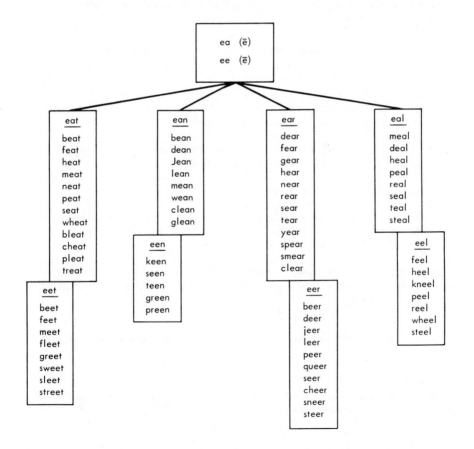

rat//?[13] It is audacious, perhaps, but enlightening, to compare this material with that produced by Theodor Geisel, hardly a linguistic scholar, in *The Cat in the Hat* (Random House).

As one critic of the linguistic approach notes:

> One danger of phonemic reading programs is that their scientific base will give them great respectability and they will gain wide use before they have been sufficiently tried. There are two other dangers. One is that fuller application of linguistics to reading will be delayed. The other is that educators will reject linguistics while rejecting phonemic reading programs.[14]

We must be aware of the tendency to tack the magic "linguistic" label on all English and reading programs. It is important to probe further to determine how linguistic findings have been brought to bear on content presented, how linguistics has improved effectiveness of instruction. We must not hesitate to critize because we are intimidated by the reputation of those who are, sometimes for the first time, delving into the field of reading instruction. Linguistics has made a tremendous contribution to the study of English, but much rethinking and a study of applied linguistics must take place before its fullest potential is realized, particularly in the teaching of reading.

Language–experience Associated with the work of teachers in San Diego County, California, the language–experience approach to reading considers reading as part of the total language development of the child. Beginning experiences in reading evolve from experiences with oral and written language. Child-dictated experiences, child-composed sentences and stories, furnish the material for reading, as described by Lee:[15]

1. An experience common to the group—field trip, story read, an experiment, film, classroom incident, topic introduced by the teacher, a picture
2. Class discussion with sentences recorded by the teacher, aide, or students
3. Reading the composed story aloud, discussion of words
4. Duplicated copy of story used in individual and group reading experiences
5. Follow-up activities—varied reading opportunities, dictation of individual sentences according to ability, small group work to extend abilities, language study, listening to literature, extension of vocabularies

This approach to reading is distinctly different from others described, for it moves away from the prepared reading text. It appears to have the following advantages:

[13]Charles C. Fries, *Linguistics and Reading* (New York: Holt, Rinehart & Winston, Inc., 1962), p. 203.

[14]Kenneth S. Goodman, "The Linguistics of Reading," *The Elementary School Journal*, April 1964, pp. 357–58.

[15]Doris Lee, "Reading, 'Riting' and Responsibility," Speech at National Conference on Language Arts in the Elementary School, Portland, Oregon, April 10, 1981.

1. Reading material has high interest value; the child is able to read what he or she has composed, and knows the vocabulary.
2. The approach develops according to individual needs, interests, abilities; the child *wants* to read.
3. Repetition of skill instruction in separate areas of language study, for example, phonology, is eliminated through a total approach to language study.
4. Reading material reflects the child's knowledge of English grammar—sentence patterns, word order, intonation.

The chief disadvantage of the language–experience approach from the view of a teacher is that it is less highly structured. Each group of children, having varied experiential backgrounds, will produce different reading material. The teacher is required to be more flexible, and for that reason, may feel less secure in working with this spontaneous type of approach. This is the same difficulty the teacher encounters in any oral language program. Another disadvantage is that content is limited by the child's knowledge; there is no provision for vocabulary development. New concepts and vocabulary must be introduced through planned experiences, through wide reading of literature, and through incidental instruction.

Despite this demand on teacher ingenuity and skill in working with the group as it learns and develops its own materials (which makes for a more creative approach to teaching), this approach warrants careful consideration, for is it not a truly "linguistic" approach? Recognizing its limitations, it appears that the total language approach to language, composition, and reading (evolving quickly into literature) potentially incorporates all the concepts of linguistics with our knowledge of the needs of children and the best of learning theory. The language–experience approach, therefore, has much to commend it as a beginning approach to reading instruction.

Individualized reading   The individualized approach to reading is scarcely a new concept, for it was an essential part of the Progressive Movement in the 1930s. The Winnetka Plan (Illinois) is one example of these earlier attempts to individualize learning. Children read silently at their individual rates of speed, answered prepared questions on the material read, and read aloud individually to the teacher.

Another plan for individualized learning was the Dalton Plan (Massachusetts) which used a laboratory approach to encourage students to achieve self-determined contracts for units of work to be accomplished. This plan granted the student much freedom and experience in planning and in budgeting time.

Both of these plans were rigid in content, however, and goals were in terms of adult needs rather than those of the child. Contemporary attempts at individualizing reading instruction stress not only quantity of reading but also the child's motivation to read more extensively. Great varieties of reading materials are needed for a successful individualized reading program.

The individualized approach to reading has many advantages:

1. Wide use of library materials and free selection are possible.
2. Broader range of reading subjects is achieved.
3. Learning experiences are extended.
4. Reading skills are taught through small group approaches.
5. Evaluation includes personal conferences.
6. Stress is put on individual development to fullest potential.
7. The gifted student is stimulated.

There is no set prescription for the individualized program in reading. As Leland Jacobs observes:

> In the first place, "individualized reading" is not a single method with predetermined steps in procedures to be followed. It is not possible to say that every teacher who would individualize guidance in reading must do this or that. It is not feasible or desirable to present a simple, single methodological formulation of what is right in "individualized reading" which every teacher shall follow.[16]

The individualized approach to reading has had excellent results with average and superior readers. The one disadvantage noted is the inability of slow students to cope with the individualized method of working. Better readers enjoy the opportunity to read widely and to share their reading experiences with other students. They also respond to the stimulus of the individual conference.[17] We shall explore individualized reading as a means for bringing literature into the elementary school reading program in the next chapter.

A Forward-Looking Reading Program

No single approach to reading appears to have all the answers. It is interesting to note that research findings are inconclusive. Studies of individualized instruction, for example, provide findings which favor group instruction as well as findings which show the individualized approach to be best.[18] This discrepancy indicates that one must beware of research which is not carefully structured. Also, one must note the nature of the specific programs being compared. At this stage no research evidence conclusively recommends one approach to reading over another. There is a need for well-organized longitudinal studies in reading instruction.

The only recourse is to be eclectic, selecting those approaches which best serve the needs of a superior reading program, one that:

1. Begins where the student is and permits progress at individual rates of speed
2. Guarantees success from the initial experiences

[16]Leland Jacobs, "Individualized Reading Is Not a Thing," in *Individualizing Reading Practices,* ed. Alice Miel (New York: Teachers College Press, 1958).

[17]Harry Sartain, "The Roseville Experiment with Individualized Reading," *The Reading Teacher,* April 1960, p. 277.

[18]Nila B. Smith, *Reading Instruction for Today's Children* (Englewood Cliffs, N.J.: Prentice-Hall, Inc., 1963), pp. 154–59.

3. Stresses development of oral language skills and continues to be closely co-ordinated with the English program to avoid repetition, as in a well-planned phonological sequence
4. Teaches reading skills using reading material of interest to the child
5. Does not belabor the teaching of skills but moves quickly into a program of wide reading of literature with instruction in literary concepts
6. Uses multimedia to present information and to motivate reading
7. Extends abilities to think—analysis, comparison, criticism, comprehension
8. Experiments with varied approaches to meet individual needs, incorporating the best of each approach to reading
9. Stimulates real interest in reading for pleasure and information; develops habits which will extend into adulthood
10. Develops research techniques and familiarity with library tools

In developing a reading program, we might note Stauffer's advice:

> . . . one must, first, drop the notion that a basic reader program in and of itself is final and sacred. It is not. Second, one must drop the notion that time can be equated with equality. Not every group must be met every day for the same length of time. Third, the idea that a basic book recommended for a grade level must be "finished" by all pupils in a grade before they can be promoted must be discarded. Fourth, teaching reading as a *memoriter* process by presenting new words in advance of the reading and then having pupils tell back the story must be stopped. If reading is taught as a thinking process, even short basic-reader stories will be read with enthusiasm. . . . Sixth, effective skills of word attack must be taught. Basic reading books do not provide for such skill training; neither do trade books.[19]

How can we best meet the criteria we have established? Let us consider the various approaches to reading in terms of these criteria. I have observed that the language–experience approach most nearly meets the first four requirements, for beginning readers are highly motivated to read stories they have composed, and the stories can be successfully read because the vocabulary is known. Included are interesting words as well as the commonly used vocabulary, the basic sight words which the child needs to know. This reading program is closely coordinated with the English program, for children develop skills of composition and reading as a direct result of spoken language, and children have repeated opportunities to use sentence patterns and varied classes of words before formal grammar study is initiated. Emphasis is placed on the development of listening skills as well as speaking skills as the teacher introduces literature through reading aloud and provides for dramatization and sharing of experiences.

Recent research by psycholinguists increases our understanding of the reading process. They stress the fact that, although reading requires visual input, it also requires even greater input from the brain in terms of knowledge of language and of the world in general. Beginning readers, therefore,

---

[19]Russell G. Stauffer, "Individualized and Group Directed Reading Instruction," *Elementary English*, October 1960, p. 381.

know much about reading before they even begin. In summary, psycholinguists state that:

1. Only a small part of the information necessary for reading comes from the printed page.
2. Comprehension must precede the identification of individual words (reading is not primarily visual).
3. Reading is not decoding to sound.[20]

These concepts surprise teachers who have had earlier training in reading. We need to reconsider old methods in light of newer findings, keeping our minds open to fresh input. Studies show us that the young reader requires feedback more than anything else during the beginning stages. The structured drill that we offer may serve no real purpose other than to stymie the child who wants to "get on with it." Essentially the child learns to read by reading, and our task as teachers is to assist the child in reading as freely, easily, and quickly as possible.

Individualized approaches to reading consider the child's needs first, whether children work in groups or alone. Teachers are gradually developing learning centers, first a small one in the corner, then two or three, and often the whole room becomes a learning center, as shown in the illustration. As they work at self-selected tasks, children make discoveries and are excited about their work and their growth. Individual conferences between child and teacher provide a time to get acquainted, a time to talk together.

Discovery methods will encourage children to develop generalizations about phonology, syntax, and semantics. These discoveries will benefit the whole language program (including reading) and avoid the repetition of instruction. The coordination of spelling with reading and composition by presenting linguistic families—*came, game, tame, fame*—is a sound method which makes the spelling task more efficient. These aspects of language are taught in conjunction with the language–experience instruction in beginning reading rather than as three distinct "subjects"—reading, spelling, English.

As soon as children develop a basic reading vocabulary—and this stage may be reached in first or second grade, depending on background and ability—they are able to begin reading selections from literature. A core of titles can be assigned to each reading level so that children progress through the wonderful world of children's literature. Titles at the first level might include:

Maurice Sendak, *Where the Wild Things Are*. Monsters can be captivating.
Wanda Gág, *Millions of Cats*. The refrain has appeal.
Dr. Seuss, *The Cat in the Hat*. Simple vocabulary, but fun!
Else H. Minarik, *Little Bear*. Four stories, illustrated by Maurice Sendak.

[20]Frank Smith, *Psycholinguistics and Reading* (New York: Holt, Rinehart, & Winston, Inc., 1973), p. 8.

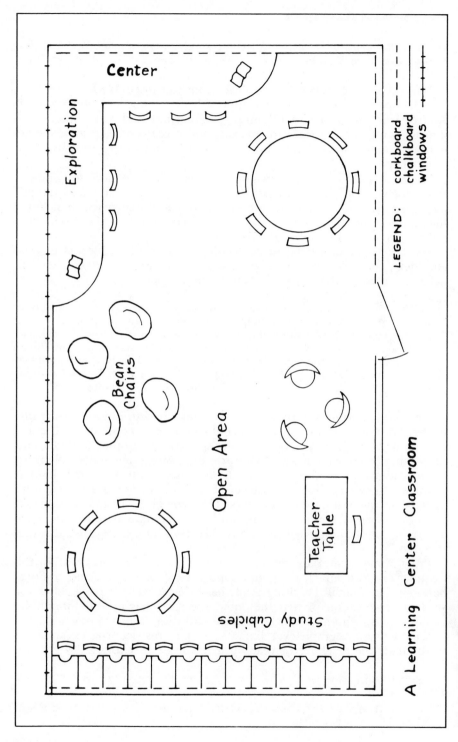

A Learning Center Classroom

Syd Hoff, *Danny and the Dinosaur*. Adventures with a museum dinosaur!
Mabel Watts, *When the Horses Galloped to London*. Imagine catching a highwayman![21]

What about vocabulary level? What about wordlists? We have too long been hampered by these scientific approaches to a child's vocabulary. Emil Andrew who comes to school chattering about space flights and other adult information that he grasps with amazing enthusiasm and eagerness should not be hemmed in by that mythical 200 words which supposedly is all he can manage.

We must credit ideas and intriguing words with some motivating power in themselves. Children are fascinated by monsters, so the "wild things" portrayed by Maurice Sendak entice them to read the story which includes such interesting words as, "rumpus," which children love. Let's seize this opportunity to make *readers* of children.

We should supply, furthermore, "grown-up" words for concepts, objects, and ideas, for children hear them and in many cases use them; they will delight in reading them, too. As Nancy Larrick points out:

> The practice of teaching children wrong names for things that have relatively simple names is certainly open to question. Indeed, if one purpose of reading is to help the child reach out and grow, why not use the exact word he will hear in school conversation and TV news reports instead of a baby-talk substitute? At first he may miss the more grown-up word in print, but the chances are that he knows it by ear. His pride in learning to read such a word may add to his self-respect and do a great deal to increase his interest in reading.[22]

The child continues to progress by reading literature of increasing difficulty. The coordination of reading and composition continues as the student reads his or her own compositions, the writing of other students, and the writing of known authors, literature. Both individual and small group approaches to the reading of literature are used, with students being encouraged to discuss literary concepts both as a writer and as one who appreciates the writing skill of others. This type of discussion is facilitated through individual conferences and student seminars. Varied reading skills are stressed as students work in other subject areas and engage in individual research.

Programmed materials can be drawn into the reading program for the teaching of word attack skills, development of vocabulary, and comprehension. The Initial Teaching Alphabet offers excellent possibilities for reading remediation in that the "new alphabet" has appeal for middle school readers who have not been successful with other approaches.

We will discard "grade level" limitations which restrict progress and tend to routinize the teaching of reading in favor of an exploratory attitude

---

[21]Elizabeth Guilfoile, *Books for Beginning Readers* (Urbana, Ill.: National Council of Teachers of English, 1962).

[22]Nancy Larrick, *A Teacher's Guide to Children's Books* (Columbus, Ohio: Charles E. Merrill Publishing Co., 1963), p. 26.

toward reading which involves three stages: (1) preparation for reading, (2) introduction to reading, and (3) independent reading. Stage 1 usually occurs during preschool and kindergarten years; stage 2 may begin in the kindergarten year and extend through first, second, and third grades; stage 3 may begin in second grade and will continue throughout life.

PREPARATION FOR READING

Encourages positive attitudes toward learning
Develops oral abilities
Provides many listening experiences
Works toward linguistic fluency and sentence expansion
Develops vocabulary—speaking and listening
Orients the child to words and books
Develops auditory and visual perception
Provides experiential backgrounds
Involves student in literature through dramatization and listening

INTRODUCTION TO READING

Coordinates writing and reading activities
Develops a program in phonology for reading and spelling
Continues to extend vocabularies—oral, written, read
Introduces poetry appreciation and composition
Continues varied listening activities, increasing attention span
Encourages creativity in all language activities
Uses small group and individual approaches
Diagnoses individual needs through conferencing
Provides a broad background in literature
Teaches all concepts in the context of reading

INDEPENDENT READING

Encourages wide reading of literature
Introduces literary concepts in poetry and prose
Uses individual and seminar approaches
Employs discovery techniques and individual research
Teaches library skills and basic library tools
Coordinates literature, language, and composition studies
Stimulates the sharing of books and book reviewing
Extends learnings through reading
Assists the student in book selection
Develops the habit of reading for pleasure and information

HELPING CHILDREN READ

The task of the teacher, as we have delineated it in the preceding section, is to facilitate reading, to help children bridge the gap between the oral language which they use with ease and the printed symbols that may be totally foreign to them. In this section we will explore teaching strategies that carry out the implications of psycholinguistic research. As Palmer recommends:

Instead of letting students become passive identifiers of letters and words, English teachers of the 80s must encourage them to become active searchers for meaning during reading. We will also need to help students expedite this process. Instead of perpetuating instruction in reading with a set of discrete and fragmented skills, we must help students go directly from graphic language to meaning—without getting needlessly bogged down in the process.[23]

Reading should be learned in as natural a manner as speech was in preschool years. Although teachers need to know the linguistic background for the reading process, children will benefit if we let them discover these concepts within the act of reading. Less time should be spent on rules and drill and more on listening to reading and on reading independently. Our classroom motto should be: "The more you read the better you read," and teaching strategies should reflect that belief.

Preparation for Reading

Perhaps the chief purpose for many parents in sending their child to school is to learn to read. It is with great expectancy on the parts of both parent and child that he or she enters first grade "ready to read." But is the child really "ready"?

Readiness *Readiness* is no clearly defined time in a child's development, for we can talk about readiness to learn almost any new skill which may be taught at varied periods of a student's life. Readiness is a state of being prepared, sufficiently mature, and mentally able to undertake a task, and being interested in attacking the learning job. We are always ready to learn something.

When is a child ready to read? We cannot state with any certainty that Al will be ready, for example, to read at the age of six, if he has an IQ of 100, for readiness varies with each individual. Albert is ready to read when he shows that he is ready, when he notices letters, asks what they are, and begins trying to read words. This state of readiness depends on a complex multiplicity of abilities which in many cases are acquired incidentally but which in other cases require formal instruction. We can prepare for reading as well as for other learning by stressing activities which develop (1) positive attitudes toward school, (2) oral language abilities, (3) experiential background, (4) visual and auditory discrimination, and (5) word and book orientation.

Positive attitudes An important aspect of preparing a child for learning is the development of a positive attitude toward learning, which for the child is usually concretely exemplified by the teacher and the school building. First experiences in the school situation must leave the child with a feeling of satisfaction, a sense of having succeeded in the adventure of

---

[23]William S. Palmer, "Reading and the Teaching of English," in *Education in the 80s: English,* ed. R. Baird Shuman (Washington, D.C.: National Education Association, 1981), p. 57.

moving out in the world. In order to produce positive feelings in the child the discerning teacher must project warmth, respect, and enthusiasm, which is conveyed through many small acts during the day:

1. Eye contact with the students, as during a story hour
2. Physical contact—in a game, a friendly pat of encouragement, a hand on the shoulder while helping
3. Direct address by name when requesting assistance, greeting, saying good-bye, calling on students to respond
4. Smiling, a touch of humor, show of enthusiasm
5. Praise for the individual and the group to promote feelings of success

Oral language   Oral language development is now recognized as a firm basis for beginning reading experiences. The interrelationship of oral language development and success in reading has been pointed out by the Task Force Report published by the National Council of Teachers of English, which recommends greater stress on oral language, for:

> Only as progress is made in the use of oral language will there be substantial improvement in reading and writing. The interdependence of these language skills has been demonstrated both in research and in practice.[24]

Walter Loban states: "Schools are beginning to be aware that research shows a powerful linkage between oral language and writing or reading—one much greater than has previously been realized."[25] The neglect of oral language instruction he attributes to the lack of clear-cut evaluation methods. It is obvious that teachers have shied away from oral instruction in favor of reading and writing possibly because oral activities are less structured. The chapters on speaking, listening, and language study offer numerous suggestions for developing oral language abilities.

How does the development of oral language prepare a child to read with greater success? One of the major contributions is in the enjoyment of language and the many ways we use language; the reading of language thus becomes a natural progression for the child who is prepared to be receptive to this new way of working with language. A second important aspect of oral language is the development of the child's concepts and vocabulary, for beginning readers will progress more surely if they are familiar with many ideas so that language to be read is understandable in meaning if not in form. The sounds of English are introduced orally, for aural discrimination between sounds is important to later identification of differences between words.

Experiential background   In the elementary school, experiential backgrounds typically vary widely in a single classroom. The horizons of some

[24]NCTE Task Force on Teaching English to the Disadvantaged, *Language Programs for the Disadvantaged* (Urbana, Ill.: National Council of Teachers of English, 1965), pp. 272–73.

[25]Walter Loban, "Oral Language Proficiency Affects Reading and Writing," *Instructor*, March 1966, p. 97.

children may be very narrow compared to the broad horizons of those who have had many opportunities to explore. The experiential background of the child is the total product of his or her way of living, environment, family origins, and will be influenced by all of the following factors and more:

Education of parents
Encouragement of child's growth
Socioeconomic status of the family
Number of books and periodicals in the home
Opportunities to travel, to explore the community
Encouragement of self-expression

The child who lacks a background that provides a wide variety of concepts must be assisted in developing experiences to supplement meager knowledge, for experiences stimulate thinking. They provide referents for the reading of new words. The classroom teacher can expand horizons through:

Educational trips—zoo, post office, fire station, library, airport, parks, nearby cities, train and bus rides
Classroom adventures—a pet, interesting person, new games, unusual objects, different foods
Multimedia—films, records, filmstrips, pictures
Reading aloud—science information, stories, news items

Visual and auditory discrimination   Before beginning the formal reading program, children need practice in making discriminations, in noting differences and likenesses. In this way they are prepared to make the more minute discriminations necessary when two similar words are encountered in reading. Experiences which help the child notice similarities and differences can be visual, as in these examples (directions are oral):

Put an X on the two shapes which are the same.

Draw a circle around the star which is biggest.

Which two letters are exactly alike?
B   b   T   B

Underline the two words which look exactly alike.
book   man   go   man

Auditory discrimination involves listening and the ability to hear differences and similarities of sound. A variety of activities will assist the child in making these discriminations:

Which word begins like FALL?
   pan   fence   hello
Which two words begin alike?
   happy   bed   horse
Which word does *not* begin like the others?
   carrot   help   candy   coffee
Can you name another word that begins like *chair*?
   Many will be suggested; some will be wrong so the teacher will need to repeat CHAIR to help the child see the difference.
   shell— The child is confusing the SH sound with CH.
   mare— The child is rhyming the ending sound rather than comparing the beginning sound.
Which word begins like SHEEP? (Closer discrimination.)
   slip   shoe   stay

Word and book orientation   As a part of readiness for learning, children are introduced to the word as a symbol which conveys meaning long before they are actually taught to read. Orientation to words is easily achieved by the use of words as identifying labels around the room: *chalkboard, Tom Turtle, Helpers, October, Mrs. Walton.* . . . These words are introduced casually with no effort to move into reading. Children will gradually show more interest, however, in knowing words, and certainly their questions along these lines should be answered, for there is little to be gained by saying "Wait" to an eager child.

In this same way children are introduced to books as something to read, and learn to hold a book right side up, to open the cover toward the left. They learn that the printed symbols are words which tell a story, that we read from left to right, and that we begin reading at the top of the page. (Later, students will be fascinated to learn that these habits are not the same for all countries or languages.) Book orientation is best achieved through the handling of books, and most children have already acquired much of this knowledge before entering school. You can present these concepts informally as you read aloud from a book. The left to right concept is reinforced as experience stories are printed on the chalkboard.

Introduction to Reading

We have already discussed in some detail various methods of teaching children to read. In this section, therefore, we shall concentrate on the development of a reading vocabulary. The recognition of words, the ability to associate the printed symbol with meaning, depends on a variety of skills as well as experiential background and listening and speaking vocabularies.

Reading is closely integrated with all language development and will be facilitated by growth in other language skills.

The most important aspect of reading developed at this time is the child's attitude toward reading. The child approaches the learning of reading with great enthusiasm; it is essential that this enthusiasm not be diminished in any way. Do we make reading such a struggle for the beginner that many children become discouraged? The important thing is to make reading a successful experience, one that is highly enjoyable and desirable. We should make sure that reading never acquires the taste of bitter medicine that may be associated with excessive emphasis on drill. Let's reconsider several aspects of reading.

Sight words   Many small words that are used frequently do not lend themselves to analysis—*a, the, who, were* . . ..These words are the ones which children must learn to recognize without hesitation if skill in reading is to be attained. Many lists have been compiled, for example, that by Edward Dolch[26] which consists of 220 words (no nouns).

There is some question whether a sight vocabulary need really be that large, however, for the newer trend of teaching words in linguistic groups would teach *all, call, fall, small* (included in the Dolch list) as part of the *all* family along with *ball, hall, tall,* and *wall.* In the same manner, *an, can,* and *ran* (from the Dolch list) would be taught with *Dan, fan, man, tan.* These words are regular in pronunciation and are readily learned on the basis of the phonogram represented.

Certainly there is a core of words which must be learned by sight, for they are not related to a linguistic family or are irregular in pronunciation—*are, been, does, from, of, one, said, very, was, what.* These words should be taught in context as much as possible rather than through drill on isolated words. Many words become "sight" words for the able readers who no longer need to analyze every word they meet. We need chiefly to provide many opportunities for the child to read and to reinforce knowledge of words through use.

> Labels used around the room can develop into phrases and sentences which include words that trouble children.
> the chalkboard
> Many helpers
> What does Tom Turtle eat?
> One fish is black. Two fish are gold.
> Introduce children to reversals, which we sometimes call PUSH-ME-PULL-ME words because they can go either direction. Interest in this study of word oddities will assist children in identifying WAS and SAW, which are just like other pairs they will discover:
> NOT—TON   SPEED—DEEPS   DRAW—WARD

[26]Edward W. Dolch, *Methods in Reading* (Champaign, Ill.: Garrard Publishing Co., 1955), pp. 373–74.

Of course, we should not spend time in class reading lists of sight words or identifying isolated words on cards. The child will learn words that are used frequently through reading them in sentences. Have children dictate their own sentences as you print them on a sheet of paper or beneath a painted picture, thus:

This is my cat
under the table.

Since this is the child's sentence, all words are familiar. In this way the beginning reader becomes at ease in reading grammatical sentences that offer syntactic clues as well as the visual forms of letters and words. The prepositional phrase is far easier to read than these words would be individually for the young reader.

Group compositions printed on the board and experience charts serve the same purpose. The child should have many opportunities to see written language that has first been spoken aloud.

Integrating Spelling and Reading

The related skills of spelling and reading obviously overlap. There is little justification for presenting these areas of study as totally unrelated subjects as is often done in the elementary school course of study and in textbook publication. If these subjects are taught in isolation, the child may never be aware of the interrelated nature of reading and spelling. An examination of spelling and reading textbooks, particularly workbooks, reveals that there is also a great deal of repetition without the benefit of coordination.

Individualized instruction and the language–experience method of teaching language arts skills permit children to discover the ways of English without this repetition. These approaches encourage children to make their own generalizations and to integrate the learnings through experimenting and observing. Here are ways of teaching that remove any stigma from English and spelling and break down the barriers among the various language arts. It is time for us to rethink old methods, to question the efficacy of time-honored tradition, and to risk letting children make choices about how and what they will learn.

Teaching phoneme-grapheme relationships   The primary-grade child usually knows the full set of English sounds but is probably not aware of these sounds until formal instruction in auditory discrimination begins in the classroom. Anne learns to relate the sounds she speaks to the written symbols that we use to represent these sounds. She learns that it is possible to write the words she can speak and, conversely, that anyone who knows the sound–symbol code can read a coded message that she has written or that someone else has written.

How can we best aid the English-speaking child who is learning to read and write? The first step is awareness of the sounds of English at the auditory level. The child needs practice in discriminating likenesses and differences among the sounds that are used regularly. We give practice like this:

Which words begin like Tom? tiger, dog, tough
Which word does *not* begin like Tom? table, tool, dust
How many words can you name that begin like Tom? toast, tub, tick, turtle, tease, tooth, . . . and so on

We begin, of course, with the most commonly used relationships between phoneme (the sound) and grapheme (the spelling of the sound). The child soon learns, for instance, that the sound heard at the beginning of *take* or the end of *sat* is spelled in the same way with one *t* symbol. Later, he or she might be introduced to the less common grapheme that appears at the end of *mitt* or *mutt*. Upper-grade students will delight in discovering even more unusual alternate spellings of this sound as in:

ptomaine	Thomas	veldt
pterodactyl	debt	

The same process is followed for each of the sounds of English as the child learns to associate the sounds of the spoken English language with written symbols working back and forth with encoding and decoding—that is, writing and reading. Through this discussion, it is easy to see how important it is to teach reading and writing together as two aspects of the same process—that is, learning to use the English code.

How can we develop the child's awareness of the sound–symbol relationship in the English language? This is a continuous process beginning with the simplest relationships that can be easily handled by first graders to more complex ones that you may discover as adults.

Minimal pairs One method the linguist uses to identify the existence of different phonemes in a language is the comparison of words that are exactly the same except for one sound, as /*pin*/ and /*fin*/. A native speaker could pronounce the word *pin* loudly, softly, with very little breath, or heavy aspiration. If, no matter how Harry says the word, he still points to a safety pin as he says /*pin*/, there is no change in meaning.

When he says /*fin*/, however, he no longer points to the safety pin but indicates the fin of a fish. Clearly he acknowledges different meanings as he says /*pin*/ when pointing to the safety pin but /*fin*/ when talking about the fish. Here is phonemic difference or two different sounds, /p/ and /f/.

Children can observe these differences in minimal pairs, too. At first present the pairs orally, thus:

Which word is an animal? *cat, hat*

Which word is something to eat? *ham, hat*
Which word tells time? *clock, click*

Rhyming words is another way of working with minimal pairs, a series of them. Ask children to name words that rhyme with *ring*. Only the initial consonant phoneme is changed as they name *sing, king, wing*.

If children name such words as *sting* or *strong,* of course, they are no longer working with *minimal* pairs because more than a single phoneme has been introduced. Contrast the phonemic spelling of these words: /riŋ/, /stiŋ/, /striŋ/. There are three, four, and five sounds in these words, respectively. Notice, however, that *ring* and *thing* contrast as minimal pairs because the grapheme *th*—as in *thing, thin, thimble*—represents a single English sound /θ/. *Ring* and *thing* are spelled phonemically, thus: /riŋ/, /θiŋ/

A sound–symbol chart A chart of sounds with corresponding symbols can be developed at varying levels of sophistication as soon as children begin associating spoken sounds with written symbols. Encourage children to discover these sounds of English themselves as they work first orally and aurally. Then have them supply the common grapheme(s) for each sound as you begin a chart like this:

SOUND	SPELLING		
	BEGINNING	MIDDLE	FINAL
/t/	ten	after	hat
/b/	box	about	cab
/p/	pat	upon	cup
/f/	fat, phone	before	half, laugh
/n/	not, knot	inside	pin

More advanced children can expand this chart fully in an exciting study of the English language. Their discoveries may include these additions:

SOUND	SPELLING		
	BEGINNING	MIDDLE	FINAL
/t/	ten, ptomaine, Thomas	after	hat, debt, veldt
/b/	box	about, Dobbs	cab, Dobb
/p/	pat	upon	cup, Lapp
/n/	not, knot, gnat pneumonia, mnemonics	inner, another, unknown	inn, on
/s/	seen, cent science, psalm	also	class, hats, ax
/g/	go, ghost, guess	legal, ago	bag, vague
/k/	cat, kite, khaki chorus, quit	act	pick, plaque

Development of these charts will lead students to make many observations regarding patterns of English orthography. Notice, for example, that the grapheme *gh* occurs in two places on the chart. Have students make a list of examples of these two sound–symbol relationships:

laugh	ghost
rough	ghastly
enough	ghetto
tough	
cough	

It is easy, of course, to develop a list of words that begin with a given initial grapheme. Here is a real incentive for using the dictionary. Development of such lists also exposes children to new vocabulary; for example, *ghastly* or *ghetto*, which may be learned incidentally by many children.

After these lists are completed, children can examine the sample words and derive generalizations regarding the appearance of this grapheme in English words.

1. When the sound /f/ is heard at the end of a word, this sound might be spelled GH.
2. When the sound /g/ is heard at the beginning of a word, this sound might be spelled GH.
3. When GH appears at the beginning of a word, it has the sound /g/.
4. When GH appears at the end of a word, it has the sound /f/.

Notice the very limited number of examples of each of these phoneme–grapheme relationships. Obviously, this spelling is not the most common spelling for either phoneme. Children can compare the number of words listed for /g/ spelled GH with those in which initial /g/ is spelled G. They may also prepare a list of words beginning with /g/ spelled GU. In this way, students will begin to observe the frequency of the various spellings. When they are uncertain about which spelling to use for this sound, the educated guess would select the most frequently used.

Students are also becoming aware of the specific words that use the less common spellings. It is not essential to memorize these words; their knowledge will gradually be reinforced through exposure.

Individualized approaches   Students can learn far more about language through individualized activities than through any formal presentation followed by drill. Use some of the following on TASK CARDS that children can select for independent study.

- ARE YOU TEED OFF? asks the question of a display which features words containing the sound TEE with emphasis on student discoveries:
  teeny   teepee   eternity   teasing   society   teaspoon
- Student-prepared word quizzes can feature interesting pairs of words that will prove intriguing to others:
  quiver, quaver   stunt, stint   boner, banner

- TWENTY-SIX SCADOO! has all students racing to write a word for each letter. Specify rules according to the ability level: each word must be at least six letters; each word must contain three syllables, etc.
- BEAT THE CLOCK requires each student to write ten (set the number according to the group) words beginning with any given sound before the second hand goes all around the clock. As the second hand approaches twelve, write the letters *tr,* for example, on the board. Each student immediately begins writing: *treat, trust, truth,* etc.
- SELF-DIAGNOSIS is an excellent means for interesting the student in bettering spelling. At the beginning of the year give students a test (never too long at any one time) of words which all should know how to spell—*said, what, who, and, that, which, them, she, can, like,* and so forth. If you don't have a list compiled, ask several students (poor spellers will be motivated by assuming this responsibility to prepare a list of words they think all should know). Repeat the test several times during the year as each tries to master the group of words. Refer to these words incidentally also to keep them in everyone's mind.
- UP IN THE AIR! the activity sheet on page 284, helps students discover the varied spellings of words that rhyme. They are guided to determine the most common spellings for the phonogram presented. The few odd words will be memorized.
- CATTY WORDS is the caption of words containing the syllable CAT. Encourage students to discover words with a similar relationship to introduce to the class: THESE WORDS ARE DOGS! *(doggerel, dogged, dogma),* HAVE YOU PAID YOUR FEES? *(fealty, coffee, phenomenon),* CAN YOU SEE? *(season, deceive, seep).*
- Each student develops a CHAIN REACTION as he or she creates a new word by changing one letter at a time, thus: *fear, dear, deaf, leaf, loaf, loan, loon, noon.*
- A WORD WHEEL is useful in the primary classroom as students try to combine initial consonant sounds with varied phonograms. Simple wheels can be made, as in the diagram, or commercial varieties are available.

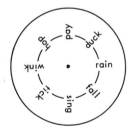

More advanced work in phonology can introduce students to examples of foreign language in English which affect our pronunciation and cause supposed irregularities in English pronunciation. Why, for example, do we look at the word *cello* which might be pronounced *sello* and say *chello?* It's an Italian word, of course, which requires the *ch* sound according to Italian linguistics. We can observe many *loan* words: plaza, prima donna, tempo, séance, requiem, mirage, per capita, piñata, boudoir, cuisine. Often we have retained the original pronunciation, but sometimes we anglicize the borrowed words as in *detour, bonbons, ensemble, adroit.*

UP IN THE AIR!   NAME _____

See how many rhymes you can find for *air*. If you really work hard, you may find 20 or more.

Now group the words you have found according to their different spellings.

AIR   CARE   BEAR   WHERE

Which spelling of this sound is most common? _____
Which spelling is very uncommon? _____
List any sets of words that are homonyms (sound alike).

_____   _____
_____   _____
_____   _____

List any words that you don't know very well.

_____

Find out what each one means and how it is used.

Dictionary study Although this skill has direct relevance for spelling, it is also vital to other subject area studies. The use of the dictionary throughout the curriculum tends to reinforce learning and also increases the value of instruction. Dictionary skills range from the most elementary to advanced skills involving specialized dictionaries with a sequence of abilities developing something like this:

1. Ability to say the alphabet letters in order
2. Use of alphabetical order in arranging words
3. Examination of the dictionary and its parts
4. Opening the dictionary to a specified letter
5. Finding a specified word
6. Using the dictionary to find acceptable spelling, pronunciation, and meaning
7. Using the dictionary to increase vocabulary (synonyms)
8. Making discoveries about words; studying etymology

Many kindergarten children come to school already able to recite the alphabet in order. Practice should be given in the use of this skill during kindergarten and first grade as the children become increasingly aware of the letters through phonics studies and beginning writing skills.

- Display the alphabet in the room in varied ways. An alphabet chart is helpful because all can see it, and the chart is available for reference as needed. Display letters in connection with appropriate pictures as knowledge of the alphabet is integrated with increasing vocabulary. A, B, C, D might be featured on a bulletin board with large pictures of an apron, baby, cat, and dog.
- Having children line up for recess in alphabetical order is a way of introducing alphabetical order. (Specify either first or last names.) As you call out, "A," all those with names beginning with A may get in line, then B, and so on. Later introduce the concept of alphabetizing the group of A names by the second letter.
- WHO CAN FOLLOW ME? is a simple game for stimulating use of alphabetical order. As the teacher (or leader) says one letter, he or she points to a student who must name the following one or two letters of the alphabet. If D is named, for example, the player names E and F.

The use of a dictionary can be started in first grade as children become accustomed to refer to a picture dictionary. Gradually the coverage of the dictionary used expands until students are introduced to the library's copy of an unabridged volume. (However, beware of employing monotonous study techniques that decrease student interest.)

- Opening the dictionary to a specific letter can be an enjoyable game as well as a learning experience. Which letters are in the middle of the alphabet? Which are near the end? Discussions of these ideas will aid the child in opening the dictionary to approximately the right place as any letter is called.
- Encourage interest in word study by encouraging student discovery. Are there words which have two pronunciations? Does the meaning change with the pronunciation? (As in the heteronyms, for example, en*trance* and *en*trance.) What words have two acceptable spellings? Do some words have many meanings?

Make illustrated charts of some words with many diverse meanings—*run, horn, hand, fly, field, beat, stock.*

• Explore synonyms for familiar words by referring to the short list of words included in many dictionary entries or by using the specialized synonym dictionary (Roget's *Thesaurus* and others). Prepare a synonym dictionary for use by class members including pages for overworked words: *walk, say, look, big, little.*

• Prepare a class book of WORD DISCOVERIES in which is included an assortment of interesting facts about words—the longest word found, words which read the same backwards and forwards (palindromes), less common homonyms *(right, wright, write, rite),* and creative uses of words in advertising.

The study of the English language is fascinating even at the stage of learning spelling. As children discover patterns and generalizations, they will begin to feel a sense of power, a feeling of control over language in a manner they may never have felt before. Language is not an esoteric subject for the study of scholars. It belongs to all of us, and we can wield it to perform many functions. This concept is important for children to understand.

It is essential also that teachers assess the reading process, the purpose of spelling, and the validity of our own information about linguistics. What are our objectives? What are the concerns of our students? Are we really using the best means to achieve the most desirable ends? Both spelling and phonics instruction deserve careful scrutiny.

Basic phonics concepts   To facilitate an integrated presentation, you need to know basic phonics concepts. The following sequence is designed to aid the child's ability to associate phoneme with grapheme and grapheme with phoneme. Activities suggested begin orally and move to writing and reading.

STEP 1: INITIAL CONSONANT PHONEMES

/b/, /d/, /f/, /h/, /j/, /k/, /l/, /m/, /n/, /p/, /r/, /t/, /v/, /w/, /y/, /z/

Bird begins with the letter *b, bird.* (Print on board.)
Can you tell me other words that begin like *bird?*
(Later) Who can tell me what letter stands for the sound we hear at the beginning of ball?
Can you tell me other words that begin with *b?*
Which word in this group does not begin with *b?*
   boy   barn   cow

CAUTION: Do not introduce too many sound–letter correspondences at one time. Begin as shown with only one sound. Review this sound the next day, and introduce one new sound, and so on. Call attention to the known sounds as they occur in other activities for excellent reinforcement.

Never present a consonant sound isolated from a word, for children may later have difficulty blending the beginning consonant and the following phonogram. The child who has been taught to say *buh* for the sound of /b/ may pronounce the word *bent* as *buh ent.*

After children know a number of consonants, a valuable practice requires them to substitute consonants to make new words. Print letters on the board as you work with them.

> With which letter–sound does ball begin? (*b*) Print *ball* on the board.
> Who can make a new word by changing /*b*/ to /*t*/? Substitute other known sounds: /*f*/, /*h*/, /*w*/.
> What letter–sound do we hear at the beginning of *hold*? (*h*)
> Can you make a new word that beings with /*t*/?
> . Let's see if we can put /*b*/ in front of these little words: *and, eat, ad, in, at.*
> Can anyone put /*b*/ in front of *ring*? in front of *right*? *link*? *low*? *lame*?

Repeated oral practice with sounds will lead to a linguistically sound approach to independent writing of words as the child learns to print in first grade.

STEP 2: UNCOMPLICATED VOWEL SOUNDS

"Short vowels": /*e*/, /*æ*/, /*i*/, /*ə*/, /*a*/, as in: hen, sat, pit, nut, got

---

The short u, /*ə*/, is called the schwa. It is also represented by other letters in unaccented syllables as the *i* in family. Some authors differentiate between the short u sound and the schwa, but there seems to be no reason to do so as the sound is a single phoneme /*ə*/.

Although the vowel sounds are presented orally in kindergarten and first grade, their real study waits until writing and reading experiences. Again we can make use of substitution.

> What vowel sound so we hear in *hat*? Can you put another *short* vowel sound in place of the *a*? What words can you make?
> hit, hot, hut. Does *het* make a word?
> If you know how to spell the word *luck* (write on the board), how would you spell *lock*? *lick*? *lack*?
> Can you read this word? (Print *miss*.)
> If we change the vowel (*moss*), what word do we have?
> If we change the vowel (*muss*), what word do we have?
> If we change the vowel (*mass*), what word do we have?

STEP 3: VOWEL DIPHTHONGS ("LONG" VOWEL SOUNDS)

"Long vowels" /*iy*/, /*ey*/, /*ay*/, /*ow*/, /*yuw*/[27] as in he, hay, ice, go, use

The linguist's designation of long vowels is confusing for the student unfamiliar with Romance languages. The first sound above, for example, is *ē*; because the *i* has that sound in Romance languages. (The letter *e* sounds like *ā*; the letter *a* sounds like *ah*; the *u* is pronounced *o͝o*). The *y*

---

[27]Linguists do not include the sound /*yuw*/ as a separate phoneme because it is actually two sounds, /*y*/ and /*uw*/, but we find it helpful to teach *ū* with the other vowels because in practice they really do "say their own names."

and *w* which follow each sound indicate a gliding sound which we make faintly after the first sound. Try saying words containing these vowel sounds to notice this effect.

A		E		I		O		U	
ai	*gain*	*ee*	*wee*	*y*	*by*	*oa*	*goat*	*u(e)*	*use*
ay	*may*	*ea*	*meat*	*uy*	*buy*	*ow*	*own*	*ew*	*few*
ei	*neigh*	*ei*	*receive*	*ei*	*height*	*oe*	*doe*	*eue*	*queue*
ey	*they*	*ie*	*believe*	*igh*	*high*				

The diphthong is a single blending sound produced by two vowels usually ending in a gliding sound (*y* or *w*). Notice the spelling and pronunciation of this word (diphthong). Do you hear the phoneme /f/? See the vowel chart for more examples of spellings of the various diphthongs.

Spellings associated with diphthongs:

OW as *now, show*
OU as *house, rough, slough, dough, could*
EW as *few, knew*
OO as *food, good*
AU as *caught*
AW as *saw*
OI as *oil*
OY as *boy*

Use inductive or discovery methods to introduce concepts of phonology also. Ask the children, for example, to begin naming words which contain *long* vowels. List twenty to thirty words on the board for examination:

name	boat	hope	slide	many
see	heel	use	seed	might
leaf	speedy	diet	write	sadly
right	kite	light	late	speech

Use a large number of samples so the class will note variations in spelling of long vowel sounds. They can make generalizations like the following derived from their observations:

1. A double *ee* is pronounced *ē*.
2. When a silent *e* is on the end of a word, the vowel before the *e* is long.
3. The letters *igh* signal a long *i* sound.
4. When two vowels are together, the first is long and the second is silent. (The group will find exceptions to this "rule" later, for example, *diet* does not fit this statement.)
5. The *y* on the end of a word is usually pronounced *ē*. (This statement may later be amended to "a word of two or more syllables" and even that generalization has exceptions. Also see the note on page 294.)

This kind of discovery activity causes the students to think as they observe language. Permit students to make their own discoveries (and their own mistakes), although the "correctness" of a recorded statement previously made by the class may be questioned when new cases are discovered. Students should be encouraged to share and to record any linguistic discoveries made as the study progresses.

STEP 4: VOWELS FOLLOWED BY R

AR as in *car*
ER as in *her*
IR as in *sir*
OR as in *for, favor*
UR as in *nurse*

The R causes the vowel to produce a sound that is neither long nor short, yet is relatively common; for example, *er*.

An E following the vowel + R signals a long vowel, thus:

$$car = care \qquad fir = fire \qquad her = here$$

In teaching vowel sounds many teachers find it practical to emphasize three sounds for each vowel, always carefully noting that these sounds are not the *only* sounds associated with each vowel. A chart like this one is helpful in clarifying what may otherwise be a most confusing subject of study for those who are just beginning to use phonic skills in reading and spelling:

	LONG	SHORT	FOLLOWED BY R
A	make	at	car
E	eat	let	her
I	ice	hit	sir
O	no	got	for
U	use	nut	purr

STEP 5: INITIAL CONSONANT BLENDS

Blends: *bl, cl, fl, gl, pl, sl*
          br, cr, dr, fr, gr, pr, tr
          sc, sk, sm, sn, sp, st, sw, tw
          scr, shr, spr, str, spl, sch, thr

The blends are introduced in the same way as the initial consonants and are blended through substitution and induction or discovery techniques.

Give students difficult words they could scarcely know how to spell. What blend do you hear at the beginning of FLUCTUATE? SMITHEREENS? STRIPLING? PRIMROSE? GROUSE? STIPEND? This is an effective way to encourage students to try spelling unknown words as well as to introduce them to some interesting words which can be explained or used in a sentence by the teacher as seems appropriate.

STEP 6: PHONOGRAMS

at	ed	it	ot	un
ate	et	in	ote	ung
ail	eat	ip	oat	ub
ain	ean	id	oar	ug
ait	eed	ing	ore	unt
an	eet	ind	on	ule
ang	end	ine	one	up
ap	ent	int	ong	ull
ag	eam	ick	ort	um
ab	en	iss	oon	uss
ad	eg	ite	ool	ut
ack	ell	ice	oom	ute

The list of phonograms is almost inexhaustible. These ending sounds may be used in conjunction with learning of initial consonants and blends. How many of the above phonograms will form a word if the letter s is placed before them: *sat, sate, sail, sang, sap,* and so on?

Use spelling games to reinforce student awareness of these patterns that occur frequently in English words.

Write a few words from one extensive family; for example, *lack, back, pack, rack, sack, Jack.* After observing the similarity, have the students expand this family as much as possible, adding: *track, clack, knack,* etc. (If the word *plaque* is suggested, send someone to the dictionary.) Examine the list when completed; have children pronounce the words. Then experiment with changing the vowel to I or O. How many will make words with the new vowel? Will spelling change at times?

STEP 7: PREFIXES

Syllables that appear at the beginnings of words often have special meanings. Knowing these prefixes not only helps students read new words more easily and understand the meaning but such knowledge also helps the student spell the first syllable of a word, thereby unlocking the spelling of the whole word. Discuss a few common prefixes such as *un* in unlock, unfasten, unhappy, unsympathetic, or *re* in return, recite, recede, reheat. Identify the meaning of each prefix, and ask students to list as many prefixes as they can.

Then have the class brainstorm a variety of words that begin with prefixes. As new prefixes are named, begin a new column so that other words that begin with the same prefix can be listed. Take time to talk about interesting words that are given as an excellent way to develop student vocabularies. On page 291 is a list of some of the more common prefixes that students might find useful.

After students have recorded a number of examples of words that begin with these prefixes, ask them to share one of their favorite words by illustrating it.

PREFIX	MEANING	EXAMPLES
ab-	away, from	absent, abstract, absurd
anti-	against	antidote, antibiotic
bi-	two, twice	bicycle, bilingual, biennial
com-, con-	together, with	compare, consecutive
contra-	against	contradict, contraband
de-	down, from	detour, depress, demean
dis-	apart, away	disable, discard, disease
ex-	out of	exit, excursion, exertion
in-, im-	not	intolerant, immobile, inactive
inter-	between	interstate, interact, intercept
intra-	into, within	intramural, intravenous
mono-	one	monorail, monotone
non-	not	noncombustible, nonprofit
per-	through	perpetuate, persevere, pertain
peri-	around	perimeter, periscope
post-	after	postgraduate, postnatal
pre-	before	prefix, predict, precook
pro-	for, forward	proceed, produce, proclaim
re-	back, again	refresh, return, reform
semi-	half	semifinalist, semiprecious
sub-	under	submarine, subway, subterranean
super-	above, over	superintendent, superstar
trans-	across	transform, transport, transcript
tri-	three	tricycle, tripod, triangle
un-	not	unable, uncertain, unhappy

Used by permission from *Elementary Teacher's Ideas and Materials Workshop,* Parker Publishing Company, April 1980, p. 5.

STEP 8: SUFFIXES

Learning the syllables that often end words is helpful, too, as students develop vocabulary and learn to spell word parts that are often used. Select one suffix and have students brainstorm as many examples as they can in five minutes. Given the suffix *less,* for example, they might suggest the following:

careless	hopeless
penniless	spotless
helpless	restless
breathless	moonless
homeless	fearless
spineless	jobless

Have the students identify the meaning of this suffix which can be added to many common words.

Then, have students name words that end with suffixes they know. Make a chart for their notebooks, thus:

SUFFIX	MEANING	EXAMPLES
-able	capable of being	understandable, manageable
-al	like	theatrical, menial, comical
-ance	state of being	remembrance, circumstance
-ant	state of being	vacant, redundant
-ary	place where	dictionary, library, aviary
-ate	to make	generate, fabricate, create
-en	made of, like	olden, golden, frighten
-ent	person who	superintendent, recipient
-er	person who	worker, baker, teacher
-est	the most	sweetest, finest, luckiest
-ood	state, condition	childhood, neighborhood
-ible	capable of being	feasible, legible, perceptible
-ic	like, made of	metallic, erratic, systematic
-ion	state of being	confusion, elation, education
-ish	like	yellowish, childish, devilish
-ist	person who	scientist, realist, pharmacist
-ity	state, condition	reality, ability, activity
-ize	to make	criticize, realize, individualize
-less	without	hopeless, careless, fearless
-ly	like	happily, coldly, freely
-ment	state of being	amazement, bewilderment
-ness	state of being	darkness, nearness, fearlessness
-or	person who	inventor, realtor, director
-ory	place	reformatory, dormitory, rectory
-ous	full of	dangerous, humorous, righteous
-some	like	handsome, wearisome, lonesome
-tude	state	attitude, gratitude, beatitude
-ward	direction	toward, forward, homeward

Reprinted by permission from *Elementary Teacher's Ideas and Materials Workshop,* Parker Publishing Company, May 1980, p. 16.

STEP 9: IRREGULAR CONSONANTS

Several letters do not represent sounds of their own. C, X, and Q, for example, always represent an alternate spelling (grapheme) of another sound (phoneme), thus:

C represents /s/ in *cent* or *science* and /k/ in *cow, picnic,* or *pack.*
X represents /ks/ in *fox* and *excuse* and /z/ in *xylophone.*
Q is usually followed by U and represents /kw/ as in *quit.*

Letters that represent two or more sounds: G and S
G represents a "hard" sound /g/ as in *gave* and represents the "soft" sound of /j/ as in *age.*
S represents several sounds as in *sit* /s/, *rose* /z/, *measure* /ž/, and *sure* /š/.

Help students make generalizations about spelling associated with these letters by using the following inquiry methods:

Ask students to list as many words that contain the /š/ phoneme as they can over a period of one day. The variety of words listed will aid vocabulary development as well as lead students to make generalizations about the spellings of this sound. They might suggest, for example: ocean, special, sugar, vacation, champagne, fissure, shell, delicious, patient, surely, national, lucious.

Write twenty to thirty words containing the letter C on the board; for example, *coal, accident, block, accuse, scale, sick, crime, custom, concave, circumstance, circle, circus, cell, cactus, cane, cigar, ace, accept.* Have the words pronounced as the class examines the list. Ask students what they notice about the group of words. They can make generalizations which will lead to the observation that C represents no sound of its own and might be considered to be a useless letter. They might also suggest this rule.

A WORTHWHILE RULE: C represents /s/ before I and E (and Y when Y substitutes for I and E), but it represents /k/ before other letters—*cake, coat, creek, cure, clean.*

STEP 10: CONSONANT DIGRAPHS

CH as in *chest, chorus* (Greek), *champagne* (French)
SH as in *short, patient, nation, ocean*
TH as in *the, thing*
WH as in *where, who*
GH as in *ghost, laugh*
PH as in *phone*
PS as in *psalm*
NG (an ending sound) as in *hang*
NK (an ending sound) as in *think*

What is the difference between a blend and a digraph? In a blend you can hear the letter sounds which blend, but in the digraph the identity of individual sounds is lost and a new sound is produced.

STEP 11: A SPECIAL FOCUS ON THE LETTER Y.

A letter which causes much confusion is Y, which represents both consonant and vowel sounds. The consonant sound is clearly identified in words like YELLOW, YACHT, YONDER. It is Y as a vowel, however, which bears clarification.

Y represents no vowel sounds of its own, but serves as an alternate spelling for I and E sounds. It would be inaccurate, therefore, to designate long and short sounds for Y, for it actually appears as both long I /ay/ and long E /iy/ as well as short I /i/. We know of no cases in which Y takes the short E /e/ sound; perhaps you will find one. Note the following examples:

LONG I

dye	hyphen	hygiene
my	cypress	type
cry	scythe	thyme
lyre	why	gyrate
lying	modify	hyacinth

LONG E	SHORT I
sadly*	crypt
playfully*	analysis
happy*	tryst
baby	cygnet
theology	nymph
identity	lyric
sticky	lynx
St. Cyr (Fr.)	rhythm
Ypres (Belg.)	oxygen
Yperite (a gas)	Ypsilanti (Michigan city)
Elysian	lynch
Lyons (Fr.)	catalyst
embryo	gypsy (the first Y)
	gymnasium
	hymn

As we scan the list of the sounds used in speaking English, we can readily note that some sounds are less confusing in that only one grapheme is usually used to denote this sound—/p/, /t/, /b/, /d/, /m/, /n/, /l/ /v/. These consonant sounds are among the first to be identified, and they cause little difficulty in spelling. For this reason we can safely teach words combining these consonants with the simpler vowel sounds—/i/, /e/, /æ/—in early spelling lessons.

> Display pictures of objects with the word printed below. Omit the beginning consonant so that children can determine which grapheme should be placed at the beginning of each word. Provide a variety—*vase, table, pony, baby, dog, mother, number, picture, log, dancer.*
>
> Practice locating blends which occur in different positions in a word as: SK in *skip, risk,* and *whiskers.* Other sounds may also be located as: SH in *shape, overshoe,* and *brush,* and CH in *chatter, branch,* and *unchain.*

As students advance in ability to identify sounds, they can explore diphthongs and consonant phonemes made by varied graphemes. Often the inductive method can be used to encourage student discovery.

> The phoneme /š/ is spelled with a wide variety of graphemes. Students can pursue a search for as many different examples as they can find. Discoveries may include: sugar, should, ocean, facial, delicious, nation, fissure, schwa, patient, chef.
>
> Focus on the symbol C by writing twenty-five words suggested by students to illustrate different sounds represented by this letter, for example:
>> coke, accident, black, ascent, accent, scale, sack, crowd, custom, cigarette, cactus, race, circus, church, circle, cast, attic

---

*The Y in the suffixes *ly* and *y* was long designated in dictionaries as a short I /i/. Usage, however, denies this pronunciation, for do we not use a *long* E to end such words? It is interesting to note that *Webster's Third New International Dictionary* (1961) lists for the first time the long E as the first pronunciation, thus: *'sadlē* or *'hapē.* Teaching this Y as a short I is confusing to students and should be avoided when the /iy/ pronunciation is used.

As students pronounce these words, divide them into groupings according to their pronunciation and spelling. Then, ask students to make generalizations about the letter c, thus:

c represents the sounds of /s/, /k/, and /s/.

It has no special sound so we really don't need it.

Before A and O, it usually sounds like /k/.

Phonic fallacies   Phonics has been severely criticized by the linguists, and some of the criticism has been justified. However, the fallacies that have been included in most presentations of phonics have largely been the result of lack of information.

In many cases teachers teach as they were taught without considering the exceptions that exist for most of the phonic generalizations that have been handed down from earlier instructors. Many examples of fallacious thinking appear in print and continue to be taught (1) in classrooms by teachers who have not been taught contemporary linguistic concepts, (2) by professors writing textbooks, who should be better informed, and (3) even by linguists who are supposed to be experts but who do not know the field of reading. Careful examination of presentations of phonics leads us to the following conclusions:

1. Very few "rules" are consistent enough to warrant teaching. Several that are consistent have been inserted within the developmental sequence. As soon as there are many exceptions, rules have little value and serve only to confuse the beginning reader or writer.
2. Sounds of single phonemes or combinations of phonemes should be pronounced in the context of a word. A consonant cannot be pronounced alone. The minute we try to say a consonant phoneme, we put a vowel sound behind it, which explains the presence of a vowel in every syllable. The number of vowel sounds heard indicates the number of syllables in a word.
3. We need to be certain of our linguistic knowledge and our ear for sounds, and we may need to reassess our understanding of phonology and the concepts we are teaching (even though they may appear in a textbook).
4. Regional variations in pronunciation exist. Because varied pronunciations are used does not mean they are "wrong." We bring them to the level of awareness because they are interesting phenomena in our language, not to evaluate them or to change the child's native speech.

The use of phonics has been aimed at aiding the beginning reader. As Smith points out, however, the language rules needed to enable a reader to predict the pronunciation of even common words are highly complex; and, even if you knew them all, you couldn't be certain a word would be correctly identified by use of phonics alone. Smith notes, furthermore:

> The question that cannot yet be answered concerns the *effectiveness* of phonics: is the limited degree of efficiency that might be attained worth acquiring? Other factors have to be taken into account related to the *cost* of trying to learn and use a phonic system. Our working memories do not have an infinite capacity and reading is not a task that can be accomplished at too leisurely a pace. Other

sources of information exist for finding out what a word in context might be, especially if the word is in the spoken vocabulary of the reader.[28]

It is true that fluent readers obviously know many phonic generalizations. They use them intuitively, usually without conscious thought. In fact, it is unlikely that they could verbalize these rules if requested to explain how to pronounce specific words. For example, how would you pronounce these words?

clique	diphthong	lachrymose
coupon	dilatory	impious
athletics	albeit	slough

Can you explain the rules on which you based your selection of a pronunciation? Work in small groups as you compare your pronunciation with that selected by other students in the class. Which pronunciation is listed in your dictionary?

Children should develop their own generalizations about language just as an adult does. The phonic concepts that we try to teach children may have meaning only to the fluent reader who has already been exposed repeatedly to written language.

Independent reading   "The more we read the better we read," is an excellent motto for the elementary school classroom. As the child develops skill with decoding, he or she begins reading independently with assistance from the teacher or a "buddy" only as needed. Good literature tends to provide its own motivation, but the wise teacher will continue to stimulate student reading and will also aid students in evaluating their own progress in reading. Some children may need individual or small group guidance to assist development in specific skills of word attack, extending vocabulary, and comprehension. The teacher should plan classroom reading instructional activities, too, to encourage interaction among students who are working independently.

Stimulating student reading   The best stimulus to wide reading is a large collection of varied titles in a well-organized central library. We can motivate student reading through a variety of strategies, thus:

- *Creative art techniques.* Students delight in creating favorite animal characters from newspaper glued in four to six layers over a two-pound coffee can or a large bottle which has been rubbed with oil. After the paper has dried, legs, antennae, tails and other needed accouterments can be added as Charlotte, Wilbur, the goose, and other barnyard friends appear. The Musicians of Bremen provide other characters for this medium.
  Paper strips glued around an armature of rolled paper or wire permits the creation of upright figures. There's skinny, rollicking Ribsy, and coming along

---

[28]Frank Smith, *Psycholinguistics and Reading* (New York: Holt, Rinehart & Winston, Inc., 1973), p. 90.

behind is Henry with a rolled newspaper in his hand. A group of students who like to work in miniature could produce the Borrowers—Pod, Homily, and Arrietty.

- *Bulletin board displays.* Let children take turns decorating a small bulletin board with the caption GUESS WHO? Displayed are pictures, drawings, small realia that suggest one book or one character. The creator then tells about the display explaining why he or she included various items.

- *Stimulating innovation.* Encourage students to utilize innovative approaches to sharing their reading. After the teacher has demonstrated more exciting ways of presenting a book to the class, students will vie to produce the more unusual presentation. Suggestions might include:

Mobile	Scroll theater
Diorama	Book jackets
Peekbox	Bookmarks
Collage	Mural
Puppetry	Literature map
Creative dramatics	Storytelling
Broadcasting	Displays
Interviewing an author	Advertisement
Poster	Filmstrips

- *Poems as songs.* The lyrics of songs are poems, a fact that we sometimes forget. Print the words of a familiar song that your children sing on a sheet so that they can read the words as a poem. As they read the words of "America, the Beautiful" or "My Country, 'Tis of Thee," they will better understand their meaning.

Students will enjoy singing our familiar songs that have been set to music such as "White Sheep," the anonymous poem that compares clouds to white sheep on a blue hill.

Anonymous   Iris M. Tiedt

White sheep, white sheep, On a blue hill.

When the wind stops, You all stand still.

When the wind blows, You walk a - way slow.

White sheep, white sheep, Where do you go?

- *The round robin book club.* An interesting way of encouraging reading is the exchange of student-owned books through a round robin book club arrangement. On a specified day each child brings one book to school, and the exchange begins. To ensure each child's receiving every book, a list is made of the children's names, and each child passes his book to the person whose name follows his own name, that is, he always passes a book to the same child. The passing of books should be regularly scheduled, perhaps once a week, for instance, every Friday. If this proves too short a time, books can be exchanged every other Friday.
- *Periodicals for young people.* There is an increasing interest in both magazines and newspapers for young people. These publications have the advantage of coming throughout the year, and for that reason tend to encourage the continuation of reading beyond the classroom. They also feature current information about interesting topics and can be used to stimulate both speaking and writing experiences. Magazines recommended for young children include:

American Forests. 1319-18th Street, N.W., Washington, D.C. 20036.
Boy's Life. New Brunswick, N.J. 08902.
Child Life. 1100 Waterway Blvd., Indianapolis, Ind. 46202.
Children's Digest. 52 Vanderbilt Avenue, New York, N.Y. 10017.
Cricket. P.O. Box 100, LaSalle, Ill. 61301.
Highlights for Children. 2300 West 5th Avenue, Columbus, Ohio 43216.
Humpty Dumpty's Magazine. 52 Vanderbilt Avenue, New York, N.Y. 10017.
Jack and Jill. Box 528, Indianapolis, Ind. 46202.
My Weekly Reader. 245 Long Hill Rd., Middletown, Conn. 06457.
National Geographic and *National Geographic School Bulletin.* 17th and M Streets, N.W., Washington, D.C. 20036.
Scholastic Magazines. 50 West 44th Street, New York, N.Y. 10036.
Science Digest. 224 West 57th Street, New York, N.Y. 10019.

- *Commercial book clubs.* A number of commercial book clubs are popular with children and encourage reading and the exchange of books, as well as the acquisition of a personal library. Several offer inexpensive hardback editions, while others specialize in paperback editions at very low prices. You can obtain information about these clubs to make available to children and parents.

Junior Literary Guild, 277 Park Avenue, New York, N.Y. 10017
Parents' Magazine's Book Clubs, 52 Vanderbilt Avenue, New York, N.Y. 10017
Scholastic Book Clubs, 50 West 44th Street, New York, N.Y. 10036

Continuing vocabulary growth Avid readers usually have no difficulty in acquiring an extensive vocabulary, but even they may require assistance with pronunciation and connotations, if not denotations, of words encountered. The study of words adds much to intellectual development at any stage, and it certainly is not limited to the reading period alone, for much effective learning about words takes place in other subject areas.

As noted frequently throughout this book, teacher interest and enthusiasm for words will be contagious. The teacher who leads the way in making discoveries and talking to children about words will make students aware of words and their meanings and help them observe intriguing features of words. Through writing and speaking experiences they come to delight in using new, less common words, in searching for synonyms and in "trying out" discoveries on classmates as well as the teacher. One girl, for example, referred to the rumblings of her stomach as "borborygmi" which mystified us all until she shared her discovery. And remember how delighted you were when you first heard of words like "expectorate" and "osculate"?

Use interesting words as you speak to children (not the above examples, perhaps); they will absorb them as their own. "You're an example of *sartorial* splendor, Mike! Do you know what that means?" Write it on the board, but let him do his own investigating. "I see Vicky has a new *coiffeur* today." "The king *abdicated* his throne." "Let's *speculate* about what might have happened if we had not entered the war." The only requirement for this approach to word study is knowledge on the part of the teacher; you may need to "grow a vocabulary" ahead of or with your students, and if you work with a group of able fifth or sixth graders, they may lead the way. Even in the primary grades we can eliminate "baby talk," avoid "talking down," and help them reach out to grasp new words to express new ideas. It's a pleasant, creative way of learning, and it's effective.

Walking words   Introduce young children to varied ways of walking through creative dramatics. As they begin walking around a circle or "following the leader" in a line, ask them if they can sneak as if they didn't want anyone to see them. Suggest that they *march* like soldiers, *tramp* like noisy boys, *scamper* like puppies playing, *stride* like tall men, *waddle* like fat bears, *strut* like peacocks. Then discuss the words and ask if they can suggest different "ways of walking." Other synonym groups can be explored also.

Favorite words   Share a group of your favorite words with the class—*scintillating, effervescent, exquisite, bombastic*—the choice is up to you! Write one of the words on the board as you say it. Ask them what they think it means. Use it in a sentence. Then invite them to share their favorite words they have discovered which they think are especially appealing. Display words which have been shared.

Word play   Spoonerisms (an inversion of beginning sounds attributed to Rev. William Spooner), Malapropisms, Wellerisms, are examples of word play that can be researched by able students.

Chain reaction   An excellent way to practice knowledge of phonics is to begin a word chain. By changing only one letter to make a new word each time, see how long the chain can be made. A chain (or more than one) can be started with children adding to it in their free time, thus:

TAME	FORT	SPOUT
tale	sort	sport
sale	port	short
pale	part	shirt
page	cart	shirk
wage	dart	shark
wade	dark	spark
wide	darn	spare
hide	dare	aspire
side	care	spine

Treasure hunt Begin a search for words of a specific nature as everyone adds to a list mounted on the bulletin board or the wordlist begun on the chalkboard. For example, begin a search for words which end in *tion, ong,* or *able* to provide practice with specific suffixes or phonograms. Lend interest to syllable practice by listing words of four, five, or six syllables. For younger children ask for words with three syllables or words with eight letters.

Borrowed English words The activity sheet below demonstrates the teaching of groups of related English words. Here words are based on a common Latin root.

VOCABULARY ACTIVITY SHEET
Borrowed English Words

Exploring Latin Roots

Root Word: BONUS   Related forms: BENE, OPTIMUS
Meaning: Good   Related forms: Well, best
Spelling in English: bon, bene, optim

Use your dictionary to find the meanings of these words:
bona fide (adjective) _____
bonny (adjective) _____
benefactor (noun) _____
benediction (noun) _____
benefit (verb) _____
benefit (noun) _____
benevolent (adjective) _____
optimist (noun) _____
optimum (adjective) _____
bon voyage (expression) _____
bonanza (noun) _____

Choose three of the words listed. Write a sentence for each one that you could use in the classroom or at home.
1. _____
_____
2. _____
_____
3. _____
_____

Plan to use each of these sentences within the next day. In class the next day tell about the situation in which you used one of the sentences.

SUMMARY

Reading instruction must be presented within the language arts program to be most effective and efficient. Developing learning activities around a theme, for example, provides purpose for listening, speaking, reading, and writing as well as the necessary thinking skills to carry out specific projects. Children need help as they begin to relate spoken language to that which is printed by them or by other authors. They need support for their attempts to gain meaning from a picture book, and they need a feeling of acceptance even as they make miscues. Too much time is spent on fragmented decoding activities that are removed from the context of reading and totally unrelated to encoding (spelling). Research points the way to a strong reading program that engages students in hearing fluent reading, reading independently supported by an able reader, and writing original literature that they can read because they composed it. The aim of all reading instruction should focus on gaining meaning from the printed word, comprehension of what has been written and what is read. Students should move as quickly as possible, therefore, into reading literature for pleasure and information, as presented in the next two chapters. They should also write original literature as described in Chapter 8.

CHALLENGE

Begin to explore on your own as you investigate the way you would like to teach reading. The teacher is the key to success in any program, so you play a very responsible role in analyzing your thinking and deciding how to carry out your philosophy of teaching. The questions that follow are designed to help you clarify your approach to reading instructions.

1. Review the goals and objectives for teaching, student needs, and what we know about effective teaching. Write three or more objectives for a strong reading program.

2. Observe a reading class in an elementary school near you. If possible, talk with the teacher about the total reading program and the kinds of activities that children typically engage in to learn how to read. Examine the teaching materials used. Write a report of your observation, noting the following:

    a. Grade level, socioeconomic level of school
    b. Factual description of reading lesson observed
    c. List of other reading experiences noted or described by teacher
    d. List of reading materials used in classroom
    e. A short critical analysis of the approach to reading observed

3. Read two or more recent articles on the teaching of reading. Check the *Education Index* in the college library for titles and sources. Look for those that report innovative practices, trends in reading instruction, or new research findings (The November/December 1981 issue of *Language Arts* focuses on "Reading Instruction"). Report orally on these articles in a small group as a way of sharing your information with other members of your class. Discuss the information shared in the large group.

EXPLORING FURTHER

Allen, P. David and Dorothy Watson, *Findings of Research in Miscue Analysis: Classroom Implications*. Urbana, Ill.: ERIC/RCS and National Council of Teachers of English, 1976.

Daniels, Steven, *How 2 Gerbils, 20 Goldfish, 200 Games, 2,000 Books and I Taught Them How to Read*. Philadelphia: Westminster Press, 1971.

Downing, John, *Reading and Reasoning*. Edinburgh and New York: Springer Publishing Co., Inc., 1979.

Heilman, Arthur W. and Elizabeth Ann Holmes, *Smuggling Language into the Teaching of Reading*. Columbus, Ohio: Charles E. Merrill Publishing Co., 1972.

Judy, Stephen N., *The ABC's of Literacy: A Guide for Parents and Educators*. New York: Oxford University Press, 1980.

————, ed., *Reading*. Lansing, Mich.: Michigan Council of Teachers of English, 1980.

McCracken, Robert and Marlene McCracken, *Reading, Writing, and Language*. Winnipeg, Canada: Pequis Publishers, 1979.

Page, William D. and Gay Su Pinnell, *Teaching Reading Comprehension*. Urbana, Ill.: National Council of Teachers of English, 1979.

Ruddell, Robert B. et al, eds., *Resources in Reading-Language Instruction*. Englewood Cliffs, N.J.: Prentice-Hall, Inc., 1974.

Smith, Frank, *Comprehension and Learning: A Conceptual Framework for Teachers*. New York: Holt, Rinehart and Winston, Inc., 1975.

————, *Reading Without Nonsense*. New York: Teachers College Press, 1978.

Spache, Evelyn B., *Reading Activities for Child Involvement*. Boston: Allyn & Bacon, 1976.

Weaver, Constance, *Psycholinguistics and Reading: From Process to Practice*. Cambridge, Mass.: Winthrop Publishing Co., 1980.

12

Through the use of words alone, the writer creates sight and sound and emotional response. By reading words alone, the reader sees, hears, and feels. Both are demonstrating an act of mentality, the connection of minds through which belief is suspended in the interest of illusion. One would be at a loss without the other.

Virginia Hamilton, *Illusion and Reality*[1]

READING LITERATURE FOR COMPREHENSION

Literature should be an integral component of the language arts program. Literature provides models for language growth, and it introduces concepts that stimulate children's thinking. Literature is part of a child's cultural heritage.

Young people need books that expand their worlds. They need fantasy to stir their imaginations, but children also "need books that present what is real. They need stories about people interacting with all the stress and emotion that accompanies human relations. They need to read about children like themselves who are coping with situations that are real to a child growing up."[2]

[1]Virginia Hamilton, *Illusion and Reality* (Lecture presented at the Library of Congress, November 17, 1975).
[2]Iris M. Tiedt, *Exploring Books with Children* (Boston: Houghton Mifflin Co., 1979), pp. 145–46.

Literature can be selected to support instruction in all areas of the curriculum. Books that portray nonstereotyped multicultural differences, showing people with the same universal hopes and problems, represent the pluralistic society in which we live. Books can help children experience empathy for different values. Books can open doors to different times and places.

BENCHMARK

Think about children's literature as you know it at this moment.

1. What are the books that you remember reading? Was reading an important part of your childhood and adolescence? Discuss this topic with others in the class.

2. How would you define children's literature?

3. Assess your own knowledge of children's literature today. Have you had a course in children's literature within the past five years? Have you read books by these authors who represent just a few of the well-known writers of children's books?

   E. B. White
   Lloyd Alexander
   Robert McCloskey
   Judy Blume
   Maurice Sendak
   Dr. Seuss

In this chapter we define children's literature, a broad field that encompasses many genres and varied media. We then discuss how to design and implement a literature program for elementary students. After completing this chapter you should be able to:

• discuss the importance of children's literature in the elementary school
• name a number of representative titles and authors in the field
• describe ways of using books across the curriculum
• tell a story to children
• plan a teaching unit around a theme using varied literature for instruction
• explain the use of literature to teach reading comprehension

LITERATURE FOR ALL CHILDREN

A teacher who knows and believes in the importance of the child's experiencing a rich literary heritage will see that good books are in the curriculum and that children hear and read literature daily.

In order to design an effective student-centered language arts program the elementary teacher must explore books for children of all levels on varied topics.

Time for Literature

Literature can appear in the elementary school classroom in many ways. It can be the material through which reading is taught. In this form literature becomes a text which is read, discussed, studied, as reading skills are practiced.

Literature is also an excellent starting point for many creative writing activities. Tall tales of Paul Bunyan, the adventures of Robin Hood, Aesop's fables serve to suggest short stories which children can write. The Moffat books by Eleanor Estes demonstrate the adventurous possibilities present in everyday happenings.

Literature is recreation as the teacher reads aloud. There are few children who do not hurry to their desks after recess as they notice the teacher seated with book in hand ready to read *The Lion, The Witch, and the Wardrobe* by C. S. Lewis (Macmillan). Other titles recommended for reading aloud include:

Mr. Popper's Penguins (Little, Brown, and Co.) by Richard and Florence Atwater.
Rabbit Hill (The Viking Press) by Robert Lawson.
The Children of Odin (The Macmillan Co.) by Padraic Colum.
Story of King Arthur and His Knights (C. Scribner's Sons) by Howard Pyle.
The Wind in the Willows (C. Scribner's Sons) by Kenneth Grahame.
Henry Huggins (Wm. Morrow and Co.) by Beverly Cleary.
The Long Winter (Harper and Row) by Laura I. Wilder.
The Witch of Blackbird Pond (Houghton Mifflin) by Elizabeth G. Speare.
Peterkin Papers (Harper and Row) by Lucretia P. Hale.
It's Perfectly True and Other Stories (Harcourt, Brace) by H. C. Andersen.

The teacher will often read a book aloud which a child could read to motivate reading. Another purpose of reading aloud is to present material that makes the child's mind reach. The child can understand ideas and vocabulary far beyond his or her reading ability, so that the first-grade child will chuckle delightedly over the antics of *Pippi Longstocking* although not able to read this book independently.

Book Selection

How do we choose books to read to a class? How do we select books for purchase by the school library? On what basis do we recommend books to students? A course in children's literature is a must for any elementary school teacher, but even that will not serve to keep the teacher's knowledge current. Frequent visits to the children's department of libraries and bookstores, reading book reviews, noting publisher's advertisements, talking to others who enjoy children's books—these are some of the ways to inform yourself about news in the children's book world.

Personal examination of each title is fun and rewarding, but because it is time-consuming, the teacher often relies on the judgment of others in selecting books. Following is a list of book selection aids which should be in the school's professional library or in the school library.

From *Pippi Longstocking* by Astrid Lindgren. Copyright 1950 by The Viking Press, Inc. Reprinted by permission of The Viking Press, Inc.

Arbuthnot, May H. et al., eds., *Children's Books Too Good to Miss* (6th ed.). Cleveland, Ohio: Western Reserve Press, 1971.

The Booklist and Subscription Books Bulletin, A Guide to Current Books. American Library Assn., 60 East Huron Street, Chicago, Illinois.

Bulletin of the Center for Children's Books, ed. Zena Sutherland. University of Chicago Press, 5801 Ellis Ave., Chicago, Ill. 60637. An excellent monthly review with evaluation and annotation of current books.

Children's Catalog. New York: H. W. Wilson. The most complete annotated listing, with regular supplements.

The Horn Book Magazine. Boston, Mass.: The Horn Book, 585 Boylston St., Boston, Mass. 02116.

Language Arts, The Official Journal of the Elementary Section of the National Council of Teachers of English. 1111 Kenyon Rd., Urbana, Ill. 61801. Especially helpful to classroom teachers (membership in NCTE).

Larrick, Nancy, ed., *A Parent's Guide to Children's Reading* (3rd ed.). Columbus, Ohio: Charles E. Merrill Publishing Co., 1969.

Root, Shelton, ed., *Adventuring with Books* (3rd ed.). Urbana, Ill.: National Council of Teachers of English, 1982. 1111 Kenyon Rd., Urbana, Ill. 61801. An up-to-date list prepared by those who know the field.

Tway, Eileen, ed., *Reading Ladders for Human Relations.* Urbana, Ill.: National Council of Teachers of English, 1981. 1111 Kenyon Rd., Urbana, Ill. 61801. An excellent annotated listing of books to further understandings among all peoples.

Let students take an active part in the selection of books, whether it is an individual selection or the purchase of a group of titles for the school library. As adults we sometimes have far different values than the children we teach. Have a stock of 3 × 5 file cards on which students (and you, too) can throughout the year note books for purchase.

Book awards   Each year selected titles in children's literature are awarded honors. Two of the most famous awards are the Newbery and Caldecott medals which were established by a publisher, Frederic G. Melcher.

The Newbery award was first given in 1922 to Hendrik Van Loon's *The Story of Mankind.* Named in honor of John Newbery, an early English publisher who is credited with "discovering" children's literature, this award is given for "distinguished literature." The award list includes many familiar titles. The full list appears on pages 415–425.

Betsy Byars. *Summer of the Swans.* Viking, (1971)
Paula Fox. *The Slave Dancer.* Bradbury. (1974)
William Armstrong. *Sounder.* Harper (1970)

The Caldecott Medal is awarded to the best picture-book of the year. Named in honor of Randolph Caldecott (1846–1886), an English illustrator of children's books, the first Caldecott Medal was awarded in 1938 to Dorothy Lathrop for *Animals of the Bible.* The illustrator in some cases is also the author. The full list of Caldecott winners appears on pages 407–415.

Maurice Sendak. *Where the Wild Things Are.* Harper. (1964)
Ed Emberley, Illus. *Drummer Hoff* by Barbara Emberley. Prentice-Hall. (1968)
Gerald McDermott. *Arrow to the Sun.* Viking. (1975)

These lists might be used as purchase lists for a beginning library. A well-established elementary school library will contain all these titles, but one must remember that books are selected for varied reasons. The Caldecott award list is composed of books for the primary grades judged on the value of their illustrations. The list of titles for the Newbery award focuses largely on books for grades four through nine with a heavy concentration of books for the junior high school level. Excellent nonfiction is also required for the school library. Titles must be evaluated, therefore, in terms of the needs of the school library as a whole.

In examining award lists, remember that many of these books were selected twenty, even thirty years ago. Some of these books do not prove as tempting today as they may have been then, as new interests and tastes develop. One wonders also whether there is not a tinge of "what adults think children should like" about awards of this nature. An interesting study could be conducted by classes to determine which books are favorites with class members. Which titles from these lists are named as favorites? Which are not, and why? Here is an opportunity to develop critical thinking as children realize that a printed list proves nothing in itself.

Young Readers

Perhaps some of the most intriguing, thought-provoking story material is appearing in books for the very youngest reader. Enhanced by artful, vivid illustrations, these books have instant appeal, first as books read to the child, and later as books to read independently.

Children entering first grade today have usually had a wide background of experiences. Their listening vocabulary is estimated at 20,000 words, and they can fully comprehend a surprising number of rather complex concepts. Through television, parental reading aloud, and talking with other children and adults, children are exposed to varied topics which little concerned the child of a generation ago.

Individual interests are varied, but in general children enjoy humor, repetition, action, and stories about real people. Youngsters who follow the astronauts through space and back again will search for books about space. Favorite books for this age group are the Dr. Seuss stories—*McElligott's Pool, Horton Hatches the Egg;* Anderson's horse stories—*Blaze and the Gypsies, Billy and Blaze;* Jerrold Beim's stories of real children—*Andy and the School Bus, Twelve O'Clock Whistle;* Marjorie Flack's animal tales—*Story about Ping, New Pet;* Margaret Johnson's *Joey and Patches, Snowshoe Paws, Stablemates;* Lois Lenski's *Cowboy Small, Little Fire Engine, Surprise for Davy;* and Hans Rey's amusing tales of *Curious George.* There are, of course, numerous other titles which could and should be named, but we shall leave that to your own exploration.

The Able Student

Grade-level categorization of books has little meaning for able readers, for they will almost certainly be reading several levels ahead of the school grade level. Many elementary school children may be reading adult literature—*Cheaper by the Dozen, Born Free, Incredible Journey, Tom Sawyer, The Hobbit,* and *The Lord of the Rings.*

The growth of able readers can focus on creativity and activities that stimulate communication. Students might organize a book club, with all members reading one specific book a week and preparing questions, observations, and ideas to discuss. Each member could take the leadership in turn to conduct a discussion or to deliver a short prepared book review. The group might also decide to present a book to the class by preparing a display, a dramatization, or a book talk.

Able students also learn much by serving as teacher aides in primary-grade classes. Older children can prepare flannel board presentations of stories that appeal to first and second graders. Puppet shows of favorite stories are also popular. Able students might organize a schoolwide campaign called EVERY CHILD A READER, which would reflect the National Right to Read Effort as the students themselves reach out to help other students learn to read.

Ethnic Minorities

Many groups of students deserve special assistance in meeting their special needs. We can promote understanding by providing more realistic pictures of minority groups and the beauty of the varied cultures that coexist within the larger culture of the nation.

Elementary school libraries need to provide numerous juvenile titles that depict characters who are black, Chinese, Japanese, Mexican-American, Puerto Rican, and so forth. Here is a portion of one list of books about Black Americans compiled by the Council on Interracial Books for Children, Inc. (9 East 40th Street, New York, N.Y. 10016).

KINDERGARTEN THROUGH SECOND GRADE:

Beim, Lorraine, and Jerrold Beim, *Two Is A Team,* illus. by Ernest Crichlow. New York: Harcourt Brace Jovanovich, Inc., 1945. $2.75. 61 pp. A simple story of friendship and cooperation between two boys which can be read independently by younger children. Only the illustrations convey the fact that one of the boys is black.

Keats, Ezra Jack, *The Snowy Day,* illus. by author. New York: Viking Press, Inc., 1962. $3.00. 32 pp. Preschool and kindergarten age children will enjoy the adventures of a little black boy as he plays in the snow. Distinguished, colorful illustrations add to the beauty of this simple story. (Film available from Weston Woods, Weston, Conn.)

————, *Whistle for Willie,* illus. by author. New York: Viking Press, Inc., 1964. $3.50. 33 pp. Another book about the hero of *The Snowy Day.* Any young child who has tried to whistle will thoroughly enjoy this beautifully illustrated picture book.

Showers, Paul, *Look at Your Eyes,* illus. by Paul Galdone. New York: Thomas Y. Crowell Co., 1962. $2.75. Through easy text and attractive illustrations, children discover, along with a young black boy, some of the basic facts about the function of the eyes. A beginning science book of general interest to young children.

THIRD THROUGH SIXTH GRADE:

Bontemps, Arna, *Frederick Douglass: Slave, Fighter, Freeman,* illus. by Harper Johnson. New York: Alfred A. Knopf, Inc., 1959. $3.00. 177 pp. A vivid, dramatic account of the life of an ex-slave whose philosophy and actions continue to have great meaning in today's society.

Brooks, Gwendolyn, *Bronzeville Boys and Girls* (poems), illus. by Ronni Solbert. New York: Harper & Row Pubs., Inc., 1956. $2.50. 40 pp. A delightful collection of poems about city children by a noted black poet and Pulitzer Prize winner. Delicate illustrations, especially of black children, capture the mood of the poetry.

Evans, Eva, *People Are Important*, illus. by Vana Earle. New York: Golden Press, 1951. $3.95. 86 pp. A factual appraisal of the world's peoples and their habits presented with a sparkling, often humorous approach.

Fritz, Jean, *Brady*, illus. by Lynd Ward. New York: Coward-McCann, Inc., 1960. $3.50. 223 pp. Excellent characterizations and a well-developed story of the underground railroad. Good supplementary reading for the study of the Civil War period.

Hughes, Langston, and Milton Meltzer, eds., *Pictorial History of the Negro in America*, rev. ed. New York: Crown Pubs., Inc., 1963. $5.95. 337 pp. The broad panorama of the history of the Black American, presented through excellent text and numerous photographs. Useful both for students, teachers, and many classroom libraries.

McGovern, Ann. *Runaway Slave*, illus. by R. M. Powers. New York: Scholastic Book Services, 1965. 212 pp. Simple, lyric prose and sensitive illustrations capture the dignity and strength of Harriet Tubman. Although primarily for third and fourth grades, it can also be handled comfortably by the "slow" or reluctant readers.

Shotwell, Louisa R. *Roosevelt Grady*. illus. by Peter Burchard. Cleveland, Ohio: World, 1963, $2.95. 151 pp. Although some events in the lives of this black migrant family may not be familiar, children in both urban and suburban communities will understand and sympathize with their hopes and dreams for a permanent home.

Sterling, Dorothy. *Mary Jane*. illus. by Ernest Crichlow. Garden City, N.J.: Doubleday, 1959. $2.95. 214 pp. A sensitive portrayal of a young girl's lonely experience as one of a small group of blacks in a junior high school that provides token integration. A realistic yet optimistic presentation which will have significance for both white and black children today.

An interesting class project is the development of an annotated list like the one just presented. Here is the nucleus of a bibliography on Mexican-American literature which could be prepared first on cards by each individual explorer and later compiled in a useful list:

Bailey, Bernadine. *Famous Latin American Liberators*. New York: Dodd, 1960. 158 pp.

———. *Picture Book of New Mexico*. New York: Albert Whitman, 1960. 26 pp.

Blecker, Sonia. *The Aztec: Indians of Mexico*. New York: Morrow, 1963. 160 pp.

———. *The Maya: Indians of Central America*. New York: Morrow, 1961. 160 pp.

Flack, Marjorie, and Larsson, Karl. *Pedro*. New York: Macmillan, 1940. 96 pp.

Goetz, Delia. *Neighbors to the South*, rev. ed. New York: Harcourt, 1959. 179 pp.

Good, Loren. *Panchito*. New York: Coward-McCann, 1955. 160 pp.

Hogner, Dorothy C. *Children of Mexico*. Boston: Heath, 1942. 64 pp.

Kidwell, Carl. *Arrow in the Sun*. New York: Viking, 1961. 254 pp.

Lay, Marion. *Wooden Saddles: The Adventures of a Mexican Boy in His Own Land*. New York: Morrow, 1939. 175 pp.

MacDonald, Etta B., and Dalrymple, Julia. *Manuel in Mexico*. Boston: Little, Brown, 1909. 118 pp.

Moon, Grace. *Tita of Mexico*. New York: Frederick A. Stokes, 1934. 213 pp.

Politi, Leo. *The Mission Bell*. New York: Scribners, 1953. 30 pp.

Rhoads, Dorothy. *The Story of Chan Yuc.* Garden City, N.J.: Doubleday, 1941. 43 pp.

Rose, Patricia. *Let's Read about Mexico.* Grand Rapids, Mich.: Fideler, 1955. 160 pp.

Sawyer, Ruth. *The Least One.* New York: Viking, 1941. 89 pp.

Schweitzer, Byrd B. *Amigo.* New York: Macmillan, 1963. 41 pp.

Thomas, Margaret L. *Carlos: Our Mexican Neighbor.* Indianapolis, Ind.: Bobbs-Merrill, 1938. 189 pp.

Wilson, Barbara K. *Fairy Tales of Mexico.* New York: Dutton, 1960. 39 pp.

Witton, Dorothy. *Crossroads for Chela.* New York: Messner, 1956. 192 pp.

Other good bibliographies about ethnic groups include:

Linskie, Rosella and Howard Rosenburg. *A Handbook for Multicultural Studies in Elementary Schools: Chicano, Black, Asian, and Native American.* R & E Research Association, 1976.

Tiedt, Pamela and Iris M. Tiedt. *Multicultural Teaching: A Handbook of Activities, Information, and Resources.* Allyn & Bacon, 1979.

Tway, Eileen, ed. *Reading Ladders for Human Relations.* American Council on Education and National Council of Teachers of English, 1981.

Women and Girls

Increasing criticism has been directed toward the image of women in children's tradebooks as well as in elementary school textbooks. This stereotyped image of women's roles and the socialization of young girls in our society places severe limitations on a young girl's expectations for her life.

Illustrations and content in children's literature help demonstrate the passive, unexciting roles that girls play, compared with the adventurous, active roles of boys. Mother is consistently depicted as a housewife in the kitchen wearing an apron. Publishers have leaned toward the production of books that would appeal to boys, stating that "girls will read books for boys, but boys won't touch books for girls." Few considered the insipid quality of "books for girls" or the fact that girls might be adversely affected by this consistent "put-down."

There is a growing movement to select books with more positive images of girls and women, books that would never include the line, "Girls can't do that." Biographies of women are also appearing with titles on Rachel Carson, Lydia Maria Child, Margaret Sanger, Dr. Florence Sabin, Bessie Smith, and Margaret Chase Smith—women who have not followed a stereotyped existence. Here is a selected list of books you might explore:

Abramovitz, Anita. *Winifred.* Steck-Vaughn Co., 1971. (Pr.-Elem.)

Alexander, Anne. *Little Foreign Devil.* Atheneum, 1970. (Elem.-Jr.)

Babbitt, Natalie. *Phoebe's Revolt.* Farrar, Straus, and Giroux, 1968. (Elem.)

Brownstone, Cecily. *All Kinds of Mothers.* McKay, 1969. (Primary)

Buckley, Mary. *Six Brothers and a Witch.* Bobbs-Merrill, 1969. (Elem.)

Burnett, Frances Hodgson. *The Secret Garden.* Lippincott, 1911. (Elem.-Jr.)

Corcoran, Barbara. *The Long Journey.* Atheneum, 1970. (Elem.)

Crockett, Mayr. *Rosanna the Goat.* Bobbs-Merrill, 1970. (Elem.)
Gaeddert, LouAnn. *Noisy Nancy and Nick.* Doubleday, 1970. (Elem.)
Gauch, Patricia Lee. *Christina Katerina and THE BOX.* Coward-McCann, 1971. (Elem.)
George, Jean C. *Julie of the Wolves.* Harper, 1972. (Elem-Jr.)
Gill, Joan. *Sara's Granny and the Groodle.* Doubleday, 1969. (Elem.)
Goffstein, M. B. *Two Piano Tuners.* Farrar, Straus, and Giroux, 1970. (Elem.)
Hall, Elizabeth. *Stand Up, Lucy.* Houghton Mifflin, 1971. (Jr.)
Hunter, Kristin. *The Soul Brothers and Sister Lou.* Scribner's Sons, 1968. (Jr.)
Klein, Norma. *Mom, the Wolfman and Me.* Avon, 1974. (Elem-Jr.)
Krasilovsky, Phyllis. *The Very Tall Little Girl.* Doubleday, 1969. (Pr.-Elem.)
Laurence. *Seymourina.* Bobbs-Merrill, 1970. (Elem.)
Lindgren, Astrid. *Pippi Longstocking.* Viking Press, 1950. (Elem.)
Malone, Mary. *Annie Sullivan.* G. P. Putnam's Sons, 1971. (Elem.)
Merriam, Eve. *Mommies at Work.* Viking Press, 1961. (Pr.-Elem.)
O'Dell, Scott. *Island of the Blue Dolphins.* Houghton Mifflin, 1960. (Elem-Jr.)
Renvoize, Jean. *A Wild Thing,* Little Brown and Co., 1971. (Sr.)
Rich, Gibson, *Firegirl.* Feminist Press, 1972. (Pr.-Elem.)
Rockwell, Anne and Harlow. *Molly's Woodland Garden.* Doubleday, 1971. (Elem.)
Sachs, Marily. *Peter and Veronica.* Doubleday, 1969. (Elem.)
Shulevitz, Uri. *Rain, Rain, Rivers.* Farrar, Straus, and Giroux, 1969. (Elem.)
Streatfield, Noel. *Thursday's Child.* Random House, 1970. (Jr.)
Swarthout, Glendon and Kathryn. *The Button Boat.* Doubleday, 1969. (Elem.-Jr.)
Swinburne, Laurence, *Detli.* Bobbs-Merrill, 1970. (Jr.)
Tallon, Robert. *The Thing in Dolores' Piano.* Bobbs-Merrill, 1970. (Elem.)
Wilson, Ellen. *American Painter in Paris: A Life of Mary Cassatt.* Farrar, Straus, and Giroux, 1971. (Jr.)
Zindel, Paul. *I Love My Mother.* Harper, 1975. (Prim.)

PLANNING A LITERATURE READING PROGRAM

Literature has always been the major component of high school and college English programs. For some reason, however, children's literature has remained on the fringe of the elementary school language arts curriculum. There seems to be little justification for this lack of emphasis. As Huck points out:

> During the most important years of their educational lives, their teachers always value literature for what it does to improve other skills or enrich other subjects. For too long now, literature in the elementary school has been a handmaiden for reading, language arts, and the social studies. The time has come to recognize what the experience of literature, as literature, may do for the child.[3]

As we consider the importance of literature programs designed for children, we need to discuss the following questions:

1. Why is there a need for a planned literature program?
2. Who is to determine a scope and sequence for this program?

[3]Charlotte Huck, *Children's Literature in the Elementary School,* 3rd ed. (New York: Holt, Rinehart & Winston, Inc., 1976), p. 704.

3.   How will literature fit into the already overcrowded curriculum?
4.   How does teaching literature differ from teaching reading?
5.   How can teachers become prepared to teach literature?

Will the study of literature, that is, analysis, destroy the child's enjoyment of a story as many purists fear? On the contrary, it has been our observation that exploring beyond the superficial story value of an author's work actually leads to greater interest in reading and aids in the development of critical thinking. Emphasis still remains on reading for enjoyment, but this enjoyment is enhanced through appreciation of the writer's skilled performance.

Literature in the Reading Program

Literature has seldom been part of the reading program in the elementary school, for reading has been dominated by the basal reader series. What are the advantages of a literature-reading program over the traditional controlled-vocabulary anthology? The use of literature in a reading program for elementary school students offers quality content to a course of study which has concentrated solely on the teaching of skills. It is time that we acknowledge the value of provocative material in exciting the student about reading. Until this excitement is present in the reading lesson, we will not develop a nation of readers.

Many titles from children's literature can be, and are being, used as reading text material. The advantages of *Pippi Longstocking, A Wrinkle in Time,* and *Johnny Tremain* over the familiar basal reader are overwhelming:

1.   Excellent writing—imagery, use of words, storytelling ability
2.   Continuity of a longer story—plot development, characterization
3.   Greater interest value—intrigue, atmosphere, entertainment
4.   Integration of literature, language, and composition studies

The only advantage undeniably present in the basal reader is controlled vocabulary. In light of our singular lack of success in producing adults who read widely, however, one wonders if the controlled vocabulary may not literally drain the vitality from the fare served our enthusiastic beginning readers. As Phyllis McGinley observes in *Sixpence in Her Shoe:*

> Whose invention was this vocabulary restriction I cannot say. Librarians deplore the trend, publishers disclaim responsibility, authors declare themselves stifled by it, children detest it. But the fact remains that somebody has set up as gospel the rule that odd words, long words, interesting words, grown-up words must be as precisely sifted out from a book for, say, five-year-olds as chaff from wheat or profanity from a television program. . . .
>
> Are children never to climb? Must they be saved from all the healthy bumps and bruises of exploration? . . . The genuine reading child . . . wants, even at six or seven or eight, gourmet fare. . . . [4]

[4]Phyllis McGinley, *Sixpence in Her Shoe* (New York: The Macmillan Company, 1964), pp. 213–14.

The Nebraska Curriculum Development Center has developed an elementary school English curriculum which focuses attention on core literature texts. The aims of this language, literature, and composition program are stated to be:

1. To teach students to comprehend the more frequent grammatical conventions
2. To teach students to comprehend the more frequent conventions of literature composed for young children—formal or generic conventions and simple rhetorical conventions
3. To teach students to control these linguistic and literary conventions in their own writing[5]

Individualized reading programs   The teaching of literature lends itself well to individualizing reading. Many teachers are experimenting with the use of trade titles, having each student read different books. The completely individualized approach to reading literature has the advantages of (1) individual selection of books, (2) progress at varied rates of speed, (3) usually greater quantity of reading, and (4) no child without something to do.

To operate with maximum effectiveness this approach requires that the teacher guide individual development through extensive student conferencing. Activities for extending learning must be planned (until they are commercially available) for each book so that students are doing more than just reading title after title. The standard book-report form hastily completed by the disinterested student is a waste of time and may actually cause children to dislike reading.

Small group seminars   Other teachers are finding that the purchase of multiple copies of several titles provides excellent material for small group approaches to literature study. This approach to literature study limits student selection but offers certain advantages for the teaching of literature: (1) use of seminar techniques in discussing a common body of reading, (2) concentration of teacher and student efforts on fewer books to be examined in depth, (3) individualized responses to independent open-ended activities for extending learning, and (4) experiences in group dynamics.

Perhaps the best method of presentation will prove to be a combination of the individualized and the small group approaches described. Neither approach actually teaches literature, for the success of these techniques lies essentially with the teacher. Teacher enthusiasm, knowledge of literature, ability to guide without domination, and wisdom in planning will, as in all of teaching, play a significant role.

Planning Literature Experiences

What procedures shall we follow in presenting a title? The techniques used will vary according to the particular books under discussion, but each literature experience will be based on the reading of a sizable portion of the

[5]Nebraska Curriculum Development Center, *A Curriculum for English; Introduction to the Elementary School Program: K–6,* Mimeographed report (Lincoln: The University of Nebraska, 1965), p. 2.

book. Books that are divided into chapters are particularly adaptable for study. A very short book might be treated as a whole. Steps in presenting the literature lesson usually follow a sequence like this:

1. *Reading a portion of the book.* Children may read silently, or they may take turns reading aloud. It is highly desirable that the teacher frequently read aloud to a group as this technique adds to the pleasure of the experience and prepares the group for immediate follow-up activities.
2. *Discussion or study of portion read.* Focus can be on any aspect of the literature being examined.
    a. vocabulary (talk about the words used, not just a list to study)
    b. theme (author's message, ideas behind the action)
    c. specific examples of imagery (similes, picturesque use of words)
    d. meaning of specific phrases or references (idioms, clichés)
    e. reaction to provocative statements
    f. discussion of action, characters, setting
3. *Extending experiences.* A variety of ideas should be suggested with each student completing several; some may be group activities.
    a. Composition
        Write a reaction to points made by the author.
        Write a story suggested by the content.
        Write poetry based on an idea presented.
    b. Language
        Discuss unusual uses of words.
        Observe description of sounds, colors, and so on.
        Study a specific sentence structure.
        Enact a portion of dialogue.
    c. Art
        Paint an imagined portrait of a character from the word picture.
        Draw a pictorial map of the setting of the story.
        Develop a mural depicting the action of the story.
        Paint one vivid scene from the action.
    d. Literature
        Read another book similar in content and compare the two.
        Read another title by the same author and compare.
        Find out about the author who wrote the story.
    e. Social studies
        Locate the setting of this story.
        At what period of history does it take place?
        Compare the life of the characters with your life—school, housing, family, clothing.

If students are reading individually, these experiences will usually be explored independently. Suggested activity sheets can be prepared so that the student can select several as he or she progresses with the book being read. Activities should be specific and should be directly related to the title read as in the sample plans of operation for three literature studies which are described subsequently.

We recommend the keeping of a reading log by each student in grades three through eight. The log is a highly individualized approach offering a challenge to the gifted student and permitting growth of the slower student. The term *log* is introduced through the explanation of its use by a ship's captain to record events during a trip. (This analogy can be extended.) Each student keeps a log in a small notebook in which he or she records:

1. Interesting new words
2. Colorful imagery
3. Written reactions to the story
4. Written answers to questions for extending learning
5. Special pages suggested—collections of synonyms, homonyms, other categories of words
6. Poetry and prose motivated by guided activities

These logs provide the teacher with a clear picture of what any student is doing (without routine book-report forms or test questions) and the progress the student is making. The logs can be used as the basis of individual conferences, or a few at a time can be read by the teacher.

Plan of operation: Grade 2 *And To Think That I Saw It on Mulberry Street* by Dr. Seuss (Vanguard, 1937)

This early work by Theodor Geisel tells the story of Marco, who usually diverts himself by imagining interesting things as he walks home from school. When he tells his father, however, his father does not appreciate the fanciful tales. The father's attitude forces Marco to face reality as he admits there was nothing but a "plain horse and wagon on Mulberry Street."

Extending learning activities This short book could be read aloud to the class if used at the beginning of the year. During the last half of the year, small groups of students could read the book together, after which it could be discussed along the lines suggested.

1. Why did Marco enjoy imagining things?
2. Which of his imaginary things did you like most?
3. Do you ever imagine things? What is your favorite imagining?
4. What did Marco's father think about imagining? Did he perhaps think Marco was lying?
5. Is imagining things the same as lying? How are they different?
6. What words do you remember from the story? Why do you remember those particular words?

Follow-up and culminating activities can be a combination of individual and group activities. Many times these activities will be suggested by the questions and interests of the children involved.

- Name all the different things Marco imagined, printing them on the board for word orientation and for experience in reading. Plan a parade down Mulberry Street to be painted cooperatively as a mural. Encourage use of the imagination; the illustrations of the book should not confine production.
- Write sentence stories about individual imaginings. Give help as needed so that each child has a story about something imagined. Crayon resist pictures of these imaginings can be produced (thin tempera wash over completed crayon picture). The picture is then shown as the story is read by each child.

- Write a group-composed letter to Marco to extend sympathy, to tell reasons for enjoying his ideas, and to share original ideas.
- Talk about color words used in the story. Have the class name other known color words. Add a few useful, but less common, examples to extend vocabularies—*scarlet, crimson, lime, olive.*

Plan of operation: Grade 4   *The Children of Green Knowe* by Lucy Boston (Harcourt, 1954)

This imaginative story of Tolly, a young boy who goes to live with his grandmother at Green Knowe, is set in Great Britain. It is rich in imagery and offers an opportunity to compare British English with American English. Although this book is not divided into chapters, it does fall easily into parts suitable for use as learning experiences. The following activities are based on the first section of the book (pp. 9–23).

1. Tolly thinks of the train as an ark floating on flood waters, and he imagines all the noises of the animals. What a noise there would be, with the lions roaring, elephants trumpeting, pigs squealing, donkeys braying, horses whinnying, bulls bellowing . . . How many additions can you make to Tolly's list? Try to think of ideas no one else will include.

    dogs *yapping*
    cats
    bears
    (Each example in this exercise uses the present participle form of a verb. Explore the varied forms of verbs as: *go, went, going, gone.*)

2. This story is set in Great Britain. Although Britishers speak the same language we do, we find that they have different ways of saying some things. On page 14, for instance, the cab driver asks Tolly whether he has any "gum boots." What are "gum boots?"
    Begin a list of examples like this one. Give an explanation in American English. Keep adding to the list:

    p. 14. gum boots   rubber boots
    p. 11. cheerio   goodby
    p. 12. windscreen   _____

3. How do you know that Tolly is used to being lonely? After reading this much of the book, what do you know about Tolly? Write a description of this boy.

4. Heavy rains are falling on the flooded countryside. On the first page of this book the author describes the rain as it appears to Tolly, "splashing against the windows and blotching downward in an ugly, dirty way." On another page she talks of the women getting off the train "into the hissing rain."
    What is your impression of rain? What does it sound like to you? Is it pleasant or unpleasant? How does it make you feel? Write your ideas about rain like this:
    RAIN is . . .
        the sprouter of bright umbrellas,
        a cozy, snugged-in feeling,

    a day for hiding games

    RAIN is . . . .
        the frizzies

Write as many ideas about rain as you wish. Your ideas will form a poem. Paint a picture of one of your ideas to go with your poem.

Plan of operation: Grade 7   *The Cat and Mrs. Cary* by Doris Gates (Viking, 1962)

The story of twelve-year-old Brad's adventures as he visits his aunt, Mrs. Cary, has a boy and a girl as leading characters. The chief character, however, is THE CAT, who condescends to live with Mrs. Cary and even to eat her food. An independent tomcat, he talks to Mrs. Cary although no one else ever hears his words. Mrs. Cary not only hears him, but replies aloud, much to the amazement of those listening. Activities for extending learning are based on Chapter 1 of this book.

1. On page 12 notice the description of THE CAT. Describe an animal which you have observed. Can you make this animal seem real? Does your animal have personality?
2. Why does THE CAT say, "When it comes to catching fish, you've never seen anything to match my equal"? (p. 15.) How would you have said the same thing? Why do you think he said it in this unusual way?
3. Read the description of the Major on page 17. Can you draw a picture of this gentleman from the word picture painted by Doris Gates? Do you like the Major? Why or why not?
4. Usually when a person speaks, we use the word "said" followed by the speaker's name to make the identity of the speaker clear to the reader as in this sentence:
    John said, "What are you doing?"
   Notice the use of dialogue on page 14. Has the author always used the word "said" to identify the speaker? In your log begin a page headed SYNONYMS FOR SAID. On this page list the words used by Doris Gates and add others that you can think of.
   What words might you substitute for "said" in these sentences? Can you suggest more than one each time?
     Susan *said,* "I need help."   *shouted*
     Mother *said,* "I have a secret."   *whispered*
     "Who will help?" *said* Paul.   *questioned*
     "Wait for me," I *said.*   *called*
     "You will see," Mr. Day *said.*   *promised*

Encouraging Reading Addiction

Most students who enroll in the first grade learn to read to a greater or lesser degree, yet it is surprising how many students in the sixth grade are not avid readers. It is obvious that children need more than the mere recognition of words to spark a sense of involvement with reading. They have to acquire a real feeling for books, the knowledge that books have something which they *need* and *want*.

It has been pointed out that the mechanical, drill-focused approach to reading may kill interest in reading at a time when enthusiasm for learning is high, and even more significant, that this readiness for learning will not be easily achieved again. Discussing this problem in reading, an expert in child psychoanalysis observes:

The long years spent by our children in mastery of the mechanics of reading rob them of pleasure and discoveries in literature, and also rob them of the possibility of *addiction,* which is one of the characteristics of the good reader. The addiction to reading is acquired at an early age—usually, I believe, under eight or nine.[6]

How do we ensure this addiction to reading? How do students acquire this sense of involvement with reading? How do we teachers motivate youngsters to read so widely that they will never lose the habit? There is no *one* answer, and there is no *right* answer; but there are many possibilities which are well worth exploring:

1. Use of exciting, quality literature in the reading program
2. Stress on stimulating coordinated reading and composition activities
3. Special attention to the reading interest of boys
4. Decrease in drill-type approaches to learning to read
5. Exposure to many, varied experiences with literature—storytelling, dramatization, discussions of books, choric speaking
6. Many opportunities to share the excitement of reading; new approaches to book reviewing
7. Teacher enthusiasm and knowledge of literature and ways of presenting literature in the classroom

Focusing attention on books *Open books for students* in varied ways, for few can resist the tempting illustrations, and the reading of a few intriguing words on a page is often enough to snag the interest of one who stops to look at a book propped open on the windowsill or a classroom table. Bookholders can be purchased or they can be made from two identical shapes cut from heavy cardboard taped together as illustrated.

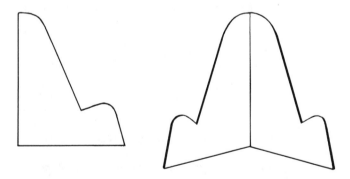

Another obvious way to open books is to *read aloud to a class.* After the last page of Mary Norton's *The Borrowers* (Harcourt) has just been completed, there will be many requests for that title and others by the same author. Showing the illustrations as the story is read is particularly important in the primary grades. The excellent illustrations by Maurice Sendak

[6]Selma Fraiberg, "The American Reading Problem," *Commentary* (June, 1965).

in Janice Udry's book, *Moon Jumpers* (Harper), for example, add much to the spell and deserve special attention.

Students can open books for each other by simply talking about a book that they have enjoyed and personally showing the book to the class or to an individual student. The Director of the Junior Book Awards for Boys' Clubs of America writes:

> There is nothing like a child for word-of-mouth advertising among his peers. The librarian may recommend a book and the youngster will read it to please her because he likes her, but if he does not like the book, wild horses can not get him to recommend it to a Clubmate. But just let one of the boys say, "you ought to read such-and-such"—and the line can form on the right for those eager to read it.[7]

Displays of books also serve to whet the reading appetites of students. A display of colorful book jackets on a bulletin board is always eye-catching. Captions can be used, for example, THE BOOK BAG (with books spilling from a real bag) or IT'S BOOK TIME (a clock face with jackets at the number spaces). Another display might consist of scattered book jackets under the caption HAVE YOU READ? As children read these books, each one adds a name tag to the cover of that book. Comparisons of total books read should definitely be avoided, with stress remaining on individual development and enjoyment of books read.

Provocative methods of presenting stories to other members of a class can be explored as the children themselves strive to "sell" others on reading a book they have enjoyed. The *preparation of a collage* about a favorite title is an excellent way of interesting others in reading the book. Imagine, for instance, what a fascinating collage could be prepared featuring *The Twenty-One Balloons* by William Pène du Bois (Viking), depicting the professor's misadventures on Krakatoa; the pictorial qualities of such a book are numerous.

Sharing books   The primary objective of reviewing or sharing books is not to "check on" student reading. Let's aim instead at multiple goals that really eliminate the need to check as we (1) stress the enjoyment of reading and sharing books, (2) encourage further reading of all kinds, and (3) stimulate critical thinking. If these goals are met, children will want to read because they find reading stimulating, entertaining, and informative. Our focus then is directly on the motivation of reading so that children will read, find it a pleasure, and wish to share their experiences with others. Sharing and book reviewing can more properly be regarded as means for motivation. In planning book review activities, we must bear these points in mind:

1.   Not all reading needs to be reviewed; students should be encouraged to read widely without the penalty of reviewing the quantity they read.
2.   Varied review techniques must be used to provide for stimulating experiences.

[7]Iris Vinton, "What Children Like to Read," *Junior Libraries,* January 1959, p. 5.

In what ways can we vary the sharing of books? Once we move away from the rigid concept of the book-report form, the possibilities for sharing books are numerous, provocative, and enriching. These approaches to book sharing can be oral or written. They can be related to other areas of the curriculum—history, geography, art, music, science, mathematics. They can take forms which branch out into more creative media. We can challenge our students to discover a different, more exciting way to share a book. Ideas will grow out of experimentation.

- The *diorama* is an excellent medium for depicting a scene from a story. Homer Price (cardboard or papier-mâché figure) could be shown with Aroma, his pet skunk, as they creep up on the robbers who are camping in the woods. The diorama also can be used to portray a scene from historical fiction or from the life of a figure in American history.
- A *mobile* can present a book by displaying the characters as well as objects or ideas essential to the story. *The 500 Hats of Bartholomew Cubbins* might, for instance, be interpreted through a mobile which features many unusual hats created in three dimensions.
- *Music* can be related to book sharing as a student or a small group of students composes a ballad about Charlotte, Wilbur, and their friends (*Charlotte's Web* by E. B. White). Older students might write a calypso or a folk song about the adventures of Huckleberry Finn or a real person about whom they have read.
- A *collage* is an intriguing method of combining art with literature. *Chitty-Chitty-Bang-Bang*, for example, might be depicted on a large poster which includes a cut-out drawing of this distinctive green car, the faces of Man-Mountain Fink, Joe, the Monster, and the twins. Portions of a map of England, the English Channel, and northern France might be worked into the background as would be other motifs taken from the story. Words can also be incorporated in the collage—*Paris, transmogrifications, Paragon Panther, Ian Fleming,* and so on.

Individualized Activities for the Learning Center

Book-centered activities are an essential part of an individualized approach to learning, which includes work in a language/reading learning center.

Using task cards Develop a set of task cards which focus on literature learning and which, of course, develop reading skills as well as those of listening, speaking, and writing. Here are some sample ideas for developing task cards. Children will be able to select the cards individually and complete as directed or with modifications made by themselves and the teacher.

TASK CARD 1

Do you know what a *bibliography* is? How can you find out?

Make a bibliography for our library about one topic that especially interests you. Your bibliography might help other students discover good books they will enjoy about this subject.

Choose topics like this—anything that interests you:

Horses	Dogs	Cats
Space travel	Mysteries	Science fiction
Living in Africa	Ocean life	Great American women

Your list can include fiction and nonfiction. If you like, you can work with another person who is interested in the same subject.

The following activities develop comprehension skills as children think about the books they have read.

TASK CARD 2

Who is your favorite author? Which books have you read by this writer? Do you know other books this author has written? Make a list of all the books written by your favorite writer.
Select two or three books by the author you have chosen. Compare them. How are they alike? How are they different? Think about:
the characters
the setting
the time in history
the length of the book
for whom is the book written
Prepare a BOOKTALK on tape about the author and the books you have reviewed. Others will enjoy listening to your comments.

TASK CARD 3

Think of a story that you like very much. Who is the most important person in the story? Is it a boy, a girl, an animal?
Imagine that you are the character in the story.
Can you tell the story as if you were that character?
Begin with the words: I am _____. I have a story to tell. Tell your story to the tape recorder. Play the story for some of your class friends.

TASK CARD 4

Choose a book that you would like to read. After you have finished reading the book, look again at the pictures.
Think about this story. What picture would you like to paint to show everyone what the story is about?
Paint a picture that shows everyone the most exciting thing that happened in the story. Show your picture to the class, and tell them about the story.

Many different kinds of task cards can be developed over a period of time to allow for developing skills. You might prepare cards on these topics featuring varied activities:

Dramatization of stories read by several students
Writing a letter to a favorite character
Advertising a book on a miniature billboard
Compiling a biography of a known author
Writing a nonfiction book about an interesting subject
Collecting poems on a specific topic
Writing another chapter to the book

Mind-mapping: A strategy that promotes comprehension   Sophie Gale, a California teacher, uses mind-mapping to help students think about a story they have read. As she comments: "Reading is an activity that uses all of the brain's capabilities. Thus, your students may read better if they use techniques that involve 'switch thinking,' using left and right hemispheres of the brain alternately." Following is her description of this technique:[8]

DEFINITION

Mind-mapping is an alternative way of taking notes or outlining. Students who use this method for recall, problem solving, or creating new material may get results with greater speed, more efficiency, and less stress. Traditional outlining primarily uses the linear, sequential thought of the left hemisphere, and that slows the process. In mind-mapping, you crisscross from left to right hemisphere to combine irregular patterns of thought with logical, analytical types of thinking.

BRANCHING

Give your students a large piece of blank paper and felt-tipped pens and ask them to write a topic in the center of the paper. To tell you all they know about this subject, have them quickly write key words associated with the subject.

As one thought generates another, branches are formed until a visual form of the thinking process emerges.

The mind-mapping technique seems to fit the kind of thinking that comes naturally to children. It is spontaneous and random, personal and creative. It is only after much effort that teachers succeed in teaching children to think logically in an orderly, sequential way as exemplified in traditional outlining.

READING

In a reading lesson of *Goldilocks and the Three Bears*, you might discuss other fanciful tales with the children, such as the names of stories in which animals are personified.

Before mind-mapping *Goldilocks,* you might:
present vocabulary
read for specific details
guide your students in discussing the illustrations
ask them to find sentences that describe Mother Bear
ask during what season of the year the story takes place
ask why they were going for a walk
ask how the bears felt upon their return to the house
ask how Goldilocks felt when she was discovered

You might also reinforce comprehension through workbook pages, duplicating masters, sentence completion worksheets, or creative art work. You might want your students to read the story aloud to enjoy the sound of the language and perhaps dramatize parts for proper inflection.

When it is time to ask your students to mind-map *Goldilocks and the Three Bears,* you will get distinct and original versions of the story that will quickly tell you what each child has absorbed. So, encourage your students to mind-map using key words.

[8]Sophie Gale, "Mind-mapping," *The Elementary Teacher's Ideas and Materials Workshop,* October 1980, pp. 15–16. Used with permission.

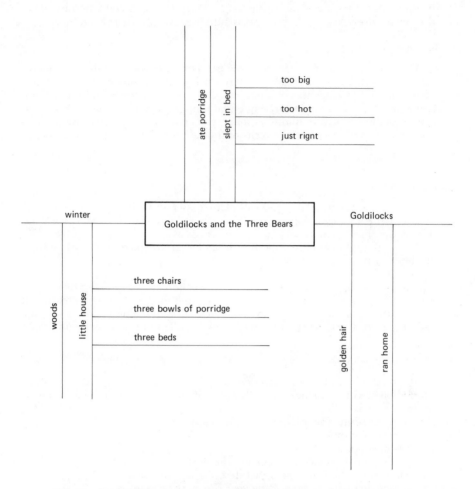

Your students will be more creative and attentive when mind-mapping is used in the classroom. They might also create new stories by replacing the time, place, characters, and events of a story with other key words.

SUMMARY

Literature is a rich resource for teaching in the elementary school. We do not always take full advantage of what is available to us as we plan the language arts program and work with language skills in other areas of the curriculum. Books can present new concepts and help students understand other people. As students read trade books, they are learning advanced reading skills. Developing a literature curriculum is one way to ensure the presence of literature in every elementary school classroom. In order to use literature effectively teachers need to know a variety of good books for children.

EXPLORING FURTHER

Applebee, Arthur N., *The Child's Concept of Story; Ages Two to Seventeen.* Chicago: University of Chicago Press, 1980.

Bingham, Jane and Grayce Scholt, *Fifteen Centuries of Children's Literature.* Westport, Conn.: Greenwood Press, Inc., 1980. An imaginative reference book that covers British and American works.

Cameron, Eleanor, *The Green and Burning Tree: On the Writing and Enjoyment of Children's Books.* Boston: Atlantic Monthly, 1969.

Cianciolo, Patricia, ed. and NCTE Committee on the Elementary School Booklist, *Adventuring with Books: A Booklist for Pre-K–Grade 8.* Urbana, Ill.: National Council of Teachers of English, 1977.

Cullinan, Bernice and M. Jerry Weiss, *Books I Read When I Was Young.* Commission on Literature. National Council of Teachers of English. New York: Avon Books, 1981.

Hopkins, Lee B., *Books Are by People* and *More Books by More People.* New York: Citation Press, 1969; 1973.

Huck, Charlotte S., *Children's Literature in the Elementary School.* New York: Holt, Rinehart and Winston, Inc., 1976.

Hunter, Mollie, *Talent Is Not Enough.* New York: Harper & Row Pubs. Inc., 1976.

International Reading Association/Children's Books Council Joint Committee, "Children's Choices for 1980," *Reading Teacher,* October 1980, reprint.

Johnson, Edna et al., *Anthology of Children's Literature* (5th ed.). Boston: Houghton Mifflin Co., 1977.

Lamme, Linda L., ed., *Literature: Making it the Foundation of Your Curriculum.* Urbana, Ill.: National Council of Teachers of English, 1981.

Somers, Albert B. and Janet E. Worthington, *Response Guides for Teaching Children's Books.* Urbana, Ill.: National Council of Teachers of English, 1979.

Sutherland, Zena et al., *Children & Books*. Glenview, Ill.: Scott, Foresman & Co., 1981.

Tiedt, Iris M., *Exploring Books With Children*. Boston: Houghton Mifflin Co., 1979.

Tiedt, Pamela L. and Iris M. Tiedt, *Multicultural Teaching*. Boston: Houghton Mifflin Co., 1979.

Townsend, John R., *A Sense of Story: Essays on Contemporary Writers for Children*. New York: J.B. Lippincott Co., 1972.

Tway, Eileen, ed., *Reading Ladders for Human Relations* (6th ed.). National Council of Teachers of English Committee on Reading Ladders for Human Relations. Washington, D.C.: American Council on Education, 1981.

White, Mary Lou, *Children's Books: The Best of the Past Decade*. Urbana, Ill.: National Council of Teachers of English, 1981.

13

Poetry is a mystery, but it is a mystery children can participate in and master. . . .

Kenneth Koch, *Wishes, Lies, and Dreams*

READING
AND WRITING POETRY
Discovering Magic and Reality

Poetry is special; it is mysterious and contains an aura of magic. Yet at the same time, poetry is real, speaking of ordinary people living together, engaged in the routines of life. When poetry enters the classroom, ordinary matters are touched with an elusive sparkle that adds excitement to learning, and children respond eagerly.

"Poetry belongs in the lives of children—all children," writes May Hill Arbuthnot in her introduction to *Time for Poetry*. She comments further:

> It is not so much the adult's job to put it there as it is to keep it there. For the newborn baby is a rhythmic being. His first cries of distress and his first gurgles of delight are cadenced. He responds to the melody and the meter of sung and spoken words long before he knows the literal meanings of those words. His early vocalizations are unworded chants that accompany his own increasingly rhythmic body movements and express the state of his being.[1]

[1]May Hill Arbuthnot, *Time for Poetry* (Glenview, Ill.: Scott, Foresman & Co., 1968), p. xv.

The purpose of this chapter is to introduce you to poetry for children and to suggest ways that you can bring poetry and children together in the classroom. The chapter is divided into two sections: The Teacher and Poetry and Bringing Children and Poetry Together. After reading the chapter and trying some of the suggested activities, you should be able to:

- present a number of concepts about poetry to children
- involve students of different ages in speaking, writing, and reading poetry
- integrate poetry into a strong language arts curriculum

THE TEACHER AND POETRY

If you enjoy poetry, you will find time for poetry in the classroom. Introduce poetry as a response to a sudden snowfall or in a science class on snakes, as a song children can sing or a rhythm they can chant, as a provocative commentary on living or a portrait of a great American.

Getting to Know Poetry

In order to familiarize yourself with the marvelous poetry available to you and to the young people whom you will teach, steep yourself in poetry for children. This is not a laborious chore, for you will find that children's poetry is not only charming and thoroughly enjoyable, but it also offers a pleasant variety ranging from nursery rhymes to poems by John Ciardi or T. S. Eliot.

Every teacher should have at least one good anthology of poetry for personal use so that it can be underlined and marked with marginal suggestions for using poems. Listed here are a number of collections:

Arbuthnot, May Hill, and Root, Shelton L., Jr. *Time for Poetry*. Glenview, Ill.: Scott, Foresman, 1968.

Austin, Mary C., and Mills, Queenie B. *The Sound of Poetry*. Boston: Allyn and Bacon, 1963.

Bissett, Donald J., ed. *Poems and Verses about Animals*. San Francisco: Chandler Publishing Co., 1967.

de Regniers, Beatrie Schenk; Moore, Eva; and White, Mary Michaels. *Poems Children Will Sit Still For*. New York: Citation Press, 1969.

Dunning, Stephen; Lueders, Edward; and Smith, Hugh, eds. *Reflections on a Gift of Watermelon Pickle*. Glenview, Ill.: Scott, Foresman, 1966.

Larrick, Nancy, ed. *On City Streets*. New York: Bantam, 1968.

Silverstein, Shel. *Where the Sidewalk Ends*. New York: Harper, 1974.

Withers, Carl. *A Rocket in My Pocket*. New York: Holt, Rinehart, and Winston, 1948.

Defining Poetry

Defining what poetry is proves difficult. Eleanor Farjeon sums up the elusive nature of poetry, thus:

> What is poetry? Who knows?
> Not the rose, but the scent of the rose;
> Not the sky, but the light of the sky;
> Not the fly, but the gleam of the fly;
> Not the sea, but the sound of the sea;
> Not myself, but something that makes me
> See, hear and feel something that prose
> Cannot; what is it? Who knows?[2]

Eleanor Farjeon

After reading a number of poems with students, you might discuss what makes a poem a poem. Examine these ideas as you guide students in making generalizations about poetry:

THE LANGUAGE OF POETRY—

More rhythmical than prose; related to music
  May rhyme, which adds to lyrical quality
Includes many images
  Fresh, original comparisons
Concentrated; fewer words

THE FORM OF POETRY—

Relatively short compared with prose
Follows certain conventions
  May capitalize first word in each line
  May indent alternate lines
  Has stanzas
Includes a number of distinctive forms

---

[2]"Poetry," from Eleanor Farjeon's *Poems for Children* (Lippincott). Copyright 1938 by Eleanor Farjeon; renewed 1966 by Gervase Farjeon. By permission of Harper & Row, Publishers, Inc.

THE CONTENT OF POETRY—

Expresses personal feelings and impressions
Views life from different perspectives
May deal with any topic

Many people consider poetry the highest form of literature in any language. It is, indeed, special. We do not, however, want to give young people the idea that poetry is beyond them, something that they cannot understand. "Instead of building a fence of formality around poetry," states Karla Kushkin, winner of the 1979 NCTE Award for Poetry for Children, "I want to emphasize its accessibility, the sound, rhythm, humor, the inherent simplicity. Poetry can be as natural and effective a form of self-expression as singing or shouting."

Concepts About Poetry

As we share poetry with students in the classroom, we can promote these understandings. We can talk with children of all ages about the following concepts related to poetry:

1. Poets are people who write to communicate their ideas to others.
2. Poets play with language in a manner not unlike a musician who plays an instrument. They strive for effects and use language with precision.
3. Good poetry contains original images and new, creative ways of looking at life.

Poets are people   You can further this understanding with students by talking about the people who write poetry for them. Show them pictures of poets and see that they know the names of these writers. Other sources of pictures of poets include *Language Arts,* the elementary journal published by the National Council of Teachers of English, book jackets on books of poetry, and other publicity material prepared by publishing houses. As you become acquainted with poets who write for young people, look for some of these names:

Dorothy Aldis	Aileen Fisher
Mary Austin	Lee Bennett Hopkins
Rhoda Bacmeister	Karla Kushkin
Dorothy Baruch	Myra Cohn Livingstone
Harry Behn	David McCord
Rowena Bennett	Eve Merriam
Elizabeth Coatsworth	Mary O'Neill
Hilda Conkling	Laura E. Richards
Eleanor Farjeon	James S. Tippett
Rachel Field	Shel Silverstein

In addition, children enjoy poetry that has been written for adults by such poets as Robert Frost, Gwendolyn Brooks, Carl Sandburg, Emily Dickinson, and Ogden Nash.

Poetry is written by widely differing poets and it is read by widely differing readers. It is inevitable, therefore, that all readers will not care for all poetry. What appeals to ten-year-old Liz, whose mind is usually traveling far from the classroom, may ring a discordant note for the teacher, whose interests are obviously not the same.

Each person brings a different background of age, sex, knowledge, and experience to the same poem. It is important that we present poetry that appeals to varied segments of the class and to consciously refrain from inflicting our own preferences on students. It is natural to share a favorite poem with the class, for teacher enthusiasm and participation adds to that of the students, but a variety of poetry is more likely to capture the interest of all.

Divergent interpretations of a single poem should also be stressed as each student is encouraged to form individual opinions of a selection, to react to it freely. We must refrain from tagging a poem as *good* or another one as *bad* so that students learn to determine for themselves whether a poem has something to offer them.

Poetry is the music of language   Its meters are related to the measures of the musical score, and many terms are common to both music and poetry; for example, *composing*. We also stress the rhythm and the music of the words as we arrange them to achieve effects similar to those of music—figures of speech, repetition, themes, patterns, rhythm. What other words are common to both poetry and music?

Onomatopoeia, a Greek word that has a certain enchantment of its own, adds to the music of poetry. "Imitative words" add to the effect of writing in both poetry and prose. Vowels and consonants produced toward the back of the mouth may combine to produce a sound effect that is broad, low-pitched, and rough as in these words: *rumble, growl, gong, howl, croak, chug, snarl.* By contrast, vowels and consonants produced toward the front of the oral cavity are often higher in pitch, giving sharper onomatopoetic effects as in: *ouch, hiss, click, bounce, whistle, jingle, rasp.* The short *u* sound combines with *l* and *m* to form soft words; for example, *lull* and *hum.*

* Prepare a bulletin board display featuring onomatopoetic or "echoic" words. Using the caption ECHOES, display examples contributed by class members.

tinkle	creak	splash
blare	bark	purr
whoosh	buzz	murmur
whisper	snore	patter
mutter	whine	shriek

* Invent new words which imitate sounds. Provide a definition for each invented word, thus:
    CLONK: the sound of a hammer on wood
    SWIZZLE: the sound of water spurting from a sprinkler
  What would you call the sound made when your soda is almost gone?
* Find examples of onomatopoeia used in poetry as in these examples:

> "The slippery slush
> As it slooshes and sloshes,
> And splishes and sploshes . . ."
>   "Galoshes" by Rhoda W. Bacmeister[3]

> . . . "He bumps
> And he jumps
> And he thumps
> And he stumps . . ."
>   "The Goblin" by Rose Fyleman[4]

Alliteration is another poetic device which adds to the melodious effects of poetry. "The repetition of the initial sound of a word in one or more closely following words" is a provocative technique if it is not overworked. Remember that alliteration is based on *sound,* not just on the repeated use of a letter—*sticks and stones, phonics fun, chic shape* (don't slip on the French *ch*).

* Experiment with writing descriptive alliterative phrases as in these examples:
    Slippery, slithery sleuth
    Proud princess Prudence
    Gloomy glowering glance
    Shining, shimmering shells
* Set out on an exploring trip to discover uses of alliteration in poetry. This type of exploratory browsing will introduce you to much poetry as you search for examples like these:

    "ribbon roads"—"The Rock" by T. S. Eliot
    "camel caravan" "mosque and minaret"—"Travel" by Robert Louis Stevenson
    "Slowly, silently, now the moon
    Walks the night in her silver shoon."—"Silver" by Walter de la Mare
    "Sing a song of seasons!"—"Autumn Fires" by Robert Louis Stevenson

Poets have long been considered "makers of music" with language as their medium. Wrote A. W. E. O'Shaughnessy:
> "We are the music-makers,
> And we are the dreamers of dreams . . ."

* Print the above lines on a large piece of construction paper for use with a display of children's poetry. The words MUSIC MAKERS or DREAMERS OF DREAMS are excellent captions for displays or titles for collections of student writing.
* Listen to the recording of Dylan Thomas reading his beautiful poetic prose "A Child's Christmas in Wales" (Caedmon TC 1002). You might also view the film of the same title produced by Marvin Lichtner.

Poets create images   The poet uses language to make unusual comparisons, to express original ways of looking at the world, new images. Imagery may take the form of similes, metaphors, and personification in poems that

---

[3]In May Hill Arbuthnot and Zena Sutherland, *The Arbuthnot Anthology of Children's Literature,* 3rd ed. (Glenview, Ill.: Scott, Foresman & Co., 1972), p. 167.
[4]Ibid., p. 125.

children can understand. You might introduce figurative language by asking students to complete this familiar simile: as quiet as a _____. Almost every student will recognize the expression that has become trite from overusage: "as quiet as a mouse." Write several fresh comparisons like these:

> As quiet as . . .
> a tiny minnow darting beneath a rock,
> five flies talking on the wall,
> two snails taking a morning walk.

Notice the pattern established by the first line, a noun followed by an action expressed in a participial phrase. Follow this same pattern as you write several ideas.

To become aware of the imagery used in poetry explore the following activities:

- As you read poetry, collect examples of imagery, words that paint pictures, thus:

    My Daddy smells like tobacco and books,
    Mother, like lavender and listerine . . ."—"Smells (Junior)" by Christopher Morley
    ". . . He is a conscious black and white
    Little symphony of night."—"The Skunk" by Robert P. Tristram Coffin
    ". . . the big, big wheels of thunder roll . . ."—"The Woodpecker" by Elizabeth Madox Roberts

- Read Emily Dickinson's poem, "I Like to See It Lap the Miles," as an example of excellent imagery and the use of intriguing words:

> I like to see it lap the miles,
> And lick the valleys up,
> And stop to feed itself at tanks;
> And then, prodigious, step
>
> Around a pile of mountains,
> And, supercilious, peer
> In shanties by the sides of roads;
> And then a quarry pare
>
> To fit its sides, and crawl between,
> Complaining all the while
> In horrid, hooting stanza;
> Then chase itself down hill
>
> And neigh like Boanerges;
> Then, punctual as a star,
> Stop—docile and omnipotent—
> At its own stable door.

After reading this poem, plan questions to stimulate the students' thinking; for example:

What is Emily Dickinson describing in this poem?
How do you know she is writing about a train?

Look at the provocative words: *supercilious, prodigious, omnipotent.* Try guessing their meanings from the context of the poem before checking with the dictionary.
Introduced here, too, is a reference to mythology, which is not often found in children's poetry. Investigate Boanerges, the Sons of Thunder.

* Compare Emily Dickinson's poem about a train with poems about trains by other poets who have compared the train differently. Rowena Bennett, for example, wrote: "A train is a dragon that roars through the dark . . ." in "A Modern Dragon." Frances Frost gives the trains human characteristics as she describes trains that ". . . whistle softly and stop to tuck each sleepy blinking town in bed!" in "Trains at Night."

Variety in Form and Subject

Variety of form is closely related to variety of subject, and we should endeavor to expose children to many different poetic forms so that their view of poetry is in no way limited. Forms of poetry will be discussed in more detail as we progress to the writing of original poems, but here are suggestions for exploring the concept that forms of poetry vary widely:

* Read poems that represent varied forms—long, short, rhymed, unrhymed—as in these examples:[5]
"Automobile Mechanics" by Dorothy Baruch
   Unrhymed free verse
"Newspaper" by Aileen Fisher
   Couplets
"How Doth the Little Crocodile" by Lewis Carroll
   Quatrains (*abab* rhyming)
* Begin a collection of poems that you especially like. You will soon have a sizable teaching anthology to use in the classroom. Try to include varied forms, for example, concrete poems like the example on page 335 or this poem that is written in a form suggested by the content.

Introducing a Poem to Children

The way you introduce poetry to students of any age requires a sense of timing and appropriateness. You need to set the stage, to create a receptive mood so that students will respond positively. How is this mood created by the teacher? It can be developed subtly by first introducing a familiar incident related to the poem or presenting an object or picture which will then suggest the poem. Sometimes we begin by writing several provocative words on the board which will lead us into the poem, or we may ask questions to stimulate a discussion.

---

[5]The poems listed here appear in Mary C. Austin and Queenie B. Mills, *The Sound of Poetry* (Boston: Allyn & Bacon, Inc., 1963).

PICTURES ON THE FLYING AIR[6]
Scott Alexander

A
poem
can play
with the wind
and dart and dance
and fly about in the mind
like a kite in the cloudy white
sky at so dizzy a height it
seems out of reach but
is waiting to be
very gently
pulled
down
to
the
page
below
by a
string
of
musical
words.

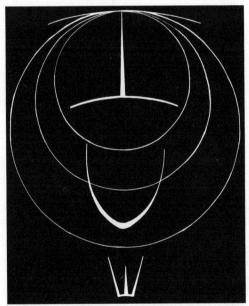

"Echo" by Richard Kostelanetz, from *Visual Language* (Brooklyn: Assembling Press, 1970). Reprinted by permission of the author.

"Now I am going to read a poem about colors," states the teacher, and the children immediately squirm. You will be more certain of a positive reaction to the poem if you provide a brief "warm-up" session. To present Christina Rosetti's lovely poem, "What Is Pink?" you might effectively begin with a discussion about colors which would arouse interest thus:

"What color is Jill's dress?" (pink)
"And what color is this flower?" (pink)
"What other things come to mind when you think of pink?
   What is pink?"
(powder, ice cream, a kitten's tongue, chilly cheeks)

From this point the discussion could easily move to several other colors and the objects they recall. Participation in the discussion has started minds working and the reading of the poem is a natural consequence.

WHAT IS PINK?
Christina Rosetti

What is pink? a rose is pink
By a fountain's brink.
What is red? a poppy's red
In its barley bed.
What is blue? the sky is blue
Where the clouds float thro'.
What is white? a swan is white
Sailing in the light.
What is yellow? Pears are yellow
Rich and ripe and mellow.
What is green? the grass is green
With small flowers between.
What is violet? clouds are violet
In the summer twilight.
What is orange? Why, an orange,
Just an orange!

Color in Poetry
Hailstones and Halibut Bones. Sterling Educational Films (241 East 34th St., New York, N.Y. 10016). Part I, 1964, 6 min., color. Part II, 1967, 7 min., color.
Both parts are excellent short films that combine artful design and color with the reading of the poems from the book by Mary O'Neill and published by Doubleday. Hailstones and halibut bones are things that are white.

A natural setting for poetry is often provided by the weather. Children who have just come in with snow still on their mittens and in their minds will be quite ready to tell the teacher excitedly of their feelings about snow. "What words can you use to describe snow?" queries the teacher. Soft, white, fluffy, cold, light, sparkling. "Let me read you a poem that talks about snow; we'll see how this poet describes snow."

Rain, wind, and sunshine can each provide an effective mood for poetry. A holiday, the season, the blooming of flowers suggest poems on varied topics. Subjects studied in the classroom will provide opportunity to relate appropriate poetry. The teacher who knows poetry, who has "the right poem at the right time," will be able to take advantage of these times for poetry and will be able to plan the right setting for an exciting experience with poetry.

Attitudes Toward Poetry

How do you feel about poetry? Do you conceive of poetry as language which is somewhat frilly, frothy, and feminine? Do you think every student ought to memorize poetry? Would you assign the memorization of a poem as a type of punishment? Do you feel that you know which poetry is "good" or "bad"? The attitudes of both teacher and student are based on past experiences with poetry. They may represent the attitudes expressed by parents and peers.

The attitude, for example, that *poetry is feminine* has led to the feeling, particularly among boys, that poetry is not something which should rightfully interest a man. Is poetry "sissy stuff"? It is if you present only poems about the blue sky, lovely flowers, pretty girls, and love. To snag the boys' interest we must clearly demonstrate that poetry is for boys; poetry is for all people.

- Note that many poets have been men. Conduct a small research study by having several boys examine six to ten anthologies of poetry, first counting the number of poets listed in the index. Then they can count the number of these names which are masculine to determine the percentage of male poets. Conducting this study themselves will impress some students who would scarcely believe your own statement of the same fact.
- Read a variety of poetry written by men: Carl Sandburg, Robert Frost, Walt Whitman, Walter de la Mare, John Masefield, James Whitcomb Riley, James Tippett, Robert Louis Stevenson, Lewis Carroll, Edward Lear, to mention only a few of the many.
- Collect pictures of men and women who write poetry. Record albums, magazine covers, articles will provide pictures which can be mounted on a bulletin board with samples of poetry as well as quotations from these men and women.
  Robert Frost: "Poetry is my kind of fooling."
  Paul Laurence Dunbar: "What's so fine as being a boy?"

The *memorization of poetry* as an end in itself has long been discarded as a method of enjoying poetry and certainly as a means of punishment. Many students voluntarily choose to memorize a poem which has particular meaning for them. Poetry is also memorized incidentally through repetition as it is recited in chorus or read frequently by individuals as a result of its appeal. Often, too, students will learn first lines or lines which are repeated in poems although the whole poem has not been memorized. Examples of lines which many children come to know include:

"Some one came knocking
At my wee, small door . . ."—Walter de la Mare: "Some One"

"The Owl and the Pussy-Cat went to sea
In a beautiful pea-green boat . . ."—Edward Lear: "The Owl and the Pussy-Cat"
"I'm hiding, I'm hiding,
And no one knows where . . ."—Dorothy Aldis: "Hiding"

The *analysis and evaluation of poetry* should not be heavily stressed with the child, for our stress is on the enjoyment of poetry. There is little doubt that the poem loses something as it is pulled apart line by line. This is not to say, on the other hand, that students should not discuss the meaning of unusual words used by the poet or that effective imagery should not be pointed out as an object of admiration. Certainly, if the class shows particular interest in the subject treated by the poem, discussion will logically develop, but we then return to the poet's "performance" as a whole.

Poetry is an experience, not a form.

Karl Shapiro

Research on Poetry Instruction

Although research of poetry instruction has not been extensive, one major study stands out. Published under the title, *Children's Poetry Preferences,* Ann Terry's study appeared in 1974.[7] This national survey reveals that poetry is neglected by most teachers and that children's enthusiasm for poetry declines as they progress through the elementary grades.

In addition, the report indicates the kinds of poetry children like. They tend to prefer humorous poetry that is narrative in style and poems that are about contemporary subjects. Of the poems children heard, the ones they liked best were:

Mummy Slept Late and Daddy Fixed Breakfast, John Ciardi
Fire! Fire! Anonymous
There Was an Old Man of Blackheath, Anonymous
Little Miss Muffett, Paul Dehn
There Once Was an Old Kangaroo, Anonymous
Hughbert and the Glue, Karla Kuskin
Betty Barter, Anonymous
Lone Dog, Irene Rutherford McLeod
Eletelephony, Laura E. Richards
Questions, Marci Ridlon

The poems they liked least were free verse and haiku. They also found imagery difficult to handle. The poems that were not well liked included:

The Red Wheelbarrow, William Carlos Williams
Haiku: "A bitter morning . . ." J. W. Hackett

[7]Ann Terry, *Children's Poetry Preferences* (Urbana, Ill.: National Council of Teachers of English Research Report, 1974).

April Rain Song, Langston Hughes
The Forecast, Dan Jaffe
Dreams, Langston Hughes
Shadows, Patricia Hubbell
The Base Stealer, Robert Francis
Haiku: "A cooling breeze . . ." Onitsura
Haiku: "What happiness . . ." Buson
December, Sanderson Vanderbilt

What does this study tell us? Clearly, we need to see that poetry is presented to children and that it is presented by a knowledgeable teacher who demonstrates enthusiasm for the poems so that children will enjoy them. In this study, for example, children heard a total of 113 poems over a period of ten days. They listened to ten to twelve poems that were taped by one reader. This method, while beneficial for research reliability, is hardly likely to bring eager responses from children. The remainder of this chapter presents instructional strategies for bringing children and poetry together.

BRINGING CHILDREN AND POETRY TOGETHER

In this section we will explore a variety of strategies for engaging students with poetry. The most direct successful method is through oral activities that involve students in responding to poetry that is read aloud by the teacher, repeating lines of their own favorites, or formally sharing poems through ensemble speaking, a voice choir.

We develop an extensive array of possibilities for guiding students in composing original poetry beginning with imaginative words and phrases, then moving to free verse, and pleasantly structured pattern poems. The writing of poetry opens doors to the reading of poetry written by others.

In this section we are stressing development of the following concepts about poetry and literature in general:

1. Children can write poetry.
2. Poetry is a way of playing with language, manipulating it to create certain effects.
3. We can respond to poetry much as we do to music—moving in time with the words, singing a poem, dramatizing the mood.
4. Not everyone likes the same poems; taste is a personal matter.
5. There are many kinds of poems. Poets write poems for varied purposes.

Presenting Poetry Orally

Begin by reading poetry aloud. Choose humorous poems or ones that have a strong rhythm to which children can respond. Select poems that have proved popular with children for many years, for example:

Sea Fever	John Masefield
Eletelephony	Laura E. Richards
Daffodils	William Wordsworth
Antonio	Laura E. Richards
My Shadow	Robert Louis Stevenson
I Think Mice Are Nice	Rose Fyleman
The Road Not Taken	Robert Frost
Child on Top of a Greenhouse	Theodore Roethke
The Elf and the Dormouse	Oliver Herford
The Clown	Dorothy Aldis
Whisky Frisky	Anonymous
There Once Was a Puffin	Florence P. Jaques
The Woodpecker	Elizabeth M. Roberts
Trains	James S. Tippett
Who Has Seen the Wind?	Christina Rossetti
Sneezles	A. A. Milne

Share poems that children know from Mother Goose. Many will inspire children to clap in time with the rhythm or to march around the room. Invite children to act out "Jack and Jill" or "Little Miss Muffet" as the rest of the class says the poem slowly and dramatically. Children of all ages should know these nursery rhymes that are part of our literary heritage.

Reading poetry together As students become familiar with poetry, encourage them to share their favorites by reading them aloud or saying ones they have memorized voluntarily. Discuss the effective reading of poetry, pointing out that sentences appear in poetry just as they do in prose. Show children how to observe the signals that punctuation provides so that the meaning of the poem is clear. Try these listening and speaking activities that will bring children and poetry together.

- A class can read poems orally together after hearing the teacher read. Stress the reading of sentences rather than lines to avoid a sing-song effect which is often associated with poetry. Try these with middle graders:

Theme in Yellow	Carl Sandburg
A Story in the Snow	Pearl R. Crouch
Brooms	Dorothy Aldis

- Children can record their reading of poetry. Each child reads one poem, either original or by known poets, which may be grouped on one theme—the season, a holiday, favorite things, vehicles, traveling. Music can be played softly to produce a pleasant background for the recording.

The voice choir The reading or speaking of poetry has much the same attributes as the singing of songs in a group. The values of the Voice Choir include:

1. Participation by even shy children
2. Sharing of enjoyable language experience
3. Group empathy developed

4. Improvement of pronunciation
5. Vocabulary development
6. Enjoyment and appreciation of poetry.

The Voice Choir does not have to be an extremely complicated matter. Almost any poem offers potential for group enjoyment. Students will be interested in experimenting with different effects with spoken poetry. Encourage suggestions of possible effects to be achieved through varied grouping of voices, different ways of interpreting lines, or even the use of sound effects when appropriate. Poetry interpretations can be varied through these techniques:

1. Use of one solo voice for a few lines
2. Division of the class into two or four groups that alternate lines or stanzas
3. Boy and girl groups or light and dark voices speak lines to vary tonal quality
4. Varied speed of lines
5. Experiment with varying pitch for unusual effect

Treat the group as a chorus, using some of the same techniques which you might use in singing. Some poems can be read in unison, but others lend themselves to part work—many verses, repetitive lines or refrains, conversation, contrasted stanzas. Students have fun saying poetry together just as they do singing songs together; they soon build up an excellent repertoire.

• A poem which is effective with older elementary school students is Lewis Carroll's "Father William," which consists of a conversation between a father and his son. The girls with higher voices can speak the young man's part with sprightly rhythm while lower voices portray the part of Father William, speaking slowly and impressively until the final verse.

FATHER WILLIAM
Lewis Carroll

"You are old, Father William," the young man said,
  "And your hair has become very white;
And yet you incessantly stand on your head—
  Do you think, at your age, it is right?"

"In my youth," Father William replied to his son,
  "I feared it might injure the brain;
But, now that I'm perfectly sure I have none,
  Why, I do it again and again."

"You are old," said the youth, "as I mentioned before,
  And have grown most uncommonly fat;
Yet you turn a back-somersault in at the door—
  Pray, what is the reason of that?"

"In my youth," said the sage, as he shook his gray locks,
  "I kept all my limbs very supple
By the use of this ointment—one shilling a box—
  Allow me to sell you a couple?"

"You are old," said the youth, "and your jaws are too weak
  For anything tougher than suet;
Yet you finished the goose, with the bones and the beak—
  Pray, how did you manage to do it?"

"In my youth," said the father, "I took to the law,
  And argued each case with my wife;
And the muscular strength which it gave to my jaw
  Has lasted the rest of my life."

"You are old," said the youth, "one would hardly suppose
  That your eye was as steady as ever;
Yet you balanced an eel on the end of your nose—
  What made you so awfully clever?"

"I have answered three questions, and that is enough,"
  Said his father. "Don't give yourself airs!
Do you think I can listen all day to such stuff?
  Be off, or I'll kick you down-stairs!"

- Even the youngest of children enjoy repeating the lines of poetry if the poem has rhythm, repetition, and some humor. Other poems which are especially suitable for speaking in a group are:
  Puppy and I: A. A. Milne (Conversation)
  Poor Old Woman: Anonymous (Refrain and Repetition)
  The Mysterious Cat: Vachel Lindsay (Repetition)
- Introduce students to the wild, wonderful verses of Shel Silverstein collected under the title: *Where the Sidewalk Ends* (Harper, 1974). He writes and illustrates fantastic, humorous poems on all kinds of subjects as you can see in this sampling:

THE CROCODILE'S TOOTHACHE

The Crocodile
Went to the dentist
And sat down in the chair,
And the dentist said, "Now tell me, sir,
Why does it hurt and where?" . . .

THE LONG-HAIRED BOY

There was a boy in our town with long hair—
I mean really long hair—
And everybody pointed at him
And laughed at him
And made fun of him.
And when he walked down the street
The people would roar
And stick their tongues out
And make funny faces
And run in and slam their door
And shout at him from the window
Until he couldn't stand it anymore. . . .

Other poems in this volume include:

"Magical Eraser"
"Recipe for a Hippopotamus Sandwich"
"With His Mouth Full of Food"
"Spaghetti"
"Sleeping Sardines"

Writing Original Poems

"Writing poetry makes children feel happy, capable, and creative. It makes them feel more open to understanding and appreciating what others have written (literature)," says Kenneth Koch in *Wishes, Lies, and Dreams.*

Prewriting activities   Read some of the poems that children have written, perhaps taken from your school publications or the local newspaper. A number of published collections of poetry written by young people are available, too. Suggest purchasing copies of these books for your school library:

Baron, Virginia O., *Here I Am!* New York: E. P. Dutton & Co., Inc., 1969.
Jordan, June and Torri Bush, comps., *The Voices of the Children.* New York: Holt, Rinehart & Winston, Inc., 1970.
Koch, Kenneth. *Rose, Where Did You Get That Red?* New York: Random House, Inc., 1979.
Kohl, Herbert and Victor H. Cruz, eds. *Stuff.* New York: World, 1970.
Lewis, Richard, ed., *Miracles.* New York: Simon and Schuster, Inc., 1966.
Merriam, Eve and Nancy Larrick, *Male and Female under 18.* New York: Avon Books, 1973.
Pellowski et al., eds., *Have You Seen a Comet? Children's Art and Writing from Around the World.* New York: John Day, 1971.

As young people come to know poetry and to see the variety of form and content that is possible, they will also perceive poetry as something they can do. As they discover poetry that appeals to them, young persons will feel at home with poetry and will be able to conceive of themselves as poets. The development of this image is the key to stimulating student-composed poetry.

Be ready to take advantage of natural opportunities that arise. When a child expresses a thought or an apt bit of imagery, say, "I like the way you said that, Phil. Let's write it on the board so everybody can enjoy it." Some teachers keep strips of manila paper on which phrases or sentences can be lettered quickly with a felt pen so that the children's words can be recorded for display on a bulletin board. Displayed with the caption POETRY PLEASES in one first grade room were these examples:

quiet as a flea at work—Sally
soft, secret sound—Phil

Our earth is round,
All water and ground—Stan
walking and talking—Margie
The bear clumped and humped,
thumped and bumped—Bob

Poetry is a word, two words, and more. The teacher must be aware of the possibilities for poetry as it occurs in natural form. When Dave brings his frog to school, for example, and calls it "my funny, funny frog," the mere repetition of Dave's phrase leads children to add other lines to produce a spontaneous class composition. " 'My funny, funny frog'—that sounds like a poem. Who can add another line?" As the first words are written on the board, someone suggests, "Hippety, hippety, hop," and another child cries excitedly, "Will he ever stop?" and there is a poem!

My funny, funny frog.
Hippety, hippety, hop.
Will he ever stop?

Beginning experiences with free verse   You cannot, of course, wait patiently for the unplanned experience in writing poetry to come. We must plan experiences which seem as natural and desirable as those which are initiated in the manner just described, but we must provide the stimulus. A sequence of experiences in the writing of poetry can be readily developed, beginning with the least complicated types of poetry for primary grades and progressing in difficulty. The emphasis in the *writing* of poetry remains on enjoyment, as was true in the *reading* of poetry. The elementary school child who is steeped in poetry will find writing original verse a natural means for expressing thoughts.

Many teachers find free verse highly successful with children who have had little experience with the writing of poetry. Beginning poets may write only one line, whereas the more able or experienced child will soon write two, three, and more lines. Why is free verse especially suited to inexperienced writers? The key word is *freedom,* for in free verse there is:

1. No rhyming to lend artificiality
2. No set pattern of rhythm or meter
3. Free variation in length of lines, form, and content
4. Emphasis on the thought expressed

The fact, too, that free verse may consist of one or many lines provides a built-in accommodation for individual abilities. The child for whom writing is laborious finds success in composing one line whereas the child for whom writing comes with greater ease may extend ideas into ten lines. For this reason the following suggestions for motivating the writing of free verse may be used at any level of ability.

• Display a large picture of a boy and girl. Ask some provocative questions: "What are these children doing? What are they thinking? Can you imagine that you are the boy or girl in the picture?" Pretending that he or she is one of the figures in the picture, each student writes the thoughts that come to mind. Again, suggest that each thought begin on a new line, thus:

> I wish I could get a new bike.
> Then I'd go like the wind—
> Down Madison Street,
> Across the Highway—
> No place would be too far for me
> If I had a bright shiny new bike.

- Use the senses to motivate the writing of poetry by providing an object that is concealed within a box or a large paper bag. To feature the concept of SOFT-NESS, for example, use a piece of soft fur or velvet. After students have felt the concealed article, ask them how it felt. When someone mentions the adjective *soft,* ask the question, "What is soft? How would you tell someone what you mean by softness?" Have each one write ideas on paper as they try to think not of how many thoughts they can write, but of *how interesting or unusual* each thought is.

WHAT IS SOFT?

> Softness is a feeling.
> Softness is velvety fur.
> Softness is a small kitten's paw.
> Softness is my mother's cheek.

- Read poems to children by poets who do not use rhyme: Hilda Conkling, Carl Sandburg, e. e. cummings, and Walt Whitman. This passage from Whitman's *Song of Myself* describes a handsome stallion which could inspire students to write poems about an animal they know.

> A gigantic beauty of a stallion, fresh and responsive to my caresses,
> Head high in the forehead, wide between the ears,
> Limbs glossy and supple, tail dusting the ground,
> Eyes full of sparkling wickedness, ears finely cut, flexibly moving.
> His nostrils dilate as my heels embrace him,
> His well-built limbs tremble with pleasure as we race around and return.

- Write these words on the board: "Rain is . . ." (Use this idea on a rainy day for best results. As appropriate, try "Snow is . . ." or "Sunshine is . . .") Then ask the class what rain means to them. Have them write their ideas on paper beginning each new idea on a fresh line (the poetry form). When completed, each child will have a poem of varied length about rain.

Type each poem on a large raindrop shape for display encouraging children to read the differing ideas about rain. Or, write a collective poem, thus:

> Rain is . . . patter on the roof,
>   . . . a day for hiding behind furniture,
>   . . . the flower maker.
> Rain is . . . the producer of unbrellas,
>   . . . the washer of leaves,
>   . . . the frizzies.

If it doesn't happen to be raining, you can show the film *Rainshowers* (distributed by Dimensions Films) which expresses many thoughts about rain.

Here are poems children wrote, beginning with "The moon is . . ."

> The moon is a white rabbit
> Jumping up and down.
> While we are asleep,
> It jumps up;
> And when we wake,
> It jumps down.
>
> > Robert Rogers

> The moon is a sun drowsing,
> but never going to sleep
> The stars are faces in the sky.
> Time is how long it takes you
> to do your homework.
>
> > Phyllis Dyer
> > Teacher: Mrs. Norville

Exploring poetry patterns   From free verse it is natural to introduce unrhymed poetry patterns. Children of all ages can produce enchanting cinquains. Other patterns will challenge more mature students.

Cinquain   Cinquains are poems of five lines. Although there are many varieties possible for five-line poetry (the limerick is one), the cinquain is a form more akin to haiku. The stress should still remain on the thought to be expressed, but the unrhymed lines of the cinquain fit these specifications, according to one version.

Line 1:   One word (which may be the title)
Line 2:   Two words (describing the title)
Line 3:   Three words (an action)
Line 4:   Four words (a feeling)
Line 5:   One word (referring to the title)

Here are examples written by college students who, like you, were venturing into poetry:

> *RAINBOW—*
>
> Sky's unbrella
> Turned upside down
> Lovely splash of color
> Aftermath.
>
> > Kaye Hawley

> *SUN—*
>
> Fiery orb
> Shooting golden arrows
> Glowing warmth nurtures growth
> Life.
>
> > Marge Sutton

A third-grade boy wrote this cinquain:

BED—

Soft, warm,
 Fun, bouncy, tumbling,
 Fun on my bed;
 Comfortable.

Mike McCord
Teacher: Frances H. Emery

Another form of the cinquain[8] based on syllables is as follows:

Line 1: Two syllables
Line 2: Four syllables
Line 3: Six syllables
Line 4: Eight syllables
Line 5: Two syllables

Following is an example of the cinquain written in the syllable format:

FUNNY—

People can seem
 So different to me
 As when they are so far away
 From me.

Evelyn Louie

Diamante The diamante (dee ah mahn' tay) was invented by Iris Tiedt, who whote in an article on exploring poetry patterns.

 If you become enthusiastic about having students write poetry, as I have been, you will find yourself searching for additional patterns to challenge students who have become involved in the composition of poetry. It was this search that led to my creation of four new poetry patterns that have proved to be very successful frames for ideas. While lending some structure, a pleasant patterning, the framework is not dominant or confining.[9]

The diamante, which many teachers have tried successfully with elementary school children, is a seven-line diamond-shaped poem that follows this pattern:

---

[8]This form has been attributed to Adelaide Crapsey, a minor American poet and author of *Verse* (Rochester: Manas Press, 1914).

[9]Iris M. Tiedt, "Exploring Poetry Patterns," *Elementary English,* December 1970, pp. 1082–85.

It is suggested, furthermore, that the poem be developed according to the following specifications:

Line 1:   subject noun (1 word)
Line 2:   adjectives (2 words)
Line 3:   participles (3 words)
Line 4:   nouns (4 words)
Line 3:   participles (3 words)
Line 2:   adjectives (2 words)
Line 1:   noun-opposite of subject (1 word)

Notice that this poem creates a contrast between two opposite concepts as in the following example:

Air
Balmy, soft
Floating, wafting, soothing,
Typhoon, wind, gale, cyclone
Twisting, howling, tearing,
Bitter, cold
Blast.

Vera Harryman

Septolet, Quinzaine, Quintain   Three additional poetry patterns invented by Iris Tiedt are the septolet, quinzaine, and quintain. These forms are described here with examples. You and students in your class are invited to create other new poetry forms.

The septolet consists of 7 lines (14 words) with a break in the pattern as indicated in this diagram.

Kitten
Padding stealthily
Amongst green grasses
Most   intent.
Bird
Ascends rapidly
Causing great disappointment.

Beverly Oldfield

The quinzaine (kanźen) consists of 15 syllables in 3 lines (7, 5, 3) which make a statement followed by a question, thus:

> Boys screaming in the distance—
> When will stillness drop
> On this dusk?
>
> Irma Johnson

The quintain (kwinten) is a syllable progression: 2, 4, 6, 8, 10, as illustrated here:

> Poems
> Read for pleasure
> Before the bright firelight
> Words meant for all those who enjoy
> Delightful, soothing, lovable music.
>
> L. Wille

Moving into rhymed forms   In this section we explore rhyming forms of poetry that children can chant or sing, read or write, or just plain enjoy. We need to teach children how to explore rhymes as a part of auditory discrimination and a skill that supports ability to spell; in this case we want them to be less limited in the ideas they can express as they try to write rhymed poetry forms.

Encourage children to share poems that they know, for most of them will contain rhymes. Include Mother Goose verses, beginning with those that are more familiar, but bringing in the less common ones, for example:

MOLLY, MY SISTER, AND I FELL OUT

> Molly, my sister, and I fell out,
> And what do you think it was all about?
> She loved coffee
> And I loved tea,
> And that was the reason we couldn't agree.

Plan speaking and listening activities that use a variety of rhymed poetry forms. Encourage children to try writing rhymed lines beginning with the couplets, as described in the following pages.

Couplet   The couplet is the simplest type of rhymed verse, and therefore offers possibilities for introducing rhyme to young writers. Many couplets are produced incidentally as children experiment with language—"Jean, Jean, your hair is green," or "Pink, pink, she drank some ink"—the jingles and rhymes of childhood. An excellent way to begin composing couplets is through group composition.

- To introduce students to the couplet and the techniques of writing rhymed poetry first discuss rhyming. Oral activities will quickly familiarize the class with the skill of rhyming as lists of rhymes are developed. Stress the following understandings:
  1. Rhymes are based on the sound, not the appearance of a word.
     day, neigh, lei, prey
     theme, dream, seem

sane, gain, reign, rein
rhyme, climb, time, I'm

2. Not all words have rhymes. (silver)
3. You must pronounce a word correctly and listen carefully to determine
    whether words really rhyme:
    sand—tan   few—too   kind—fine

* Make a class rhyming dictionary. Small groups of students take different sounds
  and think of all the words ending with that sound. One page headed "ite" would
  include words such as bite, fight, light, right, rite, sight, site, tight. Then as
  groups finish various pages, ditto and collate them to create ten to fifteen copies
  of class rhyming dictionaries—great for your poetry learning center.
* After a class has learned to rhyme easily, select an appropriate theme—the
  month, season, weather, state, event, person—about which the class will compose
  a poem together. For a beginning experience provide lines as in this example
  of a poem about Halloween.

Introduce the subject of Halloween through a discussion or the singing of
Halloween songs. Then say: "Let's write a poem about Halloween. Will you help
me?" Write a first line on the board, being sure that the line ends with an easily
rhymed word: "Ghosts and goblins are all around." Class members then suggest
possible second lines as indicated here:

Ghosts and goblins are all around. (Teacher)
An owl is hooting with mournful sound. (A child)
There are devils and demons and cats of black (Teacher)
And each one carries a great big sack. (A child)
Aren't you afraid to be out this night, (Teacher)
For devils are fearsome and cats might bite? (A child)
Oh, no, not I, for don't you know, (Teacher)
The cat is Susan, and that devil is Joe! (A child)

* Hints about group composition:
    1. Have several lines suggested each time before selecting a best one to
        be written on the board.
    2. Select lines by different people each time so that as many as possible
        have contributed to the finished product. You may also choose to have
        two poems produced at the same time so more than one line can be
        used; simply work on two boards inserting a different student line after
        the given first line each time.
    3. Children can learn to tap out the rhythm of the given line as they try
        to produce similar rhythm in the second line—the beginnings of meter.
* After a class has composed couplets together orally, the teacher can supply a
  variety of beginning lines as each student writes one or more endings for each
  line supplied. For the line, "Flowers now are growing," these examples were
  written:

> Flowers now are growing.
> And the grass is showing.
>
> Flowers now are growing.
> Gentle winds are blowing.
>
> Flowers now are growing,
> And the grass needs mowing.

Triplet   The triplet, an intriguing verse form which is not widely used, offers interesting possibilities as a form of rhymed poetry which young writers can create effectively. These three-line poems tell a brief story and are often humorous. As with the couplet, the initial experience can be a group composition. Teachers who have used this verse form have found that students are more successful if each first produces a rhyme list.

- Each child selects a word. The word selected must be one that rhymes easily, so you may choose to provide a list from which each person selects a word; for example, PLANE, JET, TRAIN, CAR, SWIM, FISH, PLAY, BOOK, SKY, RIDE, GAME, SING, BOX, FORT, EAT, DOG, CAT, BALL, SEA. The word chosen is then written at the top of a sheet of paper and a column of rhyming words is developed. Three related words are used to compose a triplet.
  A list of words rhyming with SEA suggested the following triplet:

  > Standing silent before the sea
  > I thought the water talked to me
  > Then laughed aloud with sudden glee.[10]
  >
  > Iris Tiedt

- An interesting variation developed to add to the enjoyment of writing triplets is the triangular triplet.[11] As in this example, the reader may begin reading at any point of the triangle. The poem must be composed so the lines may be read in any order.

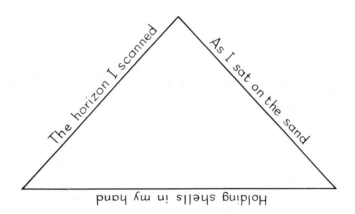

Limericks   Did you know there is a city in Ireland named Limerick through which flows the River Shannon? The limerick, which actually consists of a triplet and a couplet, is a form of verse which students usually enjoy. The

[10]Sidney Tiedt and Iris M. Tiedt, *The Elementary Teacher's Complete Ideas Handbook* (Englewood Cliffs, N.J.: Prentice-Hall, Inc., 1980), p. 93.
[11]Sidney Tiedt and Iris M. Tiedt, *Creative Writing Ideas* (San Jose, Calif.: Contemporary Press, 1964), p. 19.

form has consistently been used for humorous, nonsense verse which perhaps explains its appeal for young people. Read verses by Edward Lear and others. Write one example like the following on the board so that the form can be examined together:

> There once was a boy from Rome
> Who never used a comb.
>   His hair was a sight;
>   It never looked right!
> A boy like that should stay home!
>
> Iris Tiedt

The triplet consists of lines 1, 2, and 5, whereas lines 3 and 4 form a couplet. Students will soon observe, too, that limericks often begin with the words, "There once was . . . ," which is helpful to the beginner. Remind students to arrange the wording so that easily rhymed words end each line.

- Have students invent the strangest animal they can imagine. They can draw or paint pictures of the animals as well as write a limerick to accompany their art.

> There once was a kangeroogo,
> Who would only go where you go.
>   He ate jam and bread
>   And could stand on his head.
> He constantly read Victor Hugo.
>
> Iris Tiedt

Quatrain   The quatrain is the most commonly used verse form, perhaps because of its versatility. You can readily find examples of varied rhyme schemes—*aabb, abab, abcb,* and others. An effective method of introducing the quatrain to a class is to write several on the board with the class commenting on the similarities and the differences:

1. Quatrains contain four lines.
2. The lines are of uniform length.
3. There is rhyme.
4. The rhyme pattern varies.

Share these familiar examples:

> I eat my peas with honey;
> I've done it all my life.
> It makes the peas taste funny,
> But it keeps them on my knife!

> The rain it raineth on the just
>   And also on the unjust fella;
> But chiefly on the just, because
>   The unjust steals the just's umbrella.

- The quatrain can be arranged in varied forms for added interest. Have students create Quadrangles which, like triangular triplets, can be read from any starting point.

- Encourage students to combine forms of poetry which they know. A completed poem, for example, may consist of three quatrains and a couplet (a sonnet) or a series of quatrains may be used to form a poem of any length.

A poem written in quatrains also lends itself to music. The three stanzas of Robert Louis Stevenson's "The Swing" can be sung to this simple tune. Ask a student to play the melody on a xylophone or bells.

Additional Verses:
Verse 2:
Up in the air and over the wall,
Till I can see so wide,
Rivers and trees and cattle and all
Over the countryside.
Verse 3:
Till I look down on the garden green,
Down on the roof so brown—
Up in the air I go flying again,
Up in the air and down!

SUMMARY

Poetry has been given special emphasis as a unique form of literature that children can learn to appreciate and to produce. Concepts presented in this chapter cover background information for the teacher with a strong section on engaging students in working with poetry individually and in groups.

1. The teacher is an important key to how children feel about poetry and what they know about this form of writing.
2. Poets are human beings who write to communicate with other people. Children can participate in this communication process by reading with understanding and by creating poetry of their own.
3. Poetry study should be presented positively with emphasis on the enjoyment of each poem for what it has to offer. Every effort should be made to emphasize such elements as humor, rhythm, and descriptive language that children can respond to.
4. Children can write exciting original poetry if they first experiment with free verse and imagery, then follow poetry patterns, and last, try rhymed verse forms.

Teachers who discover poetry with children will find a joy in teaching that is akin to magic. Poetry belongs in every classroom.

CHALLENGE

Enjoy poetry as you explore. Share your findings with the other members of your class so that everyone benefits.

1. Choose at least two poems about the same topic, for example, the wind, baby animals, winter, Abraham Lincoln. Plan a lesson using those poems to stimulate student language development.

2. Teach a poem to a group of your classmates. Use specific listening and speaking strategies to involve them.

3. Try writing at least five of the poetry forms described in this chapter. Plan how you can use one of your original poems to motivate children to write poetry.

4. Investigate the work of three poets who write for children. Discover something about their lives that you can share with children. If possible, try this presentation with a group of youngsters.

EXPLORING FURTHER

Anderson, Douglas. *My Sister Looks Like a Pear; Awakening the Poetry in Young People*. New York: Hart Publishing Co., 1974.

Gensler, Kenereth and Nina Nyhart, *The Poetry Connection: An Anthology of Contemporary Poems with Ideas to Stimulate Children's Writing*. New York: Teachers & Writers Collaborative, 1978.

Kimsey, Ardis, *To Defend a Form: The Romance of Administration and Teaching in a Poetry-in-the-Schools Program*. New York: Teachers & Writers Collaborative, 1977.

Koch, Kenneth, *Rose, where did you get that red? Teaching Great Poetry to Children*. New York: Random House, Inc., 1973.

———, *Wishes, Lies and Dreams: Teaching Children to Write Poetry*. New York: Vintage, 1970.

Tiedt, Iris M. "Be Like the Bird: Exploring Poetry with Children," in *Exploring Books with Children*. Boston: Houghton Mifflin Co., 1979.

Walter, Nina, *Let Them Write Poetry*. New York: Holt, Rinehart & Winston, Inc., 1962.

PART V

Extending Language Arts Instruction

I want to encourage children to develop positive attitudes toward themselves and their abilities, to love themselves . . . I want to write stories that will allow children to fall in love with genuine Black heroes and heroines who have proved themselves to be outstanding in ability and in dedication to the cause of Black freedom . . . I want to be one of those who can choose and order words that children will want to celebrate. I want to make them shout and laugh and blink tears and care about themselves. They are our future.

Eloise Greenfield[1]

LANGUAGE ARTS ACROSS THE CURRICULUM
Interchanging Content and Methodology

The language arts program emphasizes the development of language skills and teaching the content of language and literature. In this chapter we focus on ways of interchanging content and methods of instruction among the various subjects taught in the elementary school. In the first section we will explore ways of teaching content from different areas of study as part of the language arts activities. In the second part of the chapter we will examine ways of utilizing instructional methods that are usually associated with the language arts to teach more effectively in other areas of the curriculum.

As we consider ways of correlating language arts instruction with that of other subject areas, we need to keep our goals and objectives clearly in mind. We aim to improve student languaging abilities—thinking, listening, speaking, reading, and writing. We also aim to teach concepts about language and literature. We cannot teach in any subject without using languaging abilities, but we do need to recognize that we are teaching them and not take these abilities for granted. We also need to teach concepts

---

[1]Eloise Greenfield. Acceptance Speech, Caldecott Award for *There She Come Bringing Me That Little Baby Girl,* 1975.

about language and literature consciously. The study of language can be related to other subject areas in the curriculum as students learn specialized vocabulary, information about language backgrounds of the U.S. citizenry, and other multicultural concepts. Literature offers a wealth of material for learning about the many topics introduced in the elementary school. Language arts, therefore is a rich resource for the so-called "content" subjects.

BENCHMARK

Integrating language arts instruction and instruction in other areas of the curriculum calls for ingenuity and imagination. Discuss these questions as you begin exploring the possibilities for presenting a total approach to the elementary school curriculum.

1. List a number of concepts that you think all children should learn that would help them understand themselves and others better. How can literature be used to promote such understanding?

2. What topics do students discuss in the social studies? How could their oral language skills be improved as they learned more about these topics?

3. How are language arts and music related? How can art and language arts instruction be integrated?

In this chapter you will investigate ways of interrelating language arts teaching with the total curriculum. After completing the chapter you should be able to:

- enumerate literature titles that can be used for learning in all subject areas of the curriculum
- demonstrate ways of improving language abilities through studying varied subject content
- discuss sound, yet enjoyable, language arts instructional strategies that will stimulate learning in other fields of study

INTRODUCING VARIED CONTENT IN THE LANGUAGE ARTS PROGRAM

The language arts program will be more stimulating, and therefore more effective, if instruction is centered on an interesting topic or theme. If students are to improve their listening skills, they should certainly listen to content that is exciting, and they should listen with a purpose. The same is true of speaking, reading, and writing as well as thinking development. It is important that we coordinate language arts instruction with other curricular areas. In that way, instruction will serve two goals as students learn concepts from a specific field and also improve their use of language abilities. In this section of the chapter we will focus on ways of presenting specific information through an integrated approach to teaching the language arts across the curriculum. Each of the major curricular areas will be emphasized as we explore ways of bringing language arts instruction together with the social studies, science, mathematics, art, and music.

The Social Studies

Integrating language arts instruction with social studies content is particularly easy, but it needs to be planned consciously so that teaching in both areas is effectively handled. Social studies content used to enrich and support language arts instruction can be focused around any theme or area of study, such as transportation in the United States, the changing role of women in America, or how our country was founded. A variety of examples follow.

People and places A history lesson that talks of real people who live through their biographies is far more exciting than a social studies program that relies on a single textbook. Literature—historical fiction, biography, poetry, drama, nonfiction—enriches the social studies curriculum. Selecting such literature for study in the language arts program integrates the two classes effectively as children read, listen, discuss, and write in response to the books they read. Activities focused on selected books might include the following.

• Enlarge a United States (or world) map which can be mounted on a bulletin board. As students read books, have each pin a small pennant on the map bearing the title of the book with the location revealing the setting of the story. Figures of the main characters can also be used to mark the setting, with Tom Sawyer marching beside the Mississippi and Paul Bunyan in the North Woods.
• For a novel approach to book reviewing, have students write limericks about books they've read, thus:

> Tom Sawyer was a barefoot lad;
> Far from good, not really bad.
> Aunt Polly he teased,
> Sid and Mary displeased.
> His story will make your heart glad.
>
> Iris Tiedt

• Focus attention on the achievements of individual Americans as students conduct library research. An activity sheet will help students recognize the contributions of women. In addition to preparing a research report, they might draw a portrait of one person, write a poem about one woman or a group of women, write a short biography, or prepare a skit to act out relating something about the life of the person studied. (See page 360.)

Focus on a period of time or an event Students studying the American Revolution and life in the United States at that time might work with the following activities:

1. *Focus on one person or event.* If each student chooses one specific thing to study, for example, Paul Revere, the reading and research done on this topic will naturally encompass much of the history of the times. A student from third through sixth grade could read Robert Lawson's humorous fictional biography of Paul Revere called *Mr. Revere and I* (Little, Brown) which is supposedly told by his horse, Sherry. Formerly known as Scheherazade, this talkative animal

Who's Who of American Women

Read the following list of women. How many do you know?
Most of the women listed are American. How many can you find that are not?

JANUARY
1 — Betsy Ross 1752–1836
5 — Christina Rossetti 1830–1894
6 — Joan of Arc c. 1412–1431
26 — Mary Mapes Dodge 1831–1905

FEBRUARY
3 — Gertrude Stein 1874–1946
3 — Elizabeth Black 1821–1910
9 — Amy Lowell 1874–1925
10 — Leontyne Price 1927–
15 — Susan B. Anthony 1820–1906
17 — Marian Anderson 1902–

MARCH
6 — Elizabeth Barrett Browning 1806–1861
16 — Patricia Nixon 1912–
17 — Kate Greenaway 1846–1901
21 — Phyllis McGinley 1905–
25 — Gloria Steinem 1936–

APRIL
21 — Queen Elizabeth II 1926–
21 — Charlotte Bronte 1816–1855
23 — Shirley Temple Black 1928–
25 — Ella Fitzgerald 1918–

MAY
3 — Golda Meir 1898–1981
12 — Florence Nightingale 1820–1910
20 — Dolly Madison 1768–1849
21 — Clara Barton 1821–1912
27 — Julia Ward Howe 1819–1910
27 — Amelia J. Bloomer 1818–1894

JUNE
1 — Marilyn Monroe 1926–1962
14 — Harriet Beecher Stowe 1811–1896
14 — Margaret Bourke White 1906–
16 — Katherine Graham 1917–
16 — Joyce Carol Oates 1938–
26 — Pearl S. Buck 1892–1973
27 — Helen Keller 1880–1968

JULY
6 — Della Reese 1932–
22 — Rose Kennedy 1890–
24 — Amelia Earhart 1898–1937
28 — Jacqueline Kennedy Onassis 1929–
31 — Evonne Goolegong 1951–

AUGUST
1 — Maria Mitchell 1818–1889
1 — Lucy Stone 1818–1893
12 — Katherine Lee Bates 1859–1929
31 — Maria Montessori 1870–1952

SEPTEMBER
6 — Jane Addams 1860–1935
7 — Elinor Wylie 1885–1928
14 — Margaret Sanger 1883–1966
14 — Kate Millet 1934–
19 — Rachel Field 1894–1942
25 — Barbara Walters 1931–

OCTOBER
6 — Jenny Lind 1820–1889
10 — Helen Hays 1900–
11 — Eleanor Roosevelt 1884–1962
14 — Lillian Gish 1896–1979
22 — Doris Lessing 1919–
26 — Mahalia Jackson 1911–
27 — Sylvia Plath 1932–1963
31 — Juliette Low 1860–1927

NOVEMBER
7 — Marie Curie 1867–1934
18 — Indira Gandhi 1917–
23 — Abigail Adams 1744–1818
25 — Carrie Nation 1846–1911
29 — Louisa May Alcott 1832–1888
30 — Shirley Chisholm 1924–

DECEMBER
10 — Emily Dickinson 1830–1886
14 — Margaret Chase Smith 1897–
16 — Jane Austen 1775–1817
25 — Clara Barton 1821–1912
29 — Mary Tyler Moore 1937–

Now, choose one person that you would like to know more about. Locate information in the library. Prepare a short oral report to share with your classmates. If possible, present your report on that woman's birthday.

Can you add any birthdays to this list?

was "once the most admired mount of the Queen's Own Household Cavalry." She is appalled by the activities of Paul Revere with the Sons of Liberty, but finally she realizes, as she says, "I was a Colonial! I was a Patriot, my life dedicated to the ideals of Liberty and Freedom!"

After being introduced to people and events in this comical, but factual, story, the student would be motivated to read additional books such as:

Johnny Tremain by Esther Forbes (Houghton)

And Then, What Happened, Paul Revere? by Jean Fritz (Coward)

Giving students a chance to select their own topic is better than assigning research to be done.

2. *Construct a class time line to show how events are related in time.* You might make the time line cover the years 1750–1800, fifty years that include the Revolutionary War, thus:

1750	1760	1770	1780	1790	1800

Students can include clippings from magazines or original drawings to make the display more interesting.

3. Make a poster of vocabulary items that are related to the Revolutionary period. You might group the words in categories, for example:

foods	battles
clothing	furniture
weapons	music
military positions	

What, for example, is a *crinoline* or a *camisole?* Students can illustrate various items that interest them, for instance, different kinds of uniforms. Others might want to sing or play selections of music that were popular during that time, for instance, *"Yankee Doodle."*

Notice that these words are the kinds of things that make social studies material hard to read. Yet here we have an interesting way of helping children learn to recognize these words with no particular strain because they're curious.

4. Have students make paper or cloth flags to show the historical development of the American flag, including:

The flag of 1777 (13 stars)	The 48-Star flag (48 stars)
The flag of 1818 (20 stars)	Our present flag (50 stars)

Most encyclopedias contain a good explanation of the development of the United States flag and include pictures that will help students design their miniature flags. They will discover many novel flags that they hadn't heard of before, like this one:

LIBERTY
TREE
FLAG
1775

5. Pretend that each student is a boy or girl living two hundred years ago. Each one writes a letter to a friend in England telling what life is like in the new country. They might tell about the following:

School, books, their teacher   Their father's work
The things their mother does   Activities they enjoy   A typical day

To talk about any of these ideas, of course, each student needs to know something about life in 1776. How will they find out? By reading!

Notice that in each of the above activities we *begin with the interest*, not a book that is too hard to read. This is an effective way of teaching because each student is motivated to investigate a topic. The textbook can be used as a reference book, a resource, but other resources will also be used—encyclopedia, nonfiction books about this time in history, historical fiction. Students learn how to use indexes and the table of contents as they search for information. They learn skills of reporting pertinent details and of discriminating between fact and opinion. This is truly *the inquiry method!*

6. Students could prepare an annotated bibliography of books that provide information about this period in history, both fiction and nonfiction, thus:

Berry, Brick. *Hay-Foot, Straw-Foot,* illus. by author. Viking, 1954. A story about a little drummer boy and the origins of "Yankee Doodle."

Blassingame, Wyatt. *The Story of the United States Flag.* Garrard, 1969. This informative book has diagrams and illustrations in color that reveal the history of the flags of the United States.

Bourne, Miriam Anne. *Nabby Adam's Diary,* illus. by Stephen Gammell. Coward-McCann, 1975. Nabby's diary tells of events preceding the War and of her experiences as the daughter of John Adams.

Caudill, Rebecca. *Tree of Freedom,* illus. by Dorothy Morse. Viking, 1949. The story of Stephanie, who moves with her family to the Kentucky wilderness during the Revolutionary War. She takes with her a prized possession, an apple seed, and nurtures it into her "tree of freedom."

Coatsworth, Elizabeth. *American Adventures, 1620–1945,* illus. by Robert Frankenberg. Macmillan, 1968. Seven short novels present important periods in American history. Each novel has an afterword which clearly separates historical fact from fiction.

Colver, Anne. *Bread and Butter Indian,* illus. by Garth Williams. Holt, 1964. During the Revolutionary period, Barbara develops a friendship with an Indian by sharing her bread and butter.

————. *Bread and Butter Journey,* illus. by Garth Williams. Holt, 1970. In this sequel, two families make a pioneering journey into western Pennsylvania in 1784.

Focus on a theme: diversity   As we try to promote appreciation for ethnic groups in the United States, it is helpful to talk about diversity, what it means, and how it benefits us all. We can develop an integrated language arts approach as we teach social studies concepts.

Beginning with listening   Read stories aloud that present children with pictures of different kinds of people—old and young, varied families, different races, nationalities, geographical locations, rich and poor. An excellent selection is *Sound of Sunshine, Sound of Rain* by Florence Heide (Parents). Always take time to talk about the people—their feelings, how they get along with each other, how they are like you and me, and how they are different.

Here is a very short story based on fact that you can share.

There's Nobody Like You!

The French poet, Jean Cocteau, found out early in life why diversity is better than uniformity.

As a young man, M. Cocteau was designing a stage set which required a tree as background.

He spent night after night in the theater basement cutting out individual leaves for his creation.

Then a wealthy friend, whose father owned a factory, approached him with another idea.

"Give me the design of the leaf," he said, "and in three days you will have thousands of them here."

After his friend's return, they pasted the multitude of identical leaves onto the branches.

The result, M. Cocteau recalled, was "the most boring package of flat, uninteresting forms one can see."

At last he understood why each leaf of a tree and each man in the world are different from any other.

This story is from Christoper *News Notes,* No. 187, May, 1971. Ask to be placed on the mailing list for this publication, which often contains interesting material suitable for classroom use (12 East 48th St., New York, N.Y. 10017).

Speaking about diversity Students have already begun responding orally to ideas presented in the selections you have chosen to share. To add more oral activity, have students work with role playing. Students might experiment with role reversals as girls take male roles while boys assume female roles. Any situation could be played, for example, a family going out to dinner together or riding in the car. Following this kind of role playing, discuss the difficulties encountered in playing the roles realistically.

Reading strategies Have students develop reader's theater presentations of poems or stories that attempt to break down stereotyping. Students might present excerpts from a number of books featuring minorities, for example:

Mathis, Sharon Bell, *The Hundred Penny Box.* New York: Viking Press, Inc.
O'Dell, Scott, *Island of the Blue Dolphins.* Boston: Houghton Mifflin Co.
Taylor, Theodore, *The Cay.* New York: Doubleday & Co., Inc.

See page 382 in this chapter for detailed information about reader's theater procedures.

Writing activities Ask students to write a description of a doctor. Chances are, they will describe the doctor as a man. Then read a story about a woman doctor, for example, Elizabeth Blackwell, or invite a woman physician to visit your classroom. After students talk about women as doctors, discuss their drawings and why they envisioned the doctor as a man.

Help your students compile a book of lists. Each student chooses one category of people to list, for instance:

Tennis stars	People born in February
Opera stars	Women singers
Humorous authors	Great scientists

Students research the category and find out as much as possible about the individuals listed. For each person they write a thumbnail biographical sketch. Encourage students to help each other. When the book of lists is compiled, everyone will enjoy reading the collection. Point out the variety of persons represented—age, sex, ethnic groups.

Problem solving: Group decision making Small group approaches to discussion are highly effective because student participation is greater than in a large group. The following simulation activity should be presented to the full group, which then is divided into small groups of five or six. The activity begins with individual decisions made while students are part of the large group. The second part of the activity is completed in small groups. The large group then reassembles for critiquing and evaluating the process.

DECISION BY CONSENSUS (PREPARED BY NASA)

1. Individual decision

Instructions You are a member of a space crew originally scheduled to rendezvous with a mother ship on the lighted surface of the moon. Because of mechanical difficulties, however, your ship was forced to land at a spot some two hundred miles from the rendezvous point. During the landing much of the ship and the equipment aboard were damaged, and since survival depends on reaching the mother ship, the most critical items still available must be chosen for the two-hundred-mile trip. Below are listed the 15 items left intact and undamaged after landing. Your task is to rank them in order of their importance in allowing your crew to reach the rendezvous point. Place the number 1 by the most important item, the number 2 by the second most important, and so on through number 15, the least important.

_____Box of matches
_____Food concentrate
_____50 feet of nylon rope
_____Parachute silk
_____Portable heating unit
_____Two .45-caliber pistols
_____One case of dehydrated milk
_____Two 100-pound tanks of oxygen
_____Map of the stars as seen from the moon
_____Life raft
_____Magnetic compass
_____5 gallons of water
_____Signal flares
_____First-aid kit containing injection needles
_____Solar-powered FM receiver-transmitter

2. Group consensus

This is an exercise in group decision-making. Your group is to employ the method of group consensus in reaching its decision. This means that the prediction for each of the fifteen survival items *must* be agreed upon by each group member before it becomes a part of the group decision. Consensus is difficult to reach. Therefore, not every ranking will meet with everyone's complete approval. Try, as a group, to make each ranking one with which *all* group members can at least partially agree. Here are some guides to use in reaching consensus:

1. Avoid arguing for your own individual judgments. Approach the task on the basis of logic.
2. Avoid changing your mind only in order to reach agreement and eliminate conflict. Support only solutions with which you are able to agree to some extent, at least.
3. Avoid conflict-reducing techniques such as majority vote, averaging, or trading in reaching decisions.
4. View differences of opinion as helpful rather than as a hindrance in decision-making.

On the group summary sheet place the individual rankings made earlier by each group member. Take as much time as you need in reaching your group decision.

Key Take the difference between your ranking and the ranking on the key. Add the differences. The lower the score the better. These answers are based on the best judgments that are now available to you. They are not absolute answers.

15	Box of matches	Little or no use on moon
4	Food concentrate	Supply daily food required
6	50 feet of nylon rope	Useful in tying injured together; helpful in climbing
8	Parachute silk	Shelter against sun's rays
13	Portable heating unit	Useful only if party landed on dark side of moon
11	Two .45-caliber pistols	Self-propulsion devices could be made from them
12	One case of dehydrated milk	Food; mixed with water for drinking
1	Two 100-pound tanks of oxygen	Fills respiration requirement
3	Map of the stars as seen from the moon	One of the principal means of finding directions
9	Life raft	CO_2 bottles for self-propulsion across chasms, etc.
14	Magnetic compass	Probably no magnetized poles, thus useless
2	5 gallons of water	Replenishes loss by sweating, etc.
10	Signal flares	Distress call when line of sight possible
7	First-aid kit containing injection needles	Oral pills or injection valuable
5	Solar-powered FM receiver transmitter	Distress-signal transmitter—possible communication with mother ship

3.   Critique

Following the exercise, discuss the sources of the problem-solving techniques. How often did individuals use the affective domain in working out the problem? How often did the cognitive domain dominate? What kind of balance existed? How did their knowledge of the extensional world allow them to work with the unknowns? What did they learn about their own learning styles? Did they work better in groups or alone? Did they score higher as a group, or was the individual score better? How did the scores compare with the group average? Did they enjoy the individual work more than the group work?

Science

Contemporary focus on science has led to the publication of many exciting books in the various fields of science. One of the leading writers in science for youth has been Isaac Asimov, who writes for the more advanced student.

He is author of *Building Blocks of the Universe* (Abelard) and *The Clock We Live On* (Abelard), as well as *Words of Science* (Houghton Mifflin) and adult science fiction.

Another familiar name is Herbert Zim, whose small handbooks on mammals, insects, stars, trees, birds, and so on are inexpensive and reliable reference books. Now available in paperback editions, these books are popular purchases for the young scientist who collects rocks, butterflies, or studies the stars.

Activities which relate science and literature might include the following:

1.   Literature related to science. Read the description of the life of a hermit crab told by Holling C. Holling in *Pagoo* (Houghton Mifflin). This adventure story is accompanied by superb illustrations in both black-and-white and color. Follow the reading of this book by showing the unique film *The Story of a Book* (Churchill Films) which describes the work of the Hollings in developing this idea for a book—the origin of the idea, observation of the hermit crab, preparation of illustrations, writing of the text.

Use fishnet as an attractive background for a display of books about the sea. Include some of these titles:

Brindze, Ruth. *The Rise and Fall of the Seas; the Story of the Tides.* Harcourt, Brace.
Buck, Margaret W. *Along the Seashore.* Abingdon.
Clarke, Arthur C. *The Challenge of the Sea.* Holt, Rinehart, and Winston.
Kenyon, Ley. *Discovering the Under Sea World.* Sterling.

2.   The people of science. Encourage students to read biographies of men and women of science. Gifted students will be especially interested in learning more about inventors, discoverers, scientists. Information gained can be shared by the preparation of a display which depicts the contributions of the individual.

Bigland, Eileen. *Madame Curie.* Criterion Books.
Dickinson, Alice. *Charles Darwin and Natural Selection.* Franklin Watts.
Freeman, Mae B. *The Story of Albert Einstein.* Random House.

The human speech process   Students will be interested in learning more about how human beings speak. Draw from the fields of biology and linguistics as you guide students to observe how they produce language.

The vocal tract   As a science lesson, show students an enlargement of the human head on an overhead transparency. Discuss the parts of the body that are involved in producing speech. Point out, for example, the lips and teeth as part of the mechanism for producing sounds. Identify the larynx and write the related word, laryngitis, on the board. Talk about such topics as the following:

1.   What does the uvula do? (Have students look in a mirror to locate this part of their anatomy.)
2.   What do we mean when we say, "Something went down the wrong way"?
3.   Is the nose part of the speaking system? Have students experiment by making an /m/ sound. As they make this sound, have them press their nostrils closed gently with their finger and thumb. What happens to the sound? See if they

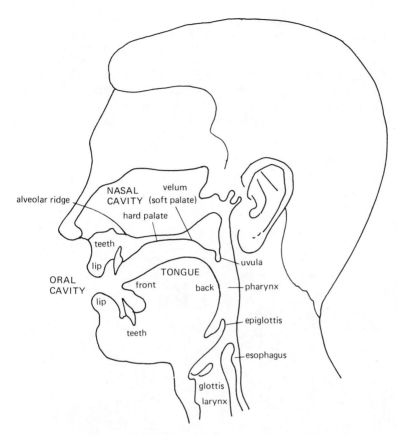

The human vocal tract.

can identify other sounds that work in the same way. (Any sound that can be hummed, a nasal sound—/m/, /n/)

4.   Compare these sets of sounds:

/t/ /d/

/p/ /b/

Have students hold their hands before their mouths as they make each sound. Ask what they notice about the pairs of sounds (/t/ and /p/ are aspirated—include a puff of air as we say them; /d/ and /b/ are made in the same way, but there is no explosion of air.)

5.   Have students make drawings of the head showing the vocal tract. (See above.) Help them identify the specific parts by pointing them out on the transparency and spelling the words aloud.

Students can research related topics about speech. Subjects of interest include:

Comparing human speech with that of animals, for example, a parrot or a chimpanzee

Comparing human communication with that of bees
How does a deaf person learn to speak? (Helen Keller)
What happens when a person's larynx is removed?

Puzzles and word activities   Content from science as well as other areas of the elementary school curriculum can be presented in a variety of puzzle forms. Children learn information but they also enjoy what they are doing. Science content and language arts skills are integrated in the following puzzle on the sun.

Our sun—a star.

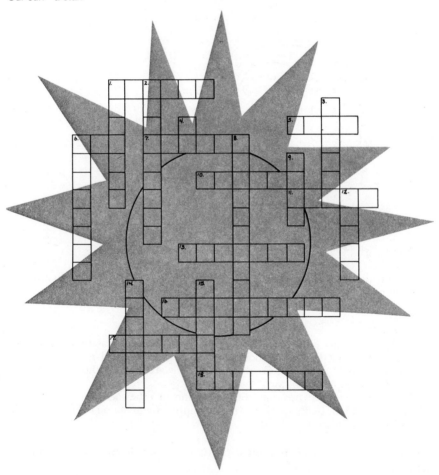

Julie Johnson, from *Elementary Teacher's Ideas and Materials Workshop*, June 1980, pp 12–13.

ACROSS

1. Without our sun, all life would perish and the air would _____.
5. Solar eclipses occur when the _____ passes between the earth and the sun.
6. The Norsemen named their _____ god Balder, the shining one.
7. Without the power of the sun, _____ would not grow.
10. Located in the Milky Way, our _____, are one hundred billion stars, one of which is our own sun.
11. Babylonians thought the sun, Shamash, gave wisdom and was the _____ of evil.
13. Our sun is large enough to fit over a _____ earths inside.
16. In 1500 B.C., a sun temple called _____ was erected in Salisbury Plain, England.
17. The Greek's sun god _____ represented music and poetry.
18. In _____ times, the sun played an important part in the lives of people as a symbol of many things.

DOWN

1. The sun is composed of gases and is like a huge nuclear _____.
2. Not only does the sun _____ moisture from the sea to give us rain; it also gives us day and night and our seasons.
3. It takes the sun 25 days to _____ once on its axis.
4. The ancient Egyptians worshipped the sun as a deity called _____.
6. Dark spots or _____ measuring up to 90,000 miles long can be seen on the surface of the sun.
8. Gaseous prominences or _____ _____ can erupt from the sun's surface to a height of about 140,000 miles.
9. Looking directly in the sun can result in the damage of your _____.
12. The diameter of the sun is about 864,000 _____.
14. Quetzalcoatl, the Aztec's sun god, was worshipped as a _____ in green feathers and was the bearer of wisdom and peace.
15. The outermost layer around the sun that looks like a halo is called the _____.

WORDS TO CHOOSE FROM

SOLAR FLARES	SUN
ENEMY	ANCIENT
APOLLO	CORONA
SERPENT	PLANTS
FREEZE	STONEHENGE
RA	EVAPORATE
MOON	MILLION
FURNACE	GALAXY
EYES	SUNSPOTS
MILES	ROTATE

ANSWERS

DOWN	ACROSS
1. FREEZE	1. FURNACE
5. MOON	2. EVAPORATE
6. SUN	3. ROTATE
7. PLANTS	4. RA
10. GALAXY	6. SUNSPOTS
11. ENEMY	8. SOLAR FLARES
13. MILLION	9. EYES
16. STONEHENGE	12. MILES
17. APOLLO	14. SERPENT
18. ANCIENT	15. CORONA

Mathematics

Many teachers are puzzled about how to relate the teaching of math with language arts. There are many interesting ways of developing language skills using information related to mathematics. Described here are just a few ideas.

The word problem

Jill ate three apples. Jack ate two apples. How many apples did they eat altogether?

Although this simple problem (3 + 2) could be solved easily by a second-grade child, it is not unusual for these same students to be confused by the problem when it is couched in the context of a story. Two approaches will help students attack this type of problem with greater success: (1) teaching the key vocabulary and (2) having students write original math stories themselves.

Key vocabulary   Prepare a sheet of easy word problems that require the use of addition to obtain the answer. Have the students work the problems independently. After most of the students have completed the computations, discuss the solutions to the problem. In each case, ask students how they knew that addition was the process called for. List the key vocabulary words on the board, for example:

altogether	total
in all	sum

After completing this list, have two students make a chart to display entitled: WORDS THAT TELL YOU TO ADD!

Repeat this learning through discovery activity for subtraction, multiplication, and division. This process is essential for primary-grade students, but it may also prove helpful to older students who still have trouble understanding how to solve word problems. Older students can use the same kind of instruction with fractions or percentages.

Writing their own stories requires students to understand the mathematical processes being used. As they describe a specific situation, they will use the vocabulary already discussed to provide a clue to the person who will read the story and work the problem.

Have students turn their story in to you with the problem worked out below. Duplicate especially good problems to share with the class. Discuss the solutions and what qualities make each one a good problem. After students have their written problems checked by you or an aid, you may wish to have students print their problems on 5 × 8 file cards. Each one can work the problem correctly on the back of the card. These cards are then used to challenge their classmates. In this way you provide drill in a stimulating way so that students learn with enjoyment.

Following directions   Many math activity sheets or construction projects require students to read directions. Try to anticipate words that may prove difficult for the group of students. Write such words on the board and discuss them with students before they undertake the activity. This instructional help will make their success more likely, an important concern of all teachers.

Mind reading, the activity on page 371, requires students to read and follow directions. The activity is fun, so motivation will be high. Introduce the more difficult words: descending, reverse order, mentally.

Have students work in pairs as they try working with several different imaginary ages. Their assignment is to try mind reading with three persons at home or in their neighborhood. Let them decide whether to reveal how mind reading works after impressing their friends.

Provide other activities of this kind to give students practice in reading and math, for example:

Calculating mileage on a road map   Shopping in the newspaper ads
Following a recipe   Playing card games

These activities can be duplicated as activity sheets if students will be figuring out the problem. You may wish to place other sets of directions on 5 × 8 file cards which can be used repeatedly at a math center to which students can go in their free time.

Mind Reading

Tell your friends you can read their minds.
Have them take any 3 descending numbers under 10 (example: 543)
Have them take the same 3 numbers in the reverse order (example: 345)
Ask them to do the following:

1. Subtract the second number from the first (the answer is always 198)
2. Subtract 58
3. Divide by 2
4. Add 30
5. Divide by 10
6. Add their age

Ask them to tell you the number they got. Mentally subtract 10 from the answer. The result is the person's age.

AN EXAMPLE

Suppose John is 9 years old and chooses the numbers 765.

	765
Subtract the reverse number	− 567
(always the same)	198
Subtract 58	− 58
Divide by 2	2/140
	70
Add 30	+ 30
Divide by 10	10/100
	10
Add his age	+ 9
	19

Mentally subtract 10 from 19.
His age is 9.

Used with permission from: Round-the-Year Puzzlers by Frank and Letha Smith ($4.50 from Contemporary Press, Box 1524, San Jose, Calif. 95109).

Reading about math topics   To further interest in the subject of mathematics, talk about math as it appears in the news. Have students bring in articles that discuss math, for example, the controversy about using metric roadsigns. Prepare a bulletin board that features such articles with the caption: FACTS AND FIGURES or WHAT'S NEW ABOUT MATH?

Present books that may interest students. Include an assortment to show students what is in the school or public library, for example:

Think Metric! by Franklyn M. Branley (Thomas Crowell, 1972)
Meter Means Measure by S. Carl Hirsch (Viking, 1973)
More New Ways with Math by Arthur Jonas (Prentice-Hall, 1964)
Graphs by Dyno Lowenstein (Watts, 1969)
Three and the Shape of Three by Arthur Razzell and K. Watts (Doubleday, 1969)
The Wonderful World of Mathematics by Lancelot Hogben (Doubleday, 1968)
The Abacus: A Pocket Computer by Jesse Dilson (St. Martins, 1968)
Sets by Irving and Ruth Adler (Day, 1967)
Math Equals: Biographies of Women Mathematicians by Teri Perl (Addison Wesley, 1978)
How to Count Like a Martian by Glory St. John (Walck, 1975)

Literature and math   Introduce students to poetry related to math, too. For young students, you may use counting rhymes or jump rope jingles that help children learn the sequence of counting, for example, the old favorite:

One, two, buckle my shoe;
Three, four, shut the door;
Five, six, pick up sticks;
Seven, eight, lay them straight;
Nine, ten, a big fat hen!

For older students, share "Arithmetic" by Carl Sandburg. After listening to his ideas about numbers, students can invent their own ideas like this:

Arithmetic is . . .
dozens of eggs and dozens of doughnuts, to eat for breakfast on Sunday morning.
Arithmetic is . . .
the stars in the sky, an infinite number that I can't even imagine.
Arithmetic is . . .
unicycles, bicycles, and tricycles—wheels going around and around.

Help students learn that mathematics is more than arithmetical computations. Introduce them to the people and the ideas that have fascinated men and women through the ages. Share your love for math with them.

Music

Music and the language arts share a common vocabulary. We speak, for example, of intonation, phrases, compositions, writing, and form in both fields. In the chapter on poetry we point out the vocabulary that relates to both poetry and music. As children sing, they should become increasingly aware of the points at which language arts and music become one. We talk, for example, of "reading" music, and we use alphabet letters to name the notes. The lyrics of songs are poems that must be read and comprehended, and we employ similar vocabulary such as "beat" or "stanza" in both poetry and music. In addition, auditory and visual discrimination are involved in reading as well as music as learners identify sound–symbol relationships. We can help students become aware of these relationships to reinforce learning in both areas.

Sound–symbol relationships   Point out the use of symbols or signs in our lives—red light–green light, stop sign. No Smoking signs, the U.S. flag, Uncle Sam, mathematic signs +, −, $, ¢. Ask students if they can name other symbols.

Then show them a piece of music (in a class music book, on a duplicated sheet, or on a transparency). Have them identify the signs or symbols used in writing music, for example:

notes—corresponding letter names ♩ ♪ ♩
notes—indication of number of beats ♩ ♪ ♩
rests ₁ ━ ♭ ♪
clef signs 𝄢
D.S., D.C. (go back to the sign; go back to the beginning)

Point out to students that music is one of the universal languages. No matter what language you speak, you can read music and play or sing the song as written.

Music and history   Have students learn songs that are associated with different periods of history, for example:

America, the Beautiful	*John Henry*
The Star-Spangled Banner	*My Darling Clementine*
Davy Crockett	*Alaska's Flag*

The following folk song describes working on a canal where barges carried freight from Albany to Buffalo in the early days of New York State's development. Have students read the words of the song to see what it tells about this operation and the period in history. Then have them look in history books to read factual descriptions of the same time, place, and means of hauling freight.

THE ERIE CANAL

I've got a mule, her name is Sal,
Fifteen miles on the Erie Canal.
She's a good old worker and a good old pal,
Fifteen miles on the Erie Canal.
We've haul'd some barges in our day,
Fill'd with lumber, coal and hay,
And we know ev'ry inch of the way
From Albany to Buffalo.

Low bridge, ev'rybody down!
Low bridge, for we're going through a town,
And you'll always know your neighbor,
You'll always know your pal,
If you ever navigated on the Erie Canal.

We better get along on our way, old gal,
Fifteen miles on the Erie Canal,
Cause you bet your life I'd never part with Sal,
Fifteen miles on the Erie Canal.

Git up there, mule, here comes a lock,
We'll make Rome 'bout six o'clock,
One more trip and back we'll go
Right back home to Buffalo.

Sing the song. Students might also dramatize this song, singing as they load the barge and then calling to the mules as they move along the canal. Some students might draw illustrations of the scenes depicted, including a portrait of the singer. Use the song as the basis for a short story about Sal and her master. Observe that this song is a monologue with the man talking about his work and then talking to his mule.

Music and poetry Discuss the relationships between music and poetry. Ask students to list words that the two have in common, for example:

lyric	beat
stanza	line
verse	pattern
phrasing	tone
rhythm	reading

Students can use information from music in which they are already involved to help them become involved in reading poetry. Play the Simon and Garfunkel song "*Richard Corey*," for example. Students enjoy the music and listen attentively to the words. You might have them transcribe the lyrics as they listen. They can discuss the story told in the lyrics. Then tell them that this song was based on a poem written by E.A. Robinson. Provide copies so they can compare the two versions, noting differences in tone and point of view.

RICHARD CORY
Edwin Arlington Robinson (1869–1935)

Whenever Richard Cory went downtown,
We people on the pavement looked at him:
He was a gentleman from sole to crown,
Clean favored, and imperially slim.

And he was always quietly arrayed,
And he was always human when he talked;
But still he fluttered pulses when he said,
"Good-morning," and he glittered when he walked.

And he was rich—yes, richer than a king—
And admirably schooled in every grace:
In fine, we thought he was everything
To make us wish that we were in his place.

So on we worked, and waited for the light,
And went without the meat, and cursed the bread;
And Richard Cory, one calm summer night,
Went home and put a bullet through his head.

Vocabulary This vocabulary activity sheet involves students in analyzing the words of "The Star-Spangled Banner." Here is an interesting way of relating social studies, vocabulary development, and music.

Music Vocabulary Sheet

Name _____

Date _____

1. What is the purpose of a national *anthem?*
2. What is the name of the national anthem of the following countries?
   France _____Germany _____
   England _____
3. Something that is "star-spangled" is: _____
   _____
4. Below is a transcript of "The Star-Spangled Banner." Some words are italicized. Using a thesaurus, find a synonym for each italicized word.

O, say can you see, by the Dawn's early light,
What so proudly we *hailed* at the twilight's last *gleaming,*
Whose broad stripes and bright stars, through the *perilous* fight,
O'er the *ramparts* we watched, were so *gallantly* streaming?
And the rockets' red glare, the bombs bursting in air,
Gave proof through the night that our flag was still there.
　　Oh, say, does that star spangled banner yet wave,
　　O'er the land of the free, and the home of the brave?

On the shore, dimly seen through the mists of the deep,
Where the *foe's haughty host* in *dread* silence *reposes,*
What is that which the breeze, o'er the towering steep,
As it fretfully blows, half conceals, half *discloses?*
Now it catches the gleam of the morning's first beam;
Full glory reflected now shines in the stream,—
　　Tis the star spangled banner. Oh! long may it wave,
　　O'er the land of the free and the home of the brave.

And where is that band who so *vauntingly* swore
That the *havoc* of war and the battle's confusion.
A home and a country should leave us no more?
Their blood has washed out their foul footstep's pollution.
No refuge could save the *hireling* and slave
From the terror of flight or the gloom of the grave;
   And the star spangled banner in triumph doth wave
   O'er the land of the free and the home of the brave.

hailed _____ gleaming _____ perilous _____ ramparts _____
gallantly _____ spangled _____ foe _____ haughty _____
host _____ dread _____ reposes _____ discloses _____
vauntingly _____ havoc _____ hireling _____

Used by permission from: *Celebrating America* by Sharon Belshaw and Candy Carter ($4.50 postpaid from Contemporary Press, Box 1524, San Jose, Calif. 95109)

Research Have students research national anthems (often included in encyclopedia articles). Small groups might research the music of different countries, presenting their findings to the class by singing, playing records, and so on.

Art

Art and language arts can be correlated to the advantage of both areas of study. Throughout this textbook we have explored ways of enhancing the study of language and literature by utilizing art activities. Additional ideas are described in this section focusing on bringing art into the language arts period.

Vocabulary development Many art activities can be developed that are directly related to reading words. Students can relate the meaning of words and the printed form of the word, thus:

This kind of wordplay is enjoyable and helps create a positive attitude toward working with words. Display student examples on a bulletin board captioned: WORDS WITH PERSONALITY. Encourage students to add to the display as they discover new examples.

An illustrated chart might feature ART WORDS that will add to student vocabulary, for instance:

complementary colors	palette
easel	template
perspective	shading
mosaic	sculpture

"*Cutting A Title*," as shown on page 379 is an interesting way of bringing art and literature together. The title of a favorite book is written carefully along the folded side of a sheet of paper. Students should write in a deliberately elongated style. When cut out, the title is opened up to form a lovely design for the cover of a retelling of the story with original illustra-

"Word Play" from *Reading Games* by Iris Tiedt ($2.50, Contemporary Press, Box 1524, San Jose, Calif. 95109)

tions. If you turn the page around, you can read the title of a popular book, *Where the Lilies Bloom* by Vera and Bill Cleaver.

Dioramas offer another artful means for bringing reading and art activities together. Constructed in a large cardboard carton, this diorama depicts *Petronella* by Jay Williams (Parents).

diorama

Art history You might introduce students to different kinds of art, for example:

impressionism
cubism

surrealism
modern

Display prints borrowed from the local library or purchased from a local art museum. Have students write short biographies of artists to display with their work. They can learn to recognize the styles of such artists as:

Van Gogh
Cezanne

Wyeth
Miró

Introduce them to the most well-known of the painters. Make a point of looking at the work of American artists also. This study can be supplemented with an exciting field trip to see paintings that may be in a local museum.

Books about art Examine some of the fine children's books that describe art techniques, crafts, and biographical presentations of noted artists. Look in the 700 section for books on everything from art history to stained glass windows. Representative examples include:

Ruskin, Ariane. *The Pantheon Story of Art for Young People*. Pantheon.
Mac Agy, Douglas. *Going for a Walk with a Line; A Step into the World of Modern Art*. Doubleday.
Glubok, Shirley. *The Art of Ancient Rome*. Harper.
Moore, Lamont. *The First Book of Architecture*. Watts.
Gaba, Lester. *Soap Sculpture*. Watts.
Weiss, Harvey. *Ceramics; From Clay to Kiln*. Young Scott Books.

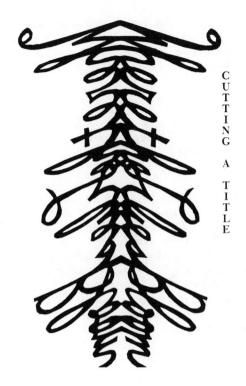

C
U
T
T
I
N
G

A

T
I
T
L
E

Slobodkin, Louis. *The First Book of Drawing*. Watts.
Awaki, Chiyo. *Origami in the Classroom*. Tuttle.
Fisher, Leonard Everett. *The Weavers*. Watts.
Chase, Alice E. *Famous Paintings; An Introduction to Art*. Platt.
Atwood, Ann. *New Moon Cove; A Collection of Photographs*. Scribner.

INJECTING LANGUAGE ARTS STRATEGIES
AND CONTENT INTO OTHER SUBJECT AREAS

Many language arts methods of teaching lend themselves to instruction in such subjects as the social studies, science, mathematics, art, and music. In this section we will focus on several types of instructional strategies that could be readily adapted to use in any area of study, for example:

Clustering to Explore a Topic
Reader's Theater Stimulates Reading and Oral Language
La Dictée: An Integrated Language Arts Approach
Vocabulary Development Across the Curriculum
Incorporating Literature in All Areas of Study
A Unit of Study: Focusing on the Future

Many other opportunities for incorporating language arts strategies across the curriculum are suggested throughout *The Language Arts Handbook*. Check the index for additional suggestions under specific subject names as well as such topics as Multicultural Teaching.

Clustering to Explore a Topic

The technique of clustering ideas is a versatile strategy that can be used across the curriculum. Use it to assess attitudes, to help students open up an idea, to determine what students know about a concept, or to outline a topic.

Exploring an idea Clustering provides an amazingly effective device for opening up an idea, a kind of warm-up exercise that prepares students for writing about a subject. It is highly individualized, drawing from each student's personal view of the world.

Introduce clustering by giving the students a word that all understand and can relate to, for example: home, school, happiness, jealousy, Christmas, ugly, friend. Work on the board together to demonstrate the technique. The given word is placed in a circle in the center of the space. Then students free-associate with this topic. Place suggested words around the center word. Words that seem to be related are written near each other to form a cluster, thus:

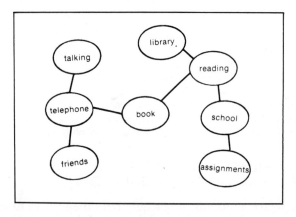

Clustering ideas around the word *book* will probably take only five–ten minutes. When most students have finished, have the class break into small groups of five–six people. Each student can share the associations with *book* orally, explaining the reason for an unusual association. The oral sharing can be followed by having each student write a paragraph focusing on one of the clusters on his or her paper.

Once students are familiar with this technique, you can use it in a variety of ways using varied content. Clustering is an excellent assessment strategy as well as a way students can probe the parameters of a subject they plan to research.

Assessing student knowledge   Clustering can be used to find out what students know (or don't know) about any subject. If you plan to introduce a new concept or area of study, have students cluster their ideas related to that concept as a kind of pretest. You may discover, for instance, that several students already have a surprising store of information that you can tap. Another student may reveal a gross misconception about the subject. This preassessment will enable you to teach the unit more effectively.

You might, for example, have students cluster independently around such words as:

magnet   rainbow
London   Texas
black   Civil War

Collect these clusters for your use in diagnosing student learning needs. Then, construct a cluster on the board with the students contributing orally as you write the words in appropriate groupings. This approach to introducing a topic stimulates student interest in the subject.

Organizing information   A student who is preparing a report on your state might cluster the ideas to aid in organizing information as in this example for California:

Reader's Theater Stimulates Reading
and Oral Language

Reader's theater is an exciting strategy for exploring and sharing literature that can be related to any subject area. It engages students in reading varied kinds of literature and then presenting it orally, an excellent culminating activity for a unit of study. Students usually work in groups as they plan a presentation, selecting and preparing material to be presented, rehearsing the production, and then making the presentation before an audience. Poetry, plays, fiction, and nonfiction can be incorporated in this type of organized oral reading by a group of students. Follow the steps described below:

STEP 1: PLANNING A PRESENTATION

Reader's theater is a strategy for making a presentation. Usually there are no props or costuming. Readers may sit on stools or chairs. It can be used with any topics or themes and with different purposes in mind. The range of possibilities includes:

Sharing stories with primary grade children
A holiday program for parents
Findings related to a period of history
Study of the life and writings of one author, for example, Mark Twain
Summary of a unit on mammals

STEP 2: SELECTING MATERIALS

Suppose, for example, you decide to participate in a Halloween program for parents. Students will need to investigate varied kinds of materials that might be used; for example:

Short stories
Excerpts from longer books
Poetry
Lyrics from songs
Factual information about superstitions
Original writing by students
Paragraphs about symbols for this holiday, for example: black cat, witch

You need also to think about timing and variety of materials to be presented. Pacing and the flow of the whole presentation will determine the kinds of materials you select—both prose and poetry, longer selections contrasted to one-liners, humor following a more serious reading.

Visit the library with the class to search out what kinds of materials are available at your school or from the local public library. Ask the librarian to suggest resources and introduce students to subject entries in the card catalog. Refer to the *Children's Catalog*, which lists books according to subjects and describes the contents and level of difficulty.

Do not try to find material that is already written in play form. Students will learn a lot by analyzing the material and deciding on how the roles should be developed. They can rewrite and arrange the material as needed.

STEP 3: PREPARING THE SCRIPT

You need multiple copies of the material to be presented. Xeroxed copies of a folktale are particularly good because you can write on the copies freely and even cut out paragraphs, as desired. As children read the story, they should be encouraged to add their own embellishments just as the ancient storytellers did.

The first step in preparing a script is to eliminate all references to the speaker (he said, she added). Since the speaker will read appropriately, these explanations are not necessary. Passages that are too long and descriptive may be shortened.

A list of the roles involved in the story should be made. In the well-known story, "Little Red Riding Hood," for example, there are:

Red Riding Hood	The wolf
Her mother	The woodsman
Her grandmother	

One person will be selected to read each role. A sixth reader will be designated as the narrator, who reads the introduction and descriptive passages. After the roles have been identified, the script can be marked with names at the left where each one begins speaking.

Seven copies of the script (one for the director) should be prepared. Scripts are mounted inside folded construction paper or manila folders so that each one is neat and does not distract from the audience's attention to the story as it is read.

STEP 4: REHEARSING THE PRODUCTION

Once the theme has been selected and materials to be presented are prepared as scripts, the show is ready for rehearsal. Students are motivated to make the presentation as good as possible, so they will practice devotedly as they polish their reading abilities. One student should act as the director, making suggestions about pacing, clarity, and so forth. The director may have assistants who observe and make suggestions.

STEP 5: THE PRESENTATION

When the reader's theater presentation has been rehearsed two to three times, it is ready to share with other groups in the school. You may want to present it to another class at the same level or to a younger group of children, depending on the content and interest level. Parents are pleased to hear children perform either in an individual classroom or before the Parent-Teacher Association.

Following is an example of the kind of story that can be adapted for reader's theater. "Molly Whuppie," taken from Joseph Jacobs' *English Fairy Tales* (Putnam, 1892), is one of the few tales in which the female is a *shero!* This tale requires a group of four girls (three princesses and the giant's wife) and a boy (the giant) plus one or two persons for narrators. Dialogue should be added freely for any of these parts as the students literally retell this old tale following the oral tradition in folklore.

Molly Whuppie

Once upon a time there was a man and a wife who had too many children, and they could not get meat for them, so they took the three youngest and left them in a wood. They travelled and travelled and could see never a house. It began to be dark, and they were hungry. At last they saw a light and made for it; it turned out to be a house. They knocked at the door, and a woman came to it, who said: "What do you want?" They said: "Please let us in and give us something to eat." The woman said: "I can't do that, as my man is a giant, and he would kill you if he comes home." They begged hard. "Let us stop for a little while," said they, "and we will go away before he comes." So she took them in, and set them down before the fire and gave them milk and bread; but just as they had begun to eat, a great knock came at the door, and a dreadful voice said:

"Fee, fie, fo, fum,
I smell the blood of some earthly one.

Who have you there, wife?" "Eh," said the wife, "it's three poor lassies cold and hungry, and they will go away. Ye won't touch 'em, man." He said nothing, but ate up a big supper, and ordered them to stay all night. Now he had three lassies of his own, and they were to sleep in the same bed with the three strangers. The youngest of the three strange lassies was called Molly Whuppie, and she was very clever. She noticed that before they went to bed the giant put straw ropes round her neck and her sisters', and around his own lassies' necks, he put gold chains. So Molly took care and did not fall asleep, but waited till she was sure every one was sleeping sound. Then she slipped out of the bed, and took the straw ropes off her own and her sisters' necks, and took the gold chains off the giant's lassies. She put the straw ropes on the giant's lassies and the gold chains on herself and her sisters, and lay down. And in the middle of the night up rose the giant, armed with a great club, and felt for the necks with the straw. It was dark. He took his own lassies out of bed on the floor, and battered them until they were dead, and then lay down again, thinking he had managed well. Molly thought it time she and her sisters were off and away, so she wakened them and told them to be quiet, and they slipped out of the house. They all got out safe, and they ran and ran, and never stopped until morning, when they saw a grand house before them. It turned out to be a king's house: so Molly went in, and told her story to the king. He said: "Well, Molly, you are a clever girl, and you have managed well; but, if you would manage better, and go back, and steal the giant's sword that hangs on the back of his bed, I would give your eldest sister my eldest son to marry." Molly said she would try. So she went back, and managed to slip into the giant's house and crept in below the bed. The giant came home, and ate up a great supper, and went to bed. Molly waited until he was snoring, and she crept out, and reached over the giant and got down the sword; but just as she got it out over the bed it gave a rattle, and up jumped the giant, and Molly ran out the door and the sword with her; and she ran, and he ran, till they came to the "Bridge of one hair"; and she got over, but he couldn't and he says, "Woe worth ye, Molly Whuppie! never ye come again." And she says: "Twice yet, carle, I'll come to Spain." So Molly took the sword to the king, and her sister was married to his son.

Well, the king he says: "Ye've managed well, Molly; but if ye would manage better, and steal the purse that lies below the giant's pillow, I would marry your second sister to my second son." And Molly said she would try. So she set out for the giant's house, and slipped in, and hid again below the bed, and waited till the giant had eaten his supper, and was snoring sound asleep. She slipped out and slipped her hand below the pillow, and got out the purse; but just as she was going out the giant wakened, and ran after her; and she ran, and he ran, till they came to the "Bridge of one hair," and she got over, but he couldn't and he said, "Woe worth ye, Molly Whuppie! never you come again." "Once yet, carle," quoth she, "I'll come to Spain." So Molly took the purse to the king, and her second sister was married to the king's second son.

After that the king says to Molly: "Molly, you are a clever girl, but if you would do better yet, and steal the giant's ring that he wears on his finger, I will give you my youngest son for yourself." Molly said she would try. So back she goes to the giant's house, and hides herself below the bed. The giant wasn't long ere he came home, and, after he had eaten a great big supper, he went to his bed, and shortly was snoring loud. Molly crept out and reached over the bed, and got hold of the giant's hand, and she pulled and she pulled until she got off the ring; but just as she got it off the giant got up, and gripped her by the hand and he says, "Now I have caught you, Molly Whuppie, and, if I had done as much ill to you as ye have done to me, what would ye do to me?"

Molly says: "I would put you into a sack, and I'd put the cat inside wi' you, and the dog aside you, and a needle and thread and a shears and I'd hang you up upon the wall, and I'd go to the wood, and choose the thickest stick I could get, and I would come home, and take you down, and hang you till you were dead."

"Well, Molly," says the giant, "I'll just do that to you."

So he gets a sack, and puts Molly into it, and the cat and the dog beside her, and a needle and thread and shears, and hangs her up upon the wall, and goes to the wood to choose a stick.

Molly she sings out: "Oh, if ye saw what I see."

"Oh," says the giant's wife, "What do ye see, Molly?"

But Molly never said a word but, "Oh, if ye saw what I see!"

The giant's wife begged that Molly would take her up into the sack till she would see what Molly saw. So Molly took the shears and cut a hole in the sack, and took out the needle and thread with her, and jumped down and helped the giant's wife up into the sack and sewed up the hole.

The giant's wife saw nothing, and began to ask to get down again; but Molly never minded, but hid herself at the back of the door. Home came the giant, and a great big tree in his hand, and he took down the sack, and began to batter it. His wife cried, "It's me, man"; but the dog barked and the cat mewed, and he did not know his wife's voice. But Molly came out from the back of the door, and the giant saw her and he after her; and he ran, and she ran, till they came to the "Bridge of one hair," and she got over but he couldn't; and he said, "Woe worth you, Molly Whuppie! never you come again." Never more, carle," quoth she, "will I come again to Spain."

So Molly took the ring to the king, and she was married to his youngest son, and she never saw the giant again.

Other stories that reverse traditional roles include the following:

Petronella by Jay Williams (Parents)
(The princess wins the prince, but who wants him?)
"The Straw Ox" a Russian tale in many collections
(The old woman is the smart one with ideas.)

La Dictée: An Integrated Language Arts Approach[2]

La dictée, an exciting, time-tested strategy for teaching composition, offers an effective, systematic method of using dictation to teach writing and reading comprehension as well as writing skills that can be used in language

---

[2]Iris M. Tiedt. *La Dictée: An Integrated Language Arts Approach to Teaching Composition.* Urbana, Ill.: ERIC, 1982.

arts classes as well as in the social studies or science classroom. *"Ecrire sous la dictée"*—to write from dictation—is described by Rollo Brown in *How the French Boy Learns to Write,* a classic study first published by Harvard University in 1915 and reprinted by the National Council of Teachers of English in 1963. By studying French methods of teaching writing, Brown hoped to aid teachers in improving composition instruction. As I have adapted it, *la dictée* focuses on teaching writing, but it also incorporates thinking, listening, and speaking skills; uses literature to provide stimulating instructional material; teaches specific content and comprehension skills; and stresses the interrelationships between reading and writing. While integrating language arts instruction, *la dictée* also offers opportunities to work across the curriculum.

La dictée is a planned presentation that requires careful selection of the dictation passage, knowledge of the literature from which the passage is taken, and development of appropriate follow-up exercises. The selection and presentation of the literature make this dictation method unique. The kinds of follow-up activities employed determine the extent of learning that will take place. This list of procedures explains how *la dictée* is used in the classroom as applied to a specific example:

1. *Select the literature to be used.* According to your purpose and the needs of your students, choose fiction or nonfiction, a trade (library) book or textbook, but do select prose that is well-written, worthy of being emulated, for example: *Dragonwings* by Laurence Yep (Harper, available in paperback)

2. *Introduce the book and author to your students.* A book suitable for preteens and teenage readers, *Dragonwings* was a Newbery Honor book in 1976. It was written by a California author who was inspired by the account of a Chinese immigrant who built a flying machine in 1909. A sensitive novel, it provides historical information about the Chinese American's cultural heritage, and therefore, is pertinent for the social studies curriculum.

   Read the book before presenting it to the students, of course. You might introduce the book by reading the first few paragraphs, beginning: "Ever since I can remember, I had wanted to know about the Land of the Golden Mountain, but my mother had never wanted to talk about it." Explain that the main character, Moon Shadow, lives in China with his mother and grandmother in the early 1900s, but his father, Windrider, lives in San Francisco's Chinatown. Fascinating information about the writing of this book is available in "Writing Dragonwings" by Laurence Yep,[3] which could be read to junior and senior high school students.

3. *Select one paragraph as the dictation passage.* Choose a paragraph that contains stimulating information. Also, examine the sentence structures and the conventions of spelling and punctuation to see that they are appropriately challenging, yet not too difficult for the class. I chose the following paragraph from *Dragonwings* because it describes an important decision, demonstrates the use of the semicolon, and shows students the difference between a common and a proper noun:

---

[3]Laurence Yep, "Writing Dragonwings," *Reading Teacher,* January 1977. Also reprinted in *Multicultural Teaching* by Pamela Tiedt and Iris Tiedt. (Boston: Allyn & Bacon, Inc. 1979).

Mother had talked quite a bit about him and so had Grandmother; but that too was not the same. They were speaking about a young man who had lived in the Middle Kingdom, not a man who had endured the hardships and loneliness of living in the demon land. I knew he made kites; but as marvelous as his kites were, he and I could not spend the rest of our lives flying kites. I was afraid of the Golden Mountain, and yet my father, who lives there, wanted me to join him. I only knew that there was a certain rightness in life—the feeling you got when you did something the way you knew you should. I owed it to Father to obey him in everything—even if it meant going to such a fearful place as the Golden Mountain. And really, how really frightening could it be if Hand Clap wanted to go back? I turned to Mother and Grandmother. "I want to go," I said.

Before reading the paragraph to the students, I explained what led up to the event described.

4.   *Read the selection aloud and discuss the meaning.* After reading the paragraph to the class, I asked questions designed to clarify the meaning, for instance:
   a.   Who are the characters participating in this scene?
   b.   Who is Hand Clap?
   c.   Who is telling the story?
   d.   What is the fearful place, The Golden Mountain? How did it get that name?
   e.   Why did Moon Shadow decide he would go to The Golden Mountain?
5.   *Dictate the paragraph to the students.* Read a sentence while students listen. Insist that they not write as you read the first time. You may want them to say the sentence aloud at this time. Then, repeat the sentence slowly as they write it. To teach good listening skills, do not repeat more than the two times described.
6.   *Have students correct their copies of the paragraph.* After dictating the full passage, read it aloud slowly as you explain special features of punctuation or spelling that may have caused difficulty. You may choose to have several students write each sentence on the chalkboard so that students see the full sentence as you discuss it. (The use of the dash in the sample passage is less common, so that few students will have used that punctuation; you may choose to use a comma.) The corrected copy of the dictation will be used as a study guide and is placed in the student's notebook.

This procedure should be repeated once a week or every other week depending on the number of followup activities you plan.

Extending *la dictée* presentations   An integral part of *la dictée* is the follow-up activity, which can focus on developing specific writing skills. One or more activities can be developed, as described in these examples.

1.   *Repetition of the same dictation.* Dictating the same passage a second time is recommended to challenge students to perfect their ability to write the sentences without error. Repeating the same passage a third or fourth time after some time has passed will reinforce the students' knowledge of the writing skills exemplified in a particular passage.
2.   *Exploring sentence patterns.* Choose one or more sentences from the passage to serve as models that students can imitate. Show them how to identify the

structural features of a sentence that form a pattern, thus: _____had ____ and so had _____; but that _____.
Then, students can use this pattern with which to construct new sentences like this one:
John had lied and so had Mildred; but that didn't make any difference now.

3. *Expanding vocabulary.* Use words from the dictated passage as the basis for vocabulary study. Discuss the meaning of such words as marvelous or loneliness, suggesting other words that we associate with these concepts. Have students explore synonyms for common words used in the passage, thus:

had talked
had described
had discussed
had told
had spoken
had shared
had conversed

Discuss how the grammatical structure of the sentence would have to be changed if the verbs listed were used instead of the one the author chose.

4. *Developing oral language.* Students can retell the happening described in this passage, trying to include as much detail as possible. They might also act out the scene expanding the dialogue as they deem appropriate.

5. *Responding to literature through writing.* This passage suggests a number of topics with which young readers can identify, for example:

How would you feel if you were Moon Shadow? Would you have made the same decision?
Write the dialogue that you think might have taken place between Moon Shadow and his father, Windrider, when they met in San Francisco.

In addition to the examples given here, you might work with sentence combining, the Cloze technique, or the Venn diagram. Each selection will suggest varied kinds of language arts activities that evolve directly out of *la dictée* procedures.

Vocabulary Development in All Subject Areas

Vocabulary study is of particular importance in that it permeates the entire elementary school curriculum. A student who has developed an inquisitive attitude toward words will reach out to the words of science, the words of history; each one will be constantly aware of the intrigue of words. The alert teacher will utilize opportunities that arise to further word interest whether they occur during the language period or in the middle of a mathematics lesson. Included in this section are suggested activities which relate interest in words to subjects other than English itself.

SCIENCE is a subject which offers many fascinating new words. Begin a study of words related to space, medicine, birds, cats, insects, and so on. Have students create a display of words with related pictures.

- *Words of Science* by Isaac Asimov (Houghton Mifflin) is an excellent collection of words in this field. The story behind each word is explained in readable fashion by a reputable scientist whom some will recognize as a writer of science fiction.
- CATEGORIES is an interesting word game that can feature knowledge in science, thus:

	Space	*Biology*
A	astronaut	ant
T		
O		
M		
I		
C		

- Word quizzes can focus attention on scientific knowledge. Have students compose questions like these:

With what word does the name of this animal rhyme? GNU _____
Where would you expect to find an EGRET? _____
What is the origin of our word HELICOPTER? _____
What does the prefix TELE mean? _____

MATHEMATICS can be helpful in furthering interest in word study as we begin thinking about the words which denote number and the processes used in computing. The study of numerology also provides fascinating words which are intriguing to the young student.

- THE ORIGIN OF NUMBER WORDS can be the title of an interesting collection of words related to numbers. Have a page for each numeral, on which are presented words related to that numeral. The page on which a large 1 is printed would bear some of these words with information about their origin:

one	primary	prime
first	unison	unicorn
solo	unity	primer
sole	unanimous	lone

This number booklet might be part of a learning center. Students could use dictionaries to expand the lists of number-related words. Later there could be an interesting class discussion of the number–word discoveries.

- The magic powers with which numbers were supposed to be endowed can provide material for challenging research. Information gathered might be presented on a bulletin board, for example, bearing a large cut-paper 3, around which is mounted information about the magic properties of this number and its influence.

    It is related to the Holy Trinity.
    Three strikes in baseball.
    Three magic wishes.
    I'll give you three guesses.
    Third time's a lucky charm.

SOCIAL STUDIES provides a wealth of word-centered activities as we discuss words in history, the history of words, words related to travel and the map, words we have borrowed from other lands and languages, words in propaganda, and so on.

- WORD CROSSINGS are provocative ways of showing relationships between words. The main word is supplied while definitions are given for the other words to be identified as in this example:

```
              F
1.   N    O    R    M    A    N    D    Y
2.        P    A    R    I    S
              N
              C
3.        S    E    I    N    E
```

The word FRANCE would be printed in place with spaces for the other letters. Definitions might be: (1) section, (2) city, (3) river. Students can construct word crossings for names of people, regions, countries, etc.

- ACROSTICS also lend themselves to words in social studies. An acrostic can be developed for a person's name, a country, river, city, and so on. Here is an acrostic for FRANCE:

```
F    R    A    N    C
R    H    O    N    E
A    L    P    S    —
N    A    P    O    L    E    O    N
C    A    L    A    I    S    —    —
E    I    F    F    E    L
```

What is the secret of this puzzle? (The first letter of each word read vertically spells a word.) Definitions are written to assist the solution of the puzzle.

- *Words on the Map* and *Words from the Myths* (Houghton Mifflin) are two titles by Isaac Asimov which explore words related to areas in the social sciences.

ART offers not only an interesting vocabulary of its own but also techniques and media for enhancing the study of words related to other subjects.

- WORD CUTTINGS are made by writing a word on the fold of a sheet of paper as indicated. The word is then cut out without disturbing the fold. Opened flat, the word cutting forms an attractive design, thus:

- WORD COLLAGES provide an unusual method for displaying words which interest students. Each student clips words from magazines selecting words on one particular theme—FRENCH WORDS, SPRING WORDS, PROVOCATIVE WORDS, R WORDS—or a potpourri of words can be included. The collection of words is then arranged over a poster with pieces of colored paper used to unite the clipped words and to add color and interest to the collage.
- WORD INTERPRETATIONS can be made by each individual. Each person selects a word—FREEDOM, MUSIC, COLOR, BLUE, TRADE, LANGUAGE, SCIENCE, HEAT, and so on. He then develops a poster on which the word appears as well as drawings which interpret the meaning of this word for the individual.
- WORD BOOKS can be tastefully enhanced by the addition of an attractive cover prepared through simple art techniques—stenciling, crayon resist, dribbling of paint in patterns, etc. The form of a booklet can also add interest to the project—the long, slim form; paper cut in an unusual shape; varied types of ties. Attention to printing and the arrangement of a title on the page will assist students in preparing a more effective booklet, a work in which they can take pride.

Poetry and other forms of literature add interest to all areas of the curriculum. As you plan any unit of study, therefore, be sure to think about how you can use literature to enhance learning. Following are ideas for incorporating poetry in the total elementary school curriculum.

Music Many familiar poems have been set to music; for example, some of the nursery rhymes, "Grandfather's Clock," Christmas carols, "Twinkle, Twinkle, Little Star," "The Star-Spangled Banner," "Home, Home, Sweet Home," and many others. Children are intrigued by seeing the verses of the songs in the form of a poem.

Interest in singing poems that someone else has set to music can lead to the selection of a poem by each child for which a melody can be written. A piano, small xylophone, or tonette will assist the students in producing the music they feel is appropriate to the poem selected. They will want to learn something about musical notation in order to write their songs with the words placed below the notes, thus:

Hum-ming bird, Hum-ming bird, With throat of ru - by red.

Come tip the blooms in Ma - ry's flow - er bed.

The original poetry of children can also be set to a melody which they can sing for the class or teach to other members of the class. This technique lends further importance to the poetry produced by the child. Their own poem set to music can be mounted inside a decorated "song sheet" to be used as a gift for their parents. Music can also be used to assist the development of an experience in either reading or writing poetry.

- Play appropriate music before reading a poem. Before reading the poem "Sea Fever," for example, play music which suggests the surf. Oriental music can set the stage for the writing of haiku.
- Music can also be played while poetry is being read. A soft musical background serves to provide a theme and unites a group of poems. Play Christmas music softly while Christmas poetry is read.
- Play records of Bob Dylan, the Beatles, or Pete Seeger. These modern poets and song writers will be very familiar to youngsters.

Art Art techniques offer varied, challenging ways to enhance the pleasure of poetry.

- Each student can select a poem to portray in a poetry broadside (poster). The poem can be typed or printed on a card or sheet of paper which is mounted on the broadside in some appropriate place. One youngster chose to print his poem, "The Balloon Man," on a bright yellow balloon which floated through the air above a town. Another concealed several poems about clouds beneath cloud shapes which were lifted to reveal the poems, "White Sheep," "The Cloud," and "Clouds."
- The collage, an abstract presentation of an idea or theme, is another excellent medium for presenting a poem. In order to construct a collage the student must first examine the poem selected for elements which can be portrayed. Some poems, for example, "The Owl and the Pussy-cat," contain many concrete references which can be included in a collage. Other poems which convey a mood will require a thoughtful use of color, texture, and shapes to help convey that mood.
- Crayons can be used to tell the story of a poem read. "See if you can draw a picture which will make the class know which poem you have in mind." Each picture can then be presented to the class to see if anyone can guess which poem is pictured. The artist can read the poem he/she selected.
- Present artful interpretations of poetry using calligraphy, as shown here.

the **Rainbow**

Boats sail on the rivers,
    And ships sail on the seas;
But clouds that sail across the sky
    Are prettier far than these.

There are bridges on the rivers,
    As pretty as you please;
But the bow that bridges heaven,
    And overtops the trees,
And builds a road from earth to sky,
    Is prettier far than these.

Christina Rossetti

Social science   Much good poetry treats topics related to the areas of history and geography. One immediately thinks of Stephen Vincent Benét and his wife, Rosemary Carr Benét, who have written many fine poems depicting the figures of American history. A collection of these poems is entitled: *Book of Americans* (Rinehart, 1933). Poems can be read aloud by either the teacher or a child to add interest to a study of history. "Abraham Lincoln" and "Nancy Hanks" are two titles which could be featured during a study of the Civil War. Other ideas relating poetry to social studies include:

- An exciting way to present background material for a study of foreign countries is through the reading of poetry by poets from these countries. Good translations of many poets are available, and it is interesting, too, to use short passages in the original language.
  Here is the refrain of a poem by Spanish poet José de Espronceda, "Canción del Pirata."

> Que es mi barco mi tesoro;
> Que es mi Dios la libertad;
> Mi ley la fuerza y el viento;
> Mi única patria la mar.

> *SONG OF THE PIRATE*
> Tr. by Iris Tiedt

> My boat is my treasure;
> Liberty is my god;
> My law the force and the wind;
> My only homeland the sea.

- Other poets can be explored as different countries are featured. Suggested here are several poets whose work is available in translation:

France: Victor Hugo
Scandinavia: Dag Hammarskjold
Russia: Yevgeny Yevtushenko, Boris Pasternak
Japan: Bashō, Buson
England: Wordsworth, Shelley

Featuring Japanese poetry in Asian studies   Haiku is a three-line verse form which originated in thirteenth-century Japan. Early masters of the form include Buson, Boncho, Moritake, Bashō, Sōkan, and many others. Authentic haiku has several distinct characteristics which have been followed rather consistently by Japanese writers and those who have translated their work:

1. The poem consists of only three lines totaling 17 syllables.
   Line 1:   5 syllables
   Line 2:   7 syllables
   Line 3:   5 syllables
2. The season, location, and references to nature are included.
3. There is no rhyme and few articles or pronouns are used.
4. The poem contrasts diverse ideas, is subtle, symbolic.

Here are two examples of haiku translated from the original Japanese:

First cold showers fall.
Even little monkey wants
A wee coat of straw

Bashō

All sky disappears
The earth's land has gone away;
Still the snowflakes fall.

Hashin

In popular use today many poets have taken liberties with this versatile verse form. American haiku have been written about a wide variety of topics, and lines have not always remained the prescribed length. Translator and poet Harry Behn comments, "Any translation into English should be, so I believe, what the author might have done if English had been his language." These rules that have grown out of Zen should be followed as much as possible in "the same packaging," but writing haiku is not a game. "It is not easy to be simple."[4]

An excellent source of information for the teacher who wants to know more about haiku is *An Introduction to Haiku* by Harold Anderson (Doubleday).

Children are most successful with this brief verse form if emphasis is rightly placed on the thoughts they are expressing rather than on the confining form. The beauty of haiku for children is that they do succeed in producing charming examples which compare well with those created by adult writers. The following examples corroborate this point.[5]

The sun shines brightly.
With its glowing flames shooting
It goes down at night.

Ricky

The old cypress tree,
So beautiful by the rocks,
Has been there for years.

Marjorie

After first thinking about an idea they wish to express, the students are encouraged to write it on paper. They can then examine their own written thought to determine how it can be divided into three parts. Experimentation with word arrangement, imagery, changing the order of the lines, and choice of words used should be encouraged as the poem is developed.

---

[4]Harry Behn *Chrysalis; Concerning Children and Poetry* (New York: Harcourt, Brace & World, Inc. 1968), p. 39.

[5]Fourth-grade children at the Van Meter School, Los Gatos, Calif.

The deceptively simple form requires more delicate handling than does free verse. Here are ideas for working with haiku in the classroom:

- One way of introducing a class to haiku is through the reading of a number of examples such as those in *Cricket Songs* by Harry Behn. After reading a number of these short poems, provide each student with a duplicate sheet (or write on the board), containing several examples of haiku. Let them discover the haiku pattern, the subject treated, and other characteristics by rereading the poems, thus:

Count the number of syllables in each line. How many syllables does each line contain?

1_____ 2_____3 _____

Is this true of each poem?_____

What season of the year is indicated in each haiku?

_____

- Japanese poetry makes us think of cherry blossoms or other spring blossoms. Use a twig of any flowering fruit tree to prepare an attractive display to motivate the writing of haiku. The flowers may be combined with pictures mounted on a bulletin board or music may be played to assist the development of a mood for haiku.
- Type haiku written by a class on a duplicating master using two long columns so that the folded sheets will produce two long, slim pages. Cut the duplicated sheets to form pages of an attractive booklet, and make a decorative cover.

- Motifs for booklet covers should be appropriate to the poetry. Students can experiment with brush stroking to simulate Japanese writing or the reeds, bamboo, flowers, and so on, associated with their art.
  The word HAIKU can be printed using letters that have an oriental appearance.
- Two films on haiku well worth investigating are:

In a Spring Garden. Pictures by Ezra Jack Keats. Weston Woods Studios, 6 min., color, n.d. (See the book on which this film is based, too: *In a Spring Garden* by Richard Lewis.)
The Day Is Two Feet Long. Weston Woods Studios, 9 min., color, 1968.

- A most rewarding art experience which correlates well with the writing of haiku is the blowing of ink with a straw. Washable black ink is applied in a swath near the bottom of an unlined file card (or any nonabsorbent paper). The wet ink is then blown with a straw to direct the ink in the desired direction. Blowing across the ink causes it to branch attractively. When the ink is dry, tiny dabs of bright tempera may be applied with a toothpick to add spring blossoms to the bare branch. The student then writes the haiku on the card below the flowering branch, and the card is used for display or as a gift for parents.

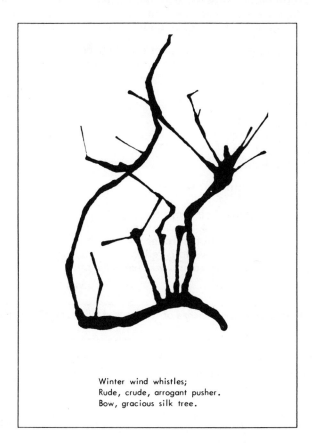

Winter wind whistles;
Rude, crude, arrogant pusher.
Bow, gracious silk tree.

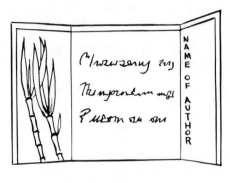

Folded slightly overlapping...
...tied with ribbon

- For an authentic presentation of haiku use rice paper (or thin onion skin or tissue paper) mounted inside colored paper. The poem is written (a felt pen will write on thin paper) together with an oriental motif—reeds, moon over water, flowering branch—and the author's name. The cover is folded so that the front flaps overlap slightly as in the sketch. A ribbon is then tied around the folder, which is ready for presentation as a gift, as shown.

Tanka are five-lined Japanese poems which contain a haiku (the first three lines). Like the haiku, they are unrhymed and follow a well-defined syllabic pattern with a total of 31 syllables for the entire poem:

Line 1:   5 syllables
Line 2:   7 syllables
Line 3:   5 syllables
Line 4:   7 syllables
Line 5:   7 syllables

Following is an example of tanka:

> Silver raindrops fall:
> A puddle of water stands.
>   Ocean before me,
> All the world is reflected.
> Look hard and you see black mud.
>
>   Irene Tabata

A beautiful book on tanka is *The Seasons of Time*, edited by Virginia O'Baron and published by Dial Press.

Poems related to all subjects   As you search through a poetry collection, note the poems that are related to topics in different subjects. Sample titles include:[6]

---

[6]Poems listed are in: *Time for Poetry* by May Hill Arbuthnot and Shelton Root, Jr. (Glenview, Ill.: Scott Foresman & Co., 1968) or *The Sound of Poetry* by Mary Austin and Queenie B. Mills (Boston: Allyn & Bacon, Inc., 1963).

Art

PICTURES TO PAINT OR DRAW

"People" Lois Lenski
"The Balloon Man" Rose Fyleman
"A Modern Dragon" Rowena Bennett
"I'd Like to Be a Lighthouse" Rachel Field
"The Purple Cow" Gelett Burgess

I never saw a purple cow;
I never hope to see one,

But I can tell you anyhow;
I'd rather see than be one!

BEAUTY

"Color" Christina Rossetti
"Brooms" Dorothy Aldis
"Morning" Emily Dickinson
"The Rainbow" Walter de la Mare
"My Heart Leaps Up" William Wordsworth
"Watching Clouds" John Farrar

Music

Science—Enrichment And Interest

Social Studies—Enrichment And Interest

The Eagle

He clasps the crag with crooked hands;
Close to the sun in lonely lands,
Ringed with the azure world, he stands.

The wrinkled sea beneath him crawls;
He watches from his mountain walls,
And like a thunderbolt he falls.

Alfred, Lord Tennyson

I HEAR AMERICA SINGING
Walt Whitman

I hear America singing, the varied carols I hear,
Those of the mechanics, each singing his as it should be,
   blithe and strong,
The carpenter singing his as he measures his plank or beam,
The mason singing his as he makes ready for work
   or leaves off work,
   The boatman singing what belongs to him in his boat,
   the deck hand singing on the steamboat deck,
The shoemaker singing as he sits on his bench, the
   hatter singing as he stands,

The wood-cutter's song, the ploughboy's on his way in the
   morning, or at noon intermission or at sundown,
The delicious singing of the mother, or the
   young wife at work, or the girl sewing or washing,
Each sings what belongs to him or her and to none else,
The day what belongs to the day—at night the party of
   young fellows, robust, friendly,
Singing with open mouths their strong melodious songs.

Mathematics—Enrichment And Interest

"Arithmetic" Carl Sandburg

"Relativity"
There once was a lady named Bright
Who traveled much faster than light.
She set out one day
In a relative way
And returned on the previous night.
Anonymous

"1,2,3" Mother Goose
"One, Two, Buckle My Shoe" Mother Goose
"Ten Little Indian Boys" M. M. Hutchinson
"The Animal Store" Rachel Field

Physical Education—Games And Movement

"The Base Stealer" Robert Francis
"Holding Hands" Lenore M. Link
"This is the way the ladies ride" Mother Goose
"London Bridge"[7]
"A Tisket, A Tasket"
Jump rope songs:
   "Teddy Bear"
   "Mother, Mother, I Am Sick"
   "Blue Bells, Cockle Sheels"

Presenting poetry as a natural part of the total curriculum is a positive way of introducing literature to children. Any collection of poetry or prose written for children will include selections that you may find useful to enrich subject matter instruction.

A Unit of Study: Focusing on the Future

For educators, the Future is Now. The students in your class will live most of their lives in the twenty-first century. We have a responsibility, therefore, for helping them look forward, for preparing them for a future we cannot

---

[7]Ask children to suggest game songs and songs for jumping rope. An interesting book to explore is Iona Opie and Peter Opie, *The Lore and Language of Schoolchildren* (New York: Oxford Univ. Press, 1967).

know with certitude. As Edwin Reischauer writes in *Toward the 21st Century for a Changing World,* "We need a profound reshaping of education if mankind is to survive in the sort of world that is fast evolving."[8]

Future probes   Cervantes wrote long ago, "Fore-warned; fore-armed." Encourage students to explore the future, to try to predict future events, to perform as futurists. They can literally develop the future and make it theirs through activities such as these:

- Design and develop a utopian or ideal school. From my experience youngsters enjoy this activity. Sometimes we talk to everybody about schools except the pupils who attend.
- List ten predictions for the next ten years. Students can list things that might happen. Another variation would be to have them make their list in order of certainty.

Remember when you make predictions, students have as good a chance of being "right" as the teacher.

- Play with time. Imagine a time machine which could be set for any time in the future. Students could then describe what life would be like for them in the year that they have selected. A variation would be a clock with a spinner. They could spin the year and then describe what it would be like. A further modification would be to have a space-type helmet which youngsters would put on. They could close their eyes and point to a year on a large chart.
- Develop a crystal ball center. Here youngsters can have fun while predicting the future. Have students look into the crystal ball and make ten predictions for the next year.
- Divide the class into two groups or committees to study some topic or institution and how it might develop in the future such as:

clothing	food
transportation	government
schools	communities
families	housing

- Develop a space center that includes a rocket where students can go to write.
- Set up a phone conference with an expert on space.
- Bring in a scientist to talk about his or her work and how it relates to the future.
- Creative writing lends itself to this kind of exploratory activity. Be sure to include task cards in your individualized writing center that focus on the future, for example:

Write a science fiction story.

If you could have any type of future, what would it be?
Write an autobiography of the *next* ten years of your life.

[8]Quoted in James Reston, "Where Are We Going?" *New York Times,* Sept. 22, 1973, p. 45.

Conjecturing We need to develop in students the art of conjecture, to create ways that youngsters can surmise about the future. A center for conjecture might be set up. It could be called "In Search of Tomorrow" or, as Bertrand De Jouvenal calls it, a surmising forum. Let's surmise about the future. Develop task cards like these:

Let your imagination go. What is it like in the year 2000—What does your personal future look like? What are you doing?
What will be the future of schools, of automobiles, of homes, and of cities?

- Have your students list ten goals that they want to achieve in the next week. They can put this in a certain place and when the time comes take them out and see if they have reached their goals. This opens up all kinds of discussion questions, questions of values, questions of long and short term goals, and how to make goals come true.
- Another possibility is to have students list their long-term goals. In activities of this nature, we are not only probing what is known as the *shallow* future, the week or the month, but also the *deep future*, ten or twenty years.
- Remember that world-shaping decisions in the year 2001 will be made by today's first graders. An activity suggested by Jerome Agel is based on the old standby, the spelling bee, but with a switch. Before the start of the bee, the teacher identifies the winner and then distributes to each student cards that have on them the words that the teacher will ask. Included on each child's card are the mistakes the teacher predicts the child will make in the bee. In effect the teacher has determined how the bee will come out before playing the game. Discuss the implications of this experience for knowing how one's life will come out. How do you really feel about having such future knowledge? Do we really want a surprise-free future? Would it spoil all the fun?

Inventing Tomorrow

HOW TO INVENT THE YEAR 2000

	A.D. 2000
Subtract this year	A.D.———
Answer	——— Years until A.D. 2000
Add your age	———
	——— your age in A.D. 2000

In A.D. 2000 I will be living in

In A.D. 2000 I will be spending most of my time

In A.D. 2000 my most significant relationship will be with

In A.D. 2000 our planet's most troublesome problems will be

From Tom McCollough, *Education in the Year 2000* (Morristown, N.J.: General Learning Press, 1974).

Resources for teaching   In preparing to teach the future, we need first to prepare ourselves. One book that I recommend is Alvin Toffler's *Future Shock*. You could read portions of this book to your students. There is a section on education, for example, that might be useful. *Future Shock* is a very readable treatment of the topic, so if you read only one book, this is it.

An excellent magazine that contains interesting, informative articles is *The Futurist*. Examine a sample copy, if possible. The address for this publication is Box 19285, Twentieth Station, Washington, D.C. 20036.

Films for the classroom   Several worthwile films are available for rental through your learning materials center.

Toward the Year 2000 (30 min., color) Distributed in the U.S. by the Film Makers (628 E. Camino Real, Arcadia, Ca 91006).

The 21st Century (30 films, approximately 30 minutes each, color). Distributed in 16mm by McGraw-Hill Films (1221 Ave. of the Americas, New York, NY 10020).

Future Shock (42 min., color) Based on Alvin Toffler's book. Distributed by McGraw-Hill Films.

Books for students   Following is a list of titles that include varied reading levels for young people exploring the future through fiction. Slobodkin's stories are easy to read while the collections of short stories edited by Damon Knight are for advanced readers. All are recommended for your school library.

A Wrinkle in Time	Madeline L'Engle
2001	Arthur C. Clark
The Promise of Space	Arthur C. Clark
S Is for Space	Ray Bradbury
Toward Infinity	Damon Knight, ed.
Worlds to Come	Damon Knight, ed.
Round Trip Space Ship	Louis Slobodkin
Space Ship under the Apple Tree	Louis Slobodkin

SUMMARY

Working with language arts across the curriculum offers exciting possibilities for the elementary school teacher. Content from the social studies, science, and mathematics adds strength to language arts instruction, while innovative instructional strategies such as reader's theater and clustering make for more effective teaching in all areas of study. Art and music enhance oral and written language arts presentations in a mutually supportive mode of instruction. A totally integrated elementary school curriculum reinforces learning and involves students in self-motivated pursuits that inject joy into the teaching–learning encounter, a benefit to both teacher and student.

EXPLORING FURTHER

Kohl, Herbert R., *Math, Writing, & Games in the Open Classroom*. New York: Random House, Inc., 1974.

Maxim, George W., *Learning Centers for Young Children: Ideas and Techniques for the Elementary School Classroom*. New York: Hart Publishing Co., 1977.

Nelson, Mary Ann, *A Comparative Anthology of Children's Literature*. New York: Holt, Rinehart & Winston, Inc., 1972.

Tiedt, Iris M. *Exploring Books with Children*. Boston: Houghton Mifflin, Inc., 1979. Many lists and suggestions throughout book; see especially the chapters on reading, social studies, and science.

Tiedt, Pamela and Iris M. Tiedt, *Multicultural Teaching: A Handbook of Activities, Information, and Resources*. Boston: Allyn & Bacon, Inc., 1979.

Tway, Eileen, ed., *Reading Ladders for Human Relations*. Washington, D.C.: American Council on Education, 1981. (6th ed.) Distributed by the National Council of Teachers of English.

Zavatsky, Bill and Ron Padgett, *The Whole Word Catalogue 1 and 2*. Teachers & Writers Collaborative. New York: McGraw-Hill Book Co., 1977.

APPENDIX

PICTURE BOOKS:
THE CALDECOTT AWARD BOOKS

Picture books for young students may often be useful with older students as well, for they may present "big ideas." Following is the list of books that have been judged outstanding in terms of illustrations each year since 1938, the winner and honor books for the Caldecott Award. Because of the emphasis on illustrations, these books tend to be appropriate for preschool and primary grade children.

1938

Dorothy P. Lathrop, illus. *Animals of the Bible* by Helen Dean Fish. Lippincott.

Honor Books:
Boris Artzybasheff. *Seven Simeons*. Viking
Robert Lawson, illus. *Four and Twenty Blackbirds* by Helen Dean Fish. Stokes.

1939

Thomas Handforth. *Mei Lei.* Doubleday.

Honor Books:
Laura Adams Armer. *The Forest Pool.* Longmans.
Robert Lawson, illus. *Wee Gillis* by Munro Leaf. Viking.
Wanda Gág. *Snow White and the Seven Dwarfs.* Coward-McCann.
Clare Newberry. *Barkis.* Harper & Row.
James Daugherty. *Andy and the Lion.* Viking.

1940

Ingri and Edgar d'Aulaire. *Abraham Lincoln.* Doubleday.

Honor Books:
Berta and Elmer Hader. *Cock-A-Doodle Doo.* Macmillan.
Ludwig Bemelmans. *Madeline.* Viking.
Lauren Ford. *The Ageless Story.* Dodd, Mead.

1941

Robert Lawson. *They Were Strong and Good.* Viking.

Honor Books:
Clare Newberry. *April's Kittens.* Harper & Row.

1942

Robert McCloskey. *Make Way For Ducklings.* Viking.

Honor Books:
Maud and Miska Petersham. *An American ABC.* Macmillan.
Velino Herrera. illus. *In My Mother's House* by Ann Nolan Clark. Viking.
Holling C. Holling. *Paddle-To-The-Sea.* Houghton Mifflin.
Wanda Gág. *Nothing At All.* Coward-McCann.

1943

Virginia Lee Burton. *The Little House.* Houghton Mifflin.

Honor Books:
Mary and Conrad Buff. *Dash and Dart.* Viking.
Clare Newberry. *Marshmallow.* Harper & Row.

1944

Louis Slobodkin, illus. *Many Moons* by James Thurber. Harcourt Brace Jovanovich.

Honor Books:
Elizabeth Orton Jones, illus. *Small Rain: Verses From the Bible* selected by Jessie Orton Jones. Viking.
Arnold E. Bare, illus. *Pierre Pigeon* by Lee Kingman, Houghton Mifflin.
Berta and Elmer Hader. *The Mighty Hunter.* Macmillan.
Jean Charlot, illus. *A Child's Good Night Book* by Margaret Wise Brown. W. R. Scott.
Plao Chan, illus. *Good Luck Horse* by Chin-Yi Chan. Whittlesey.

1945

Elizabeth Orton Jones, illus. *Prayer For A Child* by Rachel Field. Macmillan.

Honor Books:
Tasha Tudor. *Mother Goose.* Walck.
Marie Hall Ets. *In The Forest.* Viking.
Marguerite de Angeli. *Yonie Wondernose.* Doubleday.
Kate Seredy, illus. *The Christmas Anna Angel* by Ruth Sawyer. Viking.

1946

Maud and Miska Petersham. *The Rooster Crows.* Macmillan.

Honor Books:
Leonard Weisgard, illus. *Little Lost Lamb* by Golden MacDonald. Doubleday.
Marjorie Torrey, illus. *Sing Mother Goose* by Opal Wheeler. Dutton.
Ruth Gannett. *My Mother Is the Most Beautiful Woman in the World* by Becky Reyher.
    Lothrop.
Kurt Wiese. *You Can Write Chinese.* Viking.

1947

Leonard Weisgard, illus. *The Little Island* by Golden MacDonald. Doubleday.

Honor Books:
Leonard Weisgard, illus. *Rain Drop Splash* by Alvin Tresselt. Lothrop.
Jay Hyde Barnum, illus. *Boats on the River* by Marjorie Flack. Viking.
Tony Palazzo, illus. *Timothy Turtle* by Al Graham. Welch.
Leo Politi, *Pedro, The Angel of Olvera Street.* Scribner.
Marjorie Torrey, illus. *Sing In Praise: A Collection of the Best Loved Hymns* by Opal
    Wheeler. Dutton.

1948

Roger Duvoisin, illus. *White Snow, Bright Snow* by Alvin Tresselt. Lothrop.

Honor Books:
Marcia Brown. *Stone Soup.* Scribner.
Dr. Seuss. *McElligott's Pool.* Random House.
George Schreiber. *Bambino the Clown.* Viking.
Hildegard Woodward, illus. *Roger and the Fox* by Lavinia Davis. Doubleday.
Virginia Lee Burton, illus. *Song of Robin Hood* edited by Anne Malcolmson. Hough-
    ton Mifflin.

1949

Berta and Elmer Hader. *The Big Snow.* Macmillan.

Honor Books:
Robert McClosky. *Blueberries for Sal.* Viking
Helen Stone, illus. *All Around the Town* by Phyllis McGinley. Lippincott.
Leo Politi. *Juanita.* Schribner.
Kurt Wiese. *Fish in the Air.* Viking.

1950

Leo Politi. *Song of the Swallows*. Scribner.

Honor Books:
Lynd Ward, illus. *America's Ethan Allen* by Stewart Holbrook. Houghton Mifflin.
Hildegard Woodward, illus. *The Wild Birthday Cake* by Lavinia Davis. Doubleday.
Marc Simont, illus. *The Happy Day* by Ruth Krauss. Harper & Row.
Dr. Seuss. *Bartholomew and the Oobleck*. Random House.
Marcia Brown. *Henry Fisherman*. Scribner.

1951

Katherine Milhous. *The Egg Tree*. Scribner.

Honor Books:
Marcia Brown. *Dick Whittington and His Cat*. Scribner.
Nicolas, illus. *The Two Reds* by William Lipkind. Harcourt Brace Jovanovich.
Dr. Seuss. *If I Ran the Zoo*. Random House.
Helen Stone, illus. *The Most Wonderful Doll in the World* by Phyllis McGinley. Lippincott.
Clare Newberry. *T-Bone, The Baby Sitter*. Harper & Row.

1952

Nicolas, illus. *Finders Keepers* by William Lipkind. Harcourt Brace Jovanovich.

Honor Books:
Marie Hall Ets. *Mr. T. W. Anthony Woo*. Viking.
Marcia Brown. *Skipper John's Cook*. Scribner.
Margaret Bloy, illus. *All Falling Down* by Gene Zion. Harper.
William Pène du Bois. *Bear Party*. Viking.
Elizabeth Olds. *Feather Mountain*. Houghton Mifflin.

1953

Lynd Ward. *The Biggest Bear*. Houghton Mifflin.

Honor Books:
Marcia Brown, illus. and trans. *Puss in Boots* by Charles Perrault. Scribner.
Robert McCloskey. *One Morning in Maine*. Viking.
Fritz Eichenberg. *Ape In A Cape*. Harcourt Brace Jovanovich.
Margaret Bloy Graham, illus. *The Storm Book* by Charlotte Zolotow. Harper & Row.
Juliet Kepes. *Five Little Monkeys*. Houghton Mifflin.

1954

Ludwig Bemelmans. *Madeline's Rescue*. Viking.

Honor Books:
Robert McCloskey, illus. *Journey Cake, Ho!* by Ruth Sawyer. Viking.
Jean Charlot, illus. *When Will the World Be Mine?* by Miriam Schlein. Scott.
Marcia Brown, illus. *The Steadfast Tin Soldier* by Hans Christian Andersen. Scribner.
Maurice Sendak, illus. *A Very Special House* by Ruth Krauss. Harper & Row.
A. Birnbaum. *Green Eyes*. Capitol.

1955

Marcia Brown, illus. and trans. *Cinderella, Or the Little Glass Slipper* by Charles Perrault. Scribner.

Honor Books:
Marguerite de Angeli, illus. *Book of Nursery and Mother Goose Rhymes*. Doubleday.
Tibor Gergely, illus. *Wheel on the Chimney* by Margaret Wise Brown. Lippincott.
Helen Sewell, illus. *The Thanksgiving Story* by Alice Dalgliesh. Scribner.

1956

Feodor Rojankovsky, illus. *Frog Went a-Courtin'* edited by John Langstaff. Harcourt Brace Jovanovich.

Honor Books:
Marie Hall Ets. *Play With Me*. Viking.
Taro Yashima. *Crow Boy*. Viking.

1957

Marc Simont, illus. *A Tree Is Nice* by Janice May Udry. Harper & Row.

Honor Books:
Marie Hall Ets. *Mr. Penny's Race Horse*. Viking.
Tasha Tudor. *1 Is One*. Walck.
Paul Galdone, illus. *Anatole* by Eve Titus. McGraw-Hill.
James Daugherty, illus. *Gillespie and the Guards* by Benjamin Elkin. Viking.
William Pène du Bois. *Lion*. Viking.

1958

Robert McCloskey. *Time of Wonder*. Viking.

Honor Books:
Don Freeman. *Fly High, Fly Low*. Viking
Paul Galdone, illus. *Anatole and the Cat* by Eve Titus. McGraw-Hill.

1959

Barbara Cooney, illus. *Chanticleer and the Fox* adapted from Chaucer. Crowell.

Honor Books:
Antonio Frasconi. *The House That Jack Built*. Harcourt Brace Jovanovich.
Maurice Sendak, illus. *What Do You Say, Dear?* by Sesyle Joslin. Scott.
Taro Yashima. *Umbrella*. Viking.

1960

Marie Hall Ets, illus. *Nine Days to Christmas* by Marie Hall Ets and Aurora Labastida. Viking.

Honor Books:
Adrienne Adams, illus. *Houses From the Sea* by Alice E. Goudey. Scribner.
Maurice Sendak. *The Moon Jumpers* by Janice May Udry. Harper & Row.

1961

Nicholas Sidjakov, illus. *Baboushka and the Three Kings* by Ruth Robbins. Parnassus Press.

Honor Books:
Leo Lionni. *Inch by Inch*. Astor-Honor.

1962

Marcia Brown. *Once a Mouse . . .* Scribner.

Honor Books:
Peter Spier. *The Fox Went Out on a Chilly Night*. Doubleday.
Maurice Sendak. *Little Bear's Visit* by Else Holmelund Minarik. Harper & Row.
Adrienne Adams, illus. *The Day We Saw the Sun Come Up* by Alice E. Goudey. Scribner.

1963

Ezra Jack Keats. *The Snowy Day*. Viking.

Honor Books:
Bernarda Bryson, illus. *The Sun Is a Golden Earring* by Natalia M. Belting. Holt.
Maurice Sendak, illus. *Mr. Rabbit and the Lovely Present* by Charlotte Zolotow. Harper & Row.

1964

Maurice Sendak. *Where the Wild Things Are*. Harper & Row.

Honor Books:
Leo Lionni. *Swimmy*. Pantheon.
Evaline Ness, illus. *All in the Morning Early* by Sorche Nic Leodhas. Holt.
Philip Reed. *Mother Goose and Nursery Rhymes*. Atheneum.

1965

Beni Montresor, illus. *May I Bring a Friend?* by Beatrice Schenk de Regniers. Atheneum.

Honor Books:
Marvin Bileck, illus. *Rain Makes Applesauce* by Julian Scheer, Holiday.
Blair Lent, illus. *The Wave* by Margaret Hodges. Houghton Mifflin.
Evaline Ness, illus. *A Pocketful of Cricket* by Rebecca Caudill. Holt.

1966

Nonny Hogrogian, illus. *Always Room for One More* by Sorche Nic Leodhas. Holt.

Honor Books:
Roger Duvoisin, illus. *Hide and Seek Fog* by Alvin Tresselt. Lothrop.
Marie Hall Ets. *Just Me*. Viking.
Evaline Ness. *Tom Tit Tot*. Scribner.

1967

Evaline Ness. *Sam, Bangs & Moonshine*. Holt.

Honor Book:
Ed Emberley, illus. *One Wide River to Cross* by Barbara Emberley, Prentice-Hall.

1968

Ed Emberley, illus. *Drummer Hoff* by Barbara Emberley. Prentice-Hall.

Honor Books:
Leo Lionni. *Frederick*. Pantheon.
Taro Yashima. *Seashore Story*. Viking.
Ed Young, illus. *The Emperor and the Kite* by Jane Yolen. World.

1969

Uri Shulevitz, illus. *The Fool of the World and the Flying Ship* by Arthur Ransome. Farrar, Straus & Giroux.

Honor Book:
Blair Lent, illus. *Why the Sun and the Moon Live in the Sky* by Elphinstone Dayrell. Houghton Mifflin.

1970

William Steig. *Sylvester and the Magic Pebble*. Windmill/Simon & Schuster.

Honor Books:
Ezra Jack Keats. *Goggles*. Macmillan.
Leo Lionni. *Alexander and the Wind-Up Mouse*. Pantheon.
Robert Andrew Parker, illus. *Pop Corn & Ma Goodness* by Edna Mitchell Preston. Viking.
Brinton Turkle. *Thy Friend, Obadiah*. Viking.
Margot Zemach, illus. *The Judge* by Harve Zemach. Farrar, Straus & Giroux.

1971

Gail E. Haley. *A Story, A Story*. Atheneum.

Honor Books:
Blair Lent, illus. *The Angry Moon* by William Sleator. Atlantic-Little, Brown.
Arnold Lobel. *Frog and Toad Are Friends*. Harper & Row.
Maurice Sendak. *In the Night Kitchen*. Harper & Row.

1972

Nonny Hogrogian. *One Fine Day*. Macmillan.

Honor Books:
Arnold Lobel, illus. *Hildilid's Night* by Cheli Duran Ryan. Macmillan.
Janina Domanska. *If All the Seas Were One Sea*. Macmillan.
Tom Feelings, illus. *Moja Means One* by Muriel Feelings. Dial.

1973

Blair Lent, illus. *The Funny Little Woman* retold by Arlene Mosel. Dutton.

Honor Books:
Gerald McDermott. *Anansi the Spider*. Holt.
Leonard Baskin, illus. *Hosie's Alphabet* by Hosea, Tobias and Lisa Baskin. Viking.

Nancy Ekholm Burkert, illus. *Snow White and the Seven Dwarfs,* translated by Randall Jarrell. Farrar, Straus & Giroux.
Tom Bahti. *When Clay Sings* by Byrd Baylor. Scribner.

1974

Margot Zemach, illus. *Duffy and the Devil* retold by Harve Zemach. Farrar, Straus & Giroux.

Honor Books:
Susan Jeffers *Three Jovial Huntsmen: A Mother Goose Rhyme.* Bradbury.
David Macaulay. *Cathedral: The Story of Its Construction.* Houghton Mifflin.

1975

Gerald McDermott. *Arrow to the Sun.* Viking.

Honor Book:
Tom Feelings. *Jambo Means Hello: A Swahili Alphabet Book* written by Muriel Feelings. Dial.

1976

Leo and Diane Dillon, illus. *Why Mosquitoes Buzz in People's Ears* retold by Verna Ardema. Dial.

Honor Books:
Peter Parnall. *The Desert Is Theirs* by Byrd Baylor. Scribner.
Tomie de Paola. *Strega Nona.* Prentice-Hall.

1977

Leo and Diane Dillon, illus. *Ashanti to Zulu: African Traditions* by Margaret Musgrove. Dial.

Honor Books:
William Steig. *The Amazing Bone.* Farrar, Straus.
Nonny Hogrogian. *The Contest.* Greenwillow.
M. J. Goffstein. *Fish for Supper.* Dial.
Beverly B. McDermott. *The Golem.* Lippincott.
Peter Parnell, illus. *Hawk, I'm Your Brother* by Byrd Baylor. Scribner.

1978

Peter Spier, illus. *Noah's Ark.* Translated by the illustrator. Doubleday.

Honor Book:
Margot Zemach. *It Could Always Be Worse: A Yiddish Folktale.* Farrar, Strauss.

1979

Goble, Paul. *The Girl Who Loved Wild Horses.* Bradbury.

Honor Books:
Donald Crews, illus. *Freight Train.* Greenwillow.
Peter Parnall, illus. *The Way to Start a Day* by Byrd Baylor. Scribner.

1980

Barbara Cooney, illus. *Ox-Cart Man* by Donald Hall. Viking.

Honor Books:
Rachel Isadora. *Ben's Trumpet*. Greenwillow.
Uri Shulevitz. *Treasure*. Farrar, Straus.
Chris Van Allsberg. *Garden of Abdul Gaszai*. Houghton Mifflin.

1981

Arnold Lobel. *Fables*. Harper.

Honor Books:
Molly Bang. *Grey Lady and the Strawberry Snatcher*. Scholastic.
Donald Crews. *Truck*. Greenwillow.
Joseph Low. *Mice Twice*. Atheneum.
Ilse Plume. *Bremen Town Musicians*. Doubleday.

1982

Chris Van Allsburg. *Jumanji*. Houghton Mifflin.

Honor Books:
Maurice Sendak. *Outside, Over There*. Harper.
Arnold Lobel. *On Market Street*. Greenwillow.
Nancy Willard, illus. *Visit to William Blake's Inn: Poems for Innocent and Experienced Travellers*. Harcourt.

NEWBERY AWARD WINNING BOOKS

The books listed here won or were Honor Books for the Newbery Medal which has been awarded since 1922 for outstanding content in books for children. Because the emphasis is on the subject matter, rather than illustrations, the books tend to be for students in grades four through eight.

1922

Hendrik Willem van Loon. *The Story of Mankind*. Liveright.

Honor Books:
Charles Hawes. *The Great Quest*. Little, Brown.
Bernard Marshall. *Cedric The Forester*. Appleton Century Crofts.
William Bowen. *The Old Tobacco Shop*. Macmillan.
Padraic Colum. *The Golden Fleece and the Heroes Who Lived Before Achilles*. Macmillan.
Cornelia Meigs. *Windy Hill*. Macmillan.

1923

Hugh Lofting. *The Voyages of Doctor Dolittle*. Lippincott.

Honor Book: No record

1924

Charles Hawes. *The Dark Frigate*. Atlantic-Little, Brown.

Honor Book: No record

1925

Charles Finger. *Tales From Silver Lands.* Doubleday.

Honor Books:
Anne Carroll Moore. *Nicholas.* Putnam.
Anne Parrish. *Dream Coach.* Macmillan.

1926

Arthur Bowie Chrisman. *Shen of the Sea.* Dutton.

Honor Book:
Padraic Colum. *Voyagers.* Macmillan.

1927

Will James. *Smokey, The Cowhorse.* Scribner.

Honor Book: No record

1928

Dhan Gopal Mukerji. *Gayneck, The Story of a Pigeon.* Dutton.

Honor Books:
Ella Young. *The Wonder Smith and His Son.* Longmans.
Caroline Snedeker. *Downright Dencey.* Doubleday.

1929

Eric P. Kelley. *The Trumpeter of Krakow.* Macmillan.

Honor Books:
John Bennett. *Pigtail of Ah Lee Ben Loo.* Longmans.
Wanda Gág. *Millions of Cats.* Coward-McCann.
Grace Hallock. *The Boy Who Was.* Dutton.
Cornelia Meigs. *Clearing Weather.* Little, Brown.
Grace Moon. *Runaway Papoose.* Doubleday.
Elinor Whitney. *Tod of the Fens.* Macmillan.

1930

Rachel Field. *Hitty, Her First Hundred Years.* Macmillan.

Honor Books:
Jeanette Eaton. *Daughter of the Seine.* Harper & Row.
Elizabeth Miller. *Pran of Albania.* Doubleday.
Marian Hurd McNeely. *Jumping-Off Place.* Longmans.
Ella Young. *Tangle-Coated Horse and Other Tales.* Longmans.
Julia Davis Adams. *Vaino.* Dutton.
Hildegarde Swift. *Little Blacknose.* Harcourt Brace Jovanovich.

1931

Elizabeth Coatsworth. *The Cat Who Went to Heaven.* Macmillan.

Honor Books:
Anne Parrish. *Floating Island.* Harper & Row.

Alida Malkus. *The Dark Star of Itza*. Harcourt Brace Jovanovich.
Ralph Hubbard. *Queer Person*. Doubleday.
Julia Davis Adams. *Mountains Are Free*. Dutton.
Agnes Hewes. *Spice and the Devil's Cave*. Knopf.
Elizabeth Janet Gray. *Meggy MacIntosh*. Doubleday.
Herbert Best. *Garram the Hunter*. Doubleday.
Alice Lide and Margaret Johansen. *Ood-Le-Uk the Wanderer*. Little, Brown.

1932

Laura Adams Armer. *Waterless Mountain*. Longmans.

Honor Books:
Dorothy P. Lathrop. *The Fairy Circus*. Macmillan.
Rachel Field. *Calico Bush*. Macmillan.
Eunice Tietjens. *Boy of the South Seas*. Coward-McCann.
Eloise Lownsbery. *Out of the Flame*. Longmans.
Marjorie Alee. *Jane's Island*. Houghton Mifflin.
Mary Gould Davis. *Truce of the Wolf and Other Tales of Old Italy*. Harcourt Brace
   Jovanovich.

1933

Elizabeth Lewis. *Young Fu of the Upper Yangtze*. Winston.

Honor Books:
Cornelia Meigs. *Swift Rivers*. Little, Brown.
Hildegarde Swift. *The Railroad to Freedom*. Harcourt Brace Jovanovich.
Nora Burglon. *Children of the Soil*. Doubleday.

1934

Cornelia Meigs. *Invincible Louisa*. Little, Brown.

Honor Books:
Caroline Snedeker. *The Forgotten Daughter*. Doubleday.
Elsie Singmaster. *Swords of Steel*. Houghton Mifflin.
Wanda Gág. *ABC Bunny*. Coward-McCann.
Erick Berry. *Winged Girl of Knossos*. Appleton.
Sarah Schmidt. *New Land*. McBridge.
Padraic Colum. *Big Tree of Bunlahy*. Macmillan.
Agnes Hewes. *Glory of the Seas*. Knopf.
Anne Kyle. *Apprentice of Florence*. Houghton Mifflin.

1935

Monica Shannon. *Dobry*. Viking.

Honor Books:
Elizabeth Seeger. *Pageant of Chinese History*. Longmans.
Constance Rourke. *Davy Crockett*. Harcourt Brace Jovanovich.
Hilda Van Stockum. *Day on Skates*. Harper & Row.

1936

Carol Brink. *Caddie Woodlawn*. Macmillan.

Honor Books:
Phil Strong. *Honk, The Moose*. Dodd, Mead.
Kate Seredy. *The Good Master*. Viking.
Elizabeth Janet Gray. *Young Walter Scott*. Viking.
Armstrong Sperry. *All Sail Set*. Winston.

1937

Ruth Sawyer. *Roller Skates,* Viking.

Honor Books:
Lois Lenski. *Phebe Fairchild: Her Book*. Stokes.
Idwal Jones. *Whistler's Van*. Viking.
Ludwig Bemelmans. *Golden Basket*. Viking.
Margery Bianco. *Winterbound*. Viking.
Constance Rourke. *Audubon*. Harcourt Brace Jovanovich.
Agnes Hewes. *The Codfish Musket*. Doubleday.

1938

Kate Seredy. *The White Stag*. Viking.

Honor Books:
James Cloyd Bowman. *Pecos Bill*. Little, Brown.
Mabel Robinson. *Bright Island*. Random House.
Laura Ingalls. *On the Banks of Plum Creek*. Harper & Row.

1939

Elizabeth Enright. *Thimble Summer*. Rinehart.

Honor Books:
Valenti Angelo, *Nino*. Viking.
Richard and Florence Atwater. *Mr. Popper's Penguins*. Little, Brown.
Phyllis Crawford. *Hello The Boat!* Holt.
Jeanette Eaton. *Leader by Destiny: George Washington, Man and Patriot*. Harcourt Brace
  Jovanovich.

1940

James Daugherty. *Daniel Boone*. Viking.

Honor Books:
Kate Seredy. *The Singing Tree*. Viking.
Mabel Robinson. *Runner of the Mountain Tops*. Random House.
Laura Ingalls Wilder. *By the Shores of Silver Lake*. Harper & Row.
Stephen W. Meader. *Boy With a Pack*. Harcourt Brace Jovanovich.

1941

Armstrong Sperry. *Call It Courage*. Macmillan.

Honor Books:
Doris Gates. *Blue Willow*. Viking.
Mary Jane Carr. *Young Mac of Fort Vancouver*. Crowell.
Laura Ingalls Wilder. *The Long Winter*. Harper & Row.
Anna Gertrude Hall. *Nansen*. Viking.

1942

Walter D. Edmonds. *The Matchlock Gun.* Dodd, Mead.

Honor Books:
Laura Ingalls Wilder. *Little Town on the Prairie.* Harper & Row.
Genevieve Foster. *George Washington's World.* Scribner.
Lois Lenski. *Indian Captive: The Story of Mary Jemison.* Lippincott.
Eva Roe Gaggin. *Down Ryton Water.* Viking.

1943

Elizabeth Janet Gray. *Adam of the Road.* Viking.

Honor Books:
Eleanor Estes. *The Middle Moffat.* Harcourt Brace Jovanovich.
Mabel Leigh. *Have You Seen Tom Thumb?* Lippincott.

1944

Esther Forbes. *Johnny Tremain.* Houghton Mifflin.

Honor Books:
Laura Ingalls Wilder. *These Happy Golden Years.* Harper & Row.
Julia Sauer. *Fog Magic.* Viking.
Eleanor Estes. *Rufus M.* Harcourt Brace Jovanovich.
Elizabeth Yates. *Mountain Born.* Coward-McCann.

1945

Robert Lawson. *Rabbit Hill.* Viking.

Honor Books:
Eleanor Estes. *The Hundred Dresses.* Harcourt Brace Jovanovich.
Alice Dalgliesh. *The Silver Pencil.* Scribner.
Genevieve Foster. *Abraham Lincoln's World.* Scribner.
Jeanette Eaton. *Lone Journey: The Life of Roger Williams.* Harcourt Brace Jovanovich.

1946

Lois Lenski. *Strawberry Girl.* Lippincott.

Honor Books:
Marguerite Henry. *Justin Morgan Had a Horse.* Rand McNally.
Florence Crannell Means. *The Moved-Outers.* Houghton Mifflin.
Christine Weston. *Bhimsa, The Dancing Bear.* Scribner.
Katherine Shippen. *New Found World.* Viking.

1947

Carolyn Sherwin Bailey. *Miss Hickory.* Viking.

Honor Books:
Nancy Barnes *Wonderful Year.* Messner.
Mary and Conrad Buff. *Big Tree.* Viking.
William Maxwell. *The Heavenly Tenants.* Harper & Row.
Cyrus Fisher. *The Avion My Uncle Flew.* Appleton.
Eleanore Jewett. *The Hidden Treasure of Glaston.* Viking.

1948

William Pène du Bois. *The Twenty-One Balloons*. Viking.

Honor Books:
Claire Huchet Bishop. *Pancakes-Paris*. Viking.
Carolyn Treffinger. *Li Lun, Lad of Courage*. Abingdon.
Catherine Besterman. *The Quaint and Curious Quest of Johnny Longfoot*. Bobbs Merrill.
Harold Courlander. *The Cow-Tail Switch, and Other West African Stories*. Holt.
Marguerite Henry. *Misty of Chincoteague*. Rand McNally.

1949

Marguerite Henry. *King of the Wind*. Rand McNally.

Honor Books:
Holling C. Holling. *Seabird*. Houghton Mifflin.
Louise Rankin. *Daughter of the Mountains*. Viking.
Ruth S. Gannett. *My Father's Dragon*. Random House.
Arna Bontemps. *Story of the Negro*. Knopf.

1950

Marguerite de Angeli. *The Door in the Wall*. Doubleday.

Honor Books:
Rebecca Caudill. *Tree of Freedom*. Viking.
Catherine Coblentz. *The Blue Cat of Castle Town*. Longmans.
Rutherford Montgomery. *Kildee House*. Doubleday.
Genevieve Foster. *George Washington*. Scribner.
Walter and Marion Havighurst. *Song of the Pines*. Winston.

1951

Elizabeth Yates. *Amos Fortune, Free Man*. Aladdin.

Honor Books:
Mabel Leigh Hunt. *Better Known as Johnny Appleseed*. Lippincott.
Jeanette Eaton. *Gandhi, Fighter Without a Sword*. Morrow.
Clara Ingram Judson. *Abraham Lincoln, Friend of the People*. Follett.
Anne Parrish. *The Story of Appleby Capple*. Harper & Row.

1952

Eleanor Estes. *Ginger Pye*. Harcourt Brace Jovanovich.

Honor Books:
Elizabeth Baity. *Americans Before Columbus*. Viking.
Holling C. Holling. *Minn of the Mississippi*. Houghton Miffin.
Nicholas Kalashnikoff. *The Defender*. Scribner.
Julia Sauer. *The Light at Tern Rocks*. Viking.
Mary and Conrad Buff. *The Apple and the Arrow*. Houghton Mifflin.

1953

Ann Nolan Clark. *Secret of the Andes*. Viking.

Honor Books:
E. B. White. *Charlotte's Web*. Harper & Row.
Eloise McGraw. *Moccasin Trail*. Coward-McCann.
Ann Weil. *Red Sails to Capri*. Viking.
Alice Dalgliesh. *The Bears on Hemlock Mountain*. Scribner.
Genevieve Foster. *Birthdays Of Freedom*. Vol. 1. Scribner.

1954

Joseph Krumgold, *. . . And Now Miguel*. Crowell.

Honor Books:
Claire Huchet Bishop. *All Alone*. Viking.
Meindert DeJong. *Shadrach*. Harper & Row.
Meindert DeJong. *Hurray Home Candy*. Harper & Row.
Clara Ingram Judson. *Theodore Roosevelt, Fighting Patriot*. Follett.
Mary and Conrad Buff. *Magic Maize*. Houghton Mifflin.

1955

Meindert DeJong. *The Wheel on the School*. Harper & Row.

Honor Books:
Alice Dalgliesh. *Courage of Sarah Noble*. Scribner.
James Ullman. *Banner in the Sky*. Lippincott.

1956

Jean Lee Latham. *Carry On, Mr. Bowditch*. Houghton Mifflin.

Honor Books:
Marjorie Kinnan Rawlings. *The Secret River*. Scribner.
Jennie Lindquist. *The Golden Name Day*. Harper & Row.
Katherine Shippen. *Men, Microscopes, and Living Things*. Viking.

1957

Virginia Sorensen. *Miracles on Maple Hill*. Harcourt Brace Jovanovich.

Honor Books:
Fred Gipson. *Old Yeller*. Harper & Row.
Meindert DeJong. *The House of Sixty Fathers*. Harper & Row.
Clara Ingram Judson. *Mr. Justice Holmes*. Follett.
Dorothy Rhoads. *The Corn Grows Ripe*. Viking.
Marguerite de Angeli. *Black Fox of Lorne*. Doubleday.

1958

Harold Keith. *Rifles for Watie*. Thomas Y. Crowell.

Honor Books:
Mari Sandoz. *The Horsecatcher*. Westminister.
Elizabeth Enright. *Gone-Away Lake*. Harcourt Brace Jovanovich.
Robert Lawson. *The Great Wheel*. Viking.
Leo Gurko. *Tom Paine, Freedom's Apostle*. Thomas Y. Crowell.

1959

Elizabeth George Speare. *The Witch of Blackbird Pond.* Houghton Mifflin.

Honor Books:
Natalie S. Carlson. *The Family Under the Bridge.* Harper & Row.
Meindert DeJong. *Along Came a Dog.* Harper & Row.
Francis Kalnay. *Chucaro: Wild Pony of the Pampa.* Harcourt Brace Jovanovich.
William O. Steele. *The Perilous Road.* Harcourt Brace Jovanovich.

1960

Joseph Krumgold. *Onion John.* Thomas Y. Crowell.

Honor Books:
Jean George. *My Side of the Mountain.* Dutton.
Gerald W. Johnson. *America Is Born.* Morrow.
Carol Kendall. *The Gammage Cup.* Harcourt Brace Jovanovich.

1961

Scott O'Dell. *Island of the Blue Dolphins.* Houghton Mifflin.

Honor Books:
Gerald W. Johnson. *America Moves Forward.* Morrow.
Jack Schaefer. *Old Ramon.* Houghton Mifflin.
George Selden. *The Cricket in Times Square.* Farrar, Straus & Giroux.

1962

Elizabeth George Speare. *The Bronze Bow.* Houghton Mifflin.

Honor Books:
Edwin Tunis. *Frontier Living.* World.
Eloise McGraw. *The Golden Goblet.* Coward-McCann.
Mary Stolz. *Belling the Tiger.* Harper & Row.

1963

Madeleine L'Engle. *A Wrinkle in Time.* Farrar, Straus & Giroux.

Honor Books:
Sorche Nic Leodhas. *Thistle and Thyme.* Holt.
Olivia Coolidge. *Men of Athens.* Houghton Mifflin.

1964

Emily Cheney Neville. *It's Like This, Cat.* Harper & Row.

Honor Books:
Sterling North. *Rascal.* Dutton.
Ester Wier. *The Loner.* McKay.

1965

Maia Wojciechowska. *Shadow of a Bull.* Atheneum.

Honor Book:
Irene Hunt. *Across Five Aprils.* Follett.

1966

Elizabeth Borten de Treviño. *I, Juan De Pareja*. Farrar, Straus & Giroux.

Honor Books:
Lloyd Alexander. *The Black Cauldron*. Holt.
Randall Jarrell. *The Animal Family*. Pantheon.
Mary Stolz. *The Noonday Friends*. Harper & Row.

1967

Irene Hunt. *Up a Road Slowly*. Collett.

Honor Books:
Scott O'Dell. *The King's Fifth*. Houghton Mifflin.
Isaac Bashevis Singer. *Zlatch the Goat and Other Stories*. Harper & Row.
Mary K. Weik. *The Jazz Man*. Atheneum.

1968

E.L. Konigsburg. *From the Mixed-Up Files of Mrs. Basil E. Frankweiler*. Atheneum.

Honor Books:
E. L. Konigsburg. *Jennifer, Hecate, MacBeth, William McKinley, and Me, Elizabeth*. Atheneum.
Scott O'Dell. *The Black Pearl*. Houghton Mifflin.
Isaac Bashevis Singer. *The Fearsome Inn*. Scribner.
Zilpha Keatley Snyder. *The Egypt Game*. Atheneum.

1969

Lloyd Alexander. *The High King*. Holt.

Honor Books:
Julius Lester. *To Be a Slave*. Dial.
Isaac Bashevis Singer. *When Shlemiel Went to Warsaw & Other Stories*. Farrar, Straus & Giroux.

1970

William H. Armstrong. *Sounder*. Harper & Row.

Honor Books:
Sulamith Ish-Kishor. *Our Eddie*. Pantheon.
Janet Gaylord Moore. *The Many Ways of Seeing: An Introduction to the Pleasures of Art*. World.
Mary Q. Steele. *Journey Outside*. Viking.

1971

Betsy Byars. *Summer of the Swans*. Viking.

Honor Books:
Natalie Babbitt. *Knee-Knock Rise*. Farrar, Straus & Giroux.
Sylvia Louise Engdahl. *Enchantress from the Stars*. Atheneum.
Scott O'Dell. *Sing Down the Moon*. Houghton Mifflin.

1972

Robert C. O'Brien. *Mrs. Frisby and the Rats of NIMH.* Atheneum.

Honor Books:
Miska Miles. *Annie and the Old One.* Atlantic-Little, Brown.
Zilpha Keatley Snyder. *The Headless Cupid.* Atheneum.
Allan W. Eckert. *Incident at Hawk's Hill.* Little, Brown.
Virginia Hamilton. *The Planet of Junior Brown.* Macmillan.
Ursula K. LeGuin. *The Tombs of Atuan.* Atheneum.

1973

Jean Craighead George. *Julie of the Wolves.* Harper & Row.

Honor Books:
Arnold Lobel. *Frog and Toad Together.* Harper & Row.
Johanna Reiss. *The Upstairs Room.* Thomas Y. Crowell.
Zilpha Keatley Snyder. *The Witches of Worm.* Antheneum.

1974

Paula Fox. *The Slave Dancer.* Bradbury.

Honor Book:
Susan Cooper. *The Dark Is Rising.* Atheneum.

1975

Virginia Hamilton. *M. C. Higgins the Great.* Macmillan.

Honor Books:
Ellen Raskin. *Figgs & Phantoms.* Dutton.
James Lincoln Collier and Christopher Collier. *My Brother Sam Is Dead.* Four Winds Press.
Elizabeth Marie Pope. *The Perilous Gard.* Houghton Mifflin.
Bette Green. *Phillip Hall Likes Me, I Reckon Maybe.* Dial.

1976

Susan Cooper. *The Grey King.* Atheneum.

Honor Books:
Sharon Bell Mathis. *The Hundred Penny Box.* Viking.
Laurence Yep. *Dragonwings.* Harper & Row.

1977

Mildred D. Taylor. *Roll of Thunder, Hear My Cry.* Dial.

Honor Books:
William Steig. *Abel's Island.* Farrar, Straus.
Nancy Bond. *A String in the Harp.* Atheneum.

1978

Katherine Paterson. *Bridge to Terabithia.* Harper & Row.

Honor Books:
Beverly Cleary. *Ramona and Her Father*. Morrow.
Jamake Highwater. *Anpao: An American Indian Odyssey*. Lippincott.

1979

Ellen Raskin. *Westing Game*. Dutton.

Honor Book:
Katherine Paterson. *Great Gilly Hopkins*. Harper & Row.

1980

Joan Blos. *A Gathering of Days: A New England Girl's Journal*. Scribner.

Honor Books:
David Kherdian. *Road from Home: The Story of an Armenian Childhood*. Greenwillow.

1981

Katherine Paterson. *Jacob Have I Loved*. Harper & Row.

Honor Books:
Jane Langton. *Fledgling*. Harper & Row.
Madeline L'Engle. *Ring of Endless Light*. Farrar, Straus.

1982

Nancy Willard. *A Visit to William Blake's Inn: Poems for Innocent and Experienced Travellers*. Harcourt Brace Jovanovich.

Honor Books:
Aranka Siegal. *Upon the Head of a Goat: A Childhood in Hungary 1939–1944*. Farrar, Straus.
Beverly Cleary. *Ramona Quimby, Age Eight*. Morrow.

DIRECTORY OF PUBLISHERS

This handy directory of companies who publish books and other instructional materials will assist you in sending for publishers' catalogs and specific items that interest you.

Abelard, Schuman, Ltd., 666 Fifth Avenue, New York, NY 10019
Abingdon Press, 201 Eighth Avenue South, Nashville, TN 37202
ACI Films, 35 West 45 Street, New York, NY 10036
Addison-Wesley Publishing Co., Reading, MA 01867
Aims Instructional Media Services, P.O. Box 1010, Hollywood, CA 90028
Allyn & Bacon, Rockleigh, NJ 07647
American Heritage Press, 1221 Avenue of the Americas, New York, NY 10020
American Library Association, Publishing Services, 50 E. Huron St., Chicago, IL 60611
Association for Childhood Education International, 3615 Wisconsin Ave., NW, Washington, D.C. 20016
Atheneum Publishers 122 East 42d Street, New York, NY 10017

Avon Books, 959 Eighth Avenue, New York, NY 10019

Barr Films, P.O. Box 7-C, Pasadena, CA 91104

Beacon Press, 25 Beacon St., Boston, MA 02108

Bell & Howell, 2201 West Howard, Evanston, IL 60202

Bobbs-Merrill Company, 4300 W. 62d Street, Indianapolis, IN 46268

Stephen Bosustow Productions, 1649 11th Street, Santa Monica, CA 90404

The R. R. Bowker Company, Xerox Education Group, 1180 Avenue of the Americas, New York, NY 10036

Bowmar Publishing Corporation, 622 Rodier Drive, Glendale, CA 91201

Bradbury Press, 2 Overhill Road, Scarsdale, NY 10583

Brigham Young University, Motion Picture Dept., M.P.S., Provo, UT 84602

California State Department of Education. Bureau of Publications. 721 Capitol Mall, Sacramento, CA 95814.

Centron Educational Films, 1621 West Ninth, Lawrence, KS 66044

Changing Times Education Service, 1729 H Street, N.W., Washington, DC 20006

Children's Book Council, Inc., 67 Irving Place, New York, NY 10003

Childrens Press, 1224 W. Van Buren Street, Chicago, IL 60607

Churchill Films, 652 North Robertson Blvd. Los Angeles, CA 90069

Citation Press, 50 W. 44th Street, New York, NY 10036

Clearvue, 6666 North Oliphant Avenue, Chicago, IL 60631

William Collins & World Publishing Co., 2080 West 117th Street, Cleveland, OH 44111

Columbia University Press, 562 W. 113th Street, New York, NY 10025

Contemporary Press, Box 1524, San Jose, CA 95109

Coronet Instructional Media, 65 East South Water Street, Chicago, IL 60601

Council on Interracial Books for Children, 1841 Broadway, New York, NY 10023

Coward, McCann & Geoghegan, 200 Madison Avenue, New York, NY 10016

Thomas Y. Crowell Co., 666 Fifth Avenue, New York, NY 10019

Crowell-Collier Press, 640 5th Ave., New York, NY 10019

Crown Publishers, 419 Park Avenue South, New York, NY 10016

The John Day Co., 666 Fifth Avenue, New York, NY 10019

Delacorte Press, 1 Dag Hammarskjold Plaza, 245 East 47th Street, New York, NY 10017

The Dial Press, 1 Dag Hammarskjold Plaza, 245 East 47th Street, New York, NY 10017

Dilton Press, 106 Washington Ave., N. Minneapolis, MN 55401

Disney, Walt, Educational Materials, 800 Sonora Avenue, Glendale, CA 91201

Dodd, Mead & Co., 79 Madison Avenue, New York, NY 10016

Doubleday & Co., 245 Park Avenue, New York, NY 10017

Doubleday Multimedia, 1371 Reynolds Avenue, Santa Ana, CA 92705

E. P. Dutton & Co., 201 Park Avenue South, New York, NY 10003

Educational Development Corporation, 202 Lake Miriam Drive, Lakeland. FL 33803

EMC Corporation, 180 East Sixth Street, St. Paul, MN 55101

Encyclopaedia Britannica Educational Corporation, 425 North Michigan Avenue, Chicago, IL 60611

M. Evans & Co., 216 East 49th Street, New York, NY 10017

Farrar, Straus & Giroux, 19 Union Square West, New York, NY 10003

Far West Laboratory, 1855 Folsom St., San Francisco CA 94103

F. W. Faxon Company, 15 Southwest Park, Westwood, MA 02090

The Feminist Press, Box 334, Old Westbury, NY 11568

Follett Publishing Co., 1010 West Washington Blvd., Chicago, IL 60607

Four Winds Press, 50 West 44th Street, New York, NY 10036
Funk & Wagnalls, Inc., 53 E. 77th St., New York, NY 10021
Garrard Publishing Company, 1607 N. Market St., Champaign, IL 61820
General Educational Media, 350 Northern Blvd., Great Neck, NY 10021
Golden Gate Junior Books, 1247$\frac{1}{2}$ North Vista Street, Hollywood, CA 90046
Golden Press, (Western Publishing Co.), 850 Third Avenue, New York, NY 10022
Goldsholl Associates, 420 Frontage Road, Northfield, IL 60093
Grant, Allan, Productions, 808 Lockearn Street, Los Angeles, CA 90049
Greenwillow (See Morrow)
Grosset & Dunlap, 51 Madison Avenue, New York, NY 10010
Guidance Associates, 41 Washington Avenue, Pleasantville, NY 10570
G. K. Hall & Compnay, 70 Lincoln St., Boston, MA 02111
Harcourt Brace Jovanovich, 757 Third Avenue, New York, NY 10017
Harper & Row, Publishers, 10 East 53rd Street, New York, NY 10022
Harvey House, 20 Waterside Plaza, New York, NY 10010
Hastings House Publishers, 10 East 40th Street, New York, NY 10016
Hawthorn Books, 260 Madison Avenue, New York, NY 10016
Holiday House, 18 East 56th Street, New York, NY 10022
Holt, Rinehart & Winston, 383 Madison Avenue, New York, NY 10017
Horn Book, Inc., 585 Boylston St., Boston, MA 02116
Houghton Mifflin Co., 2 Park Street, Boston, MA 02107
International Reading Association, 800 Barksdale Rd., Newark, DE 19711
Alfred A. Knopf, 201 East 50th Street, New York, NY 10022
Learning Corporation of America, 711 Fifth Avenue, New York, NY 10022
Learning Resources Company, P.O. Box 3709, 202 Lake Mirian Dr., Lakeland, FL 33803
Learning Tree Filmstrips, 934 Pearl Street, P.O. Box 1590, Dept. 105, Boulder, CO 80302
Lerner Publications Company, 241 First Avenue North, Minneapolis, MN 55401
Libraries Unlimited, Box 263, Littleton, CO 80120
J. B. Lippincott Company, 521 Fifth Avenue, New York, NY 10017
Little, Brown & Co., 34 Beacon Street, Boston, MA 02106
Lothrop, Lee & Shepard Company, 105 Madison Avenue, New York, NY 10016
Macrae Smith Company, Lewis Tower Bldg., 225 S. 15th St., Philadelphia, PA 19102
Macmillan Publishing Co., 866 Third Avenue, New York, NY 10022
McGraw-Hill Book Co., 1221 Avenue of the Americas, New York, NY 10020
David McKay Company, Publishers, 750 3d Avenue, New York, NY 10017
Merrill, Charles E., Publishing Co., 1300 Alum Creek Dr., Columbus, OH 43216
Julian Messner (A Division of Simon & Schuster), 1 West 39th Street, New York, NY 10018
Miller-Brody Productions, 711 Fifth Avenue, New York, NY 10022
William Morrow & Co., 105 Madison Avenue, New York, NY 10016
National Council for the Social Studies, 1201 Sixteenth St. NW, Washington, DC 20036
National Council of Teachers of English, 1111 Kenyon Rd., Urbana, IL 61801
National Council of Teachers of Mathematics, 1906 Assoc. Dr., Reston, VA 22091
National Instructional Television, Box A, Bloomington, IN 47401
Thomas Nelson, 407 7th Ave. S., Nashville, TN 37203
Newsweek, 444 Madison Avenue, New York, NY 10022
New York Library Association, Children and Young Adult Services Section 230 W.

41st Street, Suite 1800, New York, NY 10036
New York Office of State History, State Education Dept., 99 Washington Ave., Albany, NY 12210
J. Philip O'Hara, 20 E. Huron Street, Chicago, IL 60611
Oxford Films, 1136 North Las Palmas Avenue, Los Angeles, CA 90036
Oxford University Press, 200 Madison Avenue, New York, NY 10016
Pantheon Books, 201 East 50th Street, New York, NY 10022
Parents' Magazine Press, 52 Vanderbilt Avenue, New York, NY 10017
Parnassus Press, 4080 Halleck Street, Emeryville, CA 94608
Pathescope Educational Films, 71 Weyman Avenue, New Rochelle, NY 10802
S. G. Phillips, 305 West 86th Street, New York, NY 10024
Pied Piper Productions, P.O. Box 320, Verdugo City, CA 91046
Plays, 8 Arlington Street, Boston, MA 02116
Platt & Munk, Publishers, 1055 Bronx River Avenue, Bronx, NY 10572
Prentice-Hall, Englewood Cliffs, NJ 07632
Psychology Today, Del Mar, CA 92014
G. P. Putnam's Sons, 200 Madison Avenue, New York, NY 10016
Pyramid Films Corporation, P.O. Box 1048, Santa Monica, CA 90406
Q-ED Productions, P.O. Box 1608, Burbank, CA 91507
Rand McNally & Co., P.O. Box 7600, Chicago, IL 60680
Random House Educational Media, Order Entry Department-Y, 400 Hahn Road, Westminster, MD 21157
The Reilly & Lee Co., 114 W. Illinois Street, Chicago, IL 60610
The Ronald Press Co., 79 Madison Ave., New York, NY 10016
St. Martin's Press, 175 Fifth Avenue, New York, NY 10010
Salinger Educational Media, 1635 12th Street, Santa Monica, CA 90404
Scarecrow Press, 52 Liberty St. Box 656, Metuchen, NJ 08840
Schloat Productions, 150 White Plains Road, Tarrytown, NY 10591
Schmitt, Hall & McCreary Co., 110 N. Fifth Street, Minneapolis, MN 55403
Scholastic Magazines, Audio Visual and Media Dept., 50 West 44th St., New York, NY 10036
Scott, Foresman & Co., Educational Publishers, 1900 E. Lake Ave., Glenview, IL 60025
Screen Education Enterprises, 3220 16th Avenue West, Seattle, WA 98119
Charles Scribner's Sons, 597 Fifth Street, New York, NY 10017
Scroll Press, Publishers, 129 East 94th Street, New York, NY 10028
The Seabury Press, 815 Second Avenue, New York, NY 10017
See Hear Now! Ltd., 49 Wellington Street East, Toronto M5E 1C9 Canada
Simon & Schuster Publishers, 630 5th Avenue, New York, NY 10020
Steck-Vaughn Co., Division of Intext Publishers Group, Box 2028, Austin, TX 78767
Sterling Publishing Co., 419 Park Ave. S., New York, NY 10016
Teaching Resources Films, Station Plaza, Bedford Hills, NY 10507
Technicolor, 299 Kalmus Drive, Costa Mesa, CA 92626
Troll Associates, 320 Route 17, Mahwah, NJ 07430
University of Chicago Press, 5801 Ellis Ave., Chicago, IL 60637
University of Pittsburgh Press, 127 N. Bellefield Ave., Pittsburgh, PA 15213
The Vanguard Press, 424 Madison Ave., New York, NY 10017
Van Nostrand-Reinhold Co., 450 W. 33rd Street, New York, NY 10001
The Viking Press, 625 Madison Ave., New York, NY 10022
Henry Z. Walck, Publishers, 19 Union Square W., New York, NY 10003
Walker & Co., 720 5th Ave., New York, NY 10019

The Ward Ritchie Press (Anderson, Ritchie & Simon), 3044 Riverside Dr., Los Angeles, CA 90039
Frederick Warne & Co., 101 5th Ave., New York, NY 10003
Ives Washburn, 750 3d Ave., New York, NY 10017
Franklin Watts, 730 5th Ave., New York, NY 10019
Westminster Press, Witherspoon Bldg., Philadelphia, PA 19107
Weston Woods, Weston, CT 06880
Albert Whitman & Co., 560 West Lake Street, Chicago, IL 60606
The H. W. Wilson Co., 950 University Ave., New York, NY 10452
Windmill Books, 201 Park Ave. S., New York, NY 10003
William Collins & World Publishing Co., 2080 W. 117th St., Cleveland, OH 44111
Xerox Films, 245 Long Hill Rd., Middletown, CT 06457
Young Scott Books, Reading, MA 01867

INDEX